THE KUDZU &
C-4 FUGUE

W.D. BEAMAN

UNITED WRITERS PRESS
ASHEVILLE, N.C.

United Writers Press
www.uwpnew.com

Copyright © 2025 by W.D. Beaman
First Edition

ISBN: 978-1-961813-86-1 (casebound)

ISBN: 978-1-961813-87-8 (trade paperback)

ISBN: 978-1-961813-88-5 (eBook)

Printed in the USA.

To Becky

Contents

THE KUDZU &
C-4 FUGUE

Prologue

Twenty-nine-year-old Alexis Williams Ramsay is highly trained in music and art restoration. She has a fine mezzo-soprano voice. She has an undergraduate degree in music from Furman University which was only three miles from her childhood home, a Master's Degree in art from Emory University, and a PhD in the History of Art from the University of Cambridge focusing on the restoration of paintings from the early twentieth century—primarily those of French impressionists—because her husband, Charteris Hew Ramsay, known to his friends as Hew, inherited a collection of originals from his ancestors.

Her change in majors coincided with her mother becoming the director of the Greenville County Museum of art. Alexis and Hew have three children. John, the oldest, is six. The twin girls, Elizabeth and Courtney, are three.

Hew, also twenty-nine, is a real estate developer with a focus on environmentally sensitive projects. Unlike most other developers, he only invests in projects using his own money. One of the wealthiest people in North America, he has an undergraduate degree in business from Emory University, a master's degree in Real Estate and Sustainable Development (known as an MRED) from Clemson University, and a PhD in finance from the London School of Economics. Because he is an introvert, he prefers to not publicize his PhD.

Hew is president and CEO of Eberhart North America, part of the highly successful German company, Eberhart International. Hew's late grandfather teamed with the German company on several American development projects and while Hew was a teenager, he wrote a program for construction project management that was so successful that Eberhart International hired him as a consultant.

Hew is also a very talented classical musician. His late mother taught him to play piano and organ while she was teaching keyboard instruments at Juilliard. He is teaching John to play while Alexis works with the twins, who prefer art, in her home studio. Hew's future as a performer ended when he was stabbed in the leg by a rival on his high school soccer team. He prefers the organ over the piano, but because of his injury, can no longer hold the low C on the organ pedals for any length of time.

Hew is a trim six-feet-six guy of Scottish—probably Viking—ancestry. A carbon copy of Hew, John is already taller than most six-year-old boys. Their unruly mops of blond hair can't be tamed by a comb, and their watery blue eyes immediately captivate anyone who looks into them. John is becoming a fine organist—better than Hew at his age.

Hew also works pro bono on Sundays for The Cathedral of St. Philip in Atlanta, Georgia, as an assistant for the sub-organist. The term sub-organist is one of those quirky English terms for the organist who actually plays the organ during church services as opposed to the titular organist who directs the choir. The Canon for Music, of course, is actually a fine organist too.

Hew is the assistant to the assistant. He turns pages, changes stops, pushes pistons, and sets the next score on the music desk. Hew also subs on occasion at the Catholic Cathedral of Christ the King across Peachtree Road from The Episcopal Cathedral for the Spanish Masses. Language is not a problem for Hew. Although their organist doesn't speak Spanish, Hew not only had an Hispanic nanny, but was trapped for three years in a Catholic boarding school in Bogota, Colombia, while his mother was dean of the music school in Cali. It was there that he lost his parents—they were murdered by a drug lord who was laundering money by funding the boarding and music schools.

Alexis is now head of the music and arts programs for the prestigious Atlanta Regional Academy for Technology, Art, and Music—known to the students as "A-RAT." Adults simply refer to it as the Academy. She also sings in the choir at St. Luke's Episcopal in downtown Atlanta.

Hew's fiery Scots temper sometimes flashes out through his watery blue eyes, and his unruly curly blond hair almost seems to glow red. A Gemini, his face turns red when he is angry, but Alexis—a Libra—always tries to calm him down. Five-feet-eight, she is a brunette beauty with eyes as dark as coal—and despises conflict of any sort.

After their marriage, Hew and Alexis lived in Hew's penthouse, which he designed, but they soon realized that raising kids forty floors up was not what they really wanted. So Hew and his favorite German/English architect, Johann Bergson, had designed a fine new contemporary house on a steep slope on the south side of the Chattahoochee River just north of Atlanta.

A thirty-foot music room, two levels below the great room and terrace, is larger than many hotel ballrooms. The walls also house his 10,000-volume library. Hew had a pipe organ built by Flentrop as an exact copy of the famous instrument the company had built in 1958 for Harvard University—including the extra ranks of pipes they had provided later that could be swapped out as necessary. As a boy, he had been a student in the famous St. Thomas Episcopal Choir School in New York City for several years where he sang much of the entire repertory of church music. He continued his organ studies with the sub-organist there.

He first became aware of the Harvard instrument while listening to recordings by E. Power Biggs while living in the boarding school in Bogota, Colombia. He became hooked on Baroque music because he loved the clear crisp sounds, but after having spent three years studying French Romantic music in the Catholic school in Colombia, he added a new custom built four manual virtual pipe organ console across from the Flentrop to be able to play music of other periods more authentically.

The sound is produced by a large custom built computer which sends MIDI signals to twelve top grade speakers. His music room/library was designed and engineered to make the small space sound larger than it is. It is highly reverberant and the acousticians tuned the entire space to suit the Flentrop instrument. Hew had the speakers for the virtual organ engineered to suit the space as well.

The sample sets already provide the reverberation as it actually exists in the various churches that have been digitally sampled, and the rear channel speakers provide immersive surround sound. Three of the two-story walls are lined with old leather bound books standing on solid quarter sawn oak shelves. They add diffusion and absorption to the walls. One wall is entirely made of glass panels that were slightly tilted and canted to provide more reverberation and diffusion.

The upper level is a simple three-sided balcony of books with a railing faced with lime-washed quarter sawn oak panels and rails. They are set at slight angles—not noticeable to most eyes, and are slightly canted to cancel any echo. The balcony runs behind the tall Flentrop instrument and allows access to the back doors of the organ case for ease with tuning.

The balcony opposite the organ on the other short side of the room runs behind the large rough-faced South Carolina blue silk granite fireplace. This adds reflected sound. The blocks of coursed stone are eight inches by one foot and the mortar is raked back to give the look of dry stacked stone work.

The lintel over the fire box is a massive single piece of stone. It's eight feet long and three feet high. It visually and literally supports the weight of the chimney stack above. There are two spiral stairs at either end of the balcony against the exterior wall. The north-facing exterior cantilevered-glass-walled side of the room hangs over the cliff, giving a spectacular view of the river below. The returned ends of the glass wall are also glass, making the entire window composition a square ended bay.

The great room terrace above forms a third of the top of the library/music room. The other two-thirds is under the great room itself. The structure of the walls behind the shelving units is one-foot-thick poured concrete, and the exposed ceiling is an eight-inch-thick slab of very rough, random thickness and random width board-formed concrete that was left the natural gray color. Most of the lighting is composed of warm toned LED fixtures located in the contemporary cornice above the bookshelves, but there are several pairs of 3,500-lumen color balanced dimmable LED spot lights especially designed for this space that focused on the large organ and the fireplace paintings, and there are LED strips on each of the bookshelves illuminating the books. The lighting and the concert hall quality mechanical systems were all controlled from Hew's phone and electronic tablet. The air conditioning system whispered 35 decibels of background noise.

The furniture in the room consists of international style tables and chairs. There is a forty-seven inch round glass topped pedestal dining table with matching chairs by Warren Platner upholstered in bright red Scottish cashmere wool sitting beside the glass wall. Hew uses this grouping as a library table for studying scores because the natural north light is perfect for reading even on cloudy days. There is a more formal sitting area centered in front of the fireplace on a large faded antique oriental silk rug covering part of the quarter sawn English oak floor. The grouping consists of six black leather and polished chrome Barcelona chairs designed by Mies van Der Rohe for the German Pavilion at the Barcelona International Exposition of 1929. Alexis purchased these from the Academy after the chairman stubbed his toe on one of the legs and, in a fit of rage, demanded that the chairs be thrown out. There are matching coffee and side tables and two Eames lounge chairs and ottomans in rosewood and black leather on either side the fireplace.

A large pair of John Singer Sergeant paintings of Hew's great-grandparents on their wedding day hang above the eight-foot-long natural finished wooden mantle. It was cut from an old growth tulip poplar tree that had fallen years ago in a storm on his 8,000-acre ancestral farm in Virginia. In the paintings, they are standing outside the ancient gothic doors of St. Mary's Cathedral in Edinburgh, Scotland.

Alexis and Heidi, Hew's interior designer, positioned several of Hew's large French impressionist paintings on the balcony rail to break up the long expanses of lime-washed wood.

Alexis's painting studio is above their four-car garage. The north wall is floor to ceiling glass while the south wall is covered with cabinets and storage racks. A large insulated roll-up door on the west wall allows her staff to move large paintings in from the driveway below. To the east are a full bathroom, a large stainless steel cleanup area, and a door to the service corridor and butler's pantry. The room has state-of-the-art air conditioning and ventilation systems.

Across the river from the house is a natural preserve—there are no neighbors to spoil the view. Visitors arrive by car through a large set of contemporary stainless-steel gates at the street. They wind around a large open meadow planted with native southeastern prairie grasses that might have existed before the land was planted with cotton. The ground under the grasses contains all of the deep wells for the heating and air conditioning system.

Short low, rough segments of old stonework along the side of the oval driveway appear to be left from the property's farm days and they gradually become higher and longer as visitors' cars approach the house. The south face of the house has a long fieldstone wall with a glass opening at the foyer. A long band of high windows that light the bedroom corridor separates the stone wall from the roof structure. The low sloped standing seam metal roof is covered with solar panels. The large house is a net zero building—it produces more energy than it uses and the excess is sold to the power company.

Hew invests his own trust funds in the development of real estate projects in America that are designed and constructed by Eberhart International, an environmental development, design-build, and construction management company based in Cologne, Germany. Hew and his former legal guardian, Edward Hardy, are members of the board of directors of Eberhart. As a teenager, Hew developed a building construction computer program that Eberhart still uses.

The quality of Eberhart's work is always first rate and usually wins awards. Most American developers spend money on curb appeal and eye candy and skimp on the hidden basics, while Eberhart makes sure that the bones and systems are first rate. Their philosophy is that foundations, roofs, exterior water run off systems, and mechanical and electrical/electronic systems must be as good as possible. They insist on using quality materials.

They began in collaboration with Hew's late grandfather, John Bishop XI. He was called "X.I.," pronounced as the letters X and I, based on the Roman numerals designating his place in the genealogical order.

1
SUSPENDED

"Hew, where are you?" He could tell from the sound of his wife's voice on the phone that something was wrong.

"I'm at home practicing a new composition for the organ while the house is quiet."

"Go upstairs and pour me a glass of pinot grigio and start filling the jacuzzi...no, make that my special martini...actually, make it a double. I'll be there in twenty minutes."

Damn, Hew thought, *just when I had two hours before the kids get home from school.* Hew could only practice after John was in bed. Even with a pair of expensive headphones, Hew could still hear when John was playing, so this rare afternoon was to have been golden.

Hew cancelled the call and laid both his forearms on keyboards of his four manual organ console. Known as a virtual pipe organ, it used a new concept in digital recording where engineers go into a church or cathedral—with permission—and record the sound of every pipe in its natural acoustic and produce a computer file that allows anyone who buys the file and the corresponding software to play organ music on their own instrument. The sound was better than a typical digital electronic organ and organists could recreate music on fine historic or modern instruments from around the world in the comfort of their own homes.

Hew still had pain when he was tired or stressed. Reaching low D on the pedals sometimes caused a stabbing pain, and he could only play low C on good days. No one knew whether it was real or just in his mind—or both, but either way, he'd decided not to pursue music as a major in college. Fortunately, his long thin fingers were more than adequate for the keyboards. He could easily reach an octave plus four, and years of playing the old three manual French organ in the chapel of his boarding school in Bogota—built by the master builder, Cavaillé-Coll—had made his fingers strong and flexible.

He kicked the general twelve-toe stud and raised a racket using all of the features of the Dutch sample set, venting his frustration at the interruption. When music came into his brain, he needed to let it out—at lunch, a new idea had popped up for a composition he was working on for two organs and a mezzo-soprano. He and their son John would play and Alexis would sing.

⁂

ALEXIS STORMED INTO THE HOUSE IN a whirlwind shedding her shoes, her coat, and her purse on the way into their bedroom. She'd been having a rough time at work. Her boss, Sarah Jacobsen, the head of the academy, had suddenly resigned two weeks earlier, and the board had replaced her with a politician. Alexis had initially been hired to develop the school's art studies program but she'd quickly risen in the ranks to become the head of the department.

Hew raised his eyebrows. "I'm guessing this isn't a good time for sex in the tub, is it?"

"Don't be an ass," she snarled as she ripped her clothes off and grabbed the martini, swallowing it in two gulps. "Make me another one."

"Okay. Just let the jets do their job and try to relax and gather your thoughts. Back in a minute."

He returned with a highly polished hand chased monogrammed eighteenth-century sterling silver butler's tray loaded with two antique nineteenth-century Irish crystal pitchers. One contained his favorite Scottish Botanist gin, and a dash of Dolan's French vermouth. The other contained five ounces of her favorite Tanqueray no Ten gin—enough for two more drinks—1/2 ounce of dry vermouth, and a small bottle of lavender bitters. Known as the Connaught Martini, she had first had it at the hotel in London years ago and had finally coaxed the recipe from the bartender.

10

Hew also included a sterling silver shaker, and a small modern sterling silver ice bucket with a glass liner made to prevent condensation on the silver. Two chilled modern Riedel Extreme martini glasses, a mixing glass, and a bright yellow fresh lemon with a silver lemon zester filled out the tray.

These silver pieces were inherited from his ancestors. He omitted the linen cocktail napkins assuming correctly that they would be useless beside the already wet edge of the tub. His grandfather always liked to have his cocktails mixed in front of him and presented on this same tray. Hew chuckled at the idea of "presenting" cocktails while naked in a bathtub but he was too far into it at that point.

He mixed Alexis's drink first. Hers was stirred with the mixing glass filled two-thirds full of ice and topped off with half of the pre-mixed gin and vermouth. He had learned the proportions and no longer needed a jigger. He coated the martini glass with five drops of the lavender bitters and poured the mix into the glass from about a foot above the glass. He finished it with a lemon twist and handed it to her. She purred when she took the first sip.

He then mixed his just as his buddy Charlie Hardy—almost twin brother—had taught him while they were in high school. He put the gin and vermouth into the shaker, shook it, and filled his glass. He then held the lemon over the glass as he stripped the peel off into little swirls allowing the essence of lemon to fall into the glasses.

Charlie had learned the recipe when he taught tennis at the club while they were in high school. Some of their friends now believed that shaking a martini dilutes the gin, but Hew stuck to tradition. Charlie had taught Hew to strip the lemon skin without getting the bitter white layer underneath. He positioned the lemon strips half in and half out of the side of the gently curved and sloped glass. He quickly stripped off his soccer shorts and tee shirt and joined her.

The tub was a four foot by six foot therapeutic jetted model that held 120 gallons of water. Fortunately, the on-demand gas water heater supplementing the heat from the ground water never ran cold. They both fit easily inside the tub.

Hew leaned back against the edge. "Now, please tell me what's going on."

11

Alexis sipped her martini. "Well, you know things have gotten bad since Sarah quit, but today the ax fell on me! I was sitting in my office reading the latest reports when two security officers burst in without knocking and demanded that I get up. I thought it was a joke and I said I was busy, but they looked serious so I quickly reset the password on my computer and turned it off. As I was reaching for my purse, one of the guys grabbed my arm and said, '*Now*, Alexis.' They actually frog-marched me by my elbows out of the building in front of everyone, marched me to my car, took my employee badge, and opened the parking lot gate."

"What? Were you fired? You got the old 'Don't let the doorknob hit you in the ass' treatment? You haven't done anything."

"More like the Hitler goose-step march. One of the guards told me I was on indefinite suspension for disregarding a direct order, so I take that to mean I've been fired, all because some dumb-ass idiot stole my half eaten tuna salad sandwich from the staff fridge."

"Oh, that can't be right. Have you talked to Sarah?"

"No. We've all been afraid to talk. The mood in the office has been toxic since the Mink was rammed down our throats as the new head. I know more about brain surgery than she knows about education. We assume that our cell phones are bugged. That reminds me, get me a new one immediately. Mine is an office issue. I need to copy my contacts and emails, then shut it off."

"Remind me, please. Why do y'all call her the Mink?"

"She came parading in on her first day with her nose held high wearing freshly polished black knee high boots and a full length black mink coat while carrying a five-thousand-dollar lime green leather alligator purse."

"Oh, yeah. I remember now. She ran for governor in the last election, and was defeated after she tried to pick up a man she didn't know was a reporter. The media gave her the name."

"You never listen to me! I've told you that a thousand times. It's true, but we couldn't call her that!"

"I'm sorry but you know I've tried to stay completely out of the school politics—and *all* politics for that matter. I've never actually met her." Hew refilled their glasses. She killed hers and asked for a third.

"Careful. Sip this one. You never drink two martinis, much less three. Here, hand your phone to me. I'll back it up to our home server right now." He took her phone only to discover it had already been shut down. "Bad news. They got to it first."

"Dammit. Those bastards! To Hell with them. I'm going over to Sarah's house right now and find out what she knows."

"Not after those three martinis you're not. That's all you need at the moment. Call from the kitchen line to her home land line after a while when you've sobered up a little. They can't bug that. Try to set up a lunch meeting at the penthouse. I'll get Maybell to prepare something. They won't think to look for you there."

They were lying in the tub facing each other letting the jets massage their backs. Her feet were resting on his belly. He began to massage the soles of her feet because he knew it helped her to relax. She soon began to feel drowsy. "Help me out of the tub, please, I need a nap." She was slurring her words.

He got out, dried himself off, hung his large Egyptian cotton bath sheet on the heated towel rod, and walked naked and barefooted into their bedroom to turn back the bedding. He then walked into her spacious dressing room to get her robe. He helped her out of the tub and noticed she was very drunk, so he dried her off, wrapped the colorful French silk full length bath robe around her, picked her up in his arms and carried her to their bed. Once he had laid her into their bed, he went into his dressing room and pulled on an old pair of clean baggy faded cotton soccer shorts and a faded orange round neck tee shirt—his favorite house attire of Clemson University colors. He quickly realized that his three martinis were too much on an empty stomach so rather than trying to practice, he went into the small family TV room and started watching the next episode of *Outlander*. The series is a love story using time travel and violent Scottish and American history as a backdrop, but within thirty minutes, the alcohol took over. He was fast asleep on the black leather sofa under a Scottish cashmere blanket woven with his Ramsay tartan design.

At 3:30 p.m., the kids came running in from school to watch cartoons. John was in first grade at Holy Innocents Episcopal School, and the girls were in nursery school. Douglas, their house manager, always took them to school and picked them up in the afternoon. Douglas and his wife, Maybell, their chef, had worked for Hew's grandparents, and after his grandfather X.I.'s murder, they moved to Atlanta to help Hew. The children thought of them as grandparents. Delighted to see their dad at home in the afternoon, they buried themselves under his blanket and woke him. He wrapped his arms around them and smothered them in kisses. John quickly wiggled away. He hated kissing. Hew laughed. He loved his family more than life.

2
LUNCH

Three days later, Sarah and Alexis met for lunch on the expansive west terrace of Hew's penthouse. The views south toward downtown Atlanta, west toward the Appalachian Mountains, and north toward the new high-rises in Buckhead were magnificent.

The penthouse, the top two floors of a forty-story condo building on Peachtree Road in Atlanta, Georgia, was Hew's custom-designed bachelor pad, but he now used it to house visiting dignitaries and company guests. He had moved his three manual pipe organ, his late mother's concert grand piano, the 10,000 books in his library, his eighteenth-century and nineteenth-century paintings, his French impressionist paintings, his American ancestral portraits, and the ancestral antique furniture, china, crystal, and silver to their new house. He had left most of the international style furniture and all of the bedroom furniture.

His ancestors had left him more than would fit in one house so he'd replaced the artwork in the penthouse from other pieces in his collection. They purchased new pieces of furniture for the new house.

Alexis refused to sleep in his bachelor bed. She assumed there was history there that she didn't want to think about. They had both agreed before their marriage that their love life before they met should remain private. She had nothing to tell. His would make a great movie.

Hew had financed the condo building after his grandfather died, leaving him as one of the wealthiest young men in North America. The library was a two-story space. Hew had covered the old book shelves with removable panels that matched the oak balcony rails. He thought that one of their kids might want to live there in the future, but the truth was that he simply couldn't bear to sell it and watch someone else rip it apart.

⸎

IRONICALLY, MAYBELL HAD PREPARED TUNA SALAD. She knew it was Alexis's favorite, but had no idea of the role it had played in her current situation. Maybell and her husband, Douglas, were like family to Hew and Alexis. Hew's late grandmother had overheard Maybell telling Douglas that she wished she could cook like a French chef so they sent her to the School Le Cordon Bleu in Paris. Douglas studied hotel management while she became a master chef. Douglas's quick thinking and military training had saved Hew's life after Hew had been stabbed at school.

Sarah laughed as she took a sip of her Pinot Grigio. "Well, they can't spy on us up here can they? I think we're safe. This tuna salad is to die for."

Alexis frowned. She was just picking at hers. "You don't know, do you?"

"Know what? Until you called, I've been afraid to talk with any of you all fearing for your jobs. I know they hired the Minx to take my place."

"Actually, we call her the Mink. I've been placed on indefinite suspension!"

"Oh, God. What happened?"

"Clarisa set up a camera over my objection and caught our food thief. Someone had been taking food from our employee fridge at night. She still had that surveillance camera you bought for the parking lot. I told her not to do it but you know how headstrong she can be. We had already asked James to do it and he said he would but he hadn't taken us seriously. Typical macho security man. The thief was a construction worker who came through a back door."

"The door for the expanded computer lab?"

"Yep. That's the one. James's security guy forgot to lock it at the end of the day. The construction crew was working two shifts to get the lab finished."

"But I thought we had the construction area securely contained."

"Well, it would have been if the guard had done his job."

"Did they fire him?"

"Of course not. He's a guy. You know how that works. She caught him on camera eating my half eaten tuna salad sandwich. He didn't even cut off my bite marks. Clarisa took the video to the Mink and she got the guy fired, but apparently James was mad at *ME* for failing to control my employee. Never mind *HIS* employee. He raised holy hell with me in a staff meeting. He ranted and cussed at me for over an hour calling me insubordinate. He said he had been told by the Mink to just forget about a stupid half eaten sandwich. He cited the section in the employee handbook forbidding the use of personal cameras in the school. The camera she used was not a personal camera. We bought it to try to keep the parking lot secure from drug dealers and child molesters, but we never could find the right place to mount it."

"Humph. We put that clause in the handbook because several parents didn't want their children's faces shown on social media, yet they're the very ones who stand up during a recital to video their kids on their cell phones. I know for a fact that the state laws specifically allow the use of videos and cameras to catch criminals. You'll win on that one in court. They're just waiting on the attorneys to figure out the paperwork before they fire you. Frankly, you'll have a great case when you sue. You should go ahead and contact my attorney. She's great—Edward Hardy recommended her."

"Is she new at Bishop Hardy? I know all of the women there. My brother is a partner in the Atlanta office. X.I. Bishop was Hew's grandfather and Edward and Tippy Hardy took Hew into their family after Hew's grandfather was murdered. I didn't know they did employment law."

"X.I.?"

"Yes. Everyone called him by the Roman numerals at the end of his name. He was the eleventh John Bishop. He got the nickname while he was in boarding school. I know it's weird, but it's the South. "

"I know a few odd Southern nicknames too. No, she's in private practice. She says I'll get a quick settlement because they don't want the bad publicity, and they can't allow the state assembly or the public to know about the 'extra' expenses." She made air quotation marks.

"Ah, yes, well, since I handled the publicity, it wouldn't do to let me manage that story. Speaking of story, what actually happened to you? No one knows anything."

"Actually, at the time, it seemed very innocent. Like you, I thought I was doing my job and going right by the book."

"Yeah, I followed the rules in the employee handbook to the letter and look what that has gotten me."

"I doubt the Mink even knows the handbook exists. The real problem is that a few board members were skimming the construction funds and the far right wing wanted to take control. You may remember that at my last board meeting, our consultant presented some strange numbers regarding the computer lab renovation and I questioned him about them. There was a one-hundred-thousand dollar difference and his answer didn't make sense. After the meeting, I cancelled an HR meeting so I could talk with our CFO about this strange turn of events. I was in my office with the door closed talking on the phone to our CFO about the meeting when Board Chairman Kleindic burst in without knocking and proceeded to plop his huge flabby carcass into one of my beautiful Brno cantilevered chrome and black leather office chairs."

Alexis laughed. "I've always loved those chairs. We just bought four more for our dining room—now we have twenty-four to fit the original Chippendale dining table. That now matches the number of original Chippendale chairs still at Swan Bay. Even though Mies van Der Rohe designed the tubular Brno original in 1930, in 1958, Philip Johnson had them made in a flat arm version for the Four Seasons Restaurant on Park Avenue in New York City. We prefer the flat arms. I'm surprised he would fit."

"What's Swan Bay?"

"It's Hew's ancestral tobacco farm in Virginia. They've owned it since 1650-something. The land sits on the south side of the James River and the huge antique-filled brick house is simply beautiful."

"You've got to invite me to Swan Bay. It sounds amazing."

"Well we certainly have plenty of time to do that now!"

"About Kleindic, I was afraid the chair would collapse. I held my breath for a few seconds. You should have seen him when he tried to stand and his ass was stuck! He brought the chair up off the floor."

"Oh, God. That would now be considered fat-shaming except that it's true. I wish you had had the camera." They both felt the effect of their three glasses of wine and began to howl with laughter. "Wow, the image of that will never leave my brain."

"He managed to sit back down and wriggle out of the chair but he read me the riot act before he left. Fortunately, when I managed to end my phone call, I had pushed the button on a small recorder. My attorney has the whole conversation. Those old guys figured that a woman wouldn't understand the figures. They seem to forget that my degree is in accounting. He read me the riot act about what he thought what my job description entailed and what it didn't entail. He's decided to micro-manage the school. Apparently he has decided that questioning our consultants isn't in my job description. My lawyer thinks she can get to the facts or at least ask enough uncomfortable questions to make them think we know what the extra money is for."

"Do you miss it?"

"I thought I would, but I don't. I was thinking about the carpool disaster last night. I don't need that crap in my life anymore."

"Don't remind me. What a fiasco. Libby resigned as librarian."

"I know. Poor Libby. She had worked out the perfect plan. It was a thing of efficient beauty too. She had the mothers put the book bags in the front passenger seat, the kids in the back seat, and the instruments and sports equipment in the trunk or hatchback. Two teachers could handle one car rather than the three that were required before—one if they only had book bags. The kids jumped out and grabbed their gear and off they went. The moms simply popped the trunk or hatchback when necessary. They didn't even need to get out of their cars. That was the real kicker. They could no longer gossip while they waited. Oh, how those women bitched. They called, emailed, and raised hell on social media. How dare we try to marshal their children. Poor Libby was even called a nazi!"

"Yeah, the book bag nazi. I had forgotten about that. Wait. I never thought of this before. Chairman Harry Kleindic. Isn't Klein the German word for little or small?"

This revelation and the fourth glass of wine sent them into convulsions of laughter. Maybell rushed out to check on them.

"Lord have mercy! You girls can't drive home. I'll get Douglas to drive you." She made a face. "What were his parents thinking anyway? Name a child that! Strange White folks if you ask me." She could hardly use her phone with all three of them laughing.

3
POLITICS

The following afternoon, Hew invited Charlie and Edward Hardy up to the penthouse terrace after work to discuss Alexis's situation. Hew, Edward, and Edward's son Charlie often met there, usually on Wednesdays while Alexis was at choir practice and Rosilyn played bridge. On rainy or cold afternoons they met in the old library to drink Hew's eighteen-year-old Macallan single malt Scotch and in the warm months, they drank his Botanist martinis. Both liquors were from Scotland and Hew always honored his Scottish ancestry with the Scottish toast, *Sláinte*—health. The martinis were the usual one to seven mix of gin and vermouth with a twist of fresh lemon peel served in frosty martini glasses.

Being forty floors up, and having an unobstructed vista, there was almost always a pleasant breeze. They usually smoked Cuban Cohiba Esplendido cigars. Their wives wouldn't allow the cigars anywhere near their houses. The wives considered the penthouse terrace to be harmless.

Edward Hardy carried on Hew's grandfather's law firm, Bishop Hardy. Charlie was Hew's age—he taught percussion part time in Alexis's orchestral program and was Vice President for cybersecurity at Eberhart.

In addition to the typical programming studies, the school was, at Hew's suggestion, and funded by one of his foundations, adding labs for computer hardware repair and development. It was to be a state of the art program and the only one in a public school. Alexis, Sarah, and Jacob Richards, head of the technical studies, were all great friends and worked well together.

21

Hew had moved to Atlanta after he had been stabbed by a jealous soccer teammate at his school in Alexandria, Virginia. The Hardys welcomed Hew into their family after his name was changed from John Bishop XIII to Charteris Hew Ramsay, adopting the name of an ancestral Scottish grandmother. His grandfather had done this to try to shield Hew from further repercussions, but it hadn't actually worked. Hew's parents had been murdered by a Colombian drug lord after they had accidentally stumbled into a coca field and Hew's grandfather had been murdered by a deranged US senator. Since he had no other family, Edward and Tippy Hardy had "adopted" Hew.

Hew looked at Edward."Tell me about the attorney you recommended for Sarah. Alexis got a registered termination letter in the mail this morning."

"Janet McTavish? She's top notch. But before we get into that, let me give you some background. You're not old enough to have known any of this. Long before Sarah was hired, there were two schools. One operated the vocational school, and the other operated the arts and music school. The vocational school had been founded as a private school in the 1930s by a local millionaire named L. Peter Hollis, who created a hands-on education program.

"He was known nationally in education. He believed that there was a need for a school for kids for whom a college degree wasn't an option, and he also worked to integrate the public school system. The school was very successful and led to the founding of some of Atlanta's finest and most successful companies.

"Not to be outdone, the arts community founded the other school. It too was wildly successful. Some of the graduates went on to become world class artists and performers. Both school boards were run with the majority of the members being parents, but by the late 1950s, both schools were in financial trouble. The Hollis trust funds had been terribly mismanaged by the board.

The county school board agreed to take over both schools. It was a bailout and seemed to work well until the civil rights issues of the 60s boiled over. The arts and music folks were happy to integrate knowing that many talented Black kids were not being nourished in the segregated public school system but the vocational parents were absolutely opposed to integration. Someone—I forget who—decided that having two schools was wasteful so in the true conservative north Georgia political fashion of reducing spending, they merged the two schools into one and renamed it the Atlanta Region School for Vocation, Arts, and Music. It was a combined middle and high school.

"We now understand it was also the hidden beginning of a right wing political takeover. Many educators thought that would cause problems with sexual issues with the age differences, but that never seemed to happen. The boards were merged into one parent advisory group that had no real control. The school district operated the schools just as they did all the other district schools—but this one was on two separate campuses, ten miles apart."

"That's quite a distance."

"It gets worse. To appease the liberal arts crowd, the district gave the advisory board more control of both schools with the understanding that the new board would streamline things, reduce waste, and, of course, cut costs. They somehow agreed to hire a consultant to help with the public relations of the change, but naturally, in true consultant fashion, they dictated the findings to the consultant so all he needed to do was type everything up on his letterhead and collect a fat fee.

"In reality, it didn't go as planned but by then, the media had lost interest so no one noticed what was really happening. No one lost their job or salary. They merely got a new title. Both former heads of school became department heads. All of the stationery had to be changed so an advertising company had to design a new logo. The company that was given the job was the brother of one of the state senators. Instead of repainting new logos on service vehicles and buses, the existing vehicles were considered too old and a new fleet was purchased—at a considerable expense—all from a dealer who was another senator's cousin. The excuse was that the service facilities needed to be set up to handle a single manufacturer type.

"Of course, that was nonsense, and the media had fun with it, but as usual, it ran its three-day news cycle course. The one reporter who tried to follow up was mysteriously reassigned from business to sports. The computer systems weren't compatible so all the hardware and software was replaced. Several programs were completely rewritten at massive cost. The security system was completely changed. The bottom line was that the cost savings actually added up to an extra one hundred fifty million taxpayer dollars, but it was so spread out it wasn't noticed at the time. Since the two schools were so far apart and since there were no empty offices, new spaces were leased for the new consolidated head of school and her staff. That was to appease the suburban conservatives who were now pushing for a new centrally-located campus."

"So I take it that's why they moved the offices to the new site?"

"Yes. Planning began in 1990 and it has taken decades to find a suitable site. They finally agreed on an old big box retail site that has been abandoned for years. The campus site is adjacent to a planned MARTA route.

"The two former heads of school, now department heads, had had enough and took early retirement. That's where Sarah, Jacob, and Alexis come in. They were actually able to get the school designed to their specifications. Sarah managed to get the school renamed to the Atlanta Regional Academy for Technology, Art, and Music. She believed that even though they were expanding the old industrial vocational studies to include modern computer, robotics, cyber security, and electronic courses, the time was ripe for a new image and the advisory board whole-heartedly agreed. They're only the current round of leaders who've tried to get this house in order.

"The addition of the new top management layer was discovered to have cost another three million dollars in salaries and benefits and the press started screaming. The Republicans blamed all the extra costs on the Democrats and started replacing liberal board members with conservative people.

"That's when the ugly disease of partisan politics began to really take hold. The district put Harry Kleindic in as chairman of the board. He only took the job after the district agreed to give his board autonomous control. The district was more than happy to get rid of this school because it didn't fit into their idea of a standard public school.

"Naturally, the state is still funding the whole thing. Since politicians rarely ever get into politics to help their fellow man, they had seen ways to line their own pockets with all this pending construction. At least Janet and her folks were able to control the programming and design and they moved into a new facility of which they approved."

Hew raised an eyebrow. "That's quite a story, Edward. We're actually building a new MARTA rail station at our Marietta Street project, and the school will have its own new station, but I wouldn't take the contract for the Academy. Alexis said that it could be construed as a conflict of interest since she worked there.

"Fat lot of difference that makes now. At least they hired a decent architect, but he had his hands full dealing with the construction manager. Those managers cover their fee by reducing the quality of the construction. They call it 'value engineering.' I call it taking all of the value out of the engineering. They give an initial price then once the contract is signed, they start recommending reductions. Of course the cost of construction goes down, but magically, the contractor's profit increases. Most owners don't even realize it."

Edward nodded. "That's where it all started to go north, Hew. To keep the newly-emerging Chinese contractors out of the bidding, the new board—Harry, actually—persuaded the state to allow the new school to be completely autonomous from the Atlanta school system and then got them to agree to forgo the public bid process. They found some federal funding. That meant they had to adhere to federal guidelines including the hiring of minority and small business construction companies."

"Wait. I thought the saying for things going bad was south, not north."

"Ha. Whoever heard of anything good going north?"

"But Edward, hiring minorities is a good thing, right?"

"It would certainly be except that at that point in time, most minority and small business construction companies were small outfits and worked out of their trucks. They couldn't get the insurance or bonding for a multi-million-dollar project so the politicians saw a chance to scam the system. The construction company—remember, this wasn't a public bid— hired these subcontractors by handling the insurance and paperwork for them. There were...um...let's just say, management fees, of course."

"I know about that. I also know that the original fifty-million-dollar budget doubled. The old air-conditioning system was worn out. It consisted of large air handling units located on the roof which dumped conditioned air into the huge open space. That didn't work for labs, classrooms, studios, and offices. When the contractor opened the door on the old cooling tower beside the building, he propped his aluminum ladder on the bottom condensation pan and it punched right through to the ground. At least that gave them the opportunity to upgrade to ground water source units with deep wells bored under the massive parking lots.

"Alexis was able to persuade the board to add solar panels to the flat roof which, by the way, had to be completely replaced. That gave them the opportunity to add much better insulation. Of course, the roof structure had to be beefed up to carry the weight of the extra insulation. Fortunately, the columns and foundations were up to the additional task.

"The electrical system was undersized so it was replaced entirely and the only toilets were in one corner of the building. The only truly shared spaces, other than the main offices, are the library and the food court. The food court was to have had a large clearstory set of windows, but Kleindic bullied the board to change it to a large geodesic dome. The construction managers found a way to cut the cost of the dome too. The staff referred to the bulge on the roof as 'Harry's putz.'"

Edward grinned. "Putz? That means 'penis head' if I remember my playground Yiddish correctly. I didn't know that. It was somehow kept out of the press. Once actual planning began, things heated up. The artsy crowd began to complain about the high cost of fancy tools and equipment for the vocational folks."

Hew shook his head. "I remember that fiasco. Alexis was right in the middle of that one. She managed to get it settled. I prepared a spread sheet showing the true costs of the 1000-seat theatre construction with the new sloped floor and the scenic backdrop fly loft, and the 500-seat recital hall."

"They'll settle with Sarah to stay out of court and avoid bad press."

"So, basically, Sarah really *did* simply quit."

"Yes, but actually, she saw the handwriting on the wall and got out because if the shit had hit the fan during the construction, she would have been made to take the fall—they'd have blamed it on poor management. Of course, it wasn't her poor management, but politicians seem to be bullet proof."

"That's basically what happened to Alexis, too, isn't it?'

"Yes and no. I'm not convinced that the whole story is out yet. It's too trivial in my mind. She's got a good case, and she'll get her day in court, but don't expect it to happen quickly like Sarah's. They're going to drag it out if for no other reason than to run up the legal fees. Their attorney has retained another firm to handle this. He's just going to monitor it, dream up roadblocks, and run up the fee."

"When will this all come out? The public needs to know."

"Most of it will never surface. The feds should step in, but the minority business angle makes it too politically hot with the administration in Washington. The Georgia State Assembly is doing their best to keep it buried."

"What about the new woman in Sarah's job? Alexis says she has no experience."

"She's a sad case really—a political joke at best. She was floundering about so her buddies put her in there so that she could get a wad of cash without exerting herself. She had too much information on them so they needed to keep her happy. If she can stay clean and keep her head down, she can ride it until she's ready to retire and we can't do anything about it."

"If Alexis has anything to say about it, she's toast."

"Hew, that board is just a bunch of sycophants. They just sit around the very expensive custom-made boardroom table, rubber stamp Harry's agenda items as they are directed, and look good when they're trotted out to cocktail parties and press events. There's nothing any of us can do short of running for a seat on the board, and we aren't going to do that. You, Alexis, and I need to stay out of it entirely. I can poke around, and I'll let you know what I find out, but stay away otherwise. It will run its course eventually."

"Yeah, I hear you. I hate politics anyway."

Charlie chimed in. "If they fire Alexis, I'll quit. I worry about the rest of the faculty, though. Harry and the Mink are making life difficult, but the rest of the faculty need the salaries."

Edward shrugged. "Hew, politics have served us well. You and I made a fortune from the last recession while many were going bankrupt. You were too young to understand, but your grandfather X.I. and I saw it coming and took action."

"How?"

"This very site for starters. The Democrats were in power in Washington and decided that everyone needed affordable housing."

"I've discovered the hard way that that's a politically correct word for subsidized housing."

Edward refilled their glasses. "Of course, but let's not get into that. When the Baptists sold this parcel to the developers at a highly inflated price, the developers thought nothing could fail here in this neighborhood. They didn't see the recession coming and promptly went bankrupt. The Republicans in Congress saw a way to rid the country of some of the federal banking regulations so they helped craft a bill that opened the banks to questionable loans. Wall Street picked up the loans but sold them in batches that couldn't possibly be serviced. Developers though, were grabbing money as quickly as possible. When the whole house of cards collapsed, it was tragic and much of the entire world went into recession like falling dominoes. I must admit, though, that it was comical to watch the blustering politicians hold hearings trying to blame it all on the Wall Street bankers. The bankers, knowing what the congressional fools had done, just sat there trying to act contrite. Of course, several of them had gone under so they weren't celebrating, but they weren't going to prison."

Hew nodded. "One of our associates, now my partner, recognized the opportunity to acquire this property at well below market value. She pitched it to X.I. and me. X.I. quickly bought it—much to the delight of the bank—and Eberhart Engineering and Construction started the design work. X.I. financed the whole thing from the Bishop family trust fund coffers. The number of units and the Germans' efficient design and construction almost guaranteed a sizable profit. The sale of three quarters of the units paid X.I. back. The rest was profit, and sale of units began just as the recession was ending. As you know, this was a hot market product. X.I. acted as banker, we retained an independent realtor, and we were the closing attorneys. We walked the whole planning process through an idle city planning department too."

"You didn't mention that you added a right of first refusal buyback clause to every sale."

"Everyone who used us as their loan company got a very low interest rate. That spurred sales. You're seeing the benefits of that now."

"I know. We're reselling the units at more than double the initial price. So, Hew, don't completely trash the politics. It's just unfortunate that they have landed in your bedroom. Alexis will land on her feet, so don't worry."

"I know. I just need to find a way to take her mind off of it."

4
PUPPIES

"Alexis," said Hew, "we really need to get away for a few days. You're worrying too much about your job situation. I can see it in your face. The Hardys are going to Highlands, and I'm sure they would love to have us, but I'm thinking we're overdue for a visit to Swan Bay."

She laughed. "You got the same call I did, didn't you?"

"Me?"

"You'd be a terrible poker player. I always know when you're lying."

"You got me. It's been a long time since Sebastian died and I still miss him terribly. He got me through some really bad days and I never thought I could have another dog like him, but John's been asking for a puppy, and both girls sleep with stuffed dogs every night, so yes, I got a call. Sebastian's grandpuppies are ready to leave the farm."

"I agree. Let's fly up this weekend. I think Douglas and Maybell might like to go for a visit too. Her arthritis has really been acting up. A weekend in the country might be good for both of them."

THEY FLEW UP ON FRIDAY AFTERNOON in the family's jet. Swan Bay Farm is Hew's 8000 acre ancestral tobacco farm on the south side of the James River near Clairmont, VA. His first American ancestor, Captain John Bishop, had arrived in Jamestown in 1638 to plant tobacco. This is a part of his original land patient as they call a deed in Virginia. While the farm is still in the family, Hew's grandfather, X.I. Bishop, stopped growing tobacco after winning a landmark decision against big tobacco. X.I. saw what smoking did to smoker's lungs during his time in medical school. Today the farm was a world renowned equestrian breeding center. Jeffrey and Mary Beverly run the program with the help of several first class vets. Hew hadn't told six-year-old John about the puppies, but as soon as the plane door opened, John bounded down the stairs and headed for the barns where he discovered three chocolate Lab puppies. It was love at first sight for John and the puppies.

"Dad! Dad! Mom! Come look! PUPPIES! THREE puppies. One boy and two girls. One for each of us. Look! Can we take them home? PLEASE? I'll take good care of them, I promise. You won't have to do a thing."

Maybell laughed. "Boy, you can't even pick up your dirty socks. What makes you think you're good enough to care for one dog, much less three?" She was good at baiting him and it always worked.

Alexis moaned. "No-o-o. one maybe, but not three."

Hew laughed. "Look at Elizabeth and Courtney. They've already bonded with the females. This isn't going the way I had planned, but it's all right with me."

"Are you crazy? Maybell, Douglas, and I are NOT going to clean up after three puppies."

"I understand. John and I will do it. We'll be fine."

Alexis's heart had already softened. She had grown up with black Labs. "Right. Well, John, get started. Clean up this mess in the puppy box and feed them while I watch."

"I want to name mine Johann."

Elizabeth put both hands on her hips and thrust out her three-year-old chest. "I want to name mine Princess."

"Noooo screamed her identical twin, Courtney. "I want to name *mine* Princess." She started crying.

Hew went over and sat beside her and picked her up with the tiny puppy. "Courtney, do you know what's better than a princess? A queen is better than a princess, and a queen is smarter than a princess. Maybe you could name her Queenie. How does that sound?" Courtney perked up. Crisis averted. Again.

"Douglas, let's go find ourselves some of Jeffrey's scotch and sit on the porch away from this madhouse."

Jeffrey joined them. "Hew, I've been meaning to talk with you for a while. The main house is overdue for some major restoration. The inside is fine, but the exterior woodwork has some rotten places, and the sashes are getting spongy."

"I agree. I'll get Johann on it next week. It's time to have a complete building survey done for the entire farm. We need to review the systems too. All that electronic stuff left over from the Drug Enforcement School is probably out of date and can be ripped out. I want some ideas for new uses for those buildings as well."

"I hadn't thought about that. I hate to see it go, though. We were a great team. We busted a major Colombian cartel and reclaimed hundreds of millions of dollars."

"Yeah, it was retribution for what drugs have done to my family. It wasn't nearly enough, but it helped. It had run its course for my family though after X.I. died. We lost our passion. He had been the champion for our cause, but we realized after his death that drug addicts and casual users were only increasing despite our best efforts."

"I think it would be better if Pink and I dismantled it before your guys arrive. I don't need anyone asking uncomfortable questions." Pinkney Summey had been Jeffrey's second in command while the drug enforcement team was in place.

"How's Pink doing?"

"He's great. Still single. He's living the life now."

Hew laughed. His third wee dram was kicking in.

THE NEXT MORNING AFTER A BREAKFAST that included Ms. Mamie's famous buttered biscuits and a stack of her blueberry pancakes, Hew and Jeffrey rode their ATMs out into the 8,000-acre farm to look at the condition of the buildings. After a famous farm style lunch, Hew sat in an old rocking chair on Captain John's porch of the many times restored log cabin. He was sipping his unsweetened ice tea neutralized with lemon.

John walked up, a squirming puppy cradled in his arms.

"Now, son, you know we can't take the puppies home yet."

"Sure we can. Dr. Thomas said they've been weamed."

Hew laughed. "The word is *weaned*. It means they can now eat solid food instead of their mother's milk, but they haven't been house broken yet and we don't want them in the house until they no longer pee or poop on the floor. You don't want to clean that up every few hours, do you?"

John wrinkled up his nose. "I didn't think about that, but can't they just use Sebastian's old outdoor potty?"

"Sure, but not until they've been trained."

"I want to stay here and help train them. Aunt Mary won't mind, and I promise to be good."

"The vets don't need your help, and besides, I need to send them the plans for the outdoor potty, so it will take a while." Hans Struzena, Hew's German head of engineering at Eberhart, had designed an ingenious canine toilet for Hew's condo to avoid the forty-floor trips to walk Sebastian. He devised a sloped pressure-sensitive pad of artificial grass located over a roof drain on John's terrace. It even had a small fire hydrant. When Sebastian stepped off the grass, the fire hydrant sprayed water on the pad, washed the waste away, and refilled his bowl with fresh water. Hew had another one installed outside the garage at their new house but Sebastian died of old age shortly after they moved in.

Sensing he was losing the argument, the crafty little kid changed the subject. "Dad, can I ask you another question?"

"*Can* you? Yes. *May* you? It depends."

"Dad, MAY I ask you a question?"

"Certainly. Fire away."

"What's a boing?"

Hew choked on a mouthful of tea. He stood and hung his head over the porch rail coughing and spitting until his spasms stopped. "It's a cartoon sound to simulate a bouncing spring."

"No, that's not it. Sorry, Dad. I tried to google it but the answer didn't seem right."

"Do you mean *bong*?"

"Maybe, but it's not a bell sound. I know that much."

Hew tried not to sound alarmed or accusatory. "Who's been talking to you about bongs?"

"Eddie was invited to go over to Brent Simons's house to play video games, and Brent tried to get him to suck on his bong. Brent told him it would make him feel really good and the game would come alive."

Fearful of the answer, Hew forged ahead. "Did Eddie do it?"

"No, he said he didn't want to put his mouth on something that someone else had already sucked on."

"Ah. Smart guy. Have you ever been to Brent's house?

"No, sir. He invited me, but I told him I needed to practice my music. Eddie rode his bike over—they live two blocks from his house. Once Brent started sucking on the bong, Eddie didn't like the smell so he said he needed to go home and study. Brent invited him back and told him he would sell Eddie a new bong and give him his first session for free. Brent has bong parties for the neighborhood kids because Brent's parents work until six. Brent's dad grows the brown stuff that goes in the bong on his grandmother's farm, and he lets Brent keep the money he makes."

Suddenly, the idea of John staying at the farm for a few months started to sound like a good idea to Hew. As if on cue, Johann let go a runny, puppy poop down the front of John's teeshirt. John stood up crying and started to drop the puppy. "Ewww! Gross! Oh gross."

Hew laughed again. "Stop. If you drop him and he runs off you'll have to catch him before the hawks do."

"But, Dad, it stinks."

"Yeah, but that's what babies do. Yours stunk too, but we didn't drop you on the floor. Let's go over to the garden hose and I'll wash you both down. Then you give me Johann while you go inside and take a shower. I'll go get you some dry clothes, but you must load the washing machine yourself."

"I don't know how to use the washer."

"Great time for you to learn, buddy boy. This probably won't be the last time either. Welcome to parenthood."

After showing John the wonders of a modern laundry setup, Hew quickly left him to it and moved off to one of the old drug enforcement training center barns. He stopped by and dropped Johann off with the vets, but before he put him down, he kissed the little fellow on the nose. "You may have just saved two young boys lives, little one. Welcome to our family." Hew was rewarded with a sloppy face licking.

Hew was very glad the secure internet and phone system still worked. He started to rethink the idea of ripping all of it out. He put in a call to Charlie and Edward. They were sitting on the terrace of their vacation house at Highlands, NC in the mountains north of Atlanta sipping their wee drams of Macallan 18 single malt. They couldn't believe what Hew was telling them.

Charlie was barely able to speak above a whisper. "And you're sure he said he didn't try it?"

"Yes. Positive. Is he there?"

"No, they've gone into town but I expect them back momentarily."

"Here's what I suggest, if I may. Don't confront him yet. Let's think this through first, but I think we're going to leave John up here for a while and I think Eddie should join him until we clear this up." Hew paused. "I'm not going to question John further because I don't want him to know we're actively taking this seriously. He would worry, and at the moment he's all about his new babies. Neither of them needs to be anywhere near Atlanta when the bust goes down as I'm damned well sure it will after I talk with the DEA. There will probably be lots of families involved in this if my hunch is correct, and we know all too well what drug cartels are capable of doing." Hew shuddered at the memory.

Edward broke the silence. "I'll fly with him tomorrow from here. We won't take him back to Atlanta. I want to meet with Jeffrey and get his ideas about how to approach the DEA with this. I worry about Eddie. He does love to talk and brag."

"Tell him John has three new puppies and he needs help training them."

"Actually," Charlie chimed in,"if you'll have us, I think we all should come. Eddie will love the puppies. Are there any more?" We'd love to have one too."

"Three are reserved for John and the girls. But there's one black one left from another litter. It's yours if you want it."

When Hew talked with Alexis, she agreed with the concept, so when Hew went in to tuck John into bed, he told him that he could stay and that Eddie was coming to help him.

John was ecstatic. "Dad, I really wish I had a practice organ, though.

Look at this post I found last night online. It's a nine rank mechanical action organ and it's in a climate-controlled warehouse."

Hew smiled. "We've got my mother's practice organ coming back here next week. Once it's set up, I'll teach you to tune the pipes."

John sat straight up. "Where's it been?"

"My father had it built for our apartment in New York. It was a small one manual continuo. After my grandfather had the Cali condo cleaned out, I had it set up in his pool house. I then wanted it set up here, but just have never gotten around to it. I recently wanted to add another bathroom on the second floor and rearrange the old one that opens into the center hall. I thought two en suites would be better. The historians didn't agree, so I decided to upgrade the fixtures. When they pulled out the old toilet, they found that it had a slow leak and several floor boards needed replacing. When they pulled the rotten flooring up, they discovered that the entire floor boards on the second floor had been taken up at some point and relaid ninety degrees to the original on two inch thick sleepers. That partially explains why the floor boards in the ballroom run in the short direction rather than in the long direction. I did some research in the journals and discovered a note saying that the carpenter had been paid to relay the second floor, raise the skirting, and rework the stair. We don't know why."

"But what about the organ? Where has it been?"

"It's been in the College of William and Mary's recital hall. Grandfather loaned it to Colonial Williamsburg for a series of chamber concerts for a visiting dignitary and it's been there ever since. The original palace organ was moved to the Wren Chapel during the 1920's restoration, but they wanted something small and portable to use in smaller rooms in the palace. Our organ case isn't quite stylistically right for the purists and someone has recently given them a historic 1765 English organ built by Johann Snetzler."

"I've played it," said John. "Aunt Mary took me to see it. She didn't tell me that it had belonged to my grandmother. It's only one manual with no pedal. The one in Phoenix is much larger."

"True. Maybe Bruton Parish Church would like to have it for their choir room. Hans has engineered a steel plate to fit within the depth of the old spacers to spread the load over many floor joists. The floor boards will be relaid as if nothing has changed. The carpenters will be here tomorrow to begin the work."

"Okay. I'll set my alarm for seven."

"No. I don't want you or Eddie climbing around in here while the floor is up. If you fall through, you could break your neck. Stay away until I tell you to come in. I think I'll contact the seller in Phoenix and discuss this larger organ. It might just fit here."

The seller was asking $5,000. Hew and Alexis flew out to Phoenix to look at the instrument. As had been shown in the sales pictures, everything seemed to have been carefully dismantled and expertly packed by an organ builder. The pipes were even stored in organ builder pipe trays.

Hew arranged to rent a moving pod, and have a local packing company move everything from the third floor storage unit into the pod.

As usual, all did not go exactly to plan. The pod company sent the wrong size container. It was entirely too small, but they quickly sent a larger unit the next day at no additional charge. The story was that the current owners had bought the contents of the storage unit at auction. They'd been told that the unit contained woodworker's supplies and were more than surprised to find an old pipe organ instead. They knew absolutely nothing about organs and were happy to get rid of it before the next month's rent came due.

Hew had had Jake, an expert in organ building from North Carolina, flown in on the small jet. After the flooring project was finished, several of the stable hands helped Hew and Jake move the organ into the ballroom. It took six of them eight hours to set it up. Getting everything up the long winding staircase to the second floor was a challenge, but the pipes had been carefully wrapped separately in labeled boxes.

Hew decided to locate the organ close to the west wall, leaving just enough space to walk behind the case and open the back when necessary for tuning or maintenance. The concert grand piano sat across the room under the windows beside one of the fireplaces where the natural light was perfect for reading the scores.

The ballroom was one of the largest in the state. It was much wider than the typically narrow eighteenth-century rooms. Two matching fireplaces on the end walls with ornate carvings were flanked by windows.

When the protective coverings were removed, John jumped with joy. "Dad, look! Two manuals and pedal. It's got a 16' stopped sub-bass , an 8' Gedackt on each manual, a 4' principal, a Nasat 3, a 2' Octave, a 2' rank Mixtur, a 4' Holzflute and an 8' Regal. Oh look! There's a Zimbelstern too. I've always wanted little bells." He stopped. "What's that little bellows like thing mounted up under the wind chest? It doesn't seem to do anything."

Hew smiled at his son's question. "I'm told in French it's called *anti-secousse*, which translates to anti-jolt or anti-shake. It's a small compression bellows that helps to regulate the highs and lows of the wind from the chest. Notice that it's located directly under the largest pipe on that wind chest. It supplies a little bit of pressure to help it stay constant or it absorbs small gusts. No one knows why they form, but they do. This organ also has an electric blower so we won't need a calcant to pump the wind. He built this beautiful case too."

"What's a calcant?"

"The word comes from the Latin word *calco* or the word *calx* which means heel. It means to 'tread on.' It's the way they pumped the air into the wind chest before electricity was invented."

Hew looked closely at the pipes. "I don't like this offset pedal chest pipe arrangement. I'm going to have a new diatonic chest built for them. That will place the longest pipe in the center behind the main wind chest. You, Eddie and I will paint them to match the wall color. They're too visually overpowering for this room as they are now."

John wasn't impressed. He wasn't interested in physical labor.

"I have my new tablet with a killer music app loaded now."

"What does this app do?"

"You're behind times, Dad. You've got to keep up. It's a PDF app that lets me download scores or scan in my paper scores. I can use the electronic pencil to make notes, and I turn pages by stepping on a small bluetooth-powered button set above the pedal board."

"Wow. You're too smart for a kid your age. Show me." John showed his father his latest music gadget.

"I'm amazed," said Hew. "Guess I need a new tablet. Now let's let Jake start the rough tuning. He'll need to set the temperament. Why don't you go sit at Mary's concert grand and play the notes as he directs you so he can set the temperament to match the piano in case y'all want to play duets."

Some of the pipes were in bad shape from having been moved so many times. Several were out of round. One was missing its languid. Several wood pipes needed new toes. One of the small reeds was missing. They discussed the issues and Hew decided to buy a new rank of Nasat 3 pipes.

First, they placed the pipes on the windchest. Since John was younger, lighter in weight, and as agile as a cat, they let him sit on the wind chest and plant the pipes in their respective toe boards. As he placed the second set of wooden pipes, Jake stopped him. "John, turn those wood pipes back to back rather than mouth to mouth. They will work against each other when played together if you leave them mouth to mouth."

Once the pipes were in place, Jake turned the blower on and adjusted the mechanical action to allow every pipe to speak properly. It was a long labor-intensive process but finally the instrument was ready for the finished tuning. Hew decided to let Jake teach John about tuning.

John held up his tablet. "My ForScore app has a tuner on it."

"Put it away," said Jake. "I'm going to teach you to tune by ear. It's something that you'll use forever. Let's move the bench forward so you can stand on the bench to reach those little pipes easier." He scooted the bench forward and John climbed up on it.

"Now, first, look how nicely these pipes are made. The new little tuning slides we fitted to the old pipes have flared bottom and top edges to allow you to raise or lower them without damaging the pipe. Many organ builders use aluminum to save money, but these are extremely stable and slightly thicker than aluminum ones. Do you know what voicing is?"

"No, sir, but is it like singing?"

"That's actually a very good analogy, John. I worked with each pipe to get it to sound its best just as your choir director does with every singer. Then, I adjust each pipe to blend properly with the others in the rank. It's like getting the sections of the choir to sing well together."

"Like the soprano, alto, tenor, and bass sections?"

"Yes, but there are others—like mezzo-sopranos, trebles, and counter tenors."

John puffed out his chest. "I'm a treble singer."

"And I'll bet you are very good too. Now I'm going to play a note. You tell me if it's sharp or flat." He pressed a key.

"It's sharp."

To make sure John wasn't just guessing, Jake said, "Listen again."

John listened and repeated his decision.

"Correct. Now, let your hand hover over the pipes until you hear the sound change. It will waver. Okay. Good. That's the note I'm playing. Now use the rod I gave you and carefully tap the flat metal end of the rod on the bottom of the slider and raise it up. Place the edge of your tuning rod across the top of the slide. If the beats increase, the pipe is flat. If they decrease, what do you think happens?"

"Then the pipe is sharp, sir."

"Yes. Good. Do you hear a steady tone?"

"Yes, sir."

"Good. That means it is in tune. Remember the rule of two s's. Sharp equals short. To make a pipe flatter, raise the slider and lower it to make a flat note sharper. If you're not sure, you can use the beating sound to guide you but it will take longer and you don't want your body heat to throw the whole thing out of tune.

"It will come back in tune to the temperature you tuned it to, and this room is extremely temperature stable, but the storage building was warmer than the house.

"Another thing. Remember those old churches in Europe were never heated or cooled, so those organs were never completely in tune. Don't obsess over it or tune it a lot—it's not a harpsichord."

Jake looked at Hew. "Okay, now Hew, if you will hold the keys, John and I will tune the pipes. Be sure to lift your finger off of the key when I say 'Next.' Count at least one beat before you play the next note. It will take more time, but that will allow the sound to clear my ears and brain before we start the next one."

The door opened and Edward, Charlie, and Eddie walked in. "Wow," said Edward. "Is that a new toy? I've never seen it before."

Hew nodded. "I bought it in Phoenix two weeks ago. It's a real find. Mary will love having this here. It will save her hours of travel not to mention the bad weather on the river.

"It's not quite as large as the Westover Church organ. We don't have a string stop, for instance. I asked her to research the organ since no one in Phoenix knew anything about it. She found the builder. He even wrote a very scholarly book on building a modern classical organ.

"This is his Opus 3 and his largest. He sold it to a couple who then moved from upstate New York to Sarasota, Florida, and then moved to Scottsdale near Phoenix. The builder heard that the ceilings in their new house weren't high enough for the organ so they put it in storage. Someone just stopped paying the rent on the storage unit."

Edward laughed. "John and Mary will probably fight over it now. You're practicing Zen and the art of organ tuning."

Eddie piped up. "Who's Zen? I'm starved. When's lunch?"

Hew chuckled. "You're a bottomless pit just like your old man. He's always been hungry or—" He stopped himself. "Horny" was the word he'd had in mind. "Ms. Mamie has lunch set out on the buffet." He looked around. "Where are Tippy and Rosilyn?"

"Alexis and Mary are helping them unpack."

After a huge lunch of grilled pork chops, mashed potatoes swimming in hand churned butter, green beans, homemade preserved spiced crabapples, salad, and fresh peach cobbler with hand churned vanilla ice cream, the boys ran off to the barn to see the puppies. The women drove to Williamsburg to shop, and the guys dragged themselves onto the porch of the old cabin and into the rocking chairs.

Edward broke the silence. "God, what a nightmare of a call last night! I called Jeffrey right after you hung up. He's working on a plan with the DEA and will keep our boys anonymous, but we're still worried, and that has prompted several major decisions. After Eddie went to bed, we all went out to the garden you gave us beyond the screened porch and talked very quietly for several hours.

"Rosilyn blames herself, but we don't. So don't bring it up. She just assumed that the kid's mother was a stay-at-home mom too. Here's what we're going to do. First, Tippy is going to retire from her medical practice and I'm going to scale back and ease into retirement. Second, we're going to sell our house in Atlanta to Charlie for whatever they get from the sale of their house in Decatur so we can get him out of that neighborhood. As you know, Rosilyn inherited it from her grandmother and obviously that part of the area has gone down in the last few years. This will put Eddie much closer to Holy Innocent's Episcopal School when he starts second grade in September. They can move while he's up here, assuming you'll want the boys to stay here all summer. We've also decided to never tell Eddie about the fact that we know about the drugs. He never needs to see those kids again. After all, they're all several years older, in a different school, and he didn't play with them on a regular basis."

Hew nodded. "Yes, we had assumed the boys would need to be here until school starts, but where the hell are you two going? Highlands? The Cathedral Towers? A smaller house in Atlanta? One of my condos? There aren't many small houses in your neighborhood and none of them are for sale."

"Tippy has always wanted to get back to Charleston. We've been on a waiting list at the Bishop Gadsden Episcopal Retirement Community there and they actually have an opening for a nice cottage. It's in an area called the Woodlands and the previous residents updated it and added a very nice study to the back. Tippy will leave here and fly over to start the process. I'll contact the movers."

"But Edward, you can't possibly get all your stuff into a cottage."

Edward laughed. "Well it's one of their largest, but you're right. We're going to leave most of it for Charlie and Rosilyn. His drums are still in the pool house."

Charlie nodded. "Fortunately, Rosilyn likes Tippy's style so we'll only be moving a few of her grandmother's English mahogany antiques. They'll fit right in. We aren't even going to repaint, change the rugs, or the drapes."

"Wow. That's great. Some daughters-in-law do their damnedest to separate their husband from his own family. So I take it you think the threat is real?"

"Actually, we don't really think so. After all, Eddie was only there once, but we're not going to take a chance."

Hew drove Jake over to the jet for his trip back to Charlotte and when he returned, went upstairs to play the organ only to find it horribly out of tune. "What the hell?" he yelled out loud. How could it have gone out of tune so soon? Disappointed, he stormed out and down the stairs.

Puppies

While helping the Westoever Church committee set up for the spring house tours, Alexis had rescued three cats from a ditch. She'd remembered that she still had half of a tuna sandwich from lunch in the car so she used the tuna to lure the cats into the SUV.

She'd taken the cats to the barn for the vets to treat them. She named them after three of her favorite French Impressionist painters, Claude, Pablo, and Marie. Marie Bracquemond was one of the few female painters and Alexis really admired her work.

Hew was fine with the cats but he only asked that they stay at Swan Bay. He tried to re-name the cats Deficat, Fornicat, and Magnificat but Alexis vetoed the idea immediately.

The next morning, John and Eddie ran into the ballroom and turned the organ on, not noticing the three cats following them.

Hew heard John playing and the sounds were beautiful. Everything was perfectly in tune. "What the hell?" He hurried up the stairs and as he entered the room, the three cats scampered out from the back of the organ. The organ immediately went out of tune.

"Oh, hell," said Hew. "I'll bet those damned cats were lying on the reservoir while Jake was working. Their weight changes the wind pressure. Shit. Now what?"

"If I can't use those words, neither can you."

"Sorry, John. You're right. It's just all going to need to be completely reworked and that opening at the floor will need to be closed. It's only there to allow air directly into the blower. *Merde.*"

"Dad, I know what that means too. Call Jake. Maybe there's a temporary solution."

Jake told Hew to put extra weights on the reservoir equal to the weights of the cats until he brought the new rank of Nasat 3 pipes. He would re-work everything then.

"John, you and Eddie run out to the brick pile behind Ms. Mamie's garden and bring in a few bricks," said Hew. "Rake them out with a long handled hoe. Don't stick your hands in that brick pile because there may be snakes in there soaking up the heat from the sun. See if you can find a piece of screen wire to fill the blower hole." Fifteen minutes, four bricks, and a piece of screen wire later, all was well with the organ again.

5
THE ATTORNEY

After leaving the boys at Swan Bay in the care of Jeffrey and Mary, the other six adults flew home. They dropped Edward, Charlie, and Rosilyn at the Clemson airport where they had left their car, and they drove back to Highlands. Hew and Alexis flew on to Atlanta, and Tippy flew on to Charleston. The next day, Hew and Alexis met with her new attorney.

✦

"Now Mr. Ramsay, were you physically present when Mrs. Ramsay was forcibly removed from the premises?"

"Call me Hew, please, but to answer your question, no, I was at home."

"Then I'm sure you don't want to be named in the suit or be deposed, do you?"

"No."

"Then I need you to leave. You can't be present here unless you want to run the risk of being subpoenaed."

Hew left, and the preliminary questions began. "Tell me about yourself, Mrs. Ramsay."

"Please call me Alexis. Where should I begin?"

"Wherever you're comfortable to begin, but the more I know about you and your background, the better."

Alexis sighed."If I start to bore you, just say the word. My name is Alexis Anne Williams Ramsay. I'm 30 years old. I was born in Greenville, SC. My Williams ancestors were from Wales. They worked in the slate mines in Blaenau Ffestiniog in northwestern Wales in the mountains. The Oakeley mine was the largest in the world, but for one ton of useful slate, they generated ten tons of waste. Those waste piles are huge. My ancestor was nearly killed when a slate waste pile slid down the hill in a slate avalanche. Twenty men died. He escaped, but his left arm had to be amputated which meant that he could no longer work the mines.

"Fortunately he had a highly prized tenor voice that his Welsh male choir director loved. The choirs are still the pride of the communities and there is quite a bit of competition. He was said to never have met a stranger, and apparently he had the gift of gab. The mine owners were choir members themselves, so the mine owners dressed him up and put him into sales. His descendants were natural salesmen too, so with sales expanding in the US, they sent my great-great-grandfather to Charleston, SC, and provided him with a horse and carriage.

"His ship arrived a few weeks after the 1711 hurricane devastated the city, and he began selling the highly prized Welsh royal purple roofing slates straight from the ship. Wealthy Charlestonians thought the heavy slates would be both fireproof and wind resistant. They bought the entire boat load. Those who opted to purchase the more expensive copper nails were rewarded, but those who skimped and used rustable iron nails soon regretted their decision, at which point, my great-great-grandfather sold them more slates. He quickly started a hardware business."

Janet laughed."I think one of his descendants sold me my car."

"My grandfather moved to the upstate of South Carolina and opened a hardware store north of Greenville to supply the emerging logging business. His brother continued to run the Charleston store. None of the family wanted the upstate store once grandfather retired, so he sold it. He used to laugh that even though he was a teetotaler, he outfitted all the liquor stills in upper Greenville County. He consoled himself with the knowledge that his customers bought copper goods rather than using old auto radiators. Those radiators gave people lead poisoning. My dad and his cousins are the first in his family to earn a college degree. His parents worked hard to save enough money to get him through Clemson University. He is president of a large firm of accountants. I grew up in a comfortable loving family living beside the sixteenth fairway of the Green Valley Country Club. My brother and I attended Christ Church School downtown. He's an attorney here in town."

"Doug Williams is your brother? We were in law school together. He was a great help to me."

"That's him. He's at Bishop Hardy with Edward."

"How about your mother's side?"

"My mother came from a less-well-understood ancestral background. There's a story in her family that her ancestral grandfather killed a man in France in a duel at a time when dueling was illegal. He was probably a French Protestant and his opponent had insulted his religion. He may have fled to America arriving in Charleston sometime before the American Revolution.

"The Charleston yearbook for 1886 includes a map dated 1711 that shows a family of the same name living south of Charleston on the Stono River near a place called Church Creek Flats. They disappear after that, but there was a series of uprisings of the Yamassee Indians that began on Good Friday in April of 1715. We believe that many in his family were massacred during one of those raids.

"One of his sons, we believe, survived and went west, and we pick him up in a town called Sharon, Georgia, north of Augusta, around 1820. He met a widow with four sons and married her in a civil ceremony. She was the daughter of a Roman Catholic officer who with other Catholic officers left Maryland with their families to fight with the Georgia Militia in the Revolutionary War based on the Georgia colony's gift of free land.

"Her family founded the first Roman Catholic parish in Georgia in the little town of Sharon. It was named the Church of the Blessed Purification and it's still active. When Roman Bishop John England, made his pastoral visit in 1823, he baptized, confirmed, and married my ancestor all in one day! We have a copy of his diurnal where he noted all of this."

Janet nodded. "I can believe that. I'm a Charleston Catholic girl myself and he is a legend in the state. My high school was named for him."

Alexis continued. "In 1830, the government enacted the Indian Removal Act. The Cherokee had sided with the British during the Revolutionary War. Gold was discovered in North Georgia near Dahlonega in

1828 and by 1838 all the natives were removed. The new government confiscated their land and forced them west in what's now known as the Trail of Tears."

"Hmmm," said Janet. "That's not the way I remember it from my eighth grade South Carolina history class."

"I know, but there's only so much truth the school system can feed to school children, and that part of the story isn't correct. Our South Carolina history book was written by Mary C. Simms Oliphant, granddaughter of William Gilmore Simms, himself a nineteenth-century South Carolina novelist. He was a Southern Nationalist and a staunch defender of slavery. She lived on the beautiful tree-lined James Street in an antebellum house and was a communicant of Christ Church."

"I was in Charleston last weekend," said Janet. "My sister and I had a conversation about her. A local columnist recently wrote an article about her calling her a racist."

"She was well respected in Greenville as a very refined lady."

"Well according to the article, she is now considered to be one of the state's biggest racists. Between the 1930s and the 1960s, her brand of racism was fed to all South Carolina students of the state history."

"With almost the same effect as heroin."

"I don't know if I would go that far, but she certainly had a negative effect on the people of the state that's still going on. My family won a tract of land in north Georgia near Adairsville in one of the land lotteries set up to colonize the former Indian territory. I learned this while researching my ancestors."

"My husband has researched his lineage all the way back to the thirteenth century in Scotland. I can't reliably get information before 1820 in Georgia for this branch of my family. The Union general, Sherman, burned all the courthouses, villages, and plantations along his route during his march through the South.

"My family owned one of those plantations. They had a fine old three-story house. They had stored their grain in the attic against the hard times they knew were coming. Sherman's men burned it all. There wasn't so much as a single chicken left after they passed through. But to continue, my maternal ancestor's son—my great-great-great grandfather—was captured in the Civil War and marched from Georgia to

Camp Douglas near Chicago. Today it's the site of the University of Chicago. Then, it was an unhealthy swamp and many prisoners died from the horrible conditions. Black confederate prisoners were simply shot at the gate because the Union soldiers considered that as the humane thing to do rather than put them in with the White rebels. Abraham Lincoln's government refused to give the prisoners fresh fruits or vegetables and many men contracted scurvy. My ancestor was one of those. We know this because we have his medical records and his widow's pension from the Library of Congress."

"That's sad. He died in that camp?"

"No. Actually, he somehow made it home, but he wasn't fit to work. The family was reduced to poverty. They lost most of the land to Reconstruction era taxes when Congress tried to make the South pay for the US war debts. Without slaves, there was no labor force to work the land so there were no real profits and finally, by the 1890s, when the New England textile mills started moving into northwest South Carolina to exploit the impoverished Southern labor force, some of my maternal north Georgia and western North Carolina ancestors moved to upstate South Carolina and started work in the cotton mills. Illiterate Southern men would work for much lower wages than the Yankee men and the Yankees were already starting to unionize."

"Wait. You used the term 'exploit.'"

"There had been labor riots in the North as unions began to try to organize the workers. Some owners began to try to thwart the union efforts by providing housing and other benefits to keep the workers happy, but some of these businessmen decided to move their manufacturing processes to the South. The mill owners built the villages, owned the houses, built Protestant-only churches for the workers, owned the grammar school, built a recreation center, and sold goods from the company store on credit using company scrip at very low prices to the workers. They even provided low cost simple meals from the mill canteen for the workers.

"Of course, they were making a nice profit from most of this. It was an early experiment in socialism, but if a worker did anything the mill owners didn't like, the family was immediately evicted, and their wages were garnished to pay their outstanding bills. The mills ran twenty-four hours a day with three shifts of workers so at any time, at least one-third of the work force was at home asleep. The villages were very quiet. The mills all closed down for the first week of July every year and almost everyone who could went to Myrtle Beach to play in the sand and the ocean. The elite in Greenville society, gathering at nearby Pawley's Island, though, while sitting on their screened porches sipping their martinis and bourbon and branch mixed by their Black cooks, joked that the white foam left on the beach from the waves was actually cotton lint. They called the mill workers 'lintheads.' Being a White millworker was considered just a few small steps above the Blacks."

"My Charleston Catholic ancestors were merchants. I think the plantation owners were mostly Anglicans—Episcopalians after the revolution. The Catholics, Greeks, and Jews were the merchant class, but they did own a few house slaves and others to do the heavy lifting in the shops and production areas."

"My grandmother told me that as a teen, when she and her girlfriends walked down Main Street, Greenville, the elite Whites would cross the street rather than pass or speak to the mill girls. My family worked hard to overcome the socially imposed stigma."

"When you describe it that way, I can understand. It was a hard life."

"Actually, it was better than cotton mill life in England. Remember Charles Dickens's stories? Karl Marx actually got some of his ideas while visiting an early textile mill in Manchester, England. Today, we've made peace with it. We're several generations and many miles away.

"The mills raised my great-grandparents out of abject poverty. That's my point in telling you this. I wasn't born into privilege. It was quite the opposite. After the Civil War, that side of my family had absolutely nothing. Not every White southern family lived at Tara as Margaret Mitchel's novel, *Gone with the Wind*, would have you believe. My grandfather always told us that anyone who earned a living for their family was to have our respect. My other great-grandfather...I'm sorry. If I'm going into too much detail just say the word."

"No, no. I'm fascinated. My ancestors are quite boring by comparison. I'm Catholic through and through. Continue."

"I know some people's eyes glaze over when they have to hear about someone else's ancestors. My other great-grandfather was born in a place called Cedar Mountain, North Carolina on the border with South Carolina. He could read and write and was looking for a better life than as a dirt farmer. They were the poorest of the poor Whites and couldn't afford to own a slave. His ancestors were Swiss and of the Mennonite sect, though by the time he was born, his family had joined the local Baptist congregation. His ancestors lived near Bern, Switzerland. We have those ancestry records back to the fifteenth century. The Mennonites and Amish were persecuted by both the Lutherans and the Catholics, and many were killed."

"My Catholic ancestors fled to Maryland for the same reasons. William Penn extended an opportunity for them to escape."

"My ancestor, Hans Peter Sumi was a preacher in a small community near Lancaster, PA. Actually he was the first minister in the Groffdale Mennonite Church in Earl Township, Lancaster County, He brought his wife and five children from Europe aboard the brigantine 'Richard and Elizabeth' and arrived on September 21, 1732."

"What's the difference between Mennonites and Amish?"

"Basically the Mennonites aren't as conservative. They are a subset of the Anabaptists which literally means to 'rebaptise.' They didn't believe in infant baptism and began to rebaptise adult Catholics and Protestants. One of his descendants migrated south through the Shenandoah Valley on what has become known as the Great Wagon Road.

"My great-grandfather came down out of the mountains and got a job in a new cotton mill in Greenville. My great-grandparents lived in the mill village until his retirement. One of their infant daughters is buried there in the old village cemetery. Her name was Clara. They lived in a large house next to the grammar school since Great-grandfather was the manager of what they called the Little Mill. It was a one story wood framed building across the road from the huge five-story brick mill, and they received the railroad freight cars full of raw cotton bales for initial processing.

"My grandfather was born on the village and remembers as a small boy going with his mother on nice afternoons to meet his father as he walked home. Grandfather loved to tell a story on himself. The mill burned coal to produce steam to power the machines and had a very tall brick smokestack. One afternoon, his father was late and just before his father walked under the railroad underpass on the road between the mill and their house, a huge plume of black smoke burst forth from the top of the stack. Once his father finally walked down the hill from the mill to where they were waiting, he casually remarked, 'I'm sorry I'm late. We had to fire Jack Bailey this afternoon.' My grandfather thought the black smoke came from the burning employee who had just been 'fired.' They had a great loving relationship, but Papa always referred to himself as a yellow dog Democrat."

"What is that? I don't think we had those in Charleston."

"All the White southerners were Democrats. The Yankees were Republican. Papa said they would vote for a yellow dog before they ever voted for a Republican. Of course, that changed after President Johnson signed the Civil Rights Act."

"Are you saying all Southerners are racists?"

"As retired US Senator Fritz Hollings told Ed Bradley during a TV interview, 'well, Ed, not all of us.'"

She snorted. "I remember seeing that interview on TV."

"Papa always marveled at our new fancy house. The mill village house had single bare 50-watt light bulbs hanging on a twisted pair of brown wires from the ceiling of each room.

"To this day, my mother remembers those dim lights in her grandparents' house. She can't stand dim lighting. She wouldn't allow dimmable light switches in her house."

"Papa's mother had to roll the huge white tub washing machine from the back porch to the kitchen sink to wash clothes. The kids weren't allowed into the kitchen on Mondays because she didn't want their arms to get caught in the wringer. She had to stand on a chair to remove the light bulb from the ceiling socket and screw in a little adaptor that allowed the washing machine to be plugged in. I've heard that story so many times I can still picture her standing on a chair leaning over a huge tub full of hot water trying to balance herself while screwing the little plug into the dangling light socket. Papa had nightmares that she could have been electrocuted. He was allowed to carry the baskets of wet clothes out to the clothes lines where she pinned them up with wooden clothes pins."

Janet leaned back in her chair. "Our Black maids did that too. It took two days in the Charleston summer humidity to dry clothes. If a storm brewed in the afternoon, we kids had to help haul in the still wet clothes.

I can still remember how good those dry towels smelled, though. Some-times, they even smelled like jasmine. There's a story about a brothel at 12 Short Street in Charleston. As a seaport, brothels were legal in Charleston up until the 1930's and many people who lived on Short St. still remember the house at number 12. State Senator Fielding's family owned the Black mortuary on the corner and he tells a story about his mother never leaving the clothes on the line overnight because if the police raided number 12, the men would run naked through the neigh-borhood and would grab anything they could to cover themselves."

Alexis laughed. "How's that for being environmental?"

"Yeah," said Janet, "but the sun dried clothes were as stiff as a board. As a manager, he was fortunate to have been allowed enough land to plant a small vegetable garden and raise chickens. Papa always laughed about walking barefooted as a boy in the summertime through the chick-en yard to get the eggs. His mother always had to remind him to wash the manure off his feet before he opened the back porch screened door. He also learned to wring a chicken's neck in preparation for the family's Sunday lunch. They were also fortunate to have had an enclosed bath-room on the back porch." She paused. "Please continue."

"After great-grandfather retired, one of his sons—the one who sold appliances, carpet, and TVs—bought two lots with a view of the beloved mountains. On one lot, he built his parents a house, and on the adjoin-ing lot they planted a vegetable garden and raised more chickens. There were woods below the house along a small stream and great-grandfa-ther like to take afternoon walks in those woods. They reminded him of his childhood in the mountains. He taught my grandfather, as he had been taught, to kick a fallen log to scare any critters away. He would then drop his pants and take his afternoon, um, *relief,* while sitting on the log. He also taught my grandfather how to tell the difference between leaves that were safe for wiping and the ones that were poison."

"Well that was a smart thing to know."

"I laugh when Papa tells this story. I can just see the two of them sitting there. On hot summer evenings before air-conditioning, the fam-ily gathered in the dark after supper on the large screen porch to try to cool off. After Grandmother and the women finished in the kitchen, they brought trays of sweet iced tea out for everyone. That tea was like brown sucrose because of all the sugar. Granny always said that tea had to be sweetened while the water was boiling. She said that a vigorous boiling was necessary to kill the germs and animal droppings because tea was picked and processed dry."

"We used to make sun tea by placing a gallon of water with the tea bags dangling from those little strings out in a sunny spot for a few hours."

"I remember trying that. It's a wonder we aren't all dead. All of us grandkids were usually there on the porch too. I can still remember that we played in the late afternoon shade of the pine trees until the lightening bugs came out. We caught them in jars with holes punched in the lids. Once the mosquitoes started biting, though, we quickly ran to the screened porch. He loved to have his *brood* as he called us around him with his old black Lab, Mickey, at his feet. Great-grandfather had a fine voice and when things got quiet, we would sit in the old wooden rocking chairs and watch the heat lightning dance over the distant Blue Ridge Mountains. We soon began to feel the cooler air coming from the far away rains. When Great-grandfather began to sing *Amazing Grace*, everyone knew it was his evening blessing on us all. His voice rose to sing the last verse, and then suddenly dropped to a whisper and slowed for the final words, *than when we'd first begun.* In the silence that followed, everyone knew it was a signal to go home. He died at age seventy-two from a heart attack from the effects of what we today know as brown lung disease caused by a lifetime of breathing all that cotton lint. His dog Mickey laid on the porch and cried all day."

"Yes, we've come a long way in a few generations."

"Now, Hew on the other hand has a lineage of good fortune, luck, and royal friends. He is named for one of his ancestral Scottish grandmothers, Charteris Hew Lady Elizabeth Ramsay of Clatto, Midlothan, Scotland."

"Good God! What a name. This has no bearing on your suit, but I want to hear this. It's lunchtime. Let's go off the clock and I'll take you to lunch. We won't discuss your case in public, of course. Do you know about Mary Mac's Tea Room? It's nearby."

She laughed. "Yes, let's go."

"Fine, but first, tell me about your work. What did you do on a day to day basis?"

"That'll take all day so let's drive while I talk. In a nutshell, there was no typical day. I stopped trying to plan out my days except for the obvious meetings and lesson plans. I was originally hired to consolidate and improve the art program. Members of the board wanted to make a better impression on our students.

"Two board members wanted to hold a competition for new works, but they had no idea about the money that would need to be spent. My budget was a joke so I began the slow process of increasing it.

"I quickly realized that we had two different types of art students. One type wanted to work with realistic images and the other type only wanted to work in abstract forms. I organized a changing exhibit using art work from children in other Georgia schools. It was a huge success and got national press coverage. I've been slowly adding works as my budget allowed. Unfortunately, the Republicans now in charge have decided to replace most of the abstract art. They mostly only like art if it is about dogs, ducks, horses, guns, or fish. After that program was well underway, they added head of art and music to my job description. That's an open-ended job."

"Why do you think you were terminated? Politics?"

"I don't really know. Hew and I are not political people. Sarah left because she knew too much and was tired of being bullied. I think I was in the way. I was a threat to the Mink because I knew too much about the school and had the loyalty of the faculty, but Edward has found new information. Do you know the group 'Party in A-lana'?"

"Yes. They promote the area culture. They seem to be doing well."

"The director is in sync with Kleindic. They want to downplay the symphony, opera, and art museums and make the Atlanta scene bigger than Nashville by promoting country, jazz, rock, and Motown, and all of its spinoffs. They decided that the Academy needed to stop teaching classical music and go with popular music. A year ago, they hired a man to take my place. He's been sitting on his butt just waiting. Sarah's sudden departure just opened the door for them to fire me. She would never have allowed it."

"Interesting. I'll talk with Edward. Their use of the funding may provide us with some ammunition."

❧

They soon arrived at the restaurant. Mary Mac's Tea Room was nearby on Ponce de Leon Avenue.

"Hew and I used to meet here for lunch on Fridays. We alternated between Mary Mac's and The Majestic Diner. The Majestic featured the best Greek food I've ever had. It was a haven for politicians. We even occasionally saw President Jimmy Carter there. The restaurants were both halfway between his place and my Aunt Rachel's house. She lived two blocks from campus so I saved money living with her as a day student. I left here and went on to my weekend job at the silver store in Buckhead."

"Was that Beverly Bremer's shop on Peachtree Road? They recently closed after 47 years."

"That was it. I worked there on weekends until we were married. My mother ordered silver in my pattern from that shop for years for every birthday and Christmas. She wants to start patterns for our girls, but I finally took her into our butler's pantry and started opening the custom cloth-lined silver drawers. She finally got the point. Hew inherited enough for everyone we know, but my mother is from a generation that still believes all girls need their own pattern."

"Fewer people are buying silver now. We're living in a stainless and plastic era."

"Hew has a complete set for twelve of Arne Jacobsen's stainless steel flatware that he used in his penthouse. It was designed for a hotel in Denmark and is now well known by the modern art crowd. It even has left and right-handed soup spoons. The knives look like surgeon's scalpels. We use it everyday for breakfast and lunch because John loves it, but we use our silver every week when we're all at home for family dinners in the dining room. We want to kids to learn to eat and talk like refined people. All the sterling flatware except the knives go into the dishwasher so there's no problem with keeping it polished.

"Hew went on to campus after lunch. We always had the Southern Special. He had the baked chicken breast with dressing and I had roast pork with dressing. The veggies were seasonal. We both had the peach cobbler for desert."

"Then I'll try the baked chicken breast. So how did Hew get that unusual name?"

She sighed. "His paternal ancestry dates back to at least the fourteenth century in Scotland. His maternal ancestry goes back even further. He still has cousins in Scotland whom we visit every summer. When James, son of Mary Queen of Scots, ascended to the Scottish throne, the men on both sides of Hew's family, having fought for generations in service of the Scottish crown, continued their service. One of Lady Elizabeth's relatives, John Ramsay, a page at court, saved King John's life during the battle known as the Gowrie Conspiracy. Apparently John came in to show the king a hawk he had caught in the woods and happened upon a struggle. John Ramsay killed the two conspirators and was knighted for his heroic action. There's still controversy about that battle on the fifth of August, 1660, but no one disputed that the young page saved the king's life. He even testified in court and admitted it. There's a book about it called *Blood of Kings* by a British historian named J. D. Davies. John Ramsay, by then Sir John, was a favorite of James I. Lady Elizabeth Ramsay married Sir Knight William Bishop the Elder. Scottish King James VI, as you know, became King James I, and the Ramsay family profited from the royal connection. It's mind blowing to think that had it not been for this young page, we would never have gotten the King James version of the Bible, and British, and frankly, American history, would have been very different."

"We really have no idea of what some of our ancestors went through do we? But wait, his name is Ramsay. Historians are now uncovering information that suggests that James I was gay—or at least bisexual. I suppose the conservative evangelicals will ignore this information."

"No doubt. Since no one has documented catching the king in a compromising position with young men, they'll refuse to hear it. The genealogists are telling Hew that because Sir John saved the king's life, the king bestowed many favors on the young man and the family. Sir John became Viscount Haddington among many other titles and was buried in St. Paul's Chapel at Westminster Abbey in 1662, but he doesn't have a monument. Lady Elizabeth Ramsay and Sir William Bishop's youngest son, John—don't confuse him with *Sir* John—came to Jamestown in 1638 to grow tobacco. His older brother inherited the title and all of the family land and assets. John was wildly successful and he was a shrewd business man. Hew's grandfather swore that Captain John's , as he was called, first gold coin was still in the bank vault in Switzerland."

"Um, er, he has a bank vault in Swit—" She coughed. "Switzerland?"

"Oh, I thought Edward would have told you," she said matter-of-factly. "Hew is one of the wealthiest men in North America. We try to keep it quiet."

"I don't think I've ever seen his name on one of the billionaire's lists."

"No. He has a series of trusts that are managed by his late grandfather's law firm. Edward Hardy is his local trustee and the assets of the various trusts are all kept under the threshold for billionaires. New trusts are added when necessary."

"Yes, but he still needs to pay taxes."

"I know. I suppose as my attorney you need to know this. Hew lets Edward sign any relevant legal document regarding his trust accounts using his power of attorney.

"We also have an apartment in the Carlyle Hotel in New York City. It's been in Hew's family since the hotel was built. We give anonymous charitable contributions through one of the trusts from Bishop Hardy's New York law office.

"Hew is a very introverted guy. I'm working to bring him out, but it's a challenge given his background. His parents were too busy to bond with him beyond his mother's teaching him to play music and sing. His father never wanted a child and ignored him completely. Right after Hew was born, his father got a vasectomy to keep that from happening again.

"I never met his parents or his grandfather. His parents were murdered by a drug lord in Colombia. While hiking in the Andes, they stumbled onto a cocaine processing plant. Hew was in boarding school in Bogota, and the drug lord came for him too, but his grandfather's men got him out just in time. His name at baptism was John Bishop XIII. His grandfather tried to raise him in Alexandra, VA, but ..."

"Sorry, is that thirteenth?"

"Yes." Alexis laughed. "It's not very creative. All the first-born sons were named John across thirteen generations. John played soccer on the school team but the team captain, son of a US senator, became jealous and stabbed Hew in the leg. Two other guys helped the senator's son.

Hew fought them, but X.I.—his Grandfather Bishop—decided that Hew needed to get away and change his name. That's when Edward and Tippy Hardy asked Hew to move to Atlanta. The name change almost worked except the senator found him and tried to murder him late one night while Hew was practicing the organ in St. Philip's Cathedral.

"The senator had already murdered Hew's grandfather. The gun backfired and the senator died instead. Hew has no relatives, so he inherited everything—including his mother's trusts. Oh, and Hew was the victim of at least six other murder attempts."

"God, no wonder he's a quiet guy. So how did you meet?"

She laughed. "You remember the afternoon of the ice and snow blizzard?"

"Ha. I'll never forget. I had to leave my car and walk home to Brookwood. I nearly froze to death. Hew was in the campus coffee shop drinking tea—he hates anything from Colombia, so no coffee for him. The place was crowded but he had a table for two and when I walked in, he spotted me, and when I turned away from the cashier, he stood and motioned for me to join him. He held my drink, held the chair, helped me with my book bag, and helped with my coat. I was smitten, as was he. We never looked back."

"Great story. How long have you been married?"

"We dated for nearly eight months during college and were married in my home parish church in Greenville, S.C., right after we came back from our first summer in England. Hew studied organ at Christ Church, Oxford, that summer and I studied art restoration. He's so damned sexy it took all of my resolve to stay out of his bed."

Janet smiled. "It's those blue eyes and that I've just tumbled-out-of-bed hair."

"I know. Believe me. My parents would have disowned me if I had gotten pregnant. He was unbelievably patient with me. I could tell he was experienced, but he could tell that I was not. We discussed it openly though. There are no secrets. I think the most important thing is that we have the same value system. We have three children. John is six. We both want a large family and frankly, we can afford one. Our twin girls, Elizabeth and Courtney are three."

"Nice. Tell me about them."

"John's just like his father. He looks like a smaller version. He's a highly driven gifted child. He practices his music for hours and he has Hew's temper. The girls are more like me. They love to paint and draw. John does too but he draws buildings and floor plans. He also builds models. The girls love landscapes. We all sing together at night before their bedtime. John is also helping me teach the girls. He'll sit at the piano and try to get them to sing at the proper pitch. He's very patient except when they knock over his buildings or try to bang on the organ when he's practicing."

"Sounds like typical kids. Who does the punishing?"

"Maybell and Marta, our nanny, do it while we are at work. We do it at night and on the weekends. We don't let our kids run wild. Maybell is our chef, but she's really like their grandmother. She wields a quick fly swatter across the back of their legs. One swipe is usually enough to get their attention. I do sometimes when I'm home, but they're usually pretty good kids."

"How about Hew? How is he with punishment?"

"Oh, no, not Hew. He talks and reasons. I was raised differently. I don't spend too much time trying to reason with a three-year-old — much less two of them at the same time. I go for quick results with a quick hand spank, but Hew was beaten by a priest while he was in boarding school in Colombia after defending himself from a bully. The bully was a son of a friend of the priest. It turned out that the priest's friend was a powerful drug lord. Hew's butt got infected from the beating and he spent a few days in the infirmary on his stomach while the cuts healed.

"He refuses to strike a child. He got extremely mad with John on one occasion, though. We used to buy little Golden Books to read to them. When he was five, John started using the hardbacked books to build buildings. He would stand them up and one open book would make two walls. The rectangular books never made a complete roof for the square buildings so Hew showed him how to make pitched roofs using shirt cardboard and tape. Two-year-old Elizabeth walked into his room one rainy Saturday afternoon and kicked his village over. One of the buildings had a carefully crafted church spire on top which she stepped on. She wanted to look at one of the books.

"John knocked her down. Hew heard the screaming and saw them rolling on the floor fighting. He grabbed John by the collar and sat him down in his room and took away all his books, toys, and electronic devices. He told him that he was never to hit a girl again, no matter what they did. John had to stay in his room all day and lost his privileges to practice his music for the entire week. John never played with those books again. He can hold a grudge. They're still on the top shelf in the playroom never to be read again, I'm afraid. John certainly won't, but he's graduated to Legos and Star Wars movies now with his friend, Eddie Hardy. Those two are a great team."

"This special is delicious. Did he punish Elizabeth?"

"Yes. He locked up her dolls for a week."

"Do the kids play well together now?"

"Usually—as long as it's John's idea. He's trying to teach them to play the organ."

"Three-year-old kids?"

"Yes. He took twelve glass Coca-Cola bottles and filled each with a bit of water until he got the right pitches. Then he blew across the tops making sounds. The girls loved the noise, but little by little he's gotten them to play and sing *Twinkle, Twinkle Little Star*."

"You really are a Southern girl. It sounded like you said co-cola. That's not a Charleston term. You still buy Coca-Cola in glass bottles?"

"Yes. Our house manager will only drink Coke from a six-ounce glass bottle."

"House manager. Hmmm. How did a six-year-old know to do that?"

"That's the way Hew taught him when John was three. Hew's mother taught it to him."

"Fascinating story. Maybe he can teach me to play. May I ask you a personal question?"

"Go ahead. I may not be able to answer though."

"Fair enough. I'm just wondering how you handle it all."

"All what?"

"Well, um, all that money. I wouldn't know how to begin to spend it."

"Actually, Hew and I discuss this very issue all the time. We don't spend it all. We couldn't even if we wanted to. We do have to consider our future family. We give to charities every year, but the accountants tell us how much we can give away. Sometimes we override the accountants and give more to a special cause. Hew and I decide which organization to support."

"Does it ever bother you that so much of your wealth came from enslaved labor? I only ask because my sister and I disagree on this issue. Last week, I saw a young Black woman walking down Meeting St. with the words *I'm my ancestor's wildest dream* written on the back. I noticed because she had the apostrophe in the wrong place. My sister and I wondered if that woman had any idea about the state of the lives of her contemporary relatives now living in Africa."

"Ah," said Alexis. "Only an attorney would have noticed that grammar. Well, I don't believe I'm qualified to give you an opinion. I basically feel unworthy to voice an opinion on the history of enslavement. I did not walk in their shoes. I've never felt the pain or suffering of being victimized or even discriminated against." She sighed. "I empathize with those tortured souls, but I have no basis on which to give an opinion — and perhaps no right either.

"When I first met Hew, though, I had no idea about his family or his wealth. He told me that he had no living relatives and that he had lived with the Hardys until he moved into his own apartment his freshman year. I got a hint when he offered to let me fly with him to England and I learned that he owned a flat in Oxford, but I still didn't know the true extent of his wealth. I suppose I didn't really think much about it at the time. As I matured and began to understand some of the history of Black culture, it made me sad to think that there were so many White people in this country who had been and are still so damned wrong. I never thought about it when I was growing up because we weren't wealthy. I have learned, though, that poverty isn't entirely about race. There are poor people of every race and nationality, and the Romans had a saying. *"Pecuniam non olet.'"*

"Sorry, my Latin's a little rusty."

"Money don't stink."

"It was mostly coins. The people handling it certainly stank."

"Surely you realize that our having been born White or Black is just an accident of nature. We tend to forget, and this is not an excuse by any means, but in 1619, when Africans were first shipped into Virginia, Galileo was being tried by the Catholic Inquisition for his views that the earth revolved around the sun and that a telescope wasn't witchcraft."

"What's your point?"

Alexis continued. "The world was very different then and values were very different. Slavery predates the European rise to power. Remember the Jews and the Egyptians? The entire Atlantic perimeter caused this problem. The African tribes had a role in this problem as well."

"True, but the issue today is still mostly about the American White part of the perimeter—specifically the South. Southerners bought and used the forced labor."

"I know. The early European enslavers rationalized their actions by believing they were saving the Africans from a heathen life in a Godless land by moving them to a Christian country. If you read the book *Roots*, you'll remember that the coastal African tribes sold off their captured enemies. It was an early example of what some people today are calling assisted immigration. The coastal African tribes were more than happy to sell off their prisoners."

"Yes," said Janet, "some Southerners still believe that their ancestors saved the Blacks from sin. Wealthy White Charlestonians even built a very large Presbyterian church in town mostly for their slaves. They named it Zion. The Blacks sat on the main level and the Whites owners sat in the balconies. The Episcopalians also built a small church in town for Black folks. The Presbyterian building no longer exists but the Episcopal parish is still active."

"How do you know all this?"

"During a discussion with my dad about how the people of Charleston fared during the war, he told me about a fascinating new book he recently read entitled *Days of Destruction* by two eminent contemporary South Carolina historians named Emerson and Stokes. It follows a local family of Presbyterian ministers whose son was a signalman for the Confederacy. He was stationed in St. Michael's steeple. Southern conservative Democratic Christians believed themselves to be strict orthodox Bible believers—the Bible treats slavery as a normal station of life as you know. Southerners characterized the Yankees as liberals, and many still believe this.

"The current battle, however, has shifted from slavery—few people today want to be thought of as being racist—to homosexuality, but it's the same prejudice dressed in different clothes."

"This conversation is getting too serious for a casual lunch. I do remember *Roots* from that TV series. Don't you just hate the modern sanitized descriptions?"

"It makes it seem more civilized, I suppose. I never thought about it, but I guess the same could be said of my Irish Catholic ancestors. My father's ancestors immigrated from Europe to Maryland before the Revolutionary War to escape religious persecution, but my mother's ancestors were poor Irish Catholic landless dirt farmers and after the potato famine, Ireland decided that it would be cheaper to ship them out than provide welfare for the rest of their lives. I suppose that truly was 'assisted immigration.'"

Alexis ate another bite of her lunch. "I never knew that. The Spanish first brought the African slaves to work the gold and silver mines of South America. What difference does it make whether someone was the New England builder of the slave ship, the captain of the ship, the plantation owner, or the goods importer in England? They all had the stain on their hands. Aren't the folks in Europe who ate the rice, smoked the tobacco, dyed their cloth with the Indigo, or wore cotton garments also to blame? They created the markets, in my opinion. You do know that the man who wrote the lyrics to *Amazing Grace* had been a captain of one of those slave ships."

"Yes, I've heard that. I always wonder if he ever walked under the porticos of either St. Philip's or St. Michael's churches when he was in the port of Charleston. Surely he heard the bells. How did he rationalize all that? That fact is suppressed today. Everyone sings that song without understanding why it was written."

"Hew says that John Newton, the author, had been conscripted into the Royal Navy as a young man and had no religious conviction. After serving in the navy, he took a job as captain of a slaver. He left the slave trade after he nearly died at sea during a storm and became an English abolitionist. He experienced a spiritual epiphany and became an Anglican priest and poet.

"Have we benefited from inherited wealth? Certainly. Hew wrote a research paper as a part of his PhD on the concept of effective altruism."

"I've never heard of that."

"Neither had I until he explained it. Basically, it pertains to the idea of being better at doing good. Many well intended efforts are ineffective. Suppose, as a lawyer, you decide to focus entirely on the legal needs of a small impoverished community. Certainly that will help that community, but suppose, instead, you use your talents to make as much money as you can and then give back to several charities in many communities."

"I see your point."

"I *do* feel that whenever I dress nicely or drive my SUV, some people look at me with hate or jealousy, and I know we're not perfect people—not at all. We're all born of the same clay and our only job is to love our fellow man and that sometimes seems very difficult. Well, it's impossible at times.

"I try not to be condescending. That somehow actually seems worse, but we do try to be kind. Somehow, we need to learn to talk to each other. Instead of a '*me too*' generation, we need for the next generation to be '*you too*,' and that's what we are trying to teach our kids.

"Neither you nor I asked to be born. Because Hew, for instance, is the thirteenth generation of his family in America, he has thousands of direct ancestors over those generations and who knows how many before them. Now, if any pair of those people had never met, or had gotten pregnant on a different day, he wouldn't exist.

"By the same token, the Black American population today would not exist except that their ancestors were forced together into those awful ships and into that cruel diaspora. They suffered terribly in those forced labor concentration camps we euphemistically call 'plantations.' All those light-skinned Africans are certainly the descendants of slave women who were systematically raped by their captors.

"Hew and I can't deny the past. We all need to move forward, if possible, without destroying each other's culture. Maybell believes that her ancestors probably weren't even from the same area of Africa. It's clear to her that some of her ancestors were probably enslavers. She has DNA in both sides of that issue."

"That's a hard truth to get my mind around, Alexis."

"You know, sometimes I think some of this is in our animalistic DNA."

"I believe we're better than the animals. Racism is a learned behavior."

"Don't forget, all races can be racist to the other races. It's not just a Black and White issue. Hate abounds. Hew said that once the Hispanics began working on his construction sites, the Black workers disappeared. They wouldn't work alongside the Hispanics. Even the graffiti in the portable toilets suddenly changed from English to Spanish." She laughed. "Hew has an excellent command of Spanish and Gaelic curses and porn words in several dialects. Edward Hardy's wife Tippy was born in Charleston and—"

"She can only be Tippy Mazyck. There was only one Tippy in town. She's a doctor, as I recall."

"That's her. Her brother, DeVeaux, was being given a tour of the repairs to St. Michael's tower following the devastation of Hurricane Hugo. As they walked into the base of the tower, two Black workers were arguing. They asked DeVeaux why the street was lined with media satellite trucks. He told them that there was a trial in session across the street in federal court that had attracted national media attention. A woman had been denied entry as a student into the Citadel Corps of Cadets and she was suing because her civil rights had been violated. One of the guys looked at him and said, 'She's White. She ain't got no civil rights.'"

"Yes, old prejudices die hard. I think it was Voltaire who said, 'Every man is guilty of all the good he did not do.'"

"My own ancestors had to start over after the Civil War. Did being White help? Sure, the new Southern state constitutions were rewritten to favor the Whites, but remember, and I'm *not* defending them, they had never really done much manual labor. That was the point of having slaves. It was all about cheap labor.

"Hew's first ancestral grandmother in Virginia was an English aristocrat. She had no idea about cooking or running a house. The first family slave was a Black woman who cooked and cleaned. Her descendant still works at Swan Bay. I sat down with Ms. Mamie one quiet afternoon and discussed this. She told me to stop worrying about the past because we couldn't change it. She's right. We can't change the past. We can only go forward, and I truly believe it will take love to bring us together.

"While he was a student in the Catholic boarding school, Hew learned several important things. Firstly, as he tells it, he learned the French organ literature from a very fine French organist. Secondly, he learned all about computers and computer programming from a master hacker posing as a teacher, and perhaps most importantly for his religion. Though he won't admit it, he learned about the Augustinian concept of true worship and the heart.

"His teachers were Jesuits and had a somewhat different view of religion, so naturally, being a contrarian and hating being there, Hew studied the Augustinian theories and argued with his teachers just to be annoying. He won't really admit it publicly, but he believes that the only way people can change is by changing what's in their hearts. That's extremely difficult to do. Most of them don't want to change all of their culture and why should they?"

"I certainly don't want to change mine, Alexis, and I suspect neither do you, but love alone won't feed a hungry child or pay the rent."

"Actually, I believe that love *can* feed the hungry. As for the rent, our projects have very low rent, and they are energy independent. We produce more energy than we use. People of all races need to understand that many of their problems are caused by their own bad decisions. In some ways, men are still hunter gatherers and women are the matriarchs who stay home and raise the children. That hasn't changed in some modern cultures, and until it does, nothing will change. Hew believes that today's gangs—Black, White, Hispanic, and Asian are just extensions of the continuation of the prehistoric matriarchal societies that are passed down through the generations. Those men have never understood family life consisting of a father and a mother. The gangs seem to be replacement families.

"Drugs and alcohol have played a large part of these issues. There's no simple fix. Hew's family worked for years to end the drug supplies in America, but the monster wouldn't stop growing. The demand just got worse. Hew tries by building a community center into every low-income project that can be used by the kids and the community. We provide a hot breakfast and a simple bag lunch for school. He hires the best staff to work in the centers and maintain the buildings. It's very costly, and we can see small signs of progress in his communities, but sometimes I worry that we are really just enabling a continuing systemic cultural problem. I think skin color is like the top of an iceberg."

"What do you mean?"

"I'm no sociologist, but I sometimes think that color is all we see. The real issues are under the surface. When the enslaved were forced onto the plantations, it was done without regard to cultural or even language differences. They were simply judged on the basis of color. I think White people are still doing the same thing even when we think we are trying to help. You and I chose where to live based on income and cultural issues, but when we build housing units, we assume that all Blacks or Hispanics can just live together since they're all the same color. It's plantation mentality.

"Hew learned that the hard way. He was building infill houses on vacant lots in poor neighborhoods. He helped with the framing and I even helped with the painting. The new owners provided sweat equity too. Unfortunately, we learned that the neighbors were jealous. It was the only new house on an otherwise rundown block and the neighbors simply shunned the new folks.

"No one took cultural differences into account. Hew's grandfather started giving a full college scholarship to all of the children of his employees. We have extended the program to include trade schools. America is a huge mix of cultures. I don't want anyone to make me change my culture so why should I force them to change theirs? Sarah and I used that idea with the school. We tried to incorporate the whole student body into cultural events. We never separated the technical students from the arts students. We held joint concerts and talent shows even though sometimes the music wasn't to my taste. I realize that in some ways, I'm an anachronism and I tried not to be for the sake of the younger generation's taste.

"For the far-right-wing parents, though, it was their taste or nothing. They complained bitterly if they had to sit through a few minutes of classical piano, violin, or voice during a talent show. Hew believes that music has the power to lift people's hearts, but I'm beginning to think that can only happen if the music fits their existing taste. One of the final straws was the board's demands to ban certain books. Sarah and I dug in our heels and prepared for war. We've lost that battle now.

"I can't apologize for the actions of my ancestors. They will have to answer for that. I really can't apologize for being White or for having money. It sounds disingenuous to even try. It either comes across sounding haughty or as whining. The real issue is how we move forward. We're trying, but there are no simple answers. I won't ignore the plight of other people no matter their race and I won't teach my children to hate."

"I understand Hew's thoughts on St. Augustine. We studied his book, *City of God,* in Catholic school but I must admit, I haven't thought about it in many years. Mercy. *Sursum Corda.*"

"At the Cathedral of St. Philip, the celebrant says, 'Lift up your hearts. We hear it at every Eucharist, and we respond we lift them to the Lord.'"

"Wow this is getting too deep."

"Thank you for listening. I know it wasn't very specific about my case, but once I started, I couldn't stop. I talk too much. Hew barely talks to people at all—especially to strangers. This lunch was just as delicious as I remember. I usually don't eat dessert but this peach cobbler was outstanding as always."

"Don't worry about it. I enjoyed hearing about your family. One day you can buy me a glass of wine and I'll tell you about the social and religious persecutions my Catholic ancestors fought in Charleston. Your Episcopalians were the ruling class in Charleston when I was a kid. May I take you home?"

"Oh, no. We live off of Riverside Drive on the river outside I-285. It's too far. Hew's office is on Seventeenth Street. If you don't mind running me there, I can persuade him to leave early. He likes to take off and get his quiet practice time in the empty house. Otherwise, he has to wait until we've put the kids to bed."

A week later, a process server walked into the middle of the monthly board meeting of the Academy and plopped the papers down on the table in front of the Mink. "You've been served."

6
SCMAGLEV

Just as Alexis walked into Hew's outer office, his administrative assistant was speaking to him on the phone and she waived Alexis on into Hew's office.

His office was a large corner space on the top floor of one of the Seventeenth Street buildings Eberhart had designed for his grandfather. Hew had furnished it with his favorite modern international style tables and chairs. Two walls of floor to ceiling glass looked out on Midtown Atlanta. The windows had stainless steel draperies that had been used in The Four Seasons Restaurant in New York. Hew had purchased those when the restaurant closed. Air movement from the diffusers made the draperies shimmer in the currents. The other two walls were covered in the same pale gray Scottish wool that his interior designer, Heidi, had used in his penthouse.

His desk had been designed by Warren Platner. It had a cantilevered wood-bordered leather inlaid top with a chrome pedestal rising from a thin gray granite base. His pull-up chairs were also by Platner—wire chrome frames with black wool seats and arm covers. His desk chair was a comfortable black leather and chrome unit designed by Charles Pollock. Four black leather and chrome Barcelona chairs by Mies van der Rohe were placed artfully off center on an antique silk rug and a matching coffee table. Two of his inherited Picassos hung on the wool walls—the only art in the room.

Alexis walked into Hew's office just as he picked up the phone. "Hew, there's a Mr. Sam Spencer on the phone. He said you worked together on the Alabama Street Project."

He blew Alexis a kiss and waved her toward a Barcelona chair. She enjoyed sitting in those comfortable iconic chairs even though she knew that as she aged, it would become more and more difficult to stand up after sitting there.

"Put him on, please." He whispered to Alexis, "Won't be but a minute."

"Sam Spencer. How are you? How's the railroad business?" Sam's ancestral grandfather had been the first president of the Southern Railway Company. The legendary New York banker J. P. Morgan had purchased the failing railroads in the South after the Civil War and in 1894 named Spencer the first president. Their line from Washington, DC to New Orleans had helped to rebuild Atlanta after General Sherman burned the town during the Civil War. Sam was Sam Spencer V, but he never used the roman numeral."

"I'm great thanks. Look, I know you're very busy so I'll cut to it. We had a fine, and I might add profitable, time working with Eberhart and you when we redeveloped Atlantic Station and then the Marietta Street and Inman Yard. We want to do it again. Have you ever heard of high speed rail? If not, talk with your engineering vice president, Hans, in Germany, and then get back to me. But please, keep this absolutely confidential. Hans is the only person outside of my inner circle who knows about our project."

Hew looked at Alexis and thought about afternoon sex. "Fine, Sam. I'm headed out at the moment, but I'll call him tomorrow. It's too late to try and reach him now, but you must know he doesn't speak English and my German is passable for music and simple polite conversation. Technical German is beyond me. I'll need a separate interpreter."

Sam sighed. "My lead engineer, Werner, is German also. I suppose we should meet instead. I don't want to do this by phone, but we need a very secure place to meet."

"How about at my farm in Virginia? We have a sensitive compartmented information facility."

"Why in hell do you need a SCIF on a peanut farm? Or is it tobacco?"

Hew chuckled. "That's strictly on a need-to-know basis, my friend."

"I can meet you on Monday if you can get Hans there that quickly."

"I'll call his secretary about it, but it shouldn't be a problem."

"Where's this super secret farm?"

"Oh, the farm's not a secret, but the SCIF is. It's on Cabin Point Road near Clairmont, Virginia on the south bank of the James River. We have a private air strip, but not a railroad station."

"I can fly there. Let me know where."

Hew hung up the phone and Alexis leaned forward. "Was that Sam Spencer, the railroad guy?"

"Yep. He has a little project to discuss regarding the Marietta Street property. Let's head out."

⚜

On Monday morning, Hew flew to Swan Bay. Everyone arrived by noon. Sam brought lunch prepared by his company chef and Hew took them over to the old DEA training center.

Jason Bruner, Sam's head of special projects, was impressed. "You know, Sam, if you put one of these in at Brosnan Forest and built an air strip, you could increase the number of clients who rent the place."

"We run a railroad, not an airport, but I agree about a SCIF. Get it started."

Hew cocked his head. "What's Brosnan Forest?"

"It's a fourteen-thousand-four-hundred-acre company retreat/conference/hunting preserve that my ancestral grandfather set up on railroad land near Charleston, South Carolina. We've owned it about a hundred-eighty years. The first commercial passenger train service in America ran through it between Charleston and the Savannah River. At the time, it was the longest passenger railroad in the world. We hold meetings there and rent it out to groups, but mostly it's an ecological preserve. It's home to the endangered red-cockaded woodpeckers and contains one of America's largest remaining stands of longleaf pines."

Hew nodded. "I seem to remember something about that. My friend Charlie Hardy took my son and me to see a replica of—I think it was called The Best Friend of Charleston—when we were in Charleston. One

71

of Alexis's ancestors, a 'Captain Coward,' was one of the first conductors. He actually saved the train. As Sherman's troops approached Aiken, South Carolina after burning a 'Hell and Armageddon' swath through Georgia, Captain Coward jumped on the train, fired it up and backed it down the line to the station near the Savannah River. The Confederate boys in gray actually won the battle of Aiken and Sherman moved on toward Columbia and did not burn Aiken—or find the train."

"Our connections run deeper than I knew, Hew. As the land became depleted by over-planting cotton, several Charleston business men who were losing money at their docks sent a delegation to England to 'acquire' the designs for the newly invented steam locomotive so they could intercept the cotton grown in the west from being floated down the Savannah River to the port of Savannah. That was about 1830. The train was faster than the river and not subject to flooding or drought, so it worked as planned. They had actually tried two schemes before they tried steam. One scheme would have used slaves to pull the wagons on rails, but that didn't work well because they were carrying more slaves than cotton and the slaves kept running away into the swamps. Then they tried adding sails to the freight cars. They actually built a rail line out Wentworth Street in Charleston as a test of the sails, but there simply wasn't enough wind to make it work."

"Sam, we *are* more alike than I ever knew. This is my ancestral farm. It's only eight thousand acres, but the family has lived here on this site since the early 1650s. We grew tobacco until my grandfather learned about the problems of lung cancer and stopped growing it. He started an equestrian breeding and training center to replace the tobacco income and opened these facilities we're in now as a training center for the federal drug enforcement guys. That's why this SCIF is here. He also replanted the longleaf pines. We've got about a third of the farm planted with those trees."

"I can only imagine the secrets that were passed here. Now, down to business. We only have about four hours. I had a PowerPoint presentation prepared in both English and German so we don't need to keep stopping to explain it to Hans and Werner will translate our English comments for Hans."

Hew nodded. "Proceed."

"SCMAGLEV stands for super conducting magnetic levitation and we're going to add a new train system to our mainline that will ultimately run between the ports of New York and New Orleans. It's roughly 1,050 miles between the two ports. A truck in good weather without heavy traffic can drive it in about twenty hours including stops. Airplanes are about forty percent faster than maglev trains but at much greater cost per mile, and airplanes aren't suitable for bulk freight like coal, wood chips, grain, and such. We're going to reduce that travel time to just three and a half hours."

Hew took in a sharp breath.

"The trains ride about three inches above the platform using electro-magnetic force and are propelled by magnets in the sides of the roadbed. It looks like a single lane concrete roadbed with concrete barriers on both sides."

"So it's U-shaped. Sounds like science fiction to me."

Jason chimed in. "No, it's real. The Germans have been developing it for over fifty years although the concepts are over a hundred years old. The Japanese have been leading the technology in the use of it on their trains, and they are building a long line at the moment away from their earthquake prone coast. Environmentalists are slowing them down. Much of the line goes through tunnels in the mountains and the environmentalists are protesting the waste disposal."

"The costs must be enormous, but why the secrets?"

"I'll get to that. First, though, you need to know the system we'll use isn't the German system, but the Japanese system. It's now superior to all others and is the fastest system available, but it's also the most expensive. As you know, of course, time is money. We'll insert solar panels on the roadbed. We're freight haulers only so this system will obviously speed up the delivery time and take quite a bit of congestion off the interstates. We've simply run out of land in our cities to build more highways, and too many people object to widening the old ones or building new ones."

"Back to the money."

"Okay. Well, we've run the numbers. Our system won't transport passengers. Passenger lines in America have always lost money and Americans aren't like the rest of the world when it comes to travel. We don't need to build station facilities and we don't need fancy carriages. Plus, most of the electricity consumed on a SCMAGLEV passenger train is used to power the air conditioning, food service, and the lights and outlets. We don't need any of that.

"Airplane usage costs about fifteen cents per passenger per mile. We're projecting our costs at about three cents per mile. There's also very little to repair or maintain vs. current trains and tracks. We're heavily invested in intermodal transportation so we are developing a very light-weight carriage with a polished aluminum cover that slides over the containers to reduce drag. At the moment, we still have a weight problem, but we're confident that can be overcome.

"There will be no humans on board. The computers control it all. We'll save money over the other countries because we'll use our existing real estate. Our historic line from Washington to New Orleans was double parallel tracked in the days before computers. There was a north-bound track and a south-bound track. To save on maintenance, we reorganized after we computerized and ripped out one track.

"That land has just been sitting there, so now we're going to put it to work. Because most of it has a southeastern or southern exposure, the solar panels will be efficient. Oh, and before you ask, we haven't planned to use batteries. We ran a cost analysis on batteries versus selling our power to the local utilities. The batteries are not environmentally friendly, and we'll make more power than we can use, so we'll get a very competitive rate from the power companies. We won't need expensive battery storage and maintenance facilities either so that reduces labor and construction costs."

"But what happens when the power grid goes down? You know it will in ice storm-prone areas."

Sam sighed. "Actually, that came up in a meeting last week. At this stage, we're still exploring a number of technologies, but I suspect the answer will be a computer program that can quickly switch over to all solar for the affected sectors. In that case we will need backup storage that can borrow from other unaffected sectors. That will substantially reduce the train speed in the affected areas, but they will continue to move. SCMAGLEV uses super cold magnets so the freezing weather will be an asset."

"I like that, Sam. We need to build that into all areas at least as far as south Alabama. I can try to write that computer program if you want."

"You?"

"Yep. You've given me an idea. Charlie Hardy and I will work with Hans to see if we can cobble something together. We'll sell it to you if it works."

"Ha. You'll cut me in up front, but yes, try it. I had forgotten about your prowess with code. My guys are overloaded as it is. You'll make another billion, my friend."

"Or four, but we'll need to sell it to someone else to do that."

"Oh, I suspect there are several solar companies that will want it."

Hew shrugged and Sam continued.

"The track bed will sit about thirty-five feet in the air. It will clear all highways and other obstructions, and it will be under the overhead high power lines. They're up at fifty feet or more. I'm sure we will need to pay to move a few of those in any case. It will cost on average about twenty million per mile. That's less than the Japanese cost because we own the land and aren't building passenger facilities. Interstate highways cost between six- and ten-million or more per mile depending on the terrain and complexity of bridges, and the costs are rising exponentially. But you must also consider the politics and time consumption of public meetings, regulatory and environmental reports, maintenance, etc."

Hew got lost trying to keep up with all the zeros running across his brain and he got even further lost when he tried to calculate his profit. All he knew was that he would probably surpass his ancestor's earnings by many times.

"We're being very conservative given what's at stake," said Sam. "The feds are paying with funds from several sources including Homeland Security, and we're donating the land and managing the system. We're taking a major share of the profits, of course. The government will get their taxes and the Germans and Japanese will get their share. It's all spelled out contractually."

"But the time for approvals, and hearings, and design, and—"

"Let me stop you there, Hew. It's all done. We don't need zoning or building permits to maintain or improve our rights of way. Congress began the legal process for intercity high speed rail in May of 1998 with the TEA-21. That's the Transportation Equity Act for the 21st Century. The 1969 NEPA process cleared the way with the National Environmental Policy Act. A commuter system between DC and Baltimore was approved, but it got bogged down. We don't know why, but there are tunnels that need to be built and one of them is below Washington, DC. Those are very expensive and time consuming.

"We won't need tunnels. We're good to go. All we need is a construction company that's big enough to handle this work. That's you. Oh, and we need a little easement along Marietta Street in Atlanta."

"You just casually threw in that last tidbit, didn't you? We're more than happy to discuss a contract, but tell me more about Marietta Street. We're in the process of selling a parcel to the Metropolitan Atlanta Transit Authority for a new MARTA train station on their new route. It'll be an extension of the Green Line that currently ends at Bankhead Station and it will run from the Five Points transfer station downtown to our Alabama Street development, along the railroad right of way to I-285 on to Cumberland Mall, then to the new Atlanta Braves baseball stadium, over to I-75, and then up to Marietta and Kennesaw."

"First, let me tell you a little history. Steam locomotives were extremely inefficient. They required huge amounts of coal and water and they needed major servicing every 150 miles. Atlanta was one of those service points. We sold you our old facility so now we need space for a small fleet of maintenance vehicles and we need a large elevated area for a new freight yard. We'll use the area west of your development above the existing surface yard for that, but we need a small area for access ramps for the local trucks to load and unload. The state will work with us to build a better road from our transfer yard to I-285. Also, we need office space for our mid-route computer center. We're thinking you can build us a tower along your west edge as a part of the contract."

Hew thought for a moment. "Pull up that slide with the route map and zoom in to Atlanta." When it appeared on the screen, he nodded. "Yes. Now Werner, ask Hans if we could build a linear low rise building along that west edge. That would block most of the noise from the trucks. In the Seventeenth Street condos, we had to use insulated windows to block out the train noise. Your trains seem to love running through

Atlanta in the wee hours of the morning. The banging of the couplers is one thing, but the acoustical engineers had a hell of a time mitigating those 2:00 and 3:00 a.m. diesel horns. Fortunately, we had learned our lesson when we developed Marietta Street."

Jason, Werner, and Hans discussed it for several minutes. "Hans sees no problem with that. It's a good compromise, he thinks."

"Magnetic levitation—next wave after the internal combustion engine. Fast. Trucks off the road. Very fast. Time equals money. Weather not a factor. No airport issues. Good for the environment. Now tell me about the secret part."

Sam cleared his throat again and took another sip of tea. This was the tricky part. "Let me just tell you that the president has this as one of his highest priorities."

"The president of what?"

Sam grinned. "The President of the United States! This is a matter of national pride and security. We're going to beat the Chinese and the Russians because they're using the German system. The Japanese are partners in this and they do not want their competitors to steal this technology. They want to move a few of their top engineers to America and away from the threat of being kidnapped—or worse."

Hew's blood suddenly ran cold. Sam had no idea that Hew had nearly been murdered four times by a drug family and three more times because of a stabbing. He wanted the work, but the question he had to answer now was whether the price was too high. He wanted no part of fighting Chinese or Russian hit squads or kidnappers.

Sam continued. "It's very important that this is kept secret. National security is at risk if we let them get ahead. We can't let the labor unions or mafia hear about it either. The New Orleans and New Jersey labor goons would try everything they could to stop it. The president will ask the Pentagon to classify this as a system for moving material quickly during a national crisis. He's already involved Homeland Security. He's ready to pull out all the stops."

Hew laughed. "Pull out all the stops? That's an organist's term basically meaning to play the entire instrument, but I understand your meaning here."

"I thought it meant to give it all you got. You know, loud."

Hew sighed. "We'll leave it at that. I thought you said this is secret. Does all of Washington know?"

"No, no. This is Oval Office only. Well, the Japanese ambassador and our ambassador know, and the Director of Homeland Security knows. President Eisenhower used that strategy to push the interstate highway system through and it worked like a charm. We're also keeping it from the truckers' lobbyists. We'll have to work with them at some point in time, but later is better."

"What about the politicians?"

"It's already funded, so there's no great concern there. Every year, the funding clauses get rolled over in so many agencies that no one notices. The military already has a huge budget for moving personnel and materials."

"Edward's brother-in-law says that Charleston Air Force base has a massive material transport system for supplying foreign bases. He says that most of the new motels in North Charleston are for suppliers who do business with the military."

"Yes, and we'll have a spur to the base to move those goods to the planes. Our tracks are less than a mile away. I'm only concerned that some of the politicians will want a payoff, but we will never pay. The president will need to shut them down."

Hew stood and looked around the room. "Our time is almost up, but I think I'm on board. I need to confer with our attorney, Edward."

"Of course. I remember him. Give him my best, but remember, it's secret. He can't involve his whole firm."

"He's mostly retired and living in Charleston so that won't be a problem. I'll fly to Charleston tomorrow morning."

7

EDWARD AND TIPPY

Hew's pilots flew the twin engine jet to John's Island Executive Airport near Edward and Tippy's retirement community. Because of their move to Charleston, Hew didn't see his surrogate parents nearly enough.

Edward met him at the airport and drove him to the Bishop Gadsden Episcopal Retirement Community. As they turned into the community, Hew noticed a small chapel with a brilliant blue-faced clock in its tower. "That's beautiful." he said. "What's that exterior texture?"

"Some people think it looks like a local variation of the old flint churches in England, but Tippy says it's tabby—something that was used extensively in the eighteenth century around here when oyster shells were more plentiful. Old accounts tell of the creek banks so overloaded with oysters that at low tide anyone in a small boat couldn't see over the shell banks." He paused. "That's not the case anymore. Pollution and over-farming, together with fertilizer runoff has nearly decimated the oysters."

Hew nodded. "The mortar at Swan Bay Farm was made from the lime produced by burning the crushed shells of oysters from Chesapeake Bay. The same oysters are found in Charleston. Lime mortar is wonderful stuff, but X.I. said the process was dangerous and the lime burns the skin of the masons. The medieval masons used rendered pig fat to treat their burned skin. I suspect the slaves did too."

Edward made a face. "That must have smelled to high heaven. In the old days around Charleston, they built wooden forms and filled them with compacted oyster shells. Once they had compacted them as much as they could, they poured in a wet mixture of sand, lime, and water. Then they compacted it again and moved the forms up. Once the walls were in place, they plastered the inside and the outside with a similar mixture. The wall was one chemical composition. Of course, over time, many of those buildings were left to ruin. The plaster ultimately washed off leaving only the shell core. I understand that those masons used a similar technique with their cathedrals and castles."

Edward pointed to the chapel. "The contractor here updated the process and poured a one-foot-thick concrete wall and then covered the outside in three inches of loose brown sand. A crew of Hispanic workers then stood the shells up in the sand. One of the local Episcopal bishops—the Suffragan Bishop—was fluent in Spanish. He came by and talked with the workers and blessed their work.

"Every fifteen minutes, a timer went off and they took a break and moved to a different location so they wouldn't create a pattern. Once the shells were set, the contractor poured a very wet mixture of white Portland cement that was absorbed by the sand into the form—leaving only what you see exposed. The cured concrete panels were then lifted into place. Unfortunately, the historic technique doesn't meet today's seismic codes, but this *does*."

"So, historically this was never supposed to be seen?"

"That's right, but the locals love this romantic idea of a restored ruin."

"But there aren't any shells on the tower."

"No, the tower is also tilt up concrete panels." He pointed upward. "But notice the corner quoins. They're staggered to avoid having the typical vertical joint up the corners of the walls. The panels fit together like interlaced fingers. It's so well done that it won a few national awards."

"How did they know how to do this?"

"This process was very different. It hadn't been tried before, but it was an extraordinary team of owner, contractor, tilt-up concrete sub, and architect. Notice that ragged joint above the center doors? That's actually a joint in the two concrete panels made to look like a natural crack."

Hew shook his head in approval. "That's exactly where an old wall would have cracked—the weakest point in the wall. It's a brilliant sleight of hand. The roof material looks like Welsh Royal Purple slate."

Edward looked at him, surprised. "You're correct, but how did you know that?"

"Alexis's ancestor arrived in Charleston from Wales in 1711 just a week after a major hurricane wrecked the town. He had come to try to sell slate and made a fortune. North American slates are black or blue but these purple colors are subtle and have small random streaks of a beautiful green color."

"After Hurricane Hugo, the local historians revived the use of the Welsh slate to replace the damaged roofs in town. That's why the architect knew about them. Let's stop and look inside. The acoustics are very good and there's something I think you'll like."

Edward pulled into a parking space and the two men got out of the car and entered the building through wooden doors. Hew surveyed the interior and smiled. "I can't believe it. The inside is more beautiful than the outside. That painting over the altar, wow! Those stations of the cross! And the windows are huge."

"Yes," said Edward, pleased that Hew was impressed. "We were told that these are small individual insulated panes of glass with a UV coating to reduce the fading of the interior woodwork. Sir Christopher Wren created this style of church to work with the new English *Book of Common Prayer*. He believed that people needed more natural light to read the book. In the time of the medieval church, only the priests could read. That's why the stained glass told Bible stories."

"I've seen those tablets with the Creed, the Ten Commandments, and the Lord's Prayer in old churches in England. These are large, though."

Edward nodded. "Remember that the great London fire occurred just a few years before Charleston was founded. The Wren style churches after the London fire became all the rage in the colonies. It has been said that today's Monday issue of the *New York Times* contains more information than the best read Englishman had in his library at that time. Reading was important to folks and these tablets contained the church's most essential teachings." He paused. "Plus, one of the common medical issues here with the residents is macular degeneration. These tablets are large on purpose."

Hew looked around and then stopped and gasped. "That's a three-manual Schoenstein organ console. Where's…?"

Edward pointed to the balcony over their heads.

"Wow. The pipe facade really complements the room." He looked at Edward. "May I play it?"

"Probably. Let me ask in the chaplain's office. It's just across the narthex."

While Edward stepped out of the sanctuary, Hew sat on the organ bench to review the stops. 14 voices, 16 ranks. Edward returned, closing the narthex doors. "Have at it."

Hew began with the eight-foot open diapason on the great manual and built up to full organ, topped off with the tuba, and then transitioned into the 1844 Welsh hymn tune *Hyfrydol* by Rowland Prichard. Prichard, a nineteenth-century composer and contemporary of Brahms, had composed it when he was only nineteen.

A crowd of residents had walked in to watch and listen. They spontaneously began singing the words to William Dix's *Alleluia! Sing to Jesus*, one of the two texts most often coupled with the tune.

Hew talked as he continued to play. "This instrument is larger than Schoenstein's instrument in our chapel at the cathedral, but smaller than the instrument at Holy Innocents that I played while I was a student there, but it has so much color. And the acoustics! How is that possible in such a small space?"

Edward smiled. "As I mentioned, the walls are a foot thick of solid concrete. The floor is ceramic tile on concrete, and the drywall is two layers—screwed and glued on the walls and ceiling. The ceiling is insulated, which adds mass. The metal studs are blocked between studs at two feet, four feet and eight feet in alternating vertical rows between studs. That works with a standard drywall sheet, but it also stops the walls from having harmonic vibrations.

"The walls are extremely stiff. This back wall is slanted two degrees out of parallel to the front wall to stop any echoing, and it helps create diffusion."

"How do you know so much about these acoustics?"

"The architect gave a talk. He considers this his magnum opus. Come up here and look at this huge reredos painting. Notice anything?"

"It's the presentation in the temple. It's magnificent."

"Yes. The artist is local. Look up into the top right corner on top of the hill. That's the Atlanta skyline as seen when flying into Hartsfield–Jackson."

Hew laughed. "Someone has a great sense of humor. I must admit, though, that this is stunning. The high pulpit really looks old as do those stations of the cross along the walls."

"We're told that the architect found the stations of the cross in an antique store near Atlanta that specializes in historic Catholic art from churches in the Northeast that are being closed. These were painted in oil in France in the nineteenth century and restored by Atlanta artists with the International Fine Art Conservation Studios. The American office is an offshoot of the English firm that sometimes works for the English royal family. The paintings are set within monuments that incorporate the room up-lighting and the speakers for the speech reinforcement sound system. The architect didn't want modern technology to visually intrude. Even the AC grilles, the smoke detectors, and the sprinkler heads are hidden."

"Where? Oh, wait. I see them. They're incorporated in the cornice around the blue ceiling. No one would ever notice them. That's very good. It's a well-thought-out design."

"The monuments on the walls resemble the old funerary cenotaphs in the churches downtown but the CEO here didn't want funeral art in this chapel so the architect suggested stations of the cross instead of memorials. The dismantled pulpit was just a dusty pile of lumber when the architect discovered it in a dimly lit corner of the shop owner's warehouse.

"The soundboard, however, is new. The architect designed it in the eighteenth-century Anglican style. Notice the bishop's miter on the top. The ceiling of the soundboard is painted with a compass rose. It's a symbol found in Canterbury Cathedral to remind worshippers that the Gospel—and the Anglican Communion—extends to all the corners of the globe. The original wall-mounted soundboard has been used as a medallion in the narthex ceiling.

When the director of the community saw the decorations in the pulpit woodwork, he asked what style they were. The shop owner quickly said, "*Roman.*"

The architect whispered sotto voce to the director, *"Don't worry. I know how to take the Roman out of it."*

"Well, he certainly did that. It's perfect. That blue ceiling is beautiful. Is it actually curved?"

"No. It's flat. The decorative painters from Atlanta managed to give it a subtle curved appearance. The walls and ceiling are painted with lime wash to help create the historic feel. Modern flat acrylics are too shiny for a room like this."

They finally left the chapel and drove through a beautifully manicured campus of buildings and trees back to Edward and Tippy's cottage. They settled into the den and sipped their favorite Macallan 18 single malt. Hew gave Edward a briefing complete with Sam's PowerPoint presentation. When he told Edward about the secret issues, Edward began to look concerned.

"Maybe the thing to do here is create a completely separate company. I'm just thinking out loud, but say we set it up with one of the Japanese guys as CEO. We'll give it a name. All the funds would go through Tokyo. The profit back to you could flow into our old DEA account in the Caymans and then your personal profits would go directly to your Swiss numbered account.

"You and your team must never have cell phone conversations. Set up secured land lines. Never text, use video conferencing, or email either, and any face to face meetings must be done in a SCIF. Above all, do not use a word processor. Everyone must get out their old typewriters and paper shredders. Since there's government money involved, the company will be subject to the Freedom of Information Act. Don't ever use the words, SCMAGLEV, magnetic, Japanese or German or any similar words in any of the meeting minutes, or correspondence."

"Jesus, Edward. That's old fashioned and slow as hell."

"Yeah, but it's the only way to keep you secure. Also, put Charlie on finding a first-rate security company. You will need round-the-clock protection. I suggest you start with an Israeli company. I know of one with a great local office in Atlanta." Edward paused. "This will leak out, you know. It's too big, it will involve politicians with their hands out, and there's too much construction in too many places. Sam's a master marketing salesman, but you know as well as I that his board has to know about this. They may not have been told all of it, but they have approved the concept at the very least. I suggest that when this does leak, be prepared to confront it head on with total confidence and pride. Call it a high-speed line. Never use the words 'rail' or 'tracks.' Be evasive about the exact speeds. Use something over a hundred miles per hour, saying the exact speed won't be known until the test trials."

Hew thought for a moment. "I think it's time to form my own security group within Eberhart. I'm going to contact Pink Summey. Jeffrey tells me that Pink turned down the offer to join the Secret Service. They wanted him to work in the counterfeit division and he heard a rumor that he would be sent to Kansas."

"Where is he now?"

"He's retired, living in Palm Beach, running charters of rich people out for fishing in the Gulf Stream."

"Then he's ready to get back in the action."

"We need another meeting at Swan Bay with the team. This will need to be a weekend conference."

Tippy walked in from her watercolor class in the campus art loft and Hew stood to embrace her. "Guys, let's go to the bar for happy hour, and have dinner in the commons dining room. Hew, you'll love the bar. It's paneled with the same pecky cypress as our great room in Atlanta, and the food here is five-star."

As they were walking into the dining room across from the bar, an older lady was approaching. "Hello, Jane. By yourself tonight?"

"Yes, Dave didn't feel up to it."

"Join us. Hew's wife isn't with him."

Tippy turned to Hew. "Jane was junior warden at St. Michael's downtown when they restored the church after Hurricane Hugo."

He bowed his head to her. "I'll bet you have some stories."

To Jane, Tippy said, "Hew is the sub-organist at our cathedral in Atlanta—among other things."

"Then, you'll love the story about our organ, I'm sure."

The bread and wine were served, and they studied the menu. Jane broke the silence. "My favorite St. Michael's restoration story involves the old tower clock. It was built in 1764 in London by a man named Ainsworth Thwaites and it's been ticking along ever since. It's a huge machine—about three feet by five feet by four feet tall—and it sits in a small room in the room below the bells. It was originally mounted higher up just behind the clock faces but the motion of the swinging bells during the change ringing caused the clock to go out of beat and stop running. They moved it down two levels and extended the movement rod up to the old location. After Hurricane Hugo, the vestry decided to have it restored. It had been electrified after WWII and the old pendulum was missing. The Whitechapel Bell Foundry director suggested just adding a new quartz movement, but the local architect woke up at two a.m. one night, heard the clock strike, and realized that he couldn't have a modern precise quartz movement driving the hands while the old clock still rang the bells. He was afraid that they would never be in sync and he was correct."

Their salads came. "He convinced the vestry to try for a full restoration. He called a clock company in England that Whitechapel had recommended only to be told that St. Michael's clock wasn't a Thwaites. It seems they believed that all remaining Thwaites' clocks belonged to the Crown. The architect told them that the original bill of sale and the shipping manifest were in the archives. He faxed the copies to them. The clockmakers immediately came to town on the next plane and were amazed. They agreed to restore the clock and put an auto-wind mechanism on the clock, but they needed to find the old bob to determine the amount of weight needed to drive the clock. They searched all the buildings to no avail until the old sexton told them there was a big round piece of concrete with a hole through it in the shed behind the rectory. That was it. It was the limestone bob. The clock's been running ever since."

Their prime rib arrived. "The architect also wanted to get the clock faces and hands restored. When the workers removed the old wrought copper faces, they found four small limestone pediments behind them. The details had been hacked off when the copper faces were installed, but no one living had ever seen them. Obviously the original design included details not suited for large clock faces."

The desserts arrived. "One other story involves the old weathervane. The rod was bent in the hurricane and when they removed it to restore it, they discovered that the tall rod had originally been gilded and the vane was unpainted black iron. That's just the opposite of what was there just before the hurricane. The vane was a black iron depiction of the devil with the golden lance of St. Michael run through him. It even still has a tail which now is thought of as simply the indicator of the position of the wind. Apparently, they found it offensive. The architect wanted to restore it, but he lost that argument."

"You mentioned a story about the organ."

"Oh, yes. Old age is creeping in." She laughed. "Well, the vestry had signed a contract for a new organ to be built in the Baroque north German style in our original case. The original organ had been built in London in 1764 by a German builder named Snetzler. His dated signature is still in the case. It seems that the builder they had selected had restored a Snetzler case in one of the college chapels in England. The architect casually asked Dennis, our Senior Warden, if anyone had ever heard an instrument by our Irish organ builder. Dennis realized that he had no idea unless the organist had heard one, so he contacted the builder and was invited to London to hear his latest and greatest instrument. Dennis and the architect flew to London to St. Peter's, Eaton Square. They had been invited to London's annual Organist Day and a well-known American organist was going to demonstrate the instrument. During that Saturday morning, the IRA set off a bomb in central London and destroyed the seventy-story Nat West Bank building. Our folks heard and felt the blast but had no idea what had happened until they returned to the hotel."

Tippy exclaimed, "Wow, Jane. Is that written down anywhere? Future generations might enjoy this."

"Oh, I doubt it. The current generation is all about now, not yesterday."

8
SECURITY

The team flew into Swan Bay for the weekend after Hew assured Sam that the staff had been given top security status while the DEA operation was working there. Sam, Werner, Jason, Edward, Edward's son, Charlie, Hew, Pink, Hans, and the new Japanese CEO were present. He would need a new American name, and he asked them to pick one. They decided to call him Bubba Hu.

After Edward explained his thoughts on security, they all groaned.

Sam spoke first. "Edward, forgive me, but that's a bit old fashioned. Secure, scrambled phones and data transfer are available now so I think the Japanese and German governments can get anything we need for communications. I agree with you about the words, though. If anyone requests anything through FOIA, we will comply completely."

Jason spoke up. "The Israeli security company can get us their new smartphones. They're the most secure available. The phones have military grade encryption. If you plan to continue to use this place, no offense, but all this stuff is more than fifteen years out of date. I'll admit, though, it's about as covert a location as we could find."

Pink added, "I'm in the process of replacing the entire system as we speak. It will be state of the art."

Sam groused. "Those damned phones cost $17,000 dollars each."

Hew smirked. "So don't lose yours. I've heard the WiFi is ten times faster and the cameras are great. You also need to prepare yourself for the cost of the new Israeli-designed security cameras. They're used to monitor the national power grid among other things. We'll need at least two on every support column—they are beyond expensive."

"How do you know that?"

"I know the guy in Atlanta who sells them."

Charlie agreed to hire and oversee the security company. "We may need to add our own satellites along the route too," he said. "I'm going to run the cybersecurity. Let me introduce Pink Summey. He will oversee the personal security details. The Israeli guards and drivers will cover Hew, Sam, me, and our families. Homeland Security will cover this facility. The Japanese and German governments are sending teams to cover you, Bubba, and your families and staff here as individuals."

"Is Pink your real name? Your parents must have had a great sense of humor."

Hew bristled. "Actually, his name is William Pinckney Summey. He's retired Special Forces and retired DEA. He and Jeffrey rescued me from the drug lord in Colombia. I owe him my life and I trust him completely. You will love him."

"Are we going to be held captive here?"

"No. Certainly not, and you're free to leave whenever this gets to be too much. If you or your family members want to go shopping or whatever, you will be driven and accompanied. The German government is shipping a fleet of Mercedes E Sprinter vans here. They were built in Charleston but are being armored and up-fitted with Kevlar-backed leather seats and other safety accessories in Israel. They'll have bulletproof glass, Kevlar-lined side and roof panels, an explosive-resistant undercarriage, bullet- and spike-proof tires, and hidden machine guns."

Bubba spoke up. "We'll love that. Americans drive on the wrong side of the highway."

Charlie raised his eyebrows. "Wow. I didn't know you used the English system. Anyway, Hew, Sam and I will have two vans each. And there's one more thing. We're going to ask you and all of your family members here to be fitted with a subcutaneous GPS tracker. It will be located in the back of the fatty lower portion of your ear lobe."

"I don't like everyone spying on my every move," said Bubba.

Hew took over. "I understand, and it's your decision, but we think the enemy will want you alive and talking if they kidnap you. You're of no use to them if you're dead. I've had one since I was eleven. It saved my life. It's how Pink found my parents' bodies. Our security team will only be alerted when you leave the property. They can quickly find you."

"Well, now that you've put it that way…"

Sam continued, "I don't like it either, but it is what it is, folks. Get used to it. Let's move on. Let me tell you what's developed in the last two days. We want to build a transfer terminal near the airport between the cities of Greenville and Spartanburg, South Carolina. The South Carolina State Ports Authority already has what they call their inland port there on our main line where we transfer containers. We think a branch built to the new South Carolina terminal on the old Navy base in North Charleston, South Carolina could be extremely profitable. We had planned to use our old rights of way from Charleston to Atlanta through Augusta, but we'll change that and go to the inland port instead."

"Tippy's brother lives in Charleston and he says the truck traffic on I-26 is a nightmare. They would agree to anything that would reduce that. The long slow surface trains cause delays at road crossings that infuriate the good people of North Charleston too."

"Our problem is that our right of way and trackage between Charleston and the Greenville / Spartanburg inland terminal is a narrow right of way with a single track, and while it's fine for standard traffic, we would need to straddle the line and it's somewhat circuitous between Columbia and Spartanburg. We run double stacked containers through there and we don't want to interfere with that any more than necessary. Now, while we were brainstorming that, the president called me.'

"The president of what?"

Everyone laughed at Edward. 'Sorry, we had to explain it to Hew too. You guys really don't play politics. The President of the US. Not only does he want to speed this process up, he's ready to expand it nationwide! I explained that we don't own the rights of way nationwide and he laughed and said that he owned the interstate highways so why not put it down the medians? He considers that wasted land." He paused. "Then it hit us. Interstate 26 runs from Charleston through Spartanburg, S.C. It's mostly rural with a wide median except for areas near Charleston and Columbia. The medians there are already paved."

Jason thought for a moment, then spoke. "I think we should run down the outer edge of the interstates. That will greatly reduce the interruption to the flow of traffic. In North Charleston, we can straddle our tracks and join the interstate above the I-526 intersection cloverleaf. We can join our old double main line where the interstate crosses our line near Spartanburg, SC. It's fairly straight. SCMAGLEV works best when the line is as straight as possible."

"We also quickly looked at possible national routes. The mountain ranges are, as ever, the main problem for railroads. I suspect that we might run along I-10 from New Orleans to Tucson, Arizona, and then I-8 to San Diego. Los Angeles could be a problem with the mountain range south of there. As it is, the elevation of El Paso, Texas is about 3,700 feet so we know that tunnels will be needed to get through the lower Rocky and Sierra Mountains, but hey, it's the Pres's job to get the money.

"Atlanta to Chicago has similar problems, but we think Meridian, Mississippi to Chicago via I-55 through St. Louis, Missouri might be the least expensive route.

"Birmingham, Alabama is about 1,450 feet above sea level but the grades on the current mainline are low enough that we can make mag— our system—work. El Paso will certainly need a tunnel and that will open problems that could take years to resolve."

Edward agreed. "I suspect if you get it as far as, say, San Antonio, Texas, the rest will fall in place. Texans aren't known to let a little thing like the environment stand in the way of profit. New Mexico and Arizona will go along. Your biggest problems will be in California."

"Well, hell. If we get as far as Yuma, Arizona, we'll just turn into Mexico and build a terminal in the Gulf of California."

"The Pres won't like that."

"Then it will be his job to get California in line."

They all agreed with that idea.

Hew played host for the weekend. Swan Bay's guest house, where visiting horse owners stayed, rivaled the best five-star hotels. Ms. Mamie had mostly retired from her cooking duties, but Hew now had a staff of three in the kitchen and she supervised for important events.

The group ate in the manor house dining room. "This room is spectacular—as is this manor house. Tell us about it."

"We don't refer to it as a manor. We're just an old tobacco farm at heart, but it was built in 1745. My ancestor used a young relative as the architect who went on to international fame, but the architect's design was too grand for the economy at the time so the plans were reduced. Locals call the style Tidewater Virginia Style. We're lucky that every generation saved their journals and ledgers so we have a very complete inventory. All this furniture is original Chippendale.

"My ancestors had their own ship, so tobacco went one way and furniture and silver came this way. In 1790, the western front was remodeled in the latest style and most of the old farm buildings were moved further away from the house. After dinner, I'll show you the ballroom upstairs. I'll also take you to the brick kitchen house. It and my log cabin that we passed coming over here are original to the property. They're both mid seventeenth-century—about 1652."

"Hew, think about what Jason said. This place would be ideal for our conferences. It's grand enough to entertain our Japanese and German friends as well."

Hew nodded. "I agree. We'll update the electronics and add a fresh coat of paint. I've been looking for a new use for these old buildings. Consider it done."

9
LOGISTICS

Jason opened the meeting. "Guys, I'm going to keep this short. Don't write any of this in the minutes, please. It's a moving concept—pun intended—and it might have radically changed last night. Hans, and I were sitting on your cabin porch, Hew, drinking a fine Alsatian wine from your cellar that Jeffrey showed us—none of us like American beer or bourbon—and Hans threw out a revolutionary idea during our second bottle.

We were discussing the problems with interfering with the existing lines. He thinks we, well, mostly *he*, can design a new process to construct the roadbed above the existing track while allowing the normal train service to run through the machine. Of course, the trains will run at a lower speed through the machine, but think of all the time we can save by not constantly having to move out of the way of the trains. And, this is the good part. He thinks he can use our solar powered system to move and run the machine."

"Good God! That would be amazing. We'd save millions. No. Tens of millions."

"True. He's so sure of this, he thinks he can have a prototype running by Christmas."

"Nope. That's not possible."

Hew had been listening intently and then shocked them all. "It *is* possible. I think all the components are already available but no one has put them together before. Time is becoming critical. One new Panamax ship can carry about 12,000 containers. The new North Charleston terminal has been built to handle it, the new Cooper River bridge is high enough, and the harbor channel has been deepened to fifty-two feet. They're serious."

"That's exactly right," added Jason. "We typically stack two containers onto each carrier, but six-thousand carriers is too much for one train. It would be more than thirty miles long! We have a very large carrier that was built to haul a General Electric turbine. They're built in Greenville, S.C. We're already working on a modification of the design so we can carry six containers per carriage—that's two stacks of three since we're above everything—but we'll still be running multiple trains per ship per day. These ships are changing everything about the way we handle freight.

"Now let's have a short discussion about logistics and construction sequencing. We've managed to get Homeland Security to allow us to allow Hew's company a new sub-corporation to be called Eberhart Trans-America. This will be the sole contract for construction since we can't allow every construction company in the world to have open bids. We convinced them that the Chinese construction companies will underbid everyone. Hans proposes we start with the Charlotte to Atlanta section. We can begin on both ends and in the middle. In Atlanta, we'll begin with the freight transfer yard platform."

"Johann and I have been thinking. Since the foundation costs for your new computer facility on Alabama Street will be very expensive, we'll add a high-rise office building over the computer floors. That will block the sight and sound of the freight transfer yard from our condos."

"Great idea. Hew, that'll give us room for future expansion. We'll start the first road bed south of Charlotte. Near Greer, S.C., we'll construct the interchange with the inland port with provisions for an intersection with the Charleston route. Everything in between is mostly rural. We'll need two very long, gentle curves to form a wye interchange with the existing main line. The old main line has too many curves through there anyway. We need straight and level roadbeds to maintain as much speed as possible. The through trains won't stop at this port so only the sidings will be affected. Our property group will setup a series of new companies to quietly acquire the needed rights of way. That should get the kinks worked out. We've got one farm owner who refuses to sell so we're just going to work around them. We'll use the same three-scheme approach as we move north and south.

"Hans and Jason have worked out a scheme that uses two machines to build the platform over rivers and ravines. We'll also start the Charleston route and if this new machine works out, we can use our existing right of way. Somewhere along the route, though, we need to by-pass downtown Columbia. In nineteenth century South Carolina, every road and our railroad led to Columbia. We'll tackle the line north of Charlotte last. Hans says his idea can be modified to work on the side of the interstate highways. We don't have rights of way or operate north of DC so we'll need to use the interstate idea there. We should start to consider running our route around Washington, Philadelphia, and most of northern New Jersey.

"Hew, your teams will set up precast concrete plants at the ends of the construction phases. Your team will cast all the sections and load them onto the new roadbeds and ship them to the working ends and then assemble the next section and so on and so forth."

"I like it. Let's do it. It'll save tens of millions more, and those small towns will love the lack of the noises from those freight trains that roar through blasting their horns at all of the road crossings, especially at night. Some of those houses are less than one-hundred feet from our tracks. It must be like sleeping between the rails. Also, there won't be long waits at road crossings. Only Amtrak's Crescent Limited passenger service—our historic Southern Crescent Limited—and local freight runs will remain at grade."

Eager to get away, Sam adjourned the meeting and agreed to postpone any construction until they had heard from Hans.

10
IN PARADISUM

Alexis looked at the Caller ID and answered the phone. "Good afternoon, Janet. How's my favorite attorney? I thought about calling you. It's been months."

"Yes, that's the way our judicial system works, I'm afraid. How's your family holding up?"

"Everyone's fine. The twins and I are in my studio painting. My mother is the director of the Greenville County Art Museum and she's hosting a new exhibit of 'kinderart' as she calls it. Elizabeth is painting a 'cosso' based on the painting in Hew's office and Courtney is painting a 'tisse.' Neither of them can say the names yet but they're doing a grand job if I do say so myself.

"It's blissfully quiet here. Hew's flying back from Virginia with John. We left John at the farm for the summer to learn how to care for our three new puppies. They should be home within the hour. Are they ready to settle my suit, I hope?"

"No, and that's actually why I'm calling. You're not going to like this, but they've asked the judge to dismiss your case, calling it without merit."

"I'm fighting until the very last. To hell with them all.

"I agree. I'm stalling, saying my schedule can't handle a hearing at the moment."

"Why? I want to get this behind me. I want to see them squirm."

"It's just a standard tactical ploy. They have deflected my attempts to begin depositions so I'm just fighting back. Do you know a woman named Lurleen Hargrave?"

"Yes. She works at the Academy in procurement."

"That's right. Her husband claims she's been having an affair with one of the women in the school and he claims to have witnesses. I want to hear from him before I meet with the judge."

"Whaaat? Boy, we figured that one wrong. We thought it was Mike who was having the affair."

"I don't know about that one."

"Well let me tell you—" A piercing scream came from the butler's pantry. "Can I call you back? Something's going on in the kitchen."

"I heard the scream. Go. I'll let you know what happens."

Lucinda, the new sous chef came running into the studio. Ms. Ramsay, Ms. Ramsay, come quick. Mr. Douglas fell down. I think he's dead!"

"You watch the girls!" Alexis ran down the service corridor fearing that Douglas had fallen down the two-story butler's pantry—she had always worried that one of the kids would fall over the railing. She found him face up on the floor of the main level and reached down and tenderly felt for a pulse, then dialed 911, spoke to the operator and began mouth to mouth and chest compressions, but she knew it was in vain.

The operator was still on the line, but Alexis had to hang up so she could use the phone app that Hew had invented to open the front gates and unlock the door. She could hear them at the gate, so she spoke to them over the doorbell and told them where to find her.

Hew and John walked in forty-five minutes later. John ran toward the butler's pantry with the three well trained puppies trailing behind to show Douglas. Hew found Alexis standing in the butler's pantry crying uncontrollably. Hew grabbed her and hugged her thinking that one of her parents had died.

"It's Douglas. He's—"

Hew nodded. "We passed an ambulance a few blocks back but his lights were off and he wasn't blaring his siren."

"There was no need to rush. They said he was probably dead before he hit the floor. Lucinda was with him. She said he put the teapot down, raised his hand to his head, said to tell Maybell he loved her, and collapsed."

"Oh my God. Where's Maybell?"

"She went to the grocery store. She wanted to make your favorite French onion soup tonight to welcome you home."

Hew thought for a moment. "You go on back and work with the kids. I'll break the news to Maybell. She's the closest thing to a mother I have. Douglas was like a father to me. He was a better father than JB had ever been." As he started on his way to Maybell's apartment, he saw John standing at the other stainless steel counter working on something. As he approached, he saw John vigorously rubbing an antique sterling silver tea pot. "Stop. What are you doing? You're rubbing too hard. You'll dent it."

John looked at him with tears streaming down his cheeks. "He didn't finish it. He left dried polish on it. I had to start over, dammit. It's my job now."

Hew put his arm around John, squeezed his shoulder, and kissed the top of his head. "Okay, but not so hard."

He quickly turned before John could see his own tears—his family taught its sons not to show emotion. He went to the powder room and locked the door. It took several minutes before he could face Maybell.

⁂

THE FUNERAL WAS HELD AT THE New Tabernacle Second Baptist Church in downtown Atlanta, the church Douglas and Maybell had joined when they moved to Atlanta. John asked Maybell if he could sing something for Douglas at the funeral. She nodded. "What are you going to sing, baby?"

"It's a surprise. Mr. Douglas asked me to sing it for him at his funeral. He sang it while he was teaching me to polish the silver. He made me wear gloves, though. He said the silver polish would be a bitch...um... hard to remove from the organ keys."

"That sounds just like him. But *you* polish the silver? That's a laugh. Nobody in your family ever polished their own silver. That's a servant's job."

"I didn't mind. He always made it fun. We laughed and sang songs. There was one song he said was his favorite. He said that the days of having servants do the housework were about over and I needed to know how to take care of my own stuff. He taught me to always keep my shoes shined too."

"I wondered why your shoes always looked spit-shined. He learned that in Vietnam. Always look your best, he said. Yes, Honey, sing for my Douglas."

THE SWAN BAY CROWD FLEW DOWN for the funeral. Maybell, Alexis, Ms. Mamie, Mary, and Jeffrey rode in the heavily armored van driven by two Israeli protective services guards. The Hardys drove two cars but sat with the family. Hew and John went early in a different protected van so John could practice a little.

Hew hated the security, but he knew it was necessary. Two kidnapping attempts had been reported in Tokyo at the main SCMAGLEV headquarters. Dr. Jones, the choir director, met them at the door. He took John to the choir loft and introduced him to the organist, Mostel Smith. Nearly 300 people were already in the church.

"Maybell told me you play really well," the organist told John. "I need to start the music so you just sit here on the bench with me. Have you ever played a Hammond organ?"

"No, sir."

"Okay. Just sit and watch. You'll get it. I'm classically trained myself, but I love to play my people's gospel music too."

"Yes, sir. I'll just watch you."

"Just watch and listen."

Smith began with a jazzy riff and the choir began to sway and hum. John was spellbound, but he didn't like the tremolo at all.

The church filled quickly, and the choir began to sing, "*In the Sweet By and By.*" The funeral director asked everyone to stand. As the casket was rolled down the aisle, accompanied by Hew, Edward, Charlie, Jeffrey, and two Black church members that Hew had never met as pallbearers, a single male voice in the choir began to quietly hum a single plaintive note. The choir joined the humming and moved into four-part harmony.

At first, it was mournful, but as the coffin was turned in front of the pulpit, the humming grew louder and changed into a more joyful sound.

Hew was spellbound. The humming quietly slowed in a beautiful decrescendo. The pastor stepped up to the pulpit. "Brothers and sisters, we're all here for Douglas's homegoing. We have a remembrance and if anyone else wants to say anything, you're welcome to come forward."

The only other White man in the church stepped forward. "My name is Randall Tompkins. Dougie, um, Captain Jones, was my pilot in Viet nam. He sat front seat and I sat back seat in our F-14 Tomcat. We were carrier based and our jet was new.

"The war was nearly over when it came out although we didn't know it. Dougie was one of the first men to be assigned to an F-14. One beautiful afternoon we were flying a recon mission over North Vietnam when we were hit. I passed out, but I later learned that Dougie was hit in the leg and shoulder and the plane was severely damaged.

"Somehow, though, Dougie managed to get us home. We ditched in the ocean just off the starboard side of our carrier. I don't remember being rescued, but we made it. We spent months in the hospital stateside and lost touch, but when Dougie moved to Alana, he found me. He re-membered that I was a Georgia Reb—that was his nickname for me. Reb, he said, I never thought that I could be friends with a Southern rebel.

"We spent many hours drinking his famous mint juleps—they were made with Scotch, not bourbon—and I convinced him that although I was Southern, I wasn't really a rebel." That got a laugh.

"He told me about working for the Bishops after the war and about how he and Maybell were always treated like family. He and Mr. X.I. Bishop spent long hours sitting on the terrace watching the sun set on Washington DC across the river, drinking the mint juleps and talking about war. Mr. Bishop had trained pilots before World War II so they had a lot in common.

"I wouldn't be here today except he willed us to live, and The Al-mighty had better plans for us, so I came just to say goodbye to the man who saved me and gave me time to have a wife and children."

Jumping to his feet to join five hundred others in a thunderous round of applause, tears welled in Hew's eyes. He turned to Jeffrey. "He never told me about that."

Jeffrey, the Special Forces guy, was tearing up too. "He never told me either."

Pastor Brown stepped back into the pulpit and announced, "Now we'll have a special song from Mr. John X.I. Bishop's great-grandson, John Bishop Ramsay."

John had been watching Mr. Smith's technique with this organ console. He didn't really like the sound, so during the remembrance, he googled it and figured out how to turn off the Vibrato and Leslie tones. He was afraid of the drawbars so he pushed one of the black keys on the left as he had seen the organist do, and got a soft flute-like sound. John thought it sounded vaguely like a gedackt.

He improvised an introduction and began to sing. "*I come to the garden alone, while the dew is still on the roses.*" His pure treble voice filled the back reaches of the church.

No one so much as coughed while he sang. When he got to the last verse, "*I'll stay in the garden with Him,*" the choir joined in softly humming, and when he began the last refrain, "*And He walks with me, and He talks with me, And He tells me I am His own; and the joy we share as we tarry there, None other has ever known,*" all five hundred people joined in and sang in such hushed tones, Hew thought the angels themselves were singing. Hew had never been to a funeral in a mostly-Black church before and didn't really know what to expect, but this was one of the most spirit-filled moments he had ever experienced. It moved him to get up and speak.

"My name is Hew Ramsay and..." nodding toward John, "that was my son." There was quiet, but warm applause.

"Thank you for telling us about your ordeal, Mr. Tompkins. I have never heard that story before and I've known Douglas since I was fourteen. You see, my parents were murdered by a drug lord in the Andes when they wandered into a coca field and I had to move in with my grandfather X.I. in his house in DC. My grandmother had died many years earlier so X.I., as we all called him—he was John Bishop the eleventh, but that's another story—raised me. The problem was that my grandfather's main office was in Manhattan, so he was away most of the week. That left Maybell and Douglas, who truly were my parents.

"Douglas saved my life too, Mr. Tompkins. Seems like he practiced on you." That got a laugh. "You see, I played soccer and I was very good, if I may brag a bit. The team captain was jealous, and after a game where I scored the winning goal, the captain stabbed me in the leg in an attempt to end my career. It worked. But being much taller than he, I put him down—I'll spare you those details. Douglas always picked me up after school so I knew he was waiting on the street. Seeing what happened, he ran the old station wagon across the soccer field and got me into the car. The blade had hit an artery so he whipped off his leather belt and made a tourniquet and drove like a bat out of hell." He turned to the minister. Excuse me, pastor."

The pastor grinned. "That's all right. We all know about those bats." That got more laughs.

Hew had no idea that people could actually have fun at a funeral. Episcopalians were extremely reserved and uptight at a time like this. "Okay, well, anyway, we made it to the trauma center in record time for DC, and Douglas helped me through my recovery both physically and mentally." He paused. "I didn't want to call him by his first name, but he insisted, so I told him okay, but that he would have to be my best friend. In his honor, and because we're flying his body back to Virginia tomorrow to take his place beside X.I. in our family cemetery, I want to invite everyone over to my house after the service for a farewell party."

A man yelled from the congregation. "Can you make his mint juleps?"

"If I can find enough single malt on the way home I will. I know his recipe." More applause.

Maybell stood up. "Land sakes, Hew, we don't have enough food in the house to feed this crowd."

A woman stood up. "I fried up a chicken this morning for our supper tonight. I'll bring it." More women began to shout. They had cornbread, collards, soup, beans, pies, cakes, and everything else imaginable. Hew witnessed hundreds of Atlanta's finest home cooks rise to the occasion.

Pastor Brown stood to restore order. "Now, normally, Mr. Ramsay, at this point, I preach for a while." That brought howls of laughter. "But today, we've seen the Holy Spirit come among us already, and a mint julep sounds mighty fine right about now, so let's sing and have a benediction and let Douglas go on his way to Glory."

When the organist ripped into "*When the Roll is Called up Yonder,*" Hew texted his liquor supplier and ordered immediate delivery of three cases of the 18-year-old Macallan single malt. Maybell looked at Hew and motioned for them to leave before the singing stopped. On the way home, Alexis called Hew and told him to stop at the party store and get all the plastic cups, plates, and cutlery he could find.

Maybell yelled, "Get ice too, Hew. Get at least twenty bags."

After leaving the store, Hew turned to John. "That was a beautiful tribute. How did you know how to manage that organ? I've never heard anything like that before."

"Douglas came over to the bench and showed me what to do. He sang in the choir there for years."

"Um, okay. What do you mean he came over?"

"He got out of his casket and sat down beside me and I just knew what to do. On the last refrain, he put his arm around my shoulder and just floated off out of the room in a small white cloud. Maybell saw him too. We just smiled at each other. She winked at me, looked up as he passed, and waved goodbye."

Hew didn't know what to say, so he just rode on. He needed to discuss this with one of the priests at St. Philip's before he said the wrong thing to his son.

⚜

THEY MANAGED TO BEAT THE CROWD. Maybell, Mamie, Mary, and Alexis were in full battle mode. Maybell had the family car stop at the grocery store so she could buy a cart load of tea bags, sugar, sleeves of plastic cups, and lemons. Mamie got a buggy-load of toilet paper, and Alexis got a buggy-load of paper napkins. The security driver was not amused. He was even less amused when told to expect five hundred unvetted people to show up within the next hour. Pink was not happy either. He didn't like spontaneous events. Hew had set up a folding table in the foyer and put out the Bishop family's huge antique eighteenth-century hand chased sterling silver punchbowl.

They grabbed the plates and sent Hew to the bar table with the plastic cups filled with crushed ice. The new chef was cooking simple syrup for the juleps. While that was cooking, she muddled the mint from Maybell's high brick walled potager garden using a large antique marble mortar and pestle, and boiled gallons of water for tea. She then poured the simple syrup into the crushed mint mix.

Mamie walked over to inspect his work and made him move the bowl while she laid a heavily starched and pressed white linen table cloth on the table. "We might be using plastic, but we are not going to set that punchbowl on a bare plastic table. You know better than that. Go find that big silver punch ladle. You can't be dipping with a plastic cup. This isn't one of Jeffrey's hunting parties in the woods. Go help with the ice crushing and filling them cups. You bought the wrong ice. It never occurred to me to tell you we needed crushed ice. It's your damned recipe. Men! You are way too slow. Put a sprig of mint on top of each cup too. Get moving."

Hew called to his son. "John, I need to make the punch. I want you to stand at the front door and receive our guests. You know how."

"But, Dad, what if all those women want a hug. I hate hugs."

"I know, I do too, but grin and bear it just for today. Douglas was a hugger. The trick is to put your arm around their back and gently but firmly turn them away from the door. Then release your arm and extend your hand to the next guest and say hello. Try to send at least half of them downstairs to spread out the crowd. Maybell will be down there to receive them."

⚜

Les and Mable Wilson were sitting in his dirty old brown Ford pickup at the intersection of Riverside Drive and Breakwater Ridge Road. "This has got to be the place, Mable. It's in the book at the airport."

"I ain't seen a house yet. Except for that weird gate, it's all just woods. Her pay check shows Peachtree Road."

"I told you, woman. We cain't get in there. I checked it out. It's forty stories tall and the security's like Fort Knox."

"Well this ain't much better. I saw security cameras at both the gates. Oh, look. Here comes a bunch of cars."

"Looks like a party, or else somebody died."

"I hope it was her that died. Save us a heap of trouble."

"We haven't seen anything in the newspapers or on the TV."

"She wasn't big enough for the TV unless it was a murder or an accident. Look. There's more coming. They're all full of Black folks."

"Maybe they're having a funeralizing. This is our chance to get in."

"Woman, you've lost your mind! We ain't Black and we ain't dressed for a funeralizing. We have no idea of who's dead."

"Well, then, you find another way. What's across the river?"

"Nothing but dense woods. My rifle won't shoot nobody across that river."

"Maybe we'll go to over to South Carolina this weekend to a gun show and buy us a better gun."

All five hundred showed up. Hew had never seen so much food. The scotch-laced juleps were a hit with the whole crowd. They stayed for hours until the food ran out.

11
COCKTAILS

"**I**'m starving. I didn't get a bite to eat. So much food," said Hew.

Maybell, as usual, came to his rescue. "I put a plate in the fridge for you. Go sit down and I'll put it in the microwave."

"Absolutely not, Maybell. You go sit down. I can microwave my own food. You've got a trying few days ahead of you. Rest."

"Hew, you know I like to be busy. It takes my mind off of things."

Jeffrey poked his head through the door. "Speaking of rest, are there any more of the mint juleps? I was so busy serving I didn't get a cup."

"Fat chance," said Hew. "I do have a bottle of Macallan 25 we can open. Maybell, you and Ms. Mamie were amazing. Thank you. How did you pull that together?"

Mamie cackled. "You White folks have never done a funeralizing before. We know how to make something outta nothing. Been doing it forever. You have wakes. Nobody ever woke up from their own funeral."

John wandered in and Maybell quietly whispered. "My Douglas will wake up on the other side of Jordan tomorrow." Maybell caught his eye and winked. John smiled and winked back. He understood. They now had a secret bond that no priest would ever admit could exist. They had both seen Douglas and they knew exactly where he was.

The boy turned to Hew. "Dad, it's Thursday. I want to go to ringing practice. I've missed all summer."

"I can't go tonight, but maybe Douglas…" He stopped mid sentence. There was a moment of total silence when everyone froze.

"Land sakes," said Maybell. "I'll run him over to the cathedral. Mamie'll ride with me."

"Thank you. Charlie could have picked him up, but he's already there teaching beginners."

"I'm amazed at the way Charlie has taken to the bells."

"I'm not, Mary. If I might just brag a bit as a proud mother, he has a PhD in computer technology and he's a classically trained percussionist. Bell ringing is about numbers and rhythm. He certainly knows about both."

Edward laughed. "We moved him into the pool house to get away from those damned drums too."

"That was probably a mistake, though, Edward. It only fueled his sex life with the girl next door. There was too much privacy."

Hew, desperate to change the subject said, "Who needs a refill? We'd better text Charlie and ask him to give John a ride home. There's no need for Maybell to go back out."

"Yes, please. All I'm saying is that I'm glad he's found a creative outlet within the church."

"I've always wondered about those big drums," said Jeffrey. "How can he get different notes out of only four drums? I understand the big drum in a marching band but it only plays one note."

Mary spoke up. "Technically, they're called *timpani*." She spelled it. "That's the Italian plural. They use a foot pedal to turn the drum heads.

"Drums can be tuned?" said Jeffrey. "I thought they just played a single note. You know, bang, bang, bang."

Edward shrugged. "Good question. I know about this. Basically, there are four drums called collectively timpani or individually, timpano. The largest is thirty-two inches in diameter and the smallest is twenty-three inches. They have a pedal that allows the player to change notes quickly, but the real secret is the ear of the timpanist. Charlie trained extensively to develop his ear. It's the reason we moved him out of the house." Tippy laughed. "The ability to play in tune and change quickly is a secret that most people don't understand. He starts by setting the pedal all the way down just like an accelerator pedal in a car. This allows the drummer to tighten the first drumhead. If his lowest note is E, in the score, for instance, He will play that E on the piano, or have someone in the orchestra play it for him, or he will just use his own trained ear. He gets that sound in his head and he strikes the drum once and raises the pitch using the pedal. Then he strikes it again and slowly moves the pedal until he hears the E. Think of a whistle. The four drums can play almost two octaves from low C on the biggest drum up to high A# on the smallest. It's a real art form. Charlie can lower his head with his face very close to the drum head and sing the correct pitch. The drum head will vibrate on pitch. He actually tunes very quietly on stage."

"Well, I had no idea. I have a new appreciation for drummers now. I can also understand his ability to ring the bells with good timing."

"Johann's a great ringer too," said Hew. "Charlie has helped him improve his rhythm. You think of him as a German, but he's half English and went to public schools in England—that's private boarding schools to us. He learned to ring at the local tower there."

"That's true," added Alexis. "And Charlie's little soccer team is starting to win games. Johann and Hew help coach, though Hew can really only talk strategy due to his bad leg. Charlie understands the patterns of numbers and his rhythm and bell-handling skills make him a superb ringer and teacher. The kids love him."

"Charlie's always been a kid at heart."

"Is it just me, or does Maybell seem unusually calm? I would be in pieces if Jeffrey had died."

"That was the most spirit filled, uplifting funeral I've ever attended. I think she's at peace with it."

"For Baptists, those folks really put away that punch."

"Yeah, but Jeffrey, you know after the first batch, I reduced the Scotch and increased the sugar."

"No. Surely you didn't do that."

"I certainly did. Douglas taught me how to do it without affecting the taste. That scotch is $250 a bottle and since most Southerners don't drink Scotch, they didn't notice."

Alexis asked, "Is anyone hungry? I can make sandwiches."

"Those Scottish genes never go away, Hew."

"I'm going to take you up on the food, Alexis. This Crantini is making me drunk. Tell me how you make them, Hew."

"I keep a bottle of vodka in the fridge—not the freezer. I use the round ice molds I originally purchased for my Scotch and I fill them with cranberry juice and freeze them. I put the frozen red cranberry ball in a martini glass and pour the vodka into the glass. I then add a garnish of lemon peal. We all need our citrus vitamins."

Everyone had a good laugh as the alcohol ran through their veins.

"I'll take another refill, please. You are always talking about bell ringing but I don't understand what it's all about. Why don't you ring, Alexis?"

"That's Hew and John's thing. Besides, I'm a clapper."

"A what?"

"A clapper. We spouses and partners are the bell band groupies. We arrange all the social functions. It's a term we stole from the Grace Church Cathedral band in Charleston. It's a play on the word for applause and for the actual clapper in a bell. The social part of ringing is as important as the practice. It's our answer to the English ringers going to the pub after practice. Every English tower has a local pub, but there's not one near St. Philip's or St. Luke's, so we join them at a local restaurant after practice. We call it Thursday night Bible study."

That got another laugh.

"Let me tell you, Jeffrey. Hew and John go into too much detail. They'll talk for hours. Basically, Hew spent the summer between high school and college at Oxford studying organ with the sub-organist at the cathedral at Christ Church. He's quite a character. He's called Sinjin. That's the way the Brits pronounce St. John—short for St. John-Smith. He's been here several times. Hew heard bells being rung somewhere as he left the cathedral one evening after his practice session. He followed the sound and ran into a group of ringers just as they were leaving the church across the way from the quad. He followed them to the pub and introduced himself. Turns out, they had just returned from a trip to the states and had rung at St. Luke's, and Marietta."

"Let me just interrupt. I had my first lesson at Lincoln Cathedral where our choir was in residence."

"See what I mean? I'm telling this. Hush. He practiced bells that summer almost as much as he practiced the organ. He loved it so much that he ordered a set of twelve bells for a non-existent tower at St. Philip's from the Whitechapel Bell Foundry in London."

"Sadly, it's no longer in business."

"Stop interrupting."

"He had Johann design a magnificent tower. Hew was the first tower captain, but Charlie has taken over that role."

Hew took over. "The hard part for Americans is that the Brits have been ringing for several hundred years so the introduction of a few new ringers is relatively simple. Here, the ringers are almost all beginners unless there is a Brit living nearby who can help teach. Some learn faster than others and want to jump ahead into the complicated work. That can create friction and it's the job of the tower captain to keep everyone happy. I allowed the band to try anything they want on practice night when the sound control is closed, but I was very strict about only ringing to the abilities of those who show up on Sundays. I tried to limit the amount of banging and clashing on Sundays. The dinners after practice really help build friendships.

"The ringers stand in a circle on the ground floor so they can see each other's ropes. The ropes have bright woolen threads woven into them that serve as visual markers to let each ringer know which bell is ringing by the timing of it going up or down. The bells are behind the glass wall above, and the sound comes out through the vertical grillwork above that. There are electrically operated hatches above the bells so they can practice and ring peals without disturbing the neighbors."

Alexis cut in. "Hew used some of the profits from the construction program that he developed to fund it."

Mary asked, "Is it loud in the ringing room? It's very loud outside. What about the music you play? When we heard you in Charleston many years ago, it just sounded like rhythm. I didn't recognize the tune."

John spoke up. "Let me tell her. The sound is reduced by the thickness of the ceiling to just under seventy-five decibels. We can clearly hear the bells and the conductor. The sound at the mouth of the bell is about one-hundred-fifty decibels so yes, by the time it gets to your ears it's still loud." He walked over to the piano and played a twelve note scale. "The smallest bell is called the treble." He played the high note. The lowest bell is called the tenor—ours weighs 2,500 pounds. We've got extra bells so we can have a front ten, a back ten, a front six, a back six, a front eight, and a back eight, but it's always referred to as a twelve bell tower. That way it sounds good no matter how many ringers we have at a service. We play down the scale." He played it again. The lowest bell is like the big bass drum in a marching band. It sets the rhythm in most compositions. Charlie is our best tenor ringer. His rhythm is always spot on. We don't play melodies because the bells are rotating through 360 degrees and they're too slow to play repeating notes. We memorize patterns and pull our rope at the appropriate time."

"Way over my head, John—pun intended."

Everyone laughed as Hew poured the Scotch.

"How's your lawsuit coming, Alexis? Are they ready to give you a bundle of money?"

"Slowly. Very slowly. They're throwing up road blocks at every turn. We haven't even gotten them to set a date for depositions yet."

"Charlie stays in contact with the music faculty members. They can't afford to quit but they're living on pins and needles. Kleindic and the Mink are trying to change the music over to country, jazz, and rock. The current students are rebelling. The strings and brass students refuse to play any of that music. They're classically trained. There's no part for them."

"They'll probably resign at the end of this term. I don't know where they'll find teachers who are qualified, but there will be plenty of students if that happens. It's easy to learn to play four guitar chords. Lots of people can play, but they don't have teaching certificates."

"Oh, you'd be surprised at the numbers of teachers who can play a guitar extremely well. Did you ever learn the name of the guy who ate your tuna salad sandwich?"

"Oh, yes. His name is Les Wilson."

12
BURIAL

The next morning, as soon as the fasten seatbelt sign was off, Hew went over to John and asked him to join him in the galley. The family and Pastor Brown were flying to Swan Bay.

"Do you know what a requiem is?"

"No, sir, but it sounds foreign."

"It's Latin. It's part of the old Mass service music for a funeral. The last piece is played as the body is carried out of the church. It's called *In Paradisum* or Into Paradise. It's an antiphon from the Catholic Requiem Mass. I truly believe that's what you and Maybell had the unbelievable honor of actually witnessing. There's no need to ever be afraid. Douglas will never hurt you, and don't be surprised if you see him again in times of stress or even quiet, but there's no need to discuss this with others. They will never believe you."

"Tell me more about the organ I was playing."

"It's called it a Hammond. You played something called a tibia clausa. It's basically a gedackt—a capped flute. It's thought to be one of the oldest organ sounds. Mr Hammond developed the electric organ for use as a church and classical organ as a less expensive instrument than a pipe organ. Mr. Leslie heard it and being a theatre organ fan, developed the Leslie system. Mr. Hammond didn't like it, but it became very popular and it stuck. The so called gospel churches love it."

"Their organist is classically trained. Let's buy them a nicer organ in Douglas' memory."

"Interesting. I'm going to speak with the minister now. Hand me your phone." Hew started the Fauré Requiem and John turned on his noise reduction headphones.

"Reverend Brown, may we talk for a few minutes, please?"

"Only if you'll call me Clarence. I need to explain something to you too. We aren't Southern Baptists. No, sir. That's why no one objected to your liquor. We're Independent Baptists. We have our own understanding of God's word. We believe God wants us to enjoy everything he made, but in moderation, of course."

"I understand. I want to discuss the service tomorrow. We have a way of burying our folks on the farm that I hope you will agree with. When we land, our farm lads will place the body in a pine box made from trees felled by time and storms that have grown here for hundreds of years. It's symbolic of being one with the earth. Pall bearers, of which I will head, will carry the body from the plane to the house while a piper plays. Once there, the body will be placed in repose overnight, under an American flag draped over the casket. We have always used the Burial office from my first American ancestor's *Book of Common Prayer*. We will start in the drawing room and proceed to the grave. I will sing the burial sentences using the Croft composition and others will read the lessons. We would appreciate it if you would read the prayers, committal, and the blessing. I can show you the book if you like. I have it with me."

"That sounds acceptable. Yes, I would like to study it."

Hew returned to his seat for a short nap.

AFTER THE BODY HAD BEEN PLACED in the drawing room, Hew invited everyone to have a cocktail in the upstairs ballroom.

"Hew, I've been a minister of God's Holy Word for nearly fifty years, but I don't think I've ever read anything as beautiful as that burial office. I will be honored to use it. It sounds like the King James language."

"You'd better believe it. As one of my priests once said to a comment like that, '*King James I was one of us, you know.*'"

"That's a beautiful organ. Do you or Alexis play too?"

"John and I do. We recently found this one in Phoenix. John and I were wondering if we might give your church a new pipe organ in Douglas's memory?"

"Absolutely! Oh, what an honor. But I must warn you, we can't easily part with our Hammond. Pipe organs aren't designed to give us the gospel sound."

"That won't be a problem. Many churches have more than one instrument. I'll call my friend at Schoenstein in San Francisco next week. He builds an instrument that you will love. I can take you and your committee to hear two of his instruments in Atlanta next week."

Hew had learned that the military burial details still fired real weapons, with blanks, of course, but they had long ago given up on having *Taps* played live. The bugler stood at a distance away from the crowd and pushed the valves that looked real but actually played an mp3 digital recording through a speaker hidden in the bell of the instrument. He wanted the real thing for Douglas, so he flew in a dixieland Jazz band from New Orleans. At the conclusion of the service, the band trumpeter played *Taps* and then a piper played *Amazing Grace*. Hew, Alexis, and John sang. The jazz band then struck-up *When the saints go marching in*. Everyone including Maybell danced and sang all the way back to the house to another sumptuous meal.

THE FOLLOWING MONDAY, JOHN AND EDDIE started second grade at Holy Innocents Episcopal School. The issue of a bong never came up again. The entire Simons family had been arrested and were in jail. Since the boys had spent the summer at Swan Bay, they missed the media explosion. Even the mother had been lacing the powdered sugar donuts with small amounts of cocaine. The other parents were furious. The law suits were ongoing, but there were very few assets to attach. Hew and Charlie breathed a sigh of relief. They had escaped a bomb.

"I really feel sorry for those other parents. I think most of them are good people. Several of them were our neighbors. We had covered dish block parties. Rosilyn ran into one of the mothers at the mall."

"How'd that go?"

"She told Rosilyn that we were lucky that Eddie was younger and attended a different school. I think we are completely in the clear."

"Yeah, but they'll need to watch their kids very carefully now. Once someone experiences that drug high, they want to do it again. This will plague them the rest of their lives. I know both parents are in jail, but what happened with the boy?"

"Dad said that his situation is especially sad. He was given a suspended sentence because of his age. He's in foster care until they can find a better solution. The grandmother was deemed too old to take him. His paternal uncle is a drug addict living with his girlfriend, and his maternal aunt is an alcoholic living in squalor with her drunken boyfriend, so the answer is that it's unresolved."

The boys joined the soccer team at school, and Charlie began to coach a small neighborhood team in his garden. Hew had spoken with the rector at the school to make sure the organs wouldn't be available every day for John. Hew had spent almost every lunch time practicing while he was in school there and he wanted John to be more sociable.

13
CHRISTMAS

"Sam Spencer on one."

Trying to keep it light, Hew joked, "Why, Sam, old boy, how the hell are you?"

"You've been hiding something from me. It's payback time."

"Oh, I've hidden a lot of stuff from a lot of people. What now?"

"Mint juleps. I want one. Today at five. Your house."

"Where did you hear about my mint juleps?"

"From my VP of Operations. He sings in his church choir and he recently attended a party at your house. He said he's never seen anything like it. I want a tour. Oh, and congrats on your son's YouTube video. It's quite a hit."

"YouTube video? What are you talking about?"

"Come on, he's gotten over forty thousand hits so far."

Hew was typing into his search on YouTube. "I don't do much on YouTube except follow a few organists. I would never allow John to post anything. What's he doing? Here it is. Damn. That's the funeral!"

"Yeah, well, somebody did. Where do y'all live?"

"I'll text you the address."

Hew's next call was to Edward. "What do you know about YouTube?"

"Not much. I know the basics. Why?"

"Someone uploaded John's tribute at the funeral. I want it removed."

"Hold on. I'll try to find it. Ah. Wow. He's got forty thousand hits and two full length commercials. Someone's making money. Basically,

116

after four thousand hits, they start paying and if it's sponsored, well…"

"I don't care about that. I want it gone. He's too young for that kind of publicity, and besides, the audio is terrible."

"I know about the audio. YouTube offers 4k video but the audio is limited to 128 kbps. We had that discussion at the cathedral. That's why Rob decided to livestream rather than use YouTube. The choir and organ sound better on livestream. Most people will love it. I'll check, but don't hold your breath. If anyone claims a copyright on the music, YouTube pays them a royalty. I'll report it, but I doubt it will do any good. Call Pastor Brown. He might know who posted it."

"Pastor Brown has no idea. He told me that he was never going to be a TV evangelist. He doesn't record the services and he hates having his picture taken."

⁂

SAM DROVE HIS CUSTOM BLACK LAMBORGHINI Aventador LP-4 Ultimae roadster through the stainless steel gates. As he made the sweeping 180-degree turn he saw the long wall begin to rise from the woods on his right and he muttered to himself, "Where's the house?"

The wall rose to about eight feet and was partially hidden behind mature ligustrum, camellias, and azaleas. A glass covered porte-cochere began to appear beyond the plantings. Just as he approached the port-co-chere, Hew and Alexis stepped through a pair of center pivoted floor to ceiling frosted glass doors and stood under the cantilevered glass roof. Again he muttered to himself,"This is a house?"

"Is this the Batmobile? Are you really Batman? Where the hell is your security detail? I'm sorry Hilde isn't with you."

"Hello, Alexis. Great to see you again—and witty as ever. She sends her regards. She's playing bridge. Yeah, I bought it in Italy and imported to Canada. It's not yet approved for this country, but hey, you know me. I gave my detail the afternoon off. No one would know about this car."

Always the practical one, Hew parried, "It'll be fine until you kill someone."

"Probably won't matter. I'll be dead too, but it will have been fun while it lasted."

"Are you serious?"

"Oh, come on, Hew. Lighten up. No. The car's registered, insured, and taxed at my hunting lodge in Canada. I had to fly up to check on some repairs and just couldn't resist driving it back."

"This brown and gray dry stacked rock wall is beautiful. It fits with the old abandoned farm look of the grounds. Why no manicured green lawn with polo ponies? Why no *Gone With the Wind* columned southern portico?"

"We want to be inconspicuous. Our ground water source heat exchangers are under the meadow. We designed a sloped roof for solar collectors since this is south facing. Basically, the house doesn't exist."

"I'd say you achieved your goal, but that meadow looks just looks like broom sedge and beggar lice to me. I played in fields like this as a kid. My mama hated it."

"The abandoned farm look is intentional. We returned the land to something like what it would have been centuries ago. The open area is a recreated Southeastern prairie. It was cultivated by the agriculture school at Clemson University. Working with the solar panels on the roof, we generate more energy than we use. It's called regeneration. We're giving something back to the community."

"These stone pavers are stunning. What are they?"

"The stone pavers are called Winnsboro blue granite—the 'silk of the granite trade.' It comes from a quarry near Winnsboro, SC."

"Winnsboro? That's where the SC Railroad Museum is located. They've got some of our old stuff on display. I've been meaning to go."

"Yep. I give them free rent. John and the twins love to ride the old train. We used the stone to transition to the more urban interior, but they complement the grays in the wall, I think. It was used in many major monumental buildings in the late nineteenth and early twentieth centuries until architectural styles changed. The South Carolina State House, and the old post office at Meeting and Broad Streets in downtown Charleston are built with it. Now it's used under roads and railroad ties."

"Well, it looks better here than on my railroad."

"They reopened the quarry just to use it in DC for the WWII memorial."

"Then how did you get it?"

"I bought the company and started production again. We'll use a lot of it. Johann didn't want to use it in the wall because it wouldn't look as casual as the fieldstone, but I didn't like the look of the fieldstone being used for pavers, so he compromised. Come in. Alexis will walk you through the house while I finish the drinks. We'll meet on the terrace."

"Actually, is there some place secure we can talk privately?"

"The best place will be the wine cellar. I'll meet you there."

"I want Alexis to join us."

"Okay." Hew had no idea what that was about.

Alexis gave Sam a quick tour. "The foyer is paved with the same blue granite. Johann didn't want to use polished stone outside fearing that it would be too slick, but in here and with this large antique blue silk Persian rug that our interior designer, Heidi, found, we love it. The stone wall on the left is actually the chimney back for the dining room. The glass circular stair goes down two stories to the library/music room. Hew has a glass spiral stair in his old penthouse but I thought this one needed to be more graceful. Johann and Hans copied the stair in one of the old Charleston houses but in glass."

"Is it like the room in his penthouse? I've seen it."

"Yes, but much larger and taller. The ceiling in the library here is thirty feet. The room sits under the great room and the terrace."

As she walked with him into the great room, he remarked, "That ceiling looks like it rises to twenty feet."

"Good eye. It's actually sixteen feet high. Those glass panels are each fourteen by fourteen feet. The two end panels are fixed but the two center panels slide open giving us direct access to the terrace on nice days, but we can only use them after the bugs die off."

Sam grunted. "We all know about that in the South."

"The fireplace is polished blue granite and the slab of wood on the mantle came from a tulip poplar tree from Swan Bay. It matches the fireplace downstairs except this one has skylights in the roof to wash the face of the granite. The kitchen is very minimalistic. We didn't want it to intrude on the view of the river valley."

"Oh. That's the Chattahoochee, isn't it?"

"Yes, and the land beyond is protected forest so we don't have neighbors across the way. The cabinets are painted a low gloss black.

The countertops are Absolute black granite, the appliances are mat black stainless steel except for the refrigerator and matching freezer. They're behind black wood panels. The hardware is all black too."

"With all that black, how can you see anything?"

"The lighting is excellent but when the lights are off, the kitchen almost disappears."

She walked through to the bar and the butler's pantry. "Hew has one entire wall of Scotch that people have given him. Many are rare. Almost all have been tasted at least once." She still had problems walking into the pantry because of Douglas' death. "It's an open two story space. The idea is that the staff can communicate better during the meal preparations and cleanup. The everyday utensils are stored here and there is a very large sink flanked by three dishwashers. One dishwasher is a commercial bar unit with two racks for stemware. There's a separate lower level next to the garage where the catering kitchen and the pantries are located. The next level up is the space where we store most of Hew's inherited tableware. We moved some of it back into storage at Swan Bay though. Jeffrey and Mary use it several times a year when they host the horse owners and the hunt club ball. Beyond this space is the laundry and my studio."

"This is wonderful, but I'd like to go on to the wine cellar, if you don't mind."

"Sure. You know about the library/music room, and the French Impressionist paintings. The bedrooms are just rather common. There's a spiral stair here, but let's take the elevator."

"If your closet and primary bathroom are anything like those in the penthouse, they're anything but common. This elevator is large enough to hold a grand piano."

"Actually it *will* hold Hew's concert grand and my large canvasses."

"This wine cellar is wonderful. How many bottles?"

"Only about one thousand. I inherited most of them. Here's a julep for you, a pinot grigio for Alexis, and a Macallan for me. Now, what's up?"

"I worry about long range microphones and satellite pickups. I can't take a chance on being followed." Much to Hew's chagrin, Sam pulled out his cell phone and started playing a country music song at full volume. "Oh, God, this is delicious."

"It's made with single malt rather than bourbon. There's a story that before the War for Independence, four South Carolinians staying in Philadelphia for the Continental Congress meetings introduced the classic mint julep recipe to a local publican. It took off. Theirs used corn liquor. The Swan Bay recipe uses fine single malt Scotch because my grandfather hated corn liquor. It was too sweet. The secret is not to use too much simple syrup. A little dash is more than enough."

"Great story. First, I want to invite your family to join us for Christmas at Hilde's chalet in Sion, Switzerland. Hilde hates all the security so she's going to stay in Sion for the foreseeable future. That'll save us some money too. Those guys are expensive."

"Ah, what a nice offer. Thank you, but I'm afraid we couldn't leave until the 23rd at the earliest. Alexis, John, and I are scheduled to sing in Bach's Christmas Oratorio on the 22nd. A massed choir from St. Luke's and St. Philip's is singing at St. Philip's."

"That's no problem. You can fly in your jet to the Sion International Airport and we'll pick you up."

"Tell us about Sion."

"Hilde is from there. Her grandparents met after World War two and were married in the old cathedral. They moved here. He was a civil engineer with Georgia Power Company in Atlanta, but they missed home so they moved back. Hilde's American born mother married a man from Sion. Hilde returned here for boarding school. We met at Yale. Actually, her family owns vineyards with some of the finest grapes in Switzerland. Sion is in a fine valley in the Alps."

"We'll leave immediately after the performance and see you on the 23rd."

"Great. Now for the second part. I know about Alexis's situation. Hell, everyone in Atlanta knows about it, but it will work perfectly for us. We can't keep the SCMAGLEV project—oops. Forget I used that word—a secret forever so we need someone, specifically Alexis, to become our VP of marketing."

Alexis was shocked. "But Sam, why me? Don't you already have a VP for marketing? I don't know anything about railroads. My contacts won't help you. Besides, this could be dangerous for our family."

"We have a director of marketing, but he sells loaded freight cars. We have a lobbyist in DC to monitor Congress, but you are exactly what we need for this. Your diplomatic people skills are perfect, and besides, the railroad isn't that much different from your bunch of students, staff, and teachers. People are all the same. As for the danger, if there is any actual danger, you are already in the line of fire. You might as well get paid to be there."

"I'm flattered. Let me discuss this with my attorney. I'll let you know when we get to Switzerland."

"Fair enough. Plan to stay through New Years. We'll go skiing, and Hew," he was whispering now, "Hans has a prototype for us to watch in operation. We'll take the train down to Cologne the day after Christmas. I'm promised we won't be disappointed."

"I'll just have my flight crew stay. We can fly down and they can also have a Christmas vacation in Switzerland."

⁕

"Hilde, This place is magical. I hear they expect snow tonight. Our kids will be thrilled."

"Keep your fingers crossed then. There's something here in town I want to show you. It's an international treasure. It's in the cathedral where my grandparents were married."

They entered the Basilica of Notre Dame de Valere and Hew began looking at the frescos. He knew that as soon as Alexis woke from her nap she would go nuts over these paintings. John immediately spotted the organ high in a swallow's nest on the west wall.

"Look, Dad. What a beauty. How old is it?" A priest overheard the exchange and walked up. "It's thought to be the oldest playable organ in the world, young man. We believe that the case and at least three of the ranks, the Super octave 2 foot, the Quint minor 1⅓ foot, and the 1 foot Mixture II date from about 1434. Their draw knobs are on the left and the quint knob is a little tricky because the retainer has been worn down from use. The draw knobs on the right are for the newer ranks."

"But that's Gothic, sir, I mean, Father."

"Correct. The added Principal 8, the Octav 4, the Copple 2 and the Quint Major 2⅔ plus the nine pedal notes of the Subbass 16 and 8 comprise 10 ranks with 376 pipes. There's an independent Holzpfeiffen on its own chest behind the case. It's better suited for music written in the keys of D, F, or G. We know that the folding doors were painted by the famous Freiburg painter, Peter Maggenberg, between 1434 and 1437. Would you like to go up? We've just had it tuned for Christmas. We don't normally invite visitors to play it, but Hilde and Sam are two of our favorite seasonal parishioners."

"Yes, please. My son and I are both organists. We have a three manual Flentrop at home and a small nine rank two manual at our farm."

Hilde asked, "Hew, I've never understood what those little numbers on those knobs stand for."

"I can tell her, Dad. Let me."

"John, let the grownups talk, please. Hilde, each knob is connected to a set of pipes—one pipe per note—which is also called a rank and when the knob is drawn, or pulled out, it lets wind into a channel under that set of pipes. The names differ from one country to the next, but the little numbers let us know that the longest pipe of that set is that number. So, for instance, two tells us that the longest pipe is two feet long and is therefore high pitched. Sixteen means that the longest pipe is sixteen feet long and is therefore a low sound. The pipes of a set are usually sitting in a row and when a note is pressed, a mechanical rod pulls down a valve inside the wind chest admitting air into the pipe and that note sounds."

"On newer organs, are the numbers in metric?"

"Don't even go there. That would be a nightmare for Americans."

"Hilde, I was just informed this morning that our organist is in hospital for an emergency appendectomy. Maybe Herr Ramsay would be so kind as to accompany our Midnight Christmas Mass tonight?"

"It would be my honor. What a treat! I'm very familiar with Catholic Masses, but I'm afraid I don't know your language well enough to enter at the correct times."

"Perhaps Hilde will stand with you."

"Yes, certainly, and John can pump."

John jumped. "Pump? It has to be pumped?"

Father laughed. "She's joking. It has an electric blower now, but it can still be pumped when necessary. Let me show you."

John was amazed. The organ at Swan Bay could be pumped using a small wooden handle, but he'd never bothered to try. "But it will take two people to pump these bellows."

"Yes, and they must be very sure to be in rhythm to keep the wind supply steady."

Hew improvised to get the feel of the instrument and then John did the same. "Father, we need to go back to the chalet and arrange some music for tonight. What are your preferences?"

"Perhaps a short entrance piece, the hymn *Adestes Fidelis,* and also, D'Aquin's *Nöel X.* This parish loves it and it's traditionally played here at every Christmas Mass. You may play anything you like after the Mass has ended as the people leave. Under the circumstances, we will have a spoken Mass so you don't need service music."

"As you wish, but I had a French priest as my organ teacher and I played the Spanish Mass for three years while I was in school so I can play the standard interludes and give pitches to the choir if you wish. I assume they sing Gregorian Chant. I can easily follow that. Actually, do you think you could contact my old organ teacher, Father Arturo? I have the address. I would love for him to meet my little family. We could just fly over for a few hours."

"Excellent. Yes, I will find him for you. Now, I'll go speak to my choir and cantor. Hilde can keep the key to the stair so you can practice as much as you wish. Hilde, call me if you need anything."

Hew and John retrieved their small keyboard and computer from the jet. He had a four rank sampleset of the continuo organ that Tzschockel Orgelbau had built for St. Maria Nordheim in the Netherlands that would work as a practice instrument. The sampleset contains a Gedeckt 8, a Rohrflote 4, a principal 2, and a Quint 1⅓. It had been released by Prospectum as a free sampleset. They set it up and began trying to find music for the service.

"Dad, what's a d'can noel?"

"That's the way they pronounce the composer's name." He spelled it for John. "Look him up."

John touched a few letters on his phone. "Okay. Here he is. Lou-is-Claude D'Aquin—1694-1772—Swiss. He wrote several of these. Here's the score."

"Maybe Frescobaldi's *Prelude* would work. It's relatively short, but I don't know where I'd find the music here."

"Dad, I'll get it all from the internet music shop. I'll just download it to my app on my tablet. What else are you thinking about? Oh, look, it's snowing. It's snowing. Let's wake the twins."

"Focus, Son. Find the music. Find Flor Peeter's *Choralprel: O Come All Ye Faithful*. It's a short one verse piece that's written to be played on a 8' Schalmey and a 2⅔ Nasard on one manual and soft 8 and 4' flutes on another manual, but I think I can just make it work here. That will work as an introduction to the processional hymn. Also, find the *Nöel* by Balbastre. That might be perfect as a voluntary. Actually, look for the 1582 *Personent Hodie* from the Finnish song book *Piae Cantiones* too. I can improvise on that to fit the time as the offertory."

"I'll try to find it. Oh, here it is. There's a translation of the text. 'The Son of God is gifted to man through the Blessed Virgin, and through His birth the victory of the Devil is done.' Nice one, Dad."

"Thanks. Now load the music in order while you're at it. That way, a simple turn of the page will be like a stepper. I can accompany the service music from memory. I'll just play the processional as written. I might work in the half-diminished seventh chord of Sir David Willcocks's hymn just because only you, your mother, and I will recognize it, and I simply can't imagine Christmas without it."

Alexis came out while they were working and sat in the inglenook to warm herself. "Alexis, I've just had an idea. Why don't you sing the Bach/Gounod *Ave Maria* during communion?"

"*The Prelude number 1 in C major*, BWV 846? Oh, no. I haven't practiced it in a while, but John can do it."

He explained that while John could sing it, he didn't know it as well as she did. She was still reluctant, but Hilde's mother who had been sitting quietly on the other side of the inglenook casually commented, "It's okay, dear. This parish has heard the best."

The field of battle had been set and the lines drawn. Alexis was ready to run the gauntlet in true medieval fashion. John added it to the program.

"Let's all go over to the cathedral. I need to practice singing with all that reverberation."

"Don't worry. It'll be just like all those summers in the English cathedrals except colder. Much colder."

While they were all three practicing in the cathedral during the afternoon, the beautiful dusting of snow became a blizzard with strong gusts of wind roaring down into the valley from the Alps. While Hew arranged the music for the organ, Alexis went down and wandered around studying the beautiful frescos. Just as they were ready to leave, the power went out.

As they were carefully making their way down the pitch black staircase, John turned. "Now what, Dad?"

"Oh, no worries. Catholic churches always have a large supply of candles, and you can have the extremely unique pleasure of pumping the bellows for me."

"Not by myself, I can't."

The priest had been listening from the sacristy. Thankful for his deliverance with such talent, he brought them two lighted candles. "You all sound just like angels from the realms of glory from up there. My choir always sings from down here. There's no room for them up there. Hilde will know someone who can help you, John, and now you know why we restored the bellows." He would speak to his choir and let them know about Alexis's solo. His choir was all male.

The blizzard continued. Back at the chalet, Hilde reminisced. "My father, Noah, used to pump the bellows when he was a boy. The local boys took turns and prided themselves on who got the steadiest wind pressure. The phones aren't working so let's do it the old fashioned way. Let's get the sleigh out of the barn and go ask him. Sam, you and Hew go to the barn and get the horses hooked up."

❦

"Mom, hold my phone and take a video of Mr. Noah and me in this sleigh. Eddie's gonna be so mad."

Noah told John to hand him the phone and he would video the three of them. Even though only their faces were visible from under the wool blankets and hats, he took a photo too. Hew had it copied onto a frameless polished aluminum sheet when they got home. The dim afternoon light and the blowing snow made the picture look magical.

The cathedral was freezing inside. They had arrived by sleigh as did many others. The cathedral was packed and people were standing three deep around the walls. Word had spread about the visiting American musicians who had agreed to fill in for their organist. Hilde, Noah, Alexis, John, and Hew almost had to fight to get to the spiral stair.

Hew wore gloves with the fingertips cut out. Alexis wore her full length black mink coat, a matching hat, lined black leather gloves, and black leather knee high boots. Hew had given her an early present of battery-powered heated liners for her boots. He and John wore matching full length navy blue cashmere great coats with hats, and leather boots. They had to remove their leather boots to play the pedals, but their thick Alpaca socks helped against the cold. Hew finally had to throw off his coat. The weight was restricting the movement of his arms.

Fortunately, he had also worn a bright blue cashmere sweater he had purchased in Scotland so his shoulders and trunk stayed relatively warm. Hilde, all bundled up in her brown mink, was having a great time and her entrance cues were flawless. Alexis's solo was perfect for the occasion and very well executed. The cathedral was lit entirely with hundreds of flickering candles. It was magical. There were candles beside the keyboard and in the pumping room, but the lighted tablet with the music was a Godsend. Alexis looked resplendent in the candle light. Afterward she gushed that being able to see those frescos in that original light from the organ gallery was one of the highlights of her artistic career. After Hew finished the *Noel* at the end of the Mass and saw that most of the congregation was still there listening, he quickly swapped places with John at the bellows and asked him to play something. He thought the experience would look good on his future applications to schools. John sat down, looked through his digital music file, and found his *Oxford Bach Book for Organ,* manuals only, compiled by Anne Marsden Thomas and began to play Bach's BWV 755 *Nun Freut euch, Lieben Christen gmein* (Dear Christians, let us rejoice together). Hilde recorded a video on her phone. The nave was still full so John began Bach's *Allegro* BWV 976 1st movement of Concerto in F major, after Vivaldi. Hew decided that was enough, even though John would have continued until dawn if he had his way. John was young and didn't understand the theological prejudices of church service music. Fortunately, Swiss Catholics were open minded about German church music.

"Son, we need to let Noah get to bed. It's already Christmas morning."

"Don't worry about me. I haven't had this much fun since I was a teenager. We loved to be able to stay up here and skip communion."

Hew laughed. "I had the exact same experience in boarding school. I played through every communion for three years. Of course, I'm not Catholic, so it was okay."

John had learned to pump the bellows with only a few misses, but afterward, Father thanked him for being a trooper and said that the wavering wind pressure added some old fashioned charm. "Here's a little something as a remembrance of this occasion. We don't normally do this, but I used my camcorder and videoed the service. I hope you can get this tape transferred back in the States. It's probably a little grainy with the candlelight, but the audio is digital."

As they left the cathedral, all the bells were ringing wildly. The blizzard had abated but the temperature had dropped into minus digits. Hew snuggled close to Alexis, kissed her, and wished her a Merry Christmas. John was already asleep. Hew was surprised later that Christmas morning with a new iPad Pro with the forScore app and John's extensive library already added. The girls gave him an iRig Blue Turn foot pad that worked with Bluetooth to turn the forScore pages. Charlie told Alexis that many of the symphony players had started using one. It could simply sit beside the toe studs on any of his consoles. Hew gave her a ruby and diamond choker with a matching set of earrings. The back of the plane had been loaded with wrapped presents for the kids.

14
PROTOTYPE

On the day after Christmas, Sam, Hew, and Alexis flew to Germany to meet Hans and Jason at the prototype. Alexis had agreed to Sam's offer. He asked her if she spoke German.

"Nein."

He winced. "How about Japanese?"

"Their calligraphy is beautiful, but no."

"Then I suggest you start assembling a staff of international interpreters, but keep it very small. I can't afford too much more security."

"I'll need a director of diversity, then, and I know exactly the right woman. She's Black, and she worked at the school with me."

Unhappy with this ramping up of people, he sighed, "Okay. I suppose it's nearly time to go public, but we'll do it softly."

Hew thought they were flying to Cologne. He was surprised when they boarded a helicopter and landed in a valley in the German Alps. "Sam, where are we?"

We've landed near Garmish-Parkenkirten. This meeting is completely off the record. For security reasons, the prototype has been built in a cave in the Alps near here. It works, as you will see, so we're rolling it out onto a long siding today for this demonstration."

They were met with a black Mercedes E Sprinter van with video screens inside the window panels. The screens showed videos of the passing scenery. From the exterior, it looked like a standard panel van but the back of the video display was lined with Kevlar. When they opened the door, Hew remarked, "This pale grey leather interior is beautiful."

"It was built in Charleston, South Carolina, but it was armored by the Israelis in Tel Aviv. It's one of the reasons we want to add the Charleston route. We're going to deliver two of these to Atlanta for you and two to Sam. Charleston has Boeing, Mercedes, and Volvo among others. Volvo shipped over 122,000 vehicles last year. Greenville has BMW, Lockheed, and Michelin. The dock at Charleston is always loaded with vehicles being exported and goods being delivered to the manufacturers. We haul a lot of their product in both directions."

Hew was amazed when they arrived at the cave. There was a rail line going in. Jason explained. "The Nazis used this as a place to store some of their stolen Jewish loot. We couldn't find a more perfect location for our test."

"My God! This thing is huge. It looks to be a mile long!"

"Yep. It's made of steel for the lower section and aluminum on the upper section to keep the weight down, and it's all standard technology but assembled in a unique way. We still aren't happy with the weight issues with our container modules. Hans and Jason have outdone themselves with this thing, though. It sits on the rails, but the freight trains can roll through it. Slowly, of course, but that is the key to the whole thing. It will be necessary to build the first mile the old fashioned way, but after that, the machine will back up to the first section. The augurs will drill deep holes for the piling. The piles are also the columns. The machine moves to the next location for piles while the finished precast roadbed is rolled into place overhead. The robotic arms will connect the electrical work and the machine will move on down the track while the trains roll through. There will be two of them for bridges and ravines. One will be working from one side and one from the other side to meet in the middle. It's pure genius. Let's go out. They're ready to fire it up."

"There really isn't much for Eberhart to do, is there?"

"On the contrary. You've got all the concrete piles to cast and transport. You've got to build the precast roadbed and put the magnets and solar panels in and transport them to the site. Your engineers will need to work out the precasting and transporting details. We hope to build them in an old building on the former Navy yard in Charleston. That place is just sitting there waiting to be re-discovered. They'll have to be shipped on flatbed rail cars at first until we get the first few miles set up and tested. Your team will be busy trying to keep up with Hans and Jason's monster."

The machine moved out of the cave under its own power and was switched onto the siding where the first section of elevated roadbed had been set up. It moved into place and started working. A German locomotive with three cars ran through the machine and then backed up and did it again, and the piling auger never stopped. The next roadbed section was rolled into place and all the folks went wild. They nearly knocked Hans and Jason down with their celebrating. The machine was doused with champagne as were most of the people.

"Hew, I want to go ahead and build the system as a double track main line. This machine makes that possible. I think we can build cross-overs every fifty miles or so and that will allow us to close sections as necessary for maintenance. The trains won't have to slow down in a siding as they pass either. We can move twice as many containers."

While everyone else continued to celebrate, Jason pulled Sam and him aside to tell them that terrorists had kidnapped, tortured, and murdered three employees in Tokyo. None of them were working on this project, though. Hew quickly escorted Alexis back to the helicopter. They stopped in Zurich to let Hew and Alexis off. They took a cab to the bank and Hew introduced her to the new president of the bank.

She was taken down to the vault and asked to recite the account number she had memorized shortly after their marriage. "You, Edward, and I are the only ones who know this number. The accountants take care of everything. In time, I'll bring John and the twins here."

This outer room consisted of drawers full of old ledgers and assorted family records and correspondence not contained in the journals. There's a second even larger secret room behind a movable wall."

"I've never seen so much gold! I don't remember that there was this much before."

"The old boys didn't trust currency and neither do my new guys. Everything that's not invested is converted to gold bullion."

15
MONASTERY

"I thought we were going skiing today, Dad."

"Maybe tomorrow, but today we're going to a little monastery along the Rhine in France to visit an old friend of mine named Father Arturo. I want him to meet my family. I haven't seen him since I was thirteen. He's old now, so this might be my last chance."

"Monasteries have airports?"

"No, but Eberhart has arranged for a car and driver to pick us up."

It was the same black Mercedes van.

After knocking repeatedly and waiting in the frigid air for nearly twenty minutes, a small wooden door set into a much larger wooden door opened. "May I be of assistance?"

"We are here to see Father Arturo. He's expecting us."

Without another word, the small door opened wider to allow them in. They waited another fifteen minutes and the twins were getting restless.

"John? John Bishop? Are you John Bishop, sir? You look exactly like someone I used to know!"

"Yes, Father. Did they not tell you I was coming? The cathedral in Sion called ahead and set it up." He was afraid his old teacher was having mental difficulties, but Father was still sharp as a tack.

"They said someone named Hew Ramsay wanted to visit. Since I don't know a Hew Ramsay, I wasn't terribly interested in having my day interrupted. John! Let me look at you. I thought I would never see you again in this life."

John was taken aback. He had forgotten that the priest couldn't have known about his name change. "I'm terribly sorry, Father. I had to change my name after I was removed from the school."

"Ah, yes, that. I have never understood all that. I was reassigned back here the week after."

"I'll be happy to tell you all of it, but first, allow me to introduce my family. This is my wife, Alexis, our son, John, and our twin daughters, Elizabeth and Courtney."

"What a wonderful Christmas present, John. Look at this. Come, sit by the fire and warm yourselves. This is our visitor's parlor. It's one of the few rooms that we heat here. Let me call for some coffee for us and warm milk for the little ones."

"Please, no coffee for us, but we will take tea if you have it—plain, hot, no milk or sugar, but with a slice of lemon, if possible."

Father rang a small bell and an assistant came in, took the orders, and hurried off to get the drinks. Father then turned to Alexis. "Such a stunning beauty." He reached out to touch the boy's hair. "He looks exactly like you did when you came to us. A bit younger perhaps, but the same long wiry frame, the same pale blue eyes, the same curly blond hair that no brush will ever tame, and oh, yes, those long, thin fingers. Do you play the organ too?"

"Yes, sir. We have two organs at home."

"Two? I hope one of them is French." He reached for Elizabeth and she shrieked.

"Nooooo. nooo. I want to go. I want my 'merican girl doll." Her high pitched screaming set Courtney off.

"I'll just take them back to the van while you catch up."

"Oh, please, no. Stay a while. It's been so long since I've seen a little child—and John's children. So precious. They'll warm up to me in a bit."

But they didn't. It became two full blown temper tantrums. "I see they've inherited John's temper. Perhaps you could just take them out for a little while, if that would make them happier."

"John, help your mother take them to the van."

"May I come back, Dad?"

"I'll come get you in a while. Father and I need to talk."

Hew turned back to the priest. "My parents took me out of St. Thomas's Choir School against my will, moved from Manhattan to Colombia, and dumped me in your school. I think a more appropriate word would be abandoned because I only saw them twice after that."

"My poor boy. Still carrying all that bitterness. You must let it go, my son."

"Yes, well, I have, but it comes back at strange times, like now, but I really am glad to see you. I think about you every time I play a Spanish Mass in the Catholic cathedral in Atlanta."

"Atlanta? Where is that?"

"Sorry. It's in the state of Georgia in the Southern part of the US. We live there now. But my mother was duped. She was lured to Colombia under false pretenses. I know this for a fact because when a rival drug cartel murdered Espinis, they inadvertently stole his diary. It told all. He was a vain, evil man. One of the cartel's men had been forced into service as their accountant and he was given the job of selling all of Espinis's gold and artwork. He confessed to my grandfather's law partner in their Bogota office. One of their possessions was the diary. I was able to translate it. Espinis and his half sister were laundering drug money through the music school and through your school. While they were hiking in the Andes, my parents stumbled onto a coca field and Espinis's guards murdered them."

"I'm sorry, John, er, Hew. I don't know this person, Espinis. He was a drug lord?"

"Yes. He and Father X—I'll never use his name again—were childhood friends. Their fathers were Nazis who fled to Colombia using stolen Jewish gold. Espinis's father had been part of the squads that stole the Jewish possessions. In true German fashion, he kept detailed records. All the beautiful fittings in your chapel were stolen."

"Yes, now I remember that funeral. You were ordered to play *Panis Angelicus* as I remember."

"And I did, but I followed it with Psalm 94."

"I remember the racket you made. *The Lord is a God who avenges. Oh God who avenges, shine forth.* That was gutsy. Wait. Even my organ had been stolen?"

"Yes! Espinis's father was hiding in a monastery near here on the

Rhine. The French monks, fearing the destruction of their monastery, let him talk them into allowing him to remove everything for safe keeping. The Germans bombed the monastery thinking that the Allies would use the tower as a machine gun nest. It was reduced to rubble and never rebuilt. To win favors in Colombia, he convinced the authorities to relocate the fittings to your—well, Father X's—chapel.

"Before we moved to Cali, my grandfather had us fitted with GPS trackers. His men found my parent's bodies and immediately came to rescue me. That's what the confusion was about that night. My rescue team was only about fifteen minutes ahead of Espinis's men."

"We were coming into the chapel for the service when we heard the helicopter. We ran out just as it landed and, yes, the truck broke down the gates and men came in with guns drawn. We were interrogated for hours, but no one knew anything." He was crying. "On the following Sunday, the bells rang as usual, but when we were assembled for Mass, instead of a procession, the archbishop walked out of the sacristy and into the center and told us that the school was closing immediately. He gave us all one hour to collect our possessions and walk out the front gate. All I had, of course, was my music, and I simply couldn't carry it all." He sighed. "The parents of the local boys were waiting outside. Everyone else was either given a train ticket or an airline ticket. It was over. I never knew why or what happened after that."

"I did get my diary that you forwarded to my grandfather's office. Thank you for that. I'll always treasure it."

"Unfortunately, it was the only address we had. It's where the checks came from."

"Once I had translated Espinis's diary, Luis Torres, my grandfather's Colombian law partner, immediately took it to the archbishop. He shut the place down and demolished all the buildings."

"Please, no. My organ too? It was priceless."

"No. It, the bells, the windows, and the altar were sold to a new church in South Carolina."

"Mercy! Have you been to play it?"

"Not yet." Hew laughed. "It could have been a sad story but I found out about it just in time. We were at a cocktail party and one of the guests visiting our host discovered during the evening that I'm an organist with experience at playing Catholic Masses. He is a member of the new church that's under construction and remarked that they had discovered an old chapel in Bogota that had been demolished and had purchased all of the old fittings for a steal. I asked if it had an organ and he said yes but their organist didn't want it. He convinced the church to buy a large electronic because it had more varied tonal colors. We later discovered that his boyfriend sold electronic organs."

Father was stunned. "Oh, no. What did you say?"

"I told him that I would like to know more and that I might be interested in buying it. I could see him begin to salivate. He confessed that he was chairman of the building committee and he told me that I could buy it for the cost of the new electronic organ."

"I told him that the cost to move it, repair it, and erect it in a new location would be extremely expensive, but I would look at it. I went over the next weekend and confirmed that it was our Cavaillé-Coll. I bought it for half the cost of the electronic."

"What now?"

"I don't know yet, but at least it's stored in a safe environmentally controlled fireproof warehouse."

"I'm very pleased. I know it will sing on. Continue your story."

"Espinis's half sister and nephew hunted me down and nearly got me. As I left Mass at the Cathedral of Christ the King and walked across the street and up to the Episcopal cathedral for the next service—I direct the children's choirs—those two stepped off the curb just as the bus was pulling away and they were killed."

The door opened and John ran in. "The girls are still out of control. They're driving me crazy. Mom wants to know how much longer you plan to stay."

"Hew, will you and young John stay overnight as my guests? I'd love to hear you play this instrument and I would like to give John a lesson in our French technique."

"Yes, Dad! Please? Let Mom and the girls fly back to Sion. Please?"

"Let me talk with your mother. Stay here."

136

THE BELLS WERE RINGING. "HEW AND John, it's time for the next service. Come with me to the organ loft and then we'll have some lunch in the refectory."

John was enthralled with the organ. He marveled at Father's technique. There was a smaller organ played by another monk near the monks' stalls in the choir beside the altar, but Father A played interludes from his perch high up in the west gallery. John had never seen anything like it.

The refectory was absolutely silent. The room was a masterpiece of Gothic design with Latin verses in medieval painted lettering adorning every surface. A young man about Hew's age wearing a brown habit climbed a set of narrow stone stairs set into a wall to a pulpit hanging on a side wall. When he turned and started to read, Hew recognized him.

"Father! Is that my old roommate Tomas?"

"Shh. He's reading today's rule. I forgot about him. I'll tell you later."

After the meal, the two roommates reunited. "Tomas, I tried to find you everywhere. No one knew where you were. Luis searched the records. I searched the internet. You just disappeared. I'm so glad to see you, but why here?"

"When my father was informed the school would be closing, he didn't wait. He sent his men for me because he feared that a drug lord was somehow involved. I was not there by the time it closed."

"All the way from Argentina? How did you get here?"

"My family is from here. My ancestors made wine. My relatives still do. My ancestor and his younger brother left France to start a division of the family vineyard in South America. Argentina is a word derived from the Latin word argentum which means silver or whiteness. Many Europeans moved there to mine for gold and silver. My family moved there to supply the Europeans with wine. It's been wildly successful and we have a small jet. When my father learned the truth, he sent me here to hide until he could find out more. I really began to like it here, so a few years ago, I took my vows. What about you? We thought you had been kidnapped. I'm so happy to see you're alive and have a son who looks just like you."

"That was my grandfather's men. I was taken to our family farm in Virginia and I changed my name."

The father interrupted. "I'll tell him the rest, Hew. He must go to his work in our vineyard. We can chat tonight. Now, you and John must come with me to the organ while everyone else is at work."

The organ was larger than the old chapel organ had been. Father first explained the layout of the three manuals since they were different from those John had played. "What do you like to play, John?"

"I love to play Buxtehude and Bach on my Flentrop."

"Ah. And what French music do you like?"

"I don't know any French music, but we have the Haarlem and the Hereford Cathedral samplesets on our Hauptwerk."

"What is this Hauptwerk of which you speak? It's only one manual? My English is not so good, and Hauptwerk is German for the main manual."

"No, sir. Hauptwerk is the trademark name of some digital software. It's a virtual instrument. We have a three manual and pedal console that has a large Mac computer. Engineers and organists have carefully recorded each pipe of those instruments and have captured the live sound in the room just like a CD except when put into the computer, we can play those instruments at home."

"Ah. I have heard CDs. But you do not have a French instrument like my Cavaillé-Coll here?"

"Actually, Father, as a Christmas present, Alexis gave me the software to play the instrument at Caen. We'll install it when we get home."

"Do you mean St. Etienne Abbey? Abbaye Aux Hommes? As remodeled by Cavaillé-Coll?"

"Yes, sir."

"A fine instrument. I played it when I was a student in France. So, young John, sit here in the middle. John, I mean Hew, you'll be on the left. I'll be on the right. We'll change stops and turn the pages. John, you just play the correct notes at the correct time."

"But, Father, I don't need help."

Hew laughed. "Son, it takes a committee to play this French organ. There are no pistons or toe studs. You can operate the expression pedal, though."

"What will you play for me today?"

"I have just finished a composition based on Psalm 121. I hope Dad will let me play it for our choir to sing."

"Ah, one of the Psalms of Degrees. One of my favorites."

"I don't know what a Psalm of Degree is."

"You must study the Psalms in detail if you want to write music for them. They are the Psalms from 120 to 134. They are sometimes known as Psalms of Ascents or "pilgrim songs" and are thought to have been sung as the Children of Israel traveled in the wilderness. That's not entirely correct, in my opinion, because several of them don't fit this description, but the name has stuck."

"Son, I had no idea this is what you were working on. May I video this, Father? I want to remember this moment."

"Certainly. I can manage without you."

John pulled out his tablet and opened it.

"What is this?"

"It's my music. This is the latest electronic device for storing music."

"But how do you see the rest of the score? There's only one page here."

Hew laughed. "Forgive me for laughing, Father, but I just remembered the story you told me about the young medieval monk showing his elder scribe how to read a book. Bound books were new inventions then. The young monk showed him how to turn pages, but the old guy didn't know what to do when he got to the end of the book."

"Oh, yes. I remember." He laughed. "The young scribe closed the book, flipped it over and opened it again."

John didn't understand the story. He sat there studying the console and trying to understand the French stop names, but he believe Hew's explanation of the console controls when he tried a few stops. After a hauntingly beautiful gently rolling introduction on a light flute tone, John began to sing. *I will lift up mine eyes until the hills.*

When he finished, Father A exclaimed, "This is amazing. You've managed to capture the idea of the Jews wandering and seeing the hills of Judea for the first time. Your use of the two-foot flute is absolutely perfect. Only a shepherd would have had such a flute. So sublimely simple as only a child can do. I wish I had a copy."

"That's easy, sir. Give me your email address and I'll send it to you."

"Alas, technology has passed me by, but you can send it to our librarian and he can print it for me."

"I'll send the video too and you can watch it after we've left."

"Ask Tomas for the details. John let's have a lesson while your dad talks with his old roommate. Let's back up a few hundred years and look at Couperin's *Tierce en taille.* Tierce is a mutation with the longest pipe being 1⅗ foot. It supports the fifth of the eight-foot harmonic series on the manuals. It's very French, but the English call it the seventeenth. Couperin lived from 1668 until 1733 and, yes, he was born a few years before Bach. I just happen to have the score right here for another student. We only have a few hours, and I want to teach you a little about French registration."

John had just discovered the world of French music, and he had also discovered the beauty of French organs. While John practiced, Hew and Tomas sat in the visitor's reception room by the fire and sampled Tomas's family Alsatian wine and the monk's Alsatian wine. Hew couldn't decide which he liked so he decided to buy cases of both. "Father will tell you about my rescue and the events that led to the closing of the school so let me tell you a little about life after that. There is no school near our farm so I had to go to Washington, DC and live with my grandfather. He understood that I had no intention of going to another boarding school so he enrolled me into a local day academy. I played soccer, football as you know it, but the captain didn't like me. He and two of his friends stabbed me in the leg ending my soccer days. They went to prison where one of the guys, the team captain, was murdered. His father was a US senator. He found me in Atlanta and tried to murder me, but his old gun backfired and he killed himself instead. It was a bloody awful mess right on the fair linen of the altar. He had murdered my grandfather too, so the Edward Hardy, my grandfather's law partner in the Atlanta office, took me in and I moved to Atlanta. Their son Charlie became my best friend."

The wine flowed and finally, John and Father came in and Father announced that it was dinner time.

Father let John play an interlude for Compline that night. John was ecstatic. As they took their leave the next morning, John hugged Father and thanked him. Hew gave Tomas his contact information and they agreed to stay in touch. He whispered,"I want to know how he gets on here. He must be 95 now. Especially if..."

"Yes. I understand."

Alexis snuggled up to Hew under their down comforters. "I'm really glad you and John had a good time. Father really was surprised to see you."

"I'm sorry the girls acted up."

"It's okay. Elizabeth had a slight temperature, but she's fine now. There's something I want to ask you and don't say no until we talk it through.

Oh, God, he thought. *Here it comes. Payback.*

"I got a text today from Mavis about the St. Luke's choir. Dr. Roberts has resigned as Organist Choirmaster at St. Luke's effectively at the end of the month. Seems his partner has taken a job in Portland, Oregon and Dr. Roberts will become the organist choirmaster at the Chapel of the Episcopal Seminary of the Northwest. The new dean is a priest he worked with years ago. He's promised him a new organ. He will also be teaching seminarians to read publicly."

"Hmmm. Let me sleep on that. He should find a great musical community there. Trinity Cathedral has a fine choral program and a relatively new 54-stop Rosales organ. I'm not saying no—yet. Seminarians can't read out loud? That's a good one."

"Try it. You'd be surprised at how difficult it is to read Rite One Prayer Book Tudor-Elizabethan English out loud. Say 'the peace that passeth all understanding.'"

"Don't be silly. The pith...P...the pe. Okay. Okay. I get your point."

Hew's phone woke him from a deep sleep at 6:30 a.m. It was Tomas calling. "Hew, you asked about Father. I'm sorry to tell you that he died in his sleep last night. It seems to have been a peaceful end."

"Oh, my God! Please, no. No. Our visit must have upset him. I'm so sorry. I never thought—"

"No, no. Don't think that for a minute. You answered questions that had troubled him for years. He—we—thought you were dead, so to see you and your beautiful family meant everything to him. Your answers put his mind to rest. I think he was ready to go. The Abbot has asked me to contact you and ask if you would be so kind as to play for the service. We don't have another organist at the moment."

"Absolutely. When is it?"

"We will celebrate the Requiem Eucharist today. It will be sung as Gregorian chant so you only need a few simple pieces."

"Wow! That's quick—and early. Why so early?"

"We don't embalm, and we don't bury our dead in coffins so it needs to be done as quickly as possible. He's in better hands than ours. We can do nothing more for him except pray for his soul."

"I understand. I'll see you in a couple of hours. I need to select the music."

He took John with him on the flight over, and with John's help, he quickly got acquainted with his new tablet. Avoiding the works of Bach, he found Bonnet's *Pastorale.* He decided a shepherd's song played on the French reed would be a fitting prelude for a shepherd. He also selected *Cantilene Religieuse ute 'Sept Pieces* by Dubois for the offertory and would sing *Panis Angelicus* by Franck during communion. Father would laugh at that. He decided he and John could sing *In Paradisum* from Fauré's Requiem at the end of the service. The monks would be gone by then with the body so this would be a prayer to God alone.

Hew discussed the funeral music with Tomas. "I don't know anything about music but I'm sure he would have approved. He was such a fine, wonderful person. We were so fortunate to have a finalist of the Prix de Rome live and play for us. We may never have another organist like him unless young John wants to study here."

"Fat chance. His mother would kill you and me for even talking about that. I knew Father had studied with Mme. Marie-Claire Alain, but the Prix was the highest award given in organ. I never knew that he had been a finalist. I'm humbled to have studied with him."

"He told me that the prize was discontinued shortly after his entry so he never got the chance to compete again, but you're right. The cantata he composed for the prize is still in use today. He was a gift from God."

"I want a copy. If I hadn't found him, I don't think I would have survived that damned school."

16
REQUIEM

Hew made the organ whisper the opening measures and the service was sublime. As the procession retired, Hew had no idea that when the monks began to hear the Fauré, they stopped under the organ loft just to listen. When the piece ended, he turned the organ off and slipped quietly down the stairs and out of the chapel back to his jet. He left the monks to bury their dead because that was not the way he wanted his last memory of his old friend to be. While John slept on the flight back to Sion, Hew broke down and silently wept.

17
GUN SHOT

"What the hell was that?" said Alexis.

Viktor was just about to turn out of the service driveway onto Riverside Drive when a small pock mark appeared on the windshield on Alexis's side of the van. "It was probably just a rock, Mrs. Ramsay. I'll have it replaced before you return from Virginia. Nothing to worry about, Ma'am."

After dropping Alexis off at St. Luke's Church for choir practice, Viktor called Pink. "Someone took a shot at us as I was pulling out on to Riverside Drive. It dinged the passenger side windshield. She saw it, but I told her it was probably a rock."

"Did you see anybody?"

"No. I did see an old rusty Ford pickup truck drive by but it was so dirty I couldn't read the license plate."

"How would anyone know who was in the van?"

"There's no way. We loaded inside the garage and I waited until she was buckled in before I opened the garage door."

"Well, get it replaced. Good thing we're going to Swan Bay. This is nuts. They must have thought it was Hew in the passenger seat, but a Chinese assassin would have used something more powerful. You think it was the mob?"

"I have no idea at this point."

"What will you tell Hew?"

"Nothing unless he asks. I'm paid to protect them. That includes keeping them from worrying about the 'what ifs.'"

"Was she upset?"

"No, she seemed to buy my story."

"I must say, though, we've got to give it to the guy. The old rusty Ford pickup was a good choice. There's only about a million of them in Georgia. Any chance of finding a shell casing?"

"We'll look once the family has left for Virginia. We'll find it unless he came back for it."

"DAMMIT, LES, I SAID WE NEEDED a better gun. Those windows must be extra strong. How'd you know it was her?"

"I watched her for two weeks. She went down to that big high fallutin' downtown church at the same time ever week so I figured it had to be her in the van. I don't have enough money for anything bigger. I tried to steal one from a van at that gun show and damn near got caught. How was I to know he had a sleeping Doberman in the damned van? I contacted a fellow near Clemson who lives in the country on the side of Lake Hartwell but he asked too damned many questions. I don't have any permits either."

"Well, we just need to come up with another way. I won't give up."

18
CONSERVATORS

"Hew, the conservators are ready to present their preliminary report of Swan Bay. Are you available near the end of next week?"

"Sure. I can be there on Thursday. I'll fly up tonight and I'll plan to stay over the weekend."

"That should give them plenty of time. Will you bring the family? Mary wants to visit with Alexis and the girls."

"Not John and me?"

Jeffrey laughed. "She said you two will hog her organ."

"So it's *her* organ now, is it?"

"Yes. She's punishing you for not setting it up years ago."

"Remind her that I got her that Bosendorfer concert grand piano for the ballroom."

"I'm just kidding you. We'd love to see everyone."

THE BRIEFING BEGAN AFTER LUNCH. THE lead conservator, Dorothy, led the meeting. "Mr. Ramsay, thank you for this opportunity. This is one of the finest sites we've ever surveyed. Most of the buildings are still in fine condition after the 1970 upgrades. The main house—I've been told you never refer to it as a manor house—is in outstanding condition. A few of the doors and windows need restoring as you suspected but that's not the main problem."

Hew stood quietly as they presented. He had to move away to avoid the fumes from their coffee.

"We have a minor concern about the porch on the old log cabin. It needs a major replacement. There are powder post beetles in several of the floor beams. None of the wood is original. Fortunately, the old square hewn tulip poplar logs of the cabin are still in great shape although the chinking needs to be replaced, and one log needs to be replaced. It's rotten on the inside. This picture shows that it was sawn rather than hewn. It's actually two loblolly pine logs butted one on top of the other to simulate the size of the original poplar log. The rot started between the butted logs. If they had just turned it ninety degrees it might still be good. We didn't find a reference to that in the journals. I might add that those journals are remarkable and contain a complete history of this farm. We've never seen anything like them."

"Dorothy, we can cut another tree if necessary but I'd rather fill the void with epoxy or something. I hate cutting old growth trees."

"Unfortunately, we don't recommend epoxy on rotten wood. The mold spores already in the wood are impossible to kill entirely so while we can fill the voids with the epoxy, the mold continues to eat away around the epoxy. There is a company in West Virginia who specializes in buildings of this type. They have several antique poplar logs at their workshop of the size that can be cut to fit. They can do the chinking too. They really are experts."

"Are these the guys I've seen on TV?"

"Yes, sir."

"Right. I'll trust them. I'll enjoy watching them work. Maybe they'll do a show here. Now, what's the real problem?"

Mary commented, "Hew, you'd better come over here and sit down. I know why you're standing. My cup has tea."

"Mr. Ramsay, the old brick kitchen is about to collapse. We've already closed it and we've shored the second floor and the roof. We'll begin bracing the walls this afternoon, but it isn't safe for occupancy."

"Dorothy, I can't believe that. Looks fine to me. It was restored by my grandfather. It can't have gotten that bad since then. What's the problem?"

"Basically, old buildings are like old people. Neither improves with age. Also, you must understand that architects are licensed to protect the welfare of people, not to save old buildings. The last restoration focused on pointing the exterior brickwork, replacing the wood shingles on the roof, and upgrading the systems and equipment. They used the wrong pointing mortar. The new mortar compounded the existing problem. Unfortunately, in those days, our profession didn't really look at the condition of the mortar inside the walls. Everyone assumed that brickwork was forever, but we've now learned that some old soft lime based mortars can break down over time if they didn't use enough lime. It wasn't an exact science back then and lime was more expensive than sand."

"Of course. We're Scots, you know."

"Roman mortar was very rich in lime. The lime never really sets and when wet, will return to its original formula. As it slowly dries, it moves into any voids. In this country, they didn't know that and used much less lime. The brick joints that were repointed suggested that water had been getting into the walls. The wonderful thing about soft lime mortar is that it will fail before the water damages the old soft brick. Too much water stored in the bricks will freeze and cause the face to spall off. They didn't repoint every joint so most of the water evaporated as it should. Modern mortars are too strong and dense for old brick. Old bricks were fired at lower temperatures. I can show you examples of where whole faces of brick have spalled off leaving a strong mortar joint in place. Unfortunately, we can't restored a brick like that. Here, the lime and sand has silently leached out of the old joints leaving large dangerous voids. We put our scopes into several places and I made my crew move away."

"Scopes? What kind of scope? I want to see in the walls."

"Have you ever had a colonoscopy? It's the same type of scope."

Hew squirmed uncomfortably in his chair. "No, but, whew. At least you don't have to do the same prep! I need some time. Let's take a break while I go look at this."

"I'll set it up, but I warn you, we can't stand there too long, and don't go inside."

"I saw the problem. What's your proposed solution?"

"Look at this image." She showed a photo on the screen that included horizontal and vertical strings that showed the bulges in the east and west walls. "These aren't obvious because of the large fruit trees around the kitchen. We suspect that there were years when the kitchen brickwork was simply ignored. We've seen it before. The interior of kitchens were more important than the exterior."

"Strings? Why not fancy lasers? So how can you replace the internal mortar."

"We can't. We had to use old-school strings because the trees were in the way. Ms Mamie told us she would shoot anyone who touched her trees. We recommend deconstructing the building and rebuilding it."

There was absolute silence in the room. Finally, Mary spoke. "Dorothy, as a member of the board of Virginia Preservation, I can assure you that you will have a difficult time getting us to agree to that. My board will just vote to leave the shoring in place until some better solution comes along in a few years. Aren't they injecting grout into old brick walls in buildings in Charleston?"

"Yes, they've used a system of drilling holes through the walls and inserting hundreds of small stainless steel perforated tubes. They then inject a special grout replacement. It's a viscous mix that fills the voids, but these bulges are too large for that solution. We couldn't ever pull that much brickwork back into plumb. In Charleston, they use large one and a half inch diameter stainless steel rods—Carpenter steel—to tie the sides together. Here, they would simply break the bricks, and we haven't even mentioned the chimney. Those bricks in the flues have long since vanished in the heat and pine tar acid, and with the voids in the brickwork, well, I hate to alarm you, but we're amazed that the wood shingles haven't burned."

"I can't believe this. Let's adjourn for lunch. Where will we eat? Where will the chefs work? Ms. Mamie will tell y'all to get the hell out of her kitchen."

Everyone laughed. Mary commented, "Oh, don't worry. She did. I had to talk with her for hours. She protested having to move out of her apartment on the second floor. Her ancestors have lived there for thirteen generations, and we promised her that she could move back once we finished, but while she won't ever admit it, she really loves her new one story apartment. We've called a food truck service last week when this happened. They should be arriving about now. They've been here everyday for a week and everyone—except Ms. Mamie—is satisfied for the short term. She cooks in her apartment, and I cook for Jeffrey and me."

They dined on pizza, Greek salad, and ice cream sandwiches.

The meeting resumed after lunch. Hew started. "This kitchen is as old as the log cabin. The first John Bishop—Captain John—built it for his aristocratic English wife but, of course, she had no experience with domestic work. Ms. Mamie's ancestor was the first Black person to work here. The kitchen dates from about 1651." He paused. "I need to sleep on this. Let's move on to the other buildings. I'm adding my architect, Johann to this group. He's going to either design a few new apartments or renovate the existing ones over at the old training center site and he will direct the design work on the kitchen. We have a new business moving into the old training center and we'll need some up-scale family housing."

When they had reviewed all the other facilities, Hew said, "Mary, it's going to be a fine evening. It's early. Let's let these folks have cocktails on the boat and sail over to Williamsburg. I'm in the mood for The Fat Canary's pork chop, but my security detail will drive me over. No one is going to attack a ferry in the middle of the James River."

AFTER A FINE DINNER, PINK DROVE one of the center's armored vans off of the James River ferry onto Highway 31. At Scotland, Virginia, he noticed a vehicle close on his tail. At Surrey, Virginia, instead of continuing straight, he made a left turn onto Colonial Trail East. Hew, from the back seat, noticed and told him he was going the wrong way. "Yeah, I know. I think we may have a tail. I'm leading him away from Swan Bay. I've alerted the Virginia State Patrol." He omitted adding that the closest patrol car was across the river in Williamsburg.

Hew began to get nervous. The more they drove, the worse his fears increased. He began to imagine a grenade fired from a hand held weapon coming through the back of the van and he was terrified. Suddenly, the following vehicle's left turn signal came on. The vehicle slowed and turned into a country lane and disappeared. "Looks like a false alarm. We'll drive on a few miles just in case we pick up another one. If we don't, we'll turn around."

"Probably just some good ole boys going home after having a few in town."

"Yeah. We all understand about having a few in town."

Ten miles later, they made a three-point turn on the deserted road and started back. Hew began to relax. As they passed the point where the vehicle turned off the highway, the road was empty. They drove past Swan Bay and into Clairmont. It was only 10:30 p.m. but the streets were deserted, so they drove back to Swan Bay. Hew was still too wired to sleep. He finally got up, turned on his computer, put his headphones on and watched videos. Somewhere in the middle of Bach's cello suites, he finally fell asleep in his recliner.

After having a quiet word to Mary the evening before to make sure everyone would have coffee, Hew scheduled the meeting to begin at 9:30. He also had an early meeting with Dorothy in the ballroom.

"I want to ask you about this flooring," he said. "As you can see, it's running ninety degrees to normal. We had a plumbing issue and had to remove several rotten boards. We discovered a series of sleepers that raised the floor two inches above the original level."

"When was it raised? Was this something that was done to accommodate the plumbing waste lines?"

"No. The date I found in the journal for the work was 1832. The bathrooms weren't installed until 1905. What's also interesting is that it appears that the boards were simply raised, turned over, and relaid."

"Then my guess is that the boards were probably so worn from all those dancing feet that they had grooves worn in them. Now I can't tell you why they would have raised the level and turned them ninety degrees unless someone didn't like the look. Those long boards would have accentuated the long room. It explains why there are no butt joints in the boards, though. The original boards would probably have been cut in one length down the room. It's curious, but it explains why the room is only eleven feet ten-inches high."

When they reconvened the group, Hew announced, "I have one word: *Resurgam*."

"My Latin is rusty, but doesn't that mean *rise again*?"

"Yes. *I shall rise again*. It was also a word used in Atlanta after the Civil War fires. It's on the city seal. Resurgens. The classical mythical bird, the Phoenix, rose strong as ever from the ashes. That's what Atlanta did.

"This is a working farm and this kitchen is critical. Mary, we can't wait until someone possibly finds a better solution. That may never happen. I'm not going to build a new kitchen somewhere else and truck the food over. We did that for years with the training center and the food was never hot enough. This has reminded me that we need to build a new food facility over there, and it can take some of the load from this old kitchen. We've never had enough bulk storage here. I thought about putting a new kitchen underground under the lawn, but I don't want vents and technical mechanical and plumbing trash poking up through the turf. There is also the issue of truck access, so no. We will rebuild. How will you deconstruct this kitchen? You don't know this, but I consider myself the current trustee. No one really owns historic property."

"We begin by carefully removing the equipment once all the shoring is secure. Then we carefully remove the roof and framing. We number every board and timber. We carefully remove any old pegs or hand forged cut nails. We then number each brick. The exterior bricks will be returned to their respective faces and places in the walls. The internal bricks will be handled the same way. It will go back in a similar manner using better lime mortar, but we really must stiffen the walls to meet current codes and that will include some discreet reinforcing. Any tie rods will have stainless steel pattress plates shaped to resemble a Swan."

"What's a pattress plate?"

"You see those old plates on the exterior of historic brick buildings. They have been used for millennia in Europe. They're all over Charleston. They are the exterior terminations for old wrought iron tie rods. They keep the rods from simply pulling through the brickwork."

"Let's not get too literal with those swans. A simple S-curve will be fine. I understand about the chimney, but I'll chop off the fingers of anyone who destroys that small beehive baking oven on the side of the fireplace. The food that she bakes can't be recreated any other way. It stays in place by whatever means necessary. Prop it up as necessary but don't deconstruct it. I don't want to see so much as a crack in the old dome. Let's get started immediately. Resurgam."

19

ST. LUKE'S

Hew and Alexis sat on their terrace having afternoon cocktails while they watched the setting sun. "That was an elegant going away party last night. I drank one too many of Dr. Roberts's martinis. The flowers were spectacular."

"Bitsy Hollingsworth certainly knows how to entertain. Her English antiques are superb but her choice of fabrics is too rich for my blood. All those heavy draperies! St. Luke's folks really do enjoy having a good time."

"Those fabrics are from the House of Scalamadre. They're highly prized in the South. The fabrics at Swan Bay are similar except your Grandfather X.I. had them custom made to match the original French silks so don't get too critical."

"I suppose if I'm going to take the job, I need to go to church with

154

you tomorrow. It's Dr. Roberts's last day so I need to hit the ground running, as they say. After the service, you can give me the grand tour. Then we'll go to the club for lunch."

"You're acting like you've never seen the place. It's not a foreign country."

"I've been to Evensongs and concerts when you sang, and I've spent many hours in the bell tower. I can find the toilets in the bell tower undercroft, but I've never been back stage. I don't even know where the choir room or the office is."

"That's not saying much. Those toilets are at nave level, but okay. That won't take long and the service is not much different from the service at the cathedral so there's no need for you to worry."

"We enter the tower at the undercroft level so I'm not a total idiot. There are toilets there too and they are exactly the same as the toilets at the nave level. Bet you didn't know that! The architect said that he's the only person in modern times to have designed a brick outhouse in downtown Atlanta. John loves the fact that the services are broadcast over the sound system into the toilets. He thinks it's the only set of toilets in the world with a ninety-rank pipe organ."

"I was told that the architect suggested that. Modern parents no longer teach their children to use the toilet before they leave home since there are public toilets everywhere now. The kids quickly learn that they can get out of the service by saying they need to use the bathroom. The sound system lets the parents hear the service while they kids do their business."

"I must say the organ sounds grand in the small tiled space. Of course, it sounds grand in the nave too."

"It's considered to be one of the finest organs in the South."

⁂

DURING LUNCH AT THE CLUB, HEW admitted, "You're right. The service isn't that much different. The service music is different, but I can learn that. The choir was, as I already knew, outstanding, and the organ is a real treasure. I've never been in there with the morning light either. Those huge stained glass windows are magnificent."

155

"Yes. One of the parishioners gives stained glass tours from time to time to visiting groups."

"I know. I've already gotten an email asking me to demonstrate the organ for the next tour. John, let's go back to the church after lunch to begin to learn our way around the organ. I'll need you to stand beside me and turn pages every Sunday."

"Dad, my arms aren't long enough. I can't reach up across five keyboards from there. Scan your music into your tablet and use your i-turn to turn the pages."

"I'm not comfortable with that yet. I prefer a page turner."

"One of the male choir members will do that for you. You're worrying too much. "

"That's a very tall console, but I guess all those stop knobs have to go somewhere. I'll start on Monday by looking through the music library after I practice to see what's available. What do you want to sing next Sunday?"

"I don't know. He wanted to leave that to you. I'll go with you and we'll find something—maybe a Bach chorale. Everyone loves those."

⚜

"I MUST SAY, HE LEFT THE extensive library in good form. The whole history of church music is here. All of Howells's services are here. I've never heard of some of these. Look at these scores. These are certainly well worn."

"I can't see them from here. What are they?"

"It's Charles Gounod's *O Divine Redeemer,* and his *Sanctus.* The publication date for *O Divine Redeemer* is 1929. There's also about thirty copies of Gounod's Sanctus from the St. Cecilia Mass. These scores are well used. Who was Hugh Hodgson?"

"Oh, Dr. Hodgson was the much loved, long serving organist here— 41 years if I remember correctly—but he wasn't here when I joined the choir. We still sing the Sanctus. He helped found the University of Georgia Music School and they named it in his honor. There's a story about him. He was a born and bred old school Southerner. One of his friends drove into his driveway to show off his brand new Lincoln Continental car. Hugh made him leave telling him, "Nothing but Cadillacs can park here."

"Wow. I'm glad those days are over. This is his organ score for *O Divine Redeemer*. It has all the stops penciled in as well as the piston changes. This will sound great on this organ. It's late Romantic French. I can see how those Edwardian era Atlanta Episcopalians would love this. Here's the English text."

O Lord! Shield me in danger, O regard me! On Thee, Lord alone will I call. O Divine Redeemer! I pray Thee, grant me pardon, and remember not, remember not my sins! Forgive me, O Divine Redeemer! Night gathers around my soul; Fearful, I cry to Thee Come to mine aid, O Lord! Hasten Thee Lord, haste to help me! Hear my cry! Save me Lord in Thy mercy.

"Hmmm, here's some markings for a tenor written in someone's hand. This piece was Gounod's last sacred song, originally named *Repentir* in French. It was written in April 1893 for voice and orchestra and is said to be one of his best. This opening note on this stop will get their attention. Let's practice this piece this week. You can sing the solo. It might endear me with some of the old folks. I don't want to blast them out on the first Sunday."

"Wimp. Go for it. They love great organ music here. They can't fire you since you're donating your salary."

"They could ask me to leave, but how about something fast and sinister for the postlude. Maybe Milos Sokola's *Passacaglia Quasi Toccata on the theme of BACH*? It's only a little over five minutes long."

"If nothing else, it'll get them to coffee hour faster."

During coffee hour, Hew had counted on Alexis to help him with introductions, but she had an emergency flare up with the twins in the nursery. He was on his own, and it was not one of his strengths. Try as he might, he just couldn't remember names. Several people approached him and he feared the worst. One said, "Mr. Ramsay, I want to thank you for the offertory. We haven't heard it in years, and it was one of my father's favorites. It was sung at his funeral."

Another jumped in. "Yes, Mr. Ramsay, I agree and I must say, your postlude was a stunner. Keep up the good work and we'll hire you on a permanent basis. When can we hear Gounod's *Sanctus*?"

⁂

"Can you get John to ringing practice at St. Luke's? I'll already be there practicing. I can't get enough of that organ. The color combinations are endless. Call me when you drive into the Courtland St. parking lot and I'll run down and open the tower undercroft door."

"How was St. Luke's ringing practice tonight?"

"Great. The band is making good progress. We had twelve tonight and they let John call some of the changes. He's going to surpass me."

"I've been thinking," said Alexis. "I want to show you something."

Oh, God, he thought. *What's she going to spring on me now?*

"Let's go sit on the terrace. I'll bring us a bottle of Magnificat."

Hmmm, this is going to be serious.

Alexis brought a silver tray with two linen cocktail napkins, two Lalique Ange wine glasses, and an opened bottle of Franciscan Magnificat red wine. The glasses had an angel's head on the stem at the base of the bowl with etched wings curving up the body of the glass. They were Hew's great-grandmother's and he was always afraid to use them for fear of breaking one. "I've been thinking of what I want to do with the money I get from my law suit."

"You can't spend it before you know how much it will be, dear."

"I know, I know, but Janet says it will be substantial. One of the things the lawyer is fighting is my pay for my health insurance. The Academy rules gave us health insurance for life and a life insurance policy, and they took mine away. That's illegal, and given my young age and my ancestry, it will buy something nice for some cause.

"I've been helping Mavis with the St. Luke's archives since I'm unemployed, and she showed me this rendering a few weeks ago."

Hew began studying the rendering. "That must be an early rendering of the new bell tower. Look at those pinnacles on the top. They really would have finished it off properly. As it is, it looks a little...modern... Protestant. Un-English. What's the little octagonal building? That was never built."

"Mavis said that as the tower was finishing construction, the pinnacle design was still being finalized. It seems that the treasurer hated the tower and tried everything in his power to stop it. He finally got his way with the pinnacles. That octagonal building was to have been a new chapel. The building behind it was to have been a new children's ministry center. I want to give that chapel."

"I hate to see things that were never finished. I'll get Edward and Johann on it."

"St. Luke's has a very strong outreach program. It's their mission. Building a chapel might be a fight."

"That's true. Bitsy told me they sometimes ignore their own property until they have a crisis. All that old terra cotta trim is causing moisture problems in the walls but the vestry refuses to believe it. If you give this, it must go to the actual building. We'll get Edward to pass it through the family foundation anonymously."

✦

A FEW WEEKS LATER, BITSY HOLLINGSWORTH approached Hew in the Parish Hall. "I want to give my late parent's parish in Helen, Georgia, a new organ and some bells like these at St. Luke's, and I'd like for you to recommend builders if you would, please. The new organist wants a French instrument and the rector wants English Edwardian. They each have a consultant, and as you can imagine, the consultants support the opinions of the person who retained them."

"Yep. People who hire consultants seem to have a way of letting them know exactly what they expect to hear. I'm not a consultant, though, and don't really want to get into that business."

"We don't need another consultant. I'm through with consultants. I'm looking for a straightforward no nonsense opinion on how to move forward. You don't have a dog in this hunt so you're perfect."

Sighing, he replied, "Let me run up there and see if it's something I might be able to help with. Is it urgent?"

"Not really, but I won't release the money until you give your opinion."

"Fine. I think I'll ask Johann to go with me. Maybe one trip will suffice."

20
SEMINARY

"Hew, this is Tom Roberts."

"How are you, Tom? How's everything in Portland?"

"That's why I'm calling. I need your advice."

"Okay, well, all's well here in Atlanta. I really love the organ and the well trained choir sings beautifully."

"I'm glad, but all is not well here."

"Oh, no. What's wrong? You want to move back? The job's still yours."

"No, no. It's not that. I guess you haven't heard, but the chapel burned to the ground on Friday."

"Oh, no! How did that happen?"

"This seminary is almost as old as the city, and the chapel was constructed with local timber. It was 100% wood with no sprinkler system or smoke alarms. It was also entirely too small for our current crowd, but the old alumni heard about our plans and went nuts. It seems that every square inch was sacred to somebody for something."

"Churches are loaded with sacred cows."

"This one certainly was. We decided to just upgrade the existing organ with a new solid state system and a new console. I insisted on adding several ranks, but some of the old guys even balked at that. We have just signed a contract with Cornel Zimmer to repair and rebuild the organ. I did express myself a few weeks ago saying that what we really needed was a good fire. Fortunately, I was away visiting friends when it burned.

"We have a joint Compline service with the Episcopal school. We alternate weeks. One of our new seminarians had been asking to be the thurifer so the dean let him do it last week for Friday's Compline. The service is late night, of course, and after the service, he dumped the hot charcoal from the thurible into the metal container in the sacristy. Apparently he didn't put the top on the container. The sexton was supposed to empty the charcoal properly, but we had a substitute sexton that night, and he threw the service sheets into the container, got busy, forgot to take the container out and...poof. It all went up rather quickly in the middle of the night."

"I get it. Y'all need to rise from the ashes. It's another Resurgam."

"Yes, and I want to interview architects. I have met Johann and was wondering about his background. Does he know anything about churches, liturgy, and music? Alexis seems to think highly of him."

"Absolutely! He went to an English boarding school at Lancing College and he sang in the choir there. He went up to Cambridge where he began his architectural studies and he sang in the Trinity College choir."

"He's certainly well trained in liturgical music then. That chapel at Lancing is spectacular, and the Trinity choir is first rate."

"He took undergraduate and graduate degrees in architecture at Cambridge with an emphasis on environmental design. That's what caused Eberhart to pursue him. After I persuaded him to move to Atlanta, he joined the choir at St. Philip's."

"That's good enough for me. I'll get the dean to call you. Eberhart will need to design and construct our new building. The dean wants something that reflects the Northwest ethos with a strong emphasis on a monastic style, but absolutely fire proof."

"I need to tell you that Oregon will not accept Johann's professional registration—or anyone else's for that matter. We've already tried that on a project in California. The architects in the states of California, Oregon, and Washington are very protective of their turf, claiming that an architect needs to know the state's seismic regulations. Of course, we all know that's the job of the structural engineers. They would make him sit for the five-day architectural exam and it's not worth it for one job. He can be a design consultant to a local firm if you can find one that will work with him."

161

A FEW WEEKS LATER, JOHANN AND Hew presented the first concept to Dean Benjamin McDonald, Dr. Thomas Roberts, and the subdean, Rev. Louise Henderson. "I want to propose a completely new idea. I propose that the exterior and interior walls will be exposed steel-formed white polished concrete. The forms are the size of large ashlar stone blocks. It will recall the look of the rendered Gothic cathedrals when they were new."

"Gothic cathedrals were rendered? With what? I've never heard that."

"Yes, many of the exteriors were completely rendered with lime stucco. The statuary and other details were painted in bright vivid colors. Think of a deck of playing cards."

"Wow. That must have been spectacular."

"It's been said that they could be seen for miles. There will be a new seminar room by the bell tower with a music suite above. You can walk above the cloister directly from the music suite to the musicians' gallery above the narthex so I will avoid having a stair cluttering the narthex. The formed concrete on the interior will help with the organ sound. Given this proposed volume, we expect about three seconds of reverberation. "

"That would be great. This room is too small for a cathedral-sized instrument."

"I agree, Dr. Roberts. Any less reverberation, though, and the organ won't have much presence. The room is the most important part of an organ."

The subdean looked at the floor waiting for someone else to commit. Tom finally said, "That curved apse will only focus the sound."

"Actually, Dr. Roberts, it's not a curve but several segments so it will diffuse the sound. I've also found a large quilt by an artist living near Clemson University in South Carolina that I think you should purchase. It will fit nicely and form a spectacular reredos. Here are photos."

The dean found his voice. "These are stunning. I'll contact her immediately. What are they called?"

"Passion, and it's already won awards."

"It's beautiful. That small turquoise triangle is evocative of the Trinity. That happens to be the name of our chapel. I do think, however, that we need something more subtle. The altar itself must be the most visually commanding piece in the room and we'll commission new Jacobean frontals in all of the seasonal liturgical colors to vest it."

Louise countered."Antependia? Pallium Altaris? Here? Some of the old boys will want to bury you under it. Remember what happened when you suggested moving the altar away from the wall?"

Ben laughed. He had relinquished the chair of the meeting of the board to debate that idea. He lost. "Yes, but time marches on and the most vocal of those board members are gone to Glory. I will resurrect the idea of a free-standing altar and we will have the table properly clothed with a full four-sided bright covering."

Hew remembered a story from Charleston. "There's a painting in Charleston of St. Philip's Church showing a communion Sunday. Actually, there are two paintings. One looks east, and the other west. They were painted to commemorate the loss by fire of the old 1711 church. The altar and all of the silver communion vessels were completely covered with a large white tablecloth. No one in the current congregation had any idea of what was under that white mound until one lady—a former Methodist—told them that her childhood church still covered the communion table that way. They were all astounded."

Ben laughed. "See Louise, even conservative Charleston Episcopalians can change given a few centuries. Hew's illustration serves to show that the idea of reverencing the Holy Table has changed over the centuries. It's at the service on Maundy Thursday when the altar is stripped, though, that we see this at its most dramatic moment. The scriptures tell us that at the crucifixion, Christ was stripped of his garments and we commemorate that."

Hew nodded. "When I was a choir boy at St. Thomas, Fifth Avenue, at the end of that service, the rector washed the altar with a stiff bristle brush. We could hear it scratching the surface of the table. When he finished, he processed to the chancel steps holding the brush high in the air. The church was almost pitch black at that point. He then slammed the brush down into the floor of the center aisle where it clamored across the tiles. The lights went out and the church was like a tomb. When the narthex lights finally came on, people couldn't wait to get out."

"Interesting," said Ben. "I may try that next year. Let's continue. A quilt must either contain all of the liturgical colors or else be very neutral."

Louise spoke up. "Perhaps we can make several hangings with one for each liturgical season."

"Well, I can design a large niche so all of the hangings are present," said Johann, "but each one is shown at the appropriate time. That will keep the sacristan from having to hang and rehang the heavy fabric and you won't need a large area to store them."

"That's a great idea, Johann. It will be like a theater fly loft."

"Similar, but they won't rise up. They will be rolled up on large rollers with cables hidden in the side walls controlled by motors. A simple flick of a switch will move each one."

Hew smiled. "I can create an app for your phones to control the motors from anywhere."

"Thanks, Hew, but no thanks," said the dean. "I already have several apps that no longer work. My Lexus had an app that let me start the car from anywhere but when everyone started changing from 3G to 5G, Lexus stopped servicing my app. Good old fashioned wall switches will be fine. But now, let's discuss all that clear glass. The trees are nice, but I wonder about keeping it clean."

"I suspected as much and I have two ideas. The glass will have a slight grey tint which will reduce any visible dirt. By way of example, here's some case studies. One is a series of carved glass panels like this."

"Is that from the bell tower/columbarium at Grace Church Cathedral in Charleston? I preached there just last Sunday."

"Yes, you have a good eye. The other idea is a series of faceted colored glass panels by the famous Atelier Loire in France. His grandfather designed the famous Prisoners of Conscience window in Salisbury Cathedral. The grandson is very talented. I've seen the window in Salisbury. It's magnificent. In my opinion, it's the finest piece of contemporary stained glass I've ever seen."

The subdean warmed up to the concept and finally spoke. "I've seen it too, Dean. I do like that. Perhaps we could use the plain tinted glass on the south nave wall, the carved glass idea in the narthex, and the faceted glass in the small nave windows. We could have twelve small openings with symbols of the apostles."

"That's an excellent suggestion, Doris. When my uncle was rector of Trinity Church Copley Square in Boston, the late great Italian architect Pietro Belluschi designed a new oval stone chapel for the church. I was about ten at the time but I remember it as being a stunning gem. Some of the stones were replaced with small random rectangular sets of colorful faceted glass. There was to have been a linear skylight on the roof to add natural light to the interior stone walls. Unfortunately, it was never built. I'm beginning to warm up to the clear glass for the south nave wall. Maybe we can add window washing to our list of seminarian penances."

That got a laugh. Johann added, "As I remember, Belluschi practiced here in Portland."

The dean was surprised at Johann's depth of understanding. "I like the raw concrete too. I think it's very spare and monastic, but I'm very concerned about the ability of the contractors to get it perfect—no offense, Hew, but with concrete you get what you get. Perhaps stone would work better on this campus."

Always the diplomat, Johann replied,"Unfortunately, we can't really design a new stone bearing wall that will meet the stringent seismic codes here, but I'll study the idea of facing the concrete with stone. Random stone work will add to the diffusion of sound, but I don't think that the glass openings should continue around the apse. I really want that wall to be simple. I do like the idea of small random-colored glass openings on that north wall. I also like the idea of the linear skylight, but I don't want it to wash out the stained glass. There's no direct sun on the north face." Hew was impressed with Johann's tact even though he knew that he had his heart set on the concrete.

Pleased that the team's ideas were being addressed, the dean continued, "This design reminds me of a quote from the great existentialist German philosopher, Paul Tillich. In an address in 1955 to American architects on theology and architecture he said, *I do not hesitate to say that I am most satisfied by church interiors—if built today—in which holy emptiness is architecturally expressed.* We Episcopalians tend to over-love our churches and fill them with all sorts of trappings that often detract entirely from the Eucharist. I particularly dislike seeing a case of shiny organ pipes acting as a reredos. I also hate shiny brass memorial plaques. They always start with the words, *To the Glory of God,* but we all know whose glory they are really dedicated to. Some of those plaques are as big as the object they gave. I agree with placing the musicians and organ in the west gallery. That's actually an early Anglican concept of Sir Christopher Wren's for parish churches. An organ used as a reredos has nothing to do with the gathering around the table. It's very Protestant in my opinion. The use of statues of saints and glass figures in windows over the altar are there to remind us that the entire church—past and present—joins us around the table at the Eucharist. I understand that a few cathedrals have the organ on a screen dividing the nave from the choir and sanctuary, but that's another matter entirely and concerns the way extremely large cathedrals are used."

"I'm always amazed at your ability to quote obscure passages of philosophy," said Dr. Roberts. "How do you do it?"

"Probably the same way you memorize entire scores of ridiculously complicated music, Tom. And Johann, I do not want wood pews under any circumstance. I want light, movable, stackable chairs—preferably metal. Sometimes we will arrange them as you have shown, but mostly, I want a monastic choir arrangement. I know with your background at Trinity College, Cambridge, you know exactly what I want, but without the risers."

"I understand, but you really will need portable risers in that case. Canterbury Cathedral has metal stacking chairs with blond wood seats and backs. They also link together with book racks between the chairs."

"I can live with that, but we'll need a storage room somewhere. We'll need a way to fasten the kneelers to the chairs too."

The subdean spoke up. "We'll need a sacristy and vesting rooms too. And what about toilets? Preferably, a private toilet off the priests' vesting room would be nice."

The dean grimaced. "Somehow, the idea of people seeing priests lift their robes at a public urinal isn't very dignified."

"The female priests don't have that problem."

No one commented on that tidbit. Seeing his pure form begin to drift away, Johann suddenly had a thought. "If we move the new chapel further down the slope, we can include an undercroft and put these services down there. The stair to the music suite can have a stair that descends to the undercroft under it."

"Oh yes," exclaimed the subdean. "We can leave the brick foundations of the old chapel in place and plant a simple lawn for use as an outdoor chapel. We can add columbarium niches along both sides of the foundation walls. We'll call it by the old medieval word *garth*—garden."

"I can sell those to the old boys for a pretty penny in a heartbeat... pun intended. You'll need to add a stair near the altar for the altar guild. They won't like having to walk through the undercroft."

"I don't want to see acolyte heads popping through the floor like gophers."

That image got a laugh. "I have planned for the sacristies to be on the nave level under the choir suite. I'll design several tea carts to move the altar ware and vestments back and forth."

"The space behind the reredos is called the retro choir in English Gothic cathedrals. Let's call it that. I like the old terms. The carts can stay there out of sight during the services. Leave enough room for acolytes to pass back and forth back there too. I don't like that black altar either. It has overtones of witchcraft to me."

"I selected a block of Absolute black granite for contrast, but we could use white Carrara marble instead."

"Do that. As I said earlier, we'll use full bright highly-colored Jacobean frontals too. The altar must be the most visually prominent object in the room. It must grab and hold one's attention through the entire service. White marble will contract nicely with the bare stone wall on Good Friday when the altar is bare."

The subdean added, "Of course, there will be a very large cross behind the altar."

Johann had a thought. "If so, it must be firmly set into the floor. I hate floating crosses. They are not 'signs in the sky' if the wires are visible. Also, there's a great difference between signs and symbols. You're not advertising anything here. Perhaps she could design a set of tapestries that can be changed to match the seasonal colors with a subtle cross set into each central panel. The cross would reveal itself through the mystery rather than grabbing one's attention as they walk in. It will change with every passing season and refresh your soul."

"Oh, my, Johann. Yes. I'll ask her to design complete sets of vestments to make everything coordinated. That'll be splendid."

Feeling slightly rebuked, the subdean changed the subject and added, "We'll need an elevator. Some of our faculty members are elderly."

"The elevator and stair will be in the bell tower adjacent to the music building. We can enclose the cloister with full windows of glass. I'll move the seminar room to the undercroft to allow for the chair and riser storeroom, and toilets to be in the adjacent music building."

"That will be nice in the Portland winters. Make them operable for the summers. I don't want to waste energy. Do you think we should have English change ringing bells in the tower?"

"We can, but you need to decide if your staff and faculty will learn to ring them. The students won't be here long enough to become proper ringers to form a decent band. Also, we can load the flat roof with solar panels and use deep wells for a ground water heating and air conditioning system. All the glass will be triple insulated."

Dr. Roberts spoke up. "I know exactly what I want for that organ."

"I can just see the trackers exposed in the narthex like a moving sculpture," exclaimed Johann.

Hew asked, "You were never a crucifer were you, Johann?"

"No, I was always in the choir. Why?"

Hew stood, formed his hands around an invisible pole and raised his arms up. Johann suddenly saw the thin delicate sculpture-like strips of wood used for the trackers get tangled in the arms of the cross. "Um, that won't work. Maybe I'll design a clear glass ceiling to go under the trackers."

"What exactly do you mean when you use the term tracker?"

"Sorry, Louise," Tom said. "In the time before electricity, there were thin strips of wood or small metal rods between the keys and the pipes and they were called trackers. They tracked the movement of the key to the pipe valve. When a key was depressed, the tracker pulled down and opened a small valve under the pipe and allowed air into that pipe."

"Thanks. That makes perfect sense."

"One more thing, Johann. I realize this is a first concept, but you don't show lighting. I really don't want to see holes in the ceiling or brass fixtures hanging everywhere."

"Actually, Dean, I do have some early thoughts. The lighting needs to do four basic things. First, we need task lighting to be able to read the books. Second, we need accent lights—spotlights if you will—to light the activities. Third, we need uprights to give definition to the space, and fourth, we need decorative lights to add sparkle. Think candles. What I have in mind is two rows of small hanging black wrought iron cubes. They would be square and divided on all sides into four small squares. The tops would have four up lights. The bottoms would have four down lights. The ones closest to the altar would have small accent lights capable of being aimed to crosslight the objects.

"The inward sides facing the nave seating would contain speakers that are digitally delayed for the speech reinforcement sound system. The digital sound will reach the ears at exactly the same time as the room sound giving a very clear sound. All the lights will be dimmable LEDs."

"I like that idea. Let's wrap this meeting up while we're ahead. We're all in agreement here. Johann, I must say that we love your concept. The idea of having everyone gathered in a single volume really reinforces the concept of the priesthood of all believers. The old chapel divided the nave into three areas with arches that blocked many sight lines and set the celebrant apart behind a rood screen that was essentially a separate room. Our modern seminarians don't need to experience that here.

"The idea of having the stone wall wrap around and focus all eyes on the Holy Table is just outstanding. It takes us back to the early church designs. The board has given me full authority to move with all deliberate speed. We won't get bogged down in committee, and God knows, Episcopalians love their committees.

"Hew and Johann, please proceed with haste. This is going to be expensive, but the church insurance fund will cover the costs. We'll say nothing about any of this until a contract is signed. Then the old boys can't stop us."

21
COLOMBIA

"Luis, I can't believe you called me to invite me back to Colombia. I thought I made myself perfectly clear that I would never spend another second in Colombia. Were four murder attempts by your people on my life not enough? NO!"

"Now, wait a minute, Hew. I understand your feelings, but just listen for one minute. Do you remember a boy in the choir that you discovered had a hearing problem?"

"Yes, I do. His name was Juan. Father A got him hearing aids. I gave him a few piano lessons. I've often wondered what became of him. Why?"

"He's the archbishop's nephew and he has never forgotten what you did for him. He's now a monsignor and the new rector of our cathedral. His first Mass here is next Sunday and the archbishop asked me to find you and ask you, as a surprise, to come play the service."

"Wow. He rose through the ranks very quickly, didn't he?"

"After your ordeal, and because no one knew what had happened to you, many of the families, fearing for their boys' lives, sent them away. The archbishop sent Juan to Rome. He studied at the Vatican and became a favorite. He's very bright and learned quickly. He has a great future in the church."

"That's great. I'm very happy for him but…"

"Wait. I'm not finished. We have a four manual organ here with 1,808 pipes built in 1890 by the Spanish organ builder Aquillino Amezua Juaristi, and it was recently rebuilt in Italy. There are some eighteenth-century pipes still in it. It has huge battle trumpets that I know you will love."

Hew was quickly searching online and found the specifications for the organ. Now he was interested. "Luis, that's a very short time window to learn Spanish music, but those trumpets intrigue me. I've never had an opportunity to play those before. I'll do it, but I want to do something else if you can arrange it. I want to visit the place in the Andes where my parents were murdered."

"I can probably arrange that. If you want to fly in early on Saturday, you can have the day to practice and you will stay with us. The archbishop and rector will treat you to lunch following the service. I will arrange a helicopter to take us up there, weather permitting, but don't expect to land. Some of the children survived the earthquake and are still living there. The government doesn't allow outside access."

Hew immediately began to research the music. He also ordered and installed a Spanish organ sampleset by Sonus Paradisi from Santanyi, Spain for his virtual organ. It had the fanfare trumpets he needed.

John wasn't happy that Hew took over the music room. Hew selected Juan Cabanilles' *Batallia Imperial* for the entrance procession, Antonio Soler's sonata *"For the Clarines"* for the offertory, and Soler's *The Emperor's Fanfare* for the retiring procession. He would improvise everything else. He finally decided that the music during communion would be the anonymous *Seven Fabordones*. The music would be loud and brassy, but after all, it was a day of celebration. After a week of intense practice, Hew began to have doubts. Alexis put them to rest.

"Hew! Stop! My ears are about to start bleeding. Are you giving a concert for people you hate, or is this really a Mass?"

"You're right, as usual. I just got so fascinated with this Spanish music that I've gotten carried away. It's too much. I think I'll keep the processional and recessional at least until I go there to practice. The rest won't really work, though. I don't know much about Spanish composers and I've really run out of time. I'll fall back to the music I played in boarding school. It's all French, but it suits the Mass. Maybe you could come with me and sing the Ave Maria for the offertory."

"I can't. I've already signed up to sing on Sunday. Besides, you'll spend all of Saturday holed up in the cathedral, and all day Sunday after

Mass flying all over God knows where. Take John. He can see a little of your background, and he sings that piece as well as I do."

❦

WHEN HEW, JOHN, AND HIS ISRAELI protective detail arrived at the cathedral on Saturday morning, the organist was practicing. "I'm so sorry to tell you, but there are four weddings and two funerals in the cathedral today in addition to the normal services. The only practice time is after nine p.m. No one told me until this morning that you were coming."

"I don't like going into churches after dark because I was nearly killed by a deranged senator, but I'll just have to make it work."

Hew was surprised to find that the original mechanical transmission system had been replaced with a new electrical system. Instead of having a console in the organ gallery, the new console was located downstairs closer to the choir.

The cathedral organist offered to have Hew play the retiring procession. Hew took his offer. He correctly sensed that the organist was in a difficult spot, and there was very little time to practice. He also sensed that his protective detail didn't really appreciate or understand organ music or a Christian Mass. John turned pages and helped with the stop changes.

After the service, Hew and John had lunch with Juan. Hew brought Juan up to date regarding his rescue from school. Juan knew the rest. John sat quietly picking at the strange food.

After lunch on Sunday, Luis gave them a quick briefing. I've hired a guy with a helicopter. We'll leave from his private helipad, but do not discuss cocaine, cartels, Espinis, your parents, or anything else regarding the real reason you're here. This is just a fun ride into the mountains for two Americans. Oh, and don't call me Luis at anytime."

"What's a cartel? What's an Espinis? What about my grandparents?"

"John, I'll tell you all about that later. Don't ask questions. For now, just enjoy the ride."

Luis, John, and Hew arrived by cab at the helipad. The protective detail was not happy but Hew assured them that they would be fine. Luis handed them big floppy sun hats and sunglasses. They looked like

173

tourists. "Put these on just in case anyone might remember two tall guys with blond mops of hair. You guys do stand out in a crowd you know."

Hew became apprehensive, but climbed into the helicopter for a breathtaking ride through the Andes. He began to regret leaving his protective detail behind, but the chopper wasn't large enough for everyone. The headphones were a tight fit over the hats. The wide brims had to be turned up over the top of the hats, but the headphones were necessary to be able to hear each other. John had never ridden in a helicopter before and he was spellbound.

Luis directed the pilot to fly south toward the Sumapaz National Nature Park and then further south toward the Parque Nacional. He rattled on about the wonderful scenery and the riches of Colombia. When they were between the two parks, he directed the pilot toward a dramatic outcropping of rock beside a shear cliff. Not wanting to give the pilot much background information about the former cocaine processing plant, Luis casually remarked, "I'm told this is the site of a great tragedy many years ago. During the largest earthquake in modern times, the entire side of the mountain slid off into the valley below. It nearly killed everyone in the little village."

"Wow," said John. "I can see people working in the field down there. What are those green plants?"

At that moment, they heard something that sounded like metal hitting the copter. John turned to ask Luis what it was just as the window beside him exploded and glass flew everywhere. John felt it and reached for his left ear only to find that his headphone cup was cracked into small pieces. He didn't see the bullet lodged in the ceiling over his head.

Hew tried to grab John, but the shoulder straps prevented him from getting him down. Hew began to wonder if this were somehow connected to the MAGLEV project. Maybe the drug lords were still after him. His mind began to run wild. The pilot took evasive measures and pulled up and away. The copter was trailing smoke, but they couldn't see it.

The pilot flew low over the highway just in case he needed to set it down quickly. His instruments told him they were in trouble, but he remained calm and was able to get them back to the heliport. He managed a hard landing. Luis called for a cab as soon as they were back in range of his cell phone. Luis and Hew thanked the pilot for his quick thinking and the pilot insisted they leave immediately saying he would talk with the authorities and tell them that he didn't have passengers. He would say that he was just out for a joy ride and someone shot at him. The protective detail almost smothered them, herded them into a hastily arranged cab, and directed the driver to Hew's jet. Hew and John were uncommonly quiet.

Once Hew and John were safely in the air and out of Colombian airspace, Hew told John the story.

"A cartel makes and distributes illegal drugs—cocaine in this case. Espinis was a nickname for one of the most notorious drug lords in Colombia. His name means 'thorn.'

"He murdered my parents. My mother was trying to record the music of the natives. She wanted to find the sounds that existed before the Spaniards arrived. They were hiking in the mountains and stumbled onto a cocaine field. They were murdered and..." He cleared his throat. "Don't worry about Espinis. Another cartel murdered him. The drug processing facility was located in a huge cave under the field. We were looking at the ruins of the lab. I think Luis was just trying to keep the pilot from knowing why we were there.

"Apparently, when Espinis cleared the land for the coca plants, he destroyed the extensive root system that helped to hold everything on the mountain in place. The thin rock cover over the lab cracked in the earthquake and sent all the workers sliding into the valley below. I just wanted to see where my parents died. That was a huge mistake. I should never have come and I certainly should never have brought you. This weekend was a disaster."

"I'm okay, Dad. Eddie's not going to believe this, though."

"John, now listen carefully. You can never tell anyone about any of this. Never. NOT EVER. Never tell anyone, and especially not your mother. Do you understand?"

"But, Dad, my friends will never have a trip like this."

"I said NEVER and I mean NEVER. Do you understand? Promise me, John. Promise me right now."

John pouted, but he promised.

꧁꧂

They walked in the front door at 8:30 p.m.. Hew had called Alexis from the airport to let her know they had arrived. She handed him a wee dram of Macallan and hugged and kissed her son.

"Mom, let go. You're crushing me. I can't breathe."

Sensing a problem, she started asking questions. Running toward the bedrooms, John yelled, "I just want to see the dogs. I'll talk later."

Hew shook his head. "I want a shower. I need to wash the jungle off of me."

She started to kiss him but pulled back quickly.

"Oh, yes," she said. "Go. I'll see you in bed."

꧁꧂

"Now tell me about it. Something is wrong."

"It really didn't work out as planned. Apparently the old archbishop has gotten a bit absentminded. It was great to see Juan. He was surprised to see me, but there were four weddings and two funerals in the cathedral on Saturday so I didn't get much practice time.

"The organist wasn't really happy to see me so I faked a lack of knowledge of Spanish and the Mass and asked if I could just play the processional. He gratefully agreed to let me play the retiring procession. I suspect he saw through my ruse, but he was gracious enough to realize that we were both in an awkward position. I should have known that the choir already had an entire program of music worked out. I just got caught up in learning to play those fantastic trumpets.

"John didn't sing which didn't really bother him at all. Lunch was great. John didn't like the food and made it obvious. We stopped at the pizza place for a slice on the way home. The trip to the murder site was eye opening but I'll never go again. Luis was a perfect host as you might imagine. I'm worn out. Let's get some sleep."

"I'm glad I didn't go. Oh, Janet called late Friday, but I forgot to tell you. They want another hearing before the judge."

꧁꧂

LUIS CALLED ON MONDAY. "The helicopter is a total loss, but I paid in cash for our trip and used a fake name so there's really nothing for you to worry about. He will be happy to get a new bird from his insurance company. I didn't know about the active coca field there and I think we just got too close. It's over now."

Sam's secretary buzzed him over the intercom. "Max Brindle on one."

"Sam, how the hell are you? Max Brindle here. I'm the director of state commerce here in South Carolina."

Sam thought to himself, *That didn't take long. We just started driving piles on Monday.* "Great, Max. Yes, I remember our last meeting several years ago. Just couldn't be better. To what do I owe this pleasure?"

"Your name came up this morning and it seemed like a good time to get together and smoke one of your Cuban Cohibas. My guys tell me y'all have some heavy duty equipment up in Greer at our inland port and you're driving piles. They've never seen anything like that machine."

"Ah, yes, that. It is on our right of way, you know. I'd love to get some of your top folks together as my guest over at Brosnan Forest for a weekend soon. We can talk, but it must be absolutely private. No recorders and no cell phones."

"How about next weekend? I think I can break everyone loose by then."

"Who do you plan to bring?"

"Oh, not a crowd. Just me and the director of the State Ports Authority—maybe one or two more."

"Bring that Clemson University vice president in charge of the old Charleston Navy base property."

"Dr. Charles Edwards. Right. I'll get 'em rounded up."

꧁꧂

Sam immediately called Hew. "The sovereign state of South Carolina has come sniffing like an old coon dog. You available for a meeting next weekend?"

"Okay. Swan Bay Center is finished and awaiting the Japanese any day now."

"Thanks, but I think we should do this on their turf. I've offered Brosnan Forest for a weekend getaway. Jason says our new SCIF is finished and tested so we should be fine. Call me and I'll have a car pick you up at the airport. Use the aviation services on the east side of the airport. It's closer to me than the other two."

꧁꧂

After a morning of deer hunting, the meeting convened after drinks that included Hew's famous mint juleps during lunch that included a fresh locally grown salad mix, freshly caught sautéed red fish from the nearby Edisto River, collard greens, and blueberry pie.

Hew detested collards. He thought the smell of them being cooked was worse than the smell coming out. There would be local venison for dinner.

Sam began a carefully orchestrated computer-generated presentation. "Thanks for coming, gentlemen. What I'm about to show you will revolutionize freight handling and railroading as we know it. It's the equivalent to the first passenger train run in America on Christmas Day 1830 of the Best Friend of Charleston, so hang on.

"This is top secret information and is protected at the highest level. James Singleton here is deputy director of Homeland Security, representing the president. If we say anything he doesn't like, he'll kill us."

A nervous giggle went through the crowd. He went through the audiovisual presentation including the test trial in Germany, the federal legislation, and a taped address by the president explaining the speed and security. "Any questions before we head back into the deer stands?"

Dr. Edwards responded. "Yes. The Best Friend of Charleston wasn't the first train in America."

"I know. It was the first passenger service, but we own the right of way now."

"The steam engine was invented by a Scot named James Watt," said Hew.

Dr Edwards continued. "Fair point. At Clemson, we have been researching Hyperloop. Why SCMAGLEV?"

"Thomas, please remove those words from the minutes. Substitute the words high-speed. Folks, don't ever use them again. We can't have the media reading our exact plans. So Dr. Edwards, you know…"

"Please call me Chuck. Everyone does."

"Okay, Chuck. Thanks. Please call me Sam. I'm just an old railroad man through and through like my daddy, his daddy before him, and his daddy before him. I like to see trains, so the idea of putting them inside a big old sewer pipe doesn't set well with me."

Max quipped,"My granddaddy said y'all invented the sleek shiny stainless steel passenger cars in the fifties. Seems like y'all started it."

"No. Well…"

Hew chimed in on the ribbing. "Yeah, Sam, you let the airlines take over because the rail industry wasn't fast enough and couldn't keep up."

They all laughed until some of them snorted. The scotch-laced juleps and the wine were beginning to set in.

Sam shut it down. "I'm not interested in the past. I'm moving into the future. They'll be left in my jet wash. But really, that system is very advanced for passenger service. My daddy got us out of the people hauling business years ago, but it seems that we're about to get back in it. It won't be publicly announced until next week, but I've just negotiated a new service with the Federal Railroad Administration. A new high-speed passenger line between Atlanta and D.C. has been approved. It will replace the current service and will eventually connect most of the east coast. Since we're already in design, all we will need to do is add this to our computer routing and build a few new stations. Hew's architect, Johann, is already into the design of those. They'll be a spectacular blend of new South and environmental design."

Chuck nodded. "I can get him a place as an adjunct lecturer with our graduate architecture students. He will have all those bright young minds at his disposal."

"That's great, Chuck. Knowing Johann as I do, he'll love that. Let's move on. The Tier One Final Environmental Impact Statement and Record of Decision has been approved. The initial route was to have been a completely new route south of Greenville and north of Columbia bypassing all the South Carolina cities."

"Yes, Sam is correct," added Hew, "but we were able to change that. Because Sam's design is so far along, it is now less expensive and will speed up the process to use the current rights of way. It can be completed earlier since there are no rights of way to purchase."

"Thank you, Hew. Chuck, the hyperloop tubes that have been developed are too small in our opinion to carry full-sized double- and triple-stacked cargo containers."

Jason interrupted. "Sam, new computer-generated studies are showing that the wind resistance on triple stacks will be too dangerous at the speeds we anticipate."

Chuck chimed in. "Our students can help with that."

"Yes. Let them study that. Thanks, Chuck. Now to continue…" He shot Jason an evil eye. "Our system will pick up or drop off the containers right from the docks in Charleston and at the inland port in Greer, and load them on flatbed carriages. We'll be out of there in a flash and we won't be blocking the roads or making loud noises."

"My God, the people of North Charleston will love you for that."

"Hell, everybody that travels I-26 between Charleston and Columbia will love you. You could run for governor when this is completed."

"Amtrak's Crescent runs on the main line through Clemson. How will this affect that? We still have students and faculty that use it."

"The Crescent as we know it will be history. This new passenger service will be a vast improvement. I'm sure the Clemson trustees have enough pull in Columbia to get a whistle stop at Clemson, but just know that the Columbia folks are fighting mad. They wanted it to come through Gervais Street." He paused. "Maybe the state can build a passenger station at the inland port to service Columbia and Charleston. I'll let you fight the politicians on that.

"As you saw, we won't interrupt service at all. Amtrak will develop their own new carriages and we'll be glad to let them use our roadbed—for a slight fee, of course. The tracks on the ground will remain to service our local businesses. As you know, many of them load their goods into the containers right at their own docks. They're the lifeblood of our business. After lunch, we'll look at numbers."

"With this new plan to Charleston, looks like the Columbia folks will get their connection."

"I don't fully understand the distribution side of all this. How will industries get their goods to this rather limited line?"

"Many of our customers already have our spurs running to their loading docks. A local freight train will still pick up the containers and if the containers are going north or south, they can be transferred at one of the transfer locations along the route. It will work in reverse too, but large industries will be relocating to land adjacent to our line."

Max frowned. "I assume you already own the property?"

"Well, some of it."

"I've got the governor on standby. May I get him down here for this? I thought this might be big, but I had no idea it would be this big. He knows about the new proposed passenger service, but this dwarfs that by a factor of ten."

"Okay, but I don't want to repeat the whole morning. Call him and brief him while he's on the way. He can join us for supper."

Chuck had been quietly formulating a pitch for a much bigger plan. He could see mega research dollars and new facilities rolling in. "I can only say that from Clemson's point of view, I believe that we will be all in, as the football folks like to say. Several of our research units will be able to help you develop this. Our advanced materials folks can help with all of the material development including things you haven't even considered yet. We're helping to develop new light weight polymer composites to use in the newer airplanes to reduce the weight of the fuselages and wings. CURI in Charleston will—"

"Excuse me," said Hew. "What are these new polymers made of?"

"Currently, we're using corn waste, but the Europeans are using grape waste from the winemaking process. It's very environmentally sound because this is typically just bio-waste. We take the fibers and combine them with a resin—epoxy if you like. They reduce the weight by about 25%."

The discussion went over Sam's head. "CURI? Sounds medical."

"Oh, I'm sorry, Sam. Too many acronyms. It stands for Clemson University Research Institute. There's plenty of room on the old Navy base for anything you need. We're currently looking for a donor to fund a new state of the art research building on the Charleston campus to give us the room we need to begin production on a large scale. You say that this is all computer controlled so our AI folks, our computer science folks, and our cybersecurity folks can help you too. Those computer guided power units will be a real target for cyber hackers.

"I need to introduce you to our dean of science. She's a powerhouse. We just signed a major contract with a partner for research into aerospace technology for fuselage design. You'll be a great fit. We can research new materials that will make your unit covers lighter, less expensive, and create less drag than even the design you are proposing. We're already involved, as an example, with the feds in advanced laser systems—that's thirty-three million dollars worth of research that you can tap into. It's for thermal protection for hypersonic vehicles—to the tune of forty million dollars over the next year—and we're working with a seventy-six-million-dollar grant for virtual and physical prototyping. Your project is a perfect fit. We'll need a few million from you, of course, but we could set up a new campus in Charleston just for mag—sorry, railroad research."

Hew could see that Sam was being played by a master greater than himself. "Chuck, don't you have a research center for solar-powered vehicles?"

"Yes. I forgot about your solar component. That group has its own campus in Greenville. It's called ICAR."

Sam was intrigued. He wanted his name on that Charleston facility. "I think we should run with this but I must warn you that until we're up and running, the various labs must never know what and how this all fits together. I'll find the money. This will need to be graduate and Ph.D. research."

"Thank you. That won't be a problem."

HEW AND SAM SAT IN SAM's private cottage after everyone left on Sunday afternoon and sipped a martini. "Here's to you, Sam. That was a brilliantly orchestrated presentation. I liked hearing Chuck say Clemson will be 'all in.' When James Singleton told the governor that Homeland Security, the Federal Railroad Administration, and the Department of Defense would fund everything, I thought the governor was going to wet his pants."

"James actually said that the president didn't want to get into a pissing contest with state politicians. The Department of Defense is going to justify it because there are six major defense properties along or near the route. One is Joint Base Charleston, two is something called Spawar, three is the small C17 inland training airbase near North, S.C., four is Shaw Air Force Base, five is the Marine Corps Air Station, and six is the Marine Recruit Depot."

"At least everyone had the good sense not to laugh even though they wanted to."

"I could see the governor beginning to understand that those facilities would not be on a base closure list anytime soon. That's how Clemson ultimately wound up with a large chunk of the old Navy base after the last round of closures. The dean of the College of Architecture saw a potential for a satellite campus in the Charleston area, pitched the proposal to the mayor of North Charleston and Clemson got the land. The university quickly took it out of her hands and created a new vice president's position."

"Yeah and, for her efforts, the guys in the state house decided to get rid of the College of Architecture by renaming it as a department. Nothing changed except the names, but those savvy Clemson folks convinced the legislators that the change saved big bucks."

"Yes, and that's all they wanted to hear. Don't worry. In a few years, it'll change back. Getting Clemson to agree to house the construction of our new carriages on their site in Charleston was great too. The students will get in on the ground floor if they follow through with the proposed new master's degree. This may be the answer to our weight problem. My guys are already talking to the Japanese folks about that. Let's go home, Hew. I've never spent this much money in my entire life."

"Suits me. My crews are working like bees to keep up with that monster machine."

"Jason's idea of embedding rails in the surface was brilliant. Not only will it buy us some time by looking like a railroad, we can put old worn out freight cars up there to house tools and small supplies. We will use the passing sidings for that. We've also learned that the trains will need wheels to get them up to speed before the magnets kick in. Instead of using airplane landing gear as originally planned, we'll just modify our current system and run on the rails. We won't be lying to the media, either. I'm outfitting a few old passenger cars to be used for meetings, food service, and toilets. Hell, I might even add a few old Pullman sleeper cars to house the workers in bad weather. Those machines work in rain, sleet, and snow. We'll also use small freight engines to deliver your concrete sections to the work site. No one will expect anything except a normal railroad operation."

"My crew would appreciate that, but how will that work with the roadbed machine? Won't those cars be in the way of delivering the concrete sections?"

"No. They will sit inside the machine on the level of the new roadbed. The existing rail service will still be at ground level. Hans and Jason have it all worked out. The new materials will be moved overhead into position."

"Then my guys wouldn't have to drive home every night, and it would give the impression that this is a typical railroad. It would save money too. Make sure the dining car includes a bar while you're at it.

"Charlie and Pink think our security program is working. Edward set up the construction company with a new corporation registered in Delaware. You've clearly positioned the railroad as a landlord at this point, and the government funds go into a large existing commercial bank in Delaware. The invoices and payroll are paid from a small construction office next to the bank. I doubt anyone in the world expects the two of us to be involved in this. We don't seem to have attracted the labor union mafia either. You've really gotten this thing worked out. How did you come up with it?"

"Oh, don't kid yourself. The union mafia guys are sniffing hard. They just haven't found Swan Bay, and the technology is so advanced those goons couldn't ever understand it. As for how I came up with it, well, it goes way back. I need another bourbon and branch water on ice for this discussion." He stood up and poured a jigger of whiskey in his glass. "The first Sam Spencer was born in 1847 on his father's cotton plantation near Columbus, Georgia. He joined the Confederate cavalry. After the war, he went to the University of Georgia and studied civil engineering. The South was a wasteland, so he swallowed his pride and moved north to become a surveyor for the railroads. The money was good."

"That must have been hard. He moved right into the land of his enemy."

"I know. I can't imagine. J.P. Morgan was buying up railroads and saw something he liked in Sam, so he made him the president of the new consolidated railroad in the South. The railroad and the cotton mills brought South Carolina back to life. The rest is history."

"But how did you arrange all this government money?"

"I didn't. My ancestors set it in motion. You've got to remember that the Civil War was officially over, but not in the hearts of the Southern people who had lost everything. By 1915, the country was turning its attention to World War I. The railroad became a big player in moving men and material once the US got involved. After WWII, Eisenhower started the interstate highway system on the basis of national security.

"My granddaddy knew immediately that these new highways would rob business from the railroads. He knew all the southern politicians so he started telling them that the truckers would bring labor unions to the South. Now, of course, southerners hated the Yankee and Chicago mafia-led unions. Granddaddy started to push for equal rights for railroads and Daddy took over the battle. It's taken several generations of hard work, but here we are today at the right time in the right place." He shook his head. "I've had one too many. I'm ready for bed."

23
ASSASSIN

Pink assembled the security detail for a monthly breakfast briefing at Swan Bay the following day. After they went over the various reports, nothing was flagged as suspicious. "I'm happy, but we must maintain our vigilance, folks. I'm not sure we're safe yet. Viktor and I will drive to Dulles Airport tonight to pick up our new Japanese engineer. His name is Minoru Tsunejuro and he wants to be called Minoru. He's developing the software for our system. He's an expert on SCMAGLEV operations."

They arrived curbside just as Minoru was leaving the building. Even though the terminal had been designed in the 1960s by the great architect, Eero Saarinen, Pink, usually a traditional type guy, always loved looking at the soaring curved glass wall and swooping roofline as he approached the building. Since he wasn't driving, he had a better opportunity to marvel at the construction, but as they approached the pickup curb, he saw a man approaching Minoru and something bright yellow drop to the pavement.

Pink recognized the Epipen since he always carried one in his pocket for his own bee sting allergy. He quickly jumped out just as the other man put his left arm around Minoru's waist. Pink put his left arm around the guy's waist and grabbed the hand with the syringe. He plunged the syringe into the belly of the stranger and watched his eyes grow wide.

Viktor opened the sliding door of the van and helped Pink get the now dying stranger into the seat. Minoru had been briefed on his pickup detail but after a twenty-two hour flight with two layovers, he was a bit groggy. He asked, "What is this? Who is this guy?"

Viktor pushed Minoru into the front seat while Pink moved into the rear seat with the attempted assassin. Viktor calmly drove away and didn't raise suspicions at the crowded curb. People were simply too busy with their own luggage to notice. "I'm Pink and this is Viktor. We're taking you to Swan Bay."

"Yes, I recognize you from the Zoom conference last week."

"Do you recognize this guy?"

"No. What happened?" Minoru spoke perfect English with an accent suggesting an education in England or Hong Kong.

"He was about to stab you with a hypodermic. I grabbed his arm and stuck *him* with it. He's dead." Pink went through the assassin's pockets. "He's a Chinese national according to this passport—if it's real. He boarded the plane with you in Tokyo so he's been tailing you ever since."

"Was he just going to leave me in the gutter? Turn around now! I want to go home."

"You'll be safer here. They obviously know who you are. You won't be safe back in Japan for a while."

Minoru wept silently. "You have saved my life. I'm forever in your debt. I'll do as you ask."

Pink asked Viktor to drive back around to the terminal. He searched the dead guy's pockets and found the baggage claim. He quickly ran in and retrieved the luggage. As he walked out the door, he saw a janitor sweeping the empty Epipen case into a dust pan. He then dumped it into a large trash cart so Pink was confident it would never be found.

"It would be better for all involved if you never mention this to anyone. It would destroy the morale of the team and hurt the project. Viktor and I will dispose of the body. No one will ever know."

"Yes, I agree. I hate these people. I thought a commercial flight would be safe with all the security. How did he get the syringe through security? Do what you must. The incident is forever forgotten."

"He had it in an Epipen case. I saw him drop the yellow case on the sidewalk. Security sees so many of these pens they don't even bother with them anymore. Obviously this one contained a quick acting poison."

After they dropped Minoru off at the Swan Bay guest house, Pink called Jason. "Can you meet us immediately? We're in the black van outside."

"Sure. What's up?"

"I'll fill you in when you get here. Bring the keys to Sam's jet."

After giving Jason the details, Pink said, "I think we need to get this stiff down to that island you told me about that Sam owns."

"Oh, I get it. You want to feed him to the alligators."

"I think that's the cleanest way to dispose of this guy."

"We could just fly out over the ocean and drop him off. That would be quicker."

"Yeah, but I don't want to take the chance of having him wash up on shore with a system full of God knows what type of poison."

"Oh. I didn't think about that. What if the alligator dies?"

"What's one more dead alligator? We need to take Swan Bay's old small single engine plane. The runway on the island is grass and it's too short for the jet. I can pilot the little plane myself. Let me run in and change clothes and get the keys."

"Don't mention this to Sam. We need to keep this quiet."

"No problem. Sam would be fine with it, but Hew would go nuts. Luckily, the caretaker and his family on the island are on vacation so the place is deserted. Sam lets them use his place in Canada during the bug season."

Jason came back out wearing snake boots and a long sleeved shirt. "Don't ask. The snakes and bugs are almost as bad as the alligators. I'll take the lead once we land."

It took a while to load the plane and top off the fuel. Jason brought large black garbage bags and they wrapped the body to prevent any body fluids from seeping out into the plane. The darkness covered their activities and after making his pre-flight inspections, they took off at dawn and headed out over the ocean.

Viktor asked, "Where exactly are we going?"

"We're headed to South Carolina. Sam owns thirty-one square miles of the most pristine ocean front island you will ever see. It was first explored by the Spanish and later became a summer resort for rich white planters. Sam's grandfather bought it so his wife could have a beach house. It's only accessible by boat or plane. She spent one night there and never returned. It was too wild for her and she hated the primitive house even though it's antebellum. It's been a hunting preserve ever since. The only inhabitants are the caretaker and his family. No one goes there this time of year. The bugs will eat you alive. I've brought bug spray. It'll help a little. We'll land near the house. Stay in the plane until I go get the pickup."

They flew down the coast and an hour and a half later, they were over Myrtle Beach. Storm clouds were towering in the west.

"That's Myrtle Beach below. We'll be landing in a few minutes. We want to get this done as soon as possible because they're predicting bad weather around noon. Pink, you and Viktor get into the truck bed with the body. Strip him naked but keep him on the plastic as long as possible. Remove any jewelry. Do not under any circumstances either step out of the truck or, God forbid, fall in. These gators can bring down a full grown buck deer or wild boar."

As they approached the house in the truck, Jason pointed to a six-foot-long rattlesnake on the front steps. "See what I mean?"

"So, uh, just how big are these alligators?"

"This pond is full of 'em. The oldest are approaching fifteen feet. When you toss this guy over the side, be careful. The females have babies in nests in the tall grass and the mamas are vicious. If you miss the pond, don't try to correct it. We'll be close enough that they can drag him into the water."

They made a perfect pitch. The splash attracted several gators. Pink and Viktor watched in horror as the gators went to work on the fresh meat. "Why all that splashing and rolling around?"

"The locals call it the death roll. The alligators are drowning their victim. They'll bury it in the mud until they're ready to eat. Have you seen enough? I need to get into the air and we still need to burn these clothes."

"Yeah, I'm convinced they got him."

"By this time tomorrow there won't be anything left except a few bone fragments and no one will go into that pond to check 'em out."

Pink and Viktor rode in the back of the pickup until they reached an old brick chimney on the side of the river. "Hop out and let's burn all this stuff in the old chimney. We're okay here. I've already checked for snakes. Put some more of this bug spray on your bare areas first."

"Why is this chimney here? It looks like it's going to wash away."

"At some point in history, this was a rice plantation. This chimney is all that remains of the old rice mill. The slaves worked the rice ponds and milled the rice. It was loaded onto boats and sent to market. They made a fortune, but the rising sea level is about to devour this chimney. Sam's working to save it. There aren't many left, but the environmentalists are giving him a fit because he wants to put a wall around it."

"The slaves got into ponds of rice plants like the one we just left?"

"Yep, although there were referred to as rice fields."

"Jesus Christ!"

They quickly doused the clothes, shoes, plastic bags, and travel documents with gasoline Jason syphoned out of the truck and burned it all. Viktor was amazed. "I've never seen anyone stick a plastic tube into a gas tank and suck out gas before. I'm impressed."

"I'm a Southern country boy. The trick is in using a clear tube so I can see the gas before it gets into my mouth. Then I just stick the tube in the jug which needs to be lower than the gas tank. Gravity does the rest. It's easy. I was born and raised just south of Charleston on Edisto Island. This place is like home to me. You'd be amazed at what we can do when we have to."

They used a small bare branch from a dying live oak that was now too close to the salt water and raked the ashes to insure that nothing incriminating remained. Then they piled into the truck cab to get away from the bugs and Jason drove back to the plane.

They were all soaked with sweat from the heat and humidity, so Jason turned the air-conditioning on high. "The wind will scatter the ashes and the rain and high tides will wash it all away."

Just as he arrived at the plane, another pickup came rumbling down the dirt road. "I know this guy. He's with the State Department of Natural Resources. Let me do the talking."

The DNR pickup rolled up beside Jason. They rolled down their windows. "Hey, Jason, I thought it might be Sam. I heard the plane land. What's up?"

Slipping into his best South Carolina low-country boy voice, Jason replied, "Hey, Jack. Ramey's on vacation. Sam wanted me to fly down and just have a quick look. These two guys work with us and have never been here before. We're getting out before the storm hits."

"Yeah, I hear you. Howdy, boys." He tipped his baseball cap and they returned the greeting. "Yeah, nobody in their right mind wants to spend a minute more than necessary here during bug season. I got to get on back to Georgetown myself. The wife's about to pop any minute. It's another boy. Give old Sam my best. You coming down for the turkey hunt this fall?"

"Congratulations. Yeah, I'll be coming with Sam and a few other guys, but I think these city boys have seen enough. There was a six-foot rattler waiting to greet us on the front steps. Viktor's ready to go."

"Well, I won't keep you and I really need to roll this glass up. These bugs are eating me alive."

Jack sped away back down the dirt road. "Do you think he'll go look?"

"Oh, hell no. I know his wife. He looks like a good old boy but she's got him by the short hairs. If he suspected anything, he would still be here talking."

"You said this is an island. How'd he get the truck here?"

"There's a ferry—a flat boat on a cable—that crosses the Intercoastal Waterway. The cable lays on the bottom to avoid interfering with normal boat traffic until the ferry is needed. He called and scheduled a crossing when he heard the plane. I forgot about that, but don't worry. We're fine."

"Maybe we should have called ahead to let him know we'd be here."

"Oh, hell no. He would have been sitting here waiting on us."

On the flight back, Viktor asked, "I wonder how alligators mate with those long tails in the way?"

Jason laughed. "All low country Southern boys learn this at an early age. The act of alligator mating is very unusual. Both sexes have a single opening called a cloaca that's used both for elimination of waste and for reproduction. The male has an organ that extends to enter the female. The mating season is an absolute orgy of multiple partners. The males can be heard for miles at night bellowing to the females."

Pink and Viktor were quiet all the way back to Swan Bay.

24
CHARLESTON

Fourteen members of England's Society of Royal Cumberland Youths were in Atlanta to ring peals at the three local towers. Whenever the group was in Atlanta, Hew rang one of the bells at St. Philip's in one of the peal attempts. He had been elected as a member several years earlier. His certificate carried the number 5061 and he proudly hung it in his home office. This time, he rang the number four bell to a peal of Stedman.

The Society members had been to Atlanta many times before on their American tours. The Oxford Guild had visited too, but not as often. After the tower was built, the Cumberlands had arranged for one of their best teachers to be in residence for the first summer to train the new cathedral band. Ron, a genial Yorkshire man, had done the same thing for the Grace Church Cathedral band in Charleston. He had made a huge difference and the ringers loved him.

Hew and Alexis always hosted the ringers at a party at their house. "He did love a chip butty, didn't he?"

Paul laughed. "Yes. Did he want it with scraps?"

"I don't remember that one. What is it?"

"It's basically a sandwich with french fries between two slices of bread. The scraps are the left-over small fried bits of potato left in the fryer. Did he constantly repeat, 'Don't worry about it yer daft apeth'?"

"Seems like I remember something like that now that you mention it."

"It's a term of endearment in Yorkshire. It affectionally means a silly fool. He would have said it in a firm but reassuring manner."

"They did nickname him Mr. Grumpy while he was in Charleston and it stuck with the Atlanta ringers, so I guess that's where it came from."

Hew and Alexis also housed some of the ringers either at their house or in Hew's penthouse. Charlie and Rosilyn also housed several. They had learned with previous trips that the Brits don't like American beer so they made sure there was plenty of wine and gin to go around.

"Hew, are you and John going to Ring Around Charleston next weekend?"

"Yes. I need to make a quick trip to check on a project I'm involved with at the old Navy Base in North Charleston. The whole family is going for a long weekend. We love Charleston and Grace Church Cathedral. I've arranged with our dean for the cathedral to pay for the entire cathedral band and their spouses to go over for the weekend. John and I will attempt our first peal together at Grace with the ringers. They'll be going to England next summer too."

"Great. Ring Around Charleston is always a grand affair. Many of the North American ringers will be there too. It's usually a warm and sunny February weekend. The Yankees, Canadians, and Brits love a chance to warm up a little. It's really great to have four towers at our disposal for the weekend. I'm told that Paul and Ron are arranging towers for your England trip. Aren't the Grace ringers joining you on that trip?"

"Yes, and so are the other two Atlanta-area ringing groups. It will be a real organizational feat if we pull it off. We'll be based in Oxford for the second week. Alexis and I own a small flat in Oxford across from Tom Tower. We bought it after our first year of marriage since we were studying there. We love it."

"Isn't Pembroke College across the road there?"

"Yes, but there's a row of flats too. We bought the one two doors down from where Dorothy L. Sayers of *The Nine Taylors* fame lived."

"Ah. Nice bit of ringing history that."

THE FOLLOWING WEEKEND, HEW FLEW THE entire St. Philip's, Marietta, and St. Luke's ringers to Charleston on the company Boeing business jet. His security detail had their hands full as he spent Friday afternoon reviewing the work on the container flatcars.

Most folks stayed in hotels near the cathedral. The Ramsays and Hardys stayed with Charlie's aunt and uncle on Tradd Street in the family bed and breakfast. The house had been in Charlie's mother's family, the Mazycks, since their ancestor fled France after the revocation of the Edict of Nantes. From the second floor parlor, they could see across the harbor to Fort Sumter and the Atlantic Ocean.

The ringing started on Friday evening. Hew and John scored their first peal together at Grace late in the evening in a method known as Cambridge. As a joke, the conductor called a variation known as a single as his first variation thinking he could trip Hew or John up and everyone could get to the pub early. Only elite bands include the single variation in a Cambridge peal.

Hew missed it but John rang it correctly and the conductor, seeing that his joke had backfired, quickly set Hew straight and the peal continued. Hew didn't miss the next one.

On Saturday morning, Hew took John out to Stella Maris Church on Sullivan's Island. Its eight new Whitechapel bells are small, but perfect for ringing peals because they don't wear the ringers out. John stood beside the conductor and after about an hour into the attempt of Grandsire Triples, both Hew and John noticed that three ringers had gone wrong. The conductor's wife was ringing beside the conductor and in exasperation whispered, "What now?"

"Just keep pulling while I try to sort it out."

The ringing got worse and continued for another thirty minutes. Finally, the conductor saw that it was pointless and yelled, "Stand." They stopped ringing, and walked out. Hew followed John.

"What a wasted morning, Dad," said John.

"Let's go walk on the beach so you can calm down. I've told you before that you can't win them all."

⚜

JEANNE, WIFE OF THE GRACE CHURCH Cathedral tower captain, took Alexis, Rosilyn, Lea, and Yvonne, one of the English ringers, to lunch at her favorite club on the waterfront in town. Lea had organized the ringing schedule for the various events in the four towers. It was almost as thankless a job as trying to herd cats, so Jeanne wanted to reward her in a small way. They all started with a bloody Mary. That loosened tongues.

"These ringers are interesting people."

"That's for sure. They're also brilliant people. Most have IQs of 145 or more."

"God! Hew never mentioned that! They could have their own Mensa chapter."

"Leaves me out."

"Me, too."

"Oh, that's not really true. You all are both brilliant people. I suspect there are a few savants though," quipped Lea.

"Tell me about those windows in the tower. Someone said they thought there was a dead mouse on the ledge."

"Dead mouse? Oh that's a good one. I haven't heard that one before, but there *is* a mouse carved into the glass."

"Why? Where is it? I hate mice."

"It's in the second panel from the left in the third row from the bottom. Those figures represent the writers of the four Gospels, Matthew, Mark, Luke, and John, but we sometimes refer to them as Matthew, Mouse, Luke, and John."

"But why a mouse?"

"The former rector and the architect had just visited Coventry Cathedral on a vacation in England while our columbarium/bell tower was under construction, and while looking at the modern west windows of carved saints in the clear glass, the rector remarked that he wanted something like that in the columbarium windows to add life to plain glass.

The architect thought it was too modern for Charleston. Fortunately, he had recently visited Lincoln Cathedral, and being amazed at the gallery of statues on the west front, decided to add stylized Gothic figures to our glass. Once the artist had finished carving—well, sand blasting—the trial figure into one of the one inch thick clear glass panels, the committee went to the studio to approve the work and were so overcome by the beauty, they asked him to add a small bit of whimsy somewhere to 'humanize' the work. They agreed on a little church mouse."

"Ahhh. I get it," said Alexis. "That's also why the figures are long and thin. They fit the aedicules."

"Fit the what? I need another bloody Mary, please."

"Let's have another round. I'm sorry, Rosilyn. You know how pedantic I tend to get when I'm explaining art. An aedicule is used in Gothic design to frame pieces of art and sculpture. It's from Latin and means 'little house.' The columns and gabled roof form an enclosure. You can see the same thing inside Grace on either side of the altar where the gilded tablets are painted. Gothic statuary is usually elongated to accentuate the verticality of the building too. I suspect that's why the figures aren't more plump as in a Renaissance type style."

"How in the world did he carve all that? It was backwards to him."

"His nickname is Lex. He has dyslexia. He said that the work isn't backwards to him."

"Since this is also a columbarium, those two angels in the second row are there to guard the tombs."

"We've nothing like this in England. The closest we come is the round tower in Basildon."

"That's one of the towers Hew visited. One of the ringers took him there while it was under construction just to see it. It and Grace were the inspiration for the design for our tower at the Cathedral of St. Philip. We've certainly made many wonderful lifelong friends with ringers, and when we go to England, our ringing friends open doors that we would never manage on our own. Hew was given a top of the dome of the lantern to the crypt tour of St. Paul's Cathedral, London, by the Clerk of the Cathedral Chapter. They opened every door and toured every chamber and closet. It was an experience of a lifetime."

"I've heard it said that learning to ring all those methods is like trying to memorize the London phone book."

"Yvonne, do Brits still have phone books? I haven't seen one in years."

"Speaking of tower design, the Grace bell frame sits on wooden blocks that insulate the metal frame from the concrete. It stops the sound of the clappers from transferring what they call clapper knock into the walls. I'm told it can otherwise be a very annoying sound. Those bolts need tightening as the wood shrinks. The other bolts need tightening from time to time too. Right after our tower was finished, Hew decided they needed a set of wrenches to work on the bells. One wrench in particular was very large so he went to a store that sold truck parts. That particular wrench cost $75.00 and being of Scottish ancestry, he wouldn't pay that for a single wrench."

"We call them spanners."

"One weekend, we were in Greenville visiting my parents, and Hew moaned about it to my dad. Dad took him to a very large roadside flea market to visit an old guy he knew who sold old tools. The guy had the wrench and offered it to Hew for $75.00. Hew still thought that was too much for one wrench. Dad spied a full set of wrenches. The largest wrench in the set was exactly what Hew was looking for so Dad asked the guy the price and the guy said, 'I'll let you have that whole set for $75.00.' Hew was ecstatic."

"That reminds me of an incident involving numbers. Several years ago, there was a funeral at Grace at 10:00 am on a Saturday. The band decided to go early to tighten the bolts and put the muffles on the clappers."

"Remind me about the muffles. Remember, I'm not a ringer. Charlie and Eddie are. I'm just a clapper. We arrange the social side of ringing since we don't have a nearby pub like the English do."

"A muffle is a leather pouch that fits on one side of the clapper. It straps around the clapper and produces a muffled echo-like sound. It's very dramatic and hauntingly beautiful."

"Yes, we ring that way all over England for funerals and Remembrance Day."

"So Chip asked me to go to the doughnut shop and pick up a dozen and a half doughnuts that were equal parts plain, chocolate, and jelly filled. When it was my turn at the counter, I told the young guy exactly that. He walked away, but returned and asked me to repeat it. He came back the third time, and after he walked away again, the guy behind me said, 'You're not going to tell him, are you?' I said I would if it were holding him up. He said, 'No, I want to watch this.' The manager came out and told me he would give me two dozen at the same price."

"That's amazing. Those guys couldn't divide eighteen by three?"

"Apparently not. They'll never be ringers."

Venting a little, Lea confessed, "Planning these weekends is difficult and time consuming. You don't realize what goes on behind the scenes. Some of these people don't understand the word no."

"Many of them are extremely picky—especially with their food," quipped Jeanne. "Let's go ahead and order. Everything here is very good, and let's get a bottle of pinot grigio."

"Spill the beans about the planning. I've wondered about that."

"We have outings, dinners, and country days in England, but these weekends are over the top."

"First, scheduling the ringing is a real act of love for ringing. It takes an electronic spreadsheet to keep it all straight."

"But you have a Ph.D."

"Yes, but not in accounting or business administration. I'm a scientist, for God's sake."

"With the ringers, the range of experience is astounding. There are absolute beginners who come for the first time and want rope handling lessons, all the way up to absolute world class experts. Some people only want to ring complicated methods that they've never rung before, and that can pose a problem with hurt feelings if enough people don't want to try it. Even with four towers, because a peal takes about three hours to ring, we just can't accommodate them all and still make sure everyone gets an adequate amount of rope time. Everyone wants to be the only novice in a band of experts too."

"Sounds complicated."

Jeanne reassured them. "It takes a master diplomat to contain all those egos. The first year, a contractor showed up on Friday morning to work in the courtyard and demanded everyone leave for reasons of safety. He wanted to erect scaffolding for the following Monday's work. Chip had to spar with the senior warden over that. They had a real battle of words. It took the rector to tell the warden and contractor to leave. The ringing weekend had been on the calendar for months. I'm on the social committee and let me tell you, planning an event with food is nearly impossible. This group—there's ninety-eight of them this year—contains vegans, vegetarians, gluten free, nut free, dairy free, carnivore—he only eats red meat—Keto, sugar free, shellfish free, and some I've never even heard of before. One guy won't eat poultry. He grew up on a chicken farm in Maryland. The vegetarians demand a vegetarian entree even though there's only three of them, and they can't agree on what they want. It couldn't just be salad, and any carb had to be gluten free to boot. Somehow, though, I think we'll be able to manage it."

"I was here two years ago and the Saturday night banquet was elegant and delicious. I heard nothing but compliments."

"Thank you, but there were a few grumblings about the cost. This year we thought about just having a few food trucks in the parking lot, but we couldn't decide on which ones so we gave that up."

They all laughed as the alcohol began to kick in.

"And then there's the sex."

"O-O-O-O, I've heard about the sex. Tell all."

They giggled when the waiter came by with the second bottle of wine. "Thank you, Lars. Bring us an ice bucket and just leave it here."

"I'd like to ring his clapper. Have you tried to sign him up, Lea?" They howled with laughter.

"No. You're changing the subject."

"Not really. You brought up the subject of sex."

"Well, being in that hotel is just like being at an English Edwardian house party weekend. It even looks Edwardian."

"It's hellishly expensive, but it's only three nights so we grin and bear it."

"Charleston hotels are all expensive. But at bedtime, the real parties begin. There are at least four hookups that I know of."

"Yes, we know about two of them, but it doesn't really bother anyone that I know of. We think its great fun and makes great gossip, just like now."

"I agree. Before the second weekend, I was looking for housing. I called one of the locals and she said she would ask her husband. He walked into the room while we were on the phone, and I heard her ask him. She explained that the couple wasn't married and his response was, 'Well, let the fornicating begin.'"

They nearly screamed with laughter. Others in the room turned to try to register their annoyance.

"You may not know about numbers three and four because they're same sex."

"That won't bother anyone either."

"All male?"

"No. One each."

"Well we've certainly become open minded in our old age."

"Speak for yourself, Alexis. I'm open minded, but I'm not old."

"Me either."

The others in the dining room turned again to see what they were laughing about. "Oh, look out the window at that large ship."

"You're changing the subject."

"Yes. I don't want to get kicked out before I've had my dessert, but really, Jeanne, you folks should be very proud of these weekends. They're the best and everyone has a great time. The social parts are as great as the ringing."

"Sometimes even better."

"Alexis, you were at one of the New Year's Eve parties as I remember."

"Yes. Those fantastic black-tie dinners were followed by ringing and champagne at midnight. What fun. You folks do throw elegant parties. The whole ringing world talks about them."

"There's a fraternity house directly across the street and at midnight on the eve of the millennium, just as the ringing began, two startled naked young people stood up on the bed, turned on a light, and looked out of the window. We all saw them in all their glory and decided that if they got pregnant with a girl, they could name her Milly."

More laughter. "Oh, stop. I'm about to wet my pants. Who knew ringing could be so much fun."

"The ladies room is through the door and on the left."

"I came to one of the Halloween parties. You had transformed the courtyard into a version of the dining hall at Christ Church, Oxford with two long lines of tables covered with white table cloths adorned with multi-branch candelabra and beautiful flowers. The blue neon lighted tower windows made a stunning backdrop. It looked like a reredos. Everyone was in costume."

"The flower guild did a beautiful job, as usual. That was the year we were graced with the Queen Mother and Wallis Simpson."

"Wha-a-at?"

"One of the ringers was dressed in drag with a long elegant dress, white gloves, an old mink coat, and old lady makeup. He arrived in a chauffeur-driven Rolls Royce with Wallis, also in drag, as her companion."

"As I remember it, the chauffeur was also one of your ringers and it was his car. You folks really know how to party. They stayed in character for the entire party. Everyone is still talking about it."

"How did Charleston get four towers? This ringing business is such an esoteric thing."

"Esoteric, is it? Alexis you do love big words. Briefly, St. Michael's bells were originally cast in London and hung in the tower in 1764. They've been reworked several times since. During repairs to the church after Hurricane Hugo, the architect discovered that the bells and frame were sitting on rotten beams. He became very concerned and the vestry approved a plan to repair the beams. The rector asked the architect to explore the option of restoring the bells for change ringing.

"In his research, the architect was directed to the Whitechapel Bell Foundry in London. He called the foundry and was astounded to learn that the foundry still had the original 1764 records. Shortly thereafter, Grace Church was in the process of designing a columbarium and the same architect suggested adding bells to the top. They had already studied the possibility of putting more bells in the old steeple but access to the belfry was difficult and there was no place for a ringing room so the columbarium/tower idea was born. In doing his research, the architect discovered that by 1751, there had been a set of four bells near Charleston in the tower at the now vanished town of Dorchester. Those bells were moved to St. Paul's Episcopal Church in Charleston after the 1776 war ended because the town of Dorchester became abandoned—probably because the low marshy ground wasn't fit for planting. St. Paul's bells and St. Michael's bells—except for St. Michael's largest bell, the fire bell, were confiscated by the Confederate government and sent away to be used as cannon metal. Once the folks at St. Paul's read the architect's research paper, they decided to buy a new set of bells. About this time, Stella Maris was celebrating its centenary, and they decided to buy bells so now we have four sets."

"Let's call an Uber and go shopping for shoes at Bob Ellis on King St. I can't drink another drop if I'm going to be gorgeous for the banquet tonight."

"I can't afford those shoes."

"It doesn't cost anything to try them on."

Alexis chimed in."I can afford them. I'm working again. I'll buy everyone a pair."

⁕

ON THE FLIGHT BACK TO ATLANTA, Hew texted Sam a cryptic message. "I was in Charleston all weekend ringing bells. I visited your property. All is well here."

25
KUDZU

The regular monthly meeting of the Brunhild Construction Group was about to begin. Hew had flown up the day before to check the progress of the Swan Bay Restoration Group. The international workforce of crafts people had been carefully vetted and were subcontractors to Eberhart.

He had had a difficult time with Ms. Mamie. When the construction crew deconstructed the kitchen walls, they inadvertently let the deer into her potager—the high brick walls on three sides kept the deer and rabbits out of her vegetables. Nets and chicken wire were periodically strung over the top to keep the birds, squirrels and other critters out. The kitchen formed the fourth wall.

Mary had called Hew and insisted that he fly up immediately to console her. That walled vegetable garden had been built by Hew's first American ancestor, Captain John Bishop, for Mamie's first enslaved ancestor. Her family had fed the farm folks there for generations and the deer had wiped out the current crop in one night. She had ranted and cried for over an hour.

"You stupid city folks think your food comes in boxes and cans from a store. I worked my fingers to the bone raising all that food!"

Hew finally calmed her by telling her that as an act of contrition, the crew had paid for a landscape archaeologist to come in with a team of students and excavate the garden. At first, she was resistant but the young scientist won her over simply by sitting and listening to her stories about her family and their work in the garden. He didn't understand how the soil level of a walled garden could stay the same over the centuries without massive amounts of labor to remove and replenish it. His team had carried out phytolithic studies and found multiple periods of planting since about 1660.

With a twinkle in her eye, she laughed and finally told him about their secret garden "tea" parties. Early on, they had started making compost tea as a way of avoiding the back-breaking labor of having to remove all of the soil. Because they considered manure to be nasty, her ancestors never used animal manure except for small amounts of chicken manure naturally left when the chickens were let in to eat the grubs—beetle larvae—and other insects.

At planting time, the earth was always plowed and the chickens were brought in for a week or two before planting started. They recycled all of the spent plant matter—tomato bushes, bean vines, carrot tops, and other materials into compost and the oldest compost was placed in burlap bags and steeped in barrels of tepid river water until the water turned brown and smelled like rich earth.

It's a tricky process to get right and temperature is critical. The technique was passed down through the generations of family cooks. The water must be constantly stirred to keep it aerated and the "tea" must not be applied to the soil during the hottest part of the day. That was the "tea party" part. They sat around telling stories drinking tea and eating sweets as they took turns stirring the pot. They usually waited until late afternoon to apply the solution to the soil.

Dr. Scott was fascinated and asked if she meant leftover cooked vegetables. She quickly told him in no uncertain terms that there were never any leftovers from her cooking. The farm hands ate it all. Hew, she said, was the only tricky eater at Swan Bay but it wasn't his fault because he had been raised in New York City.

Dr. Scott had studied the history of fertilization and knew it was nearly as old as civilization. He also knew that it had basically been lost in early America. Both George Washington and Thomas Jefferson had dabbled in using manure for fertilizer but the practice was not considered to have been widespread. Early Americans simply cleared more land when the old land failed to produce at previous levels.

The study was record-breaking and he assured Mamie that her ancestors would be fully credited for their planting skills. Basically, they had rotated their crops and, based on a hunch developed from asking more questions, Scott's further excavations revealed the foundations of a second-walled garden that had allowed the crops to be rotated before crop management was fully understood. Historians were just beginning to understand how creative those early Africans were.

In South Carolina, the Africans were now being credited with developing the rice culture. Rice has been grown in Africa for millennia and the wetlands around Charleston were perfect for the crop. Hew was, of course, astounded. He had no idea that any of this had ever taken place. He also remembered an entry in the family journals describing that as a young man, his great-grandfather had had the second garden torn out after a winter ice storm had felled trees around it and destroyed most of the walls. He had a hole dug and used the bricks to line a new swimming pool.

Using a windmill, he pumped water up from the James River to keep the pool fresh and replenished and his friends loved it. Ms Mamie told them that her grandmother had been so mad that she refused to plant his favorite black Russian heirloom tomatoes and they've never been planted there since. When asked why, her grandmother had simply said that the ground must have been cursed by the storm.

Hew knew better than to argue with her. His grandfather had relined the pool with fiberglass and installed a filtration system. Hew had recently removed the old disintegrating brick and fiberglass and replaced it with steel reinforced concrete.

She had also taken Dr. Scott into her root cellar, where she explained the process of preserving vegetables. Dr. Scott had heard of this process, but she showed him shelves loaded with glass jars of vegetables, pickles, and relishes. One wall contained glass jars of seeds. Her ancestors had developed a system of planting that reserved some material for seed for the next year and had always planted enough for canning for the winter months. Being a young academically minded city guy himself, he was astounded. Hew asked her if she still had seeds for the black Russian heirloom tomatoes. She answered coyly, "I might."

These seeds alone provided material for detailed studies. The microscopic soil studies showed the presence of species of plants long after they had been harvested. The plants left silica deposits in the soil that are unique and datable. DNA showed the exact species. After much discussion, the scientists were able to get Hew to agree to test the DNA of some of the skeletal remains in the family cemetery. Using ground penetrating radar, they scanned the graves that had dates on the tombstones that related to the silica in the soil samples. They were searching for evidence of the effects of diet on their health. No bodies were exhumed. They simply drove tiny probes into the teeth in the sculls. The results were spectacular. Virginia Tech used the research in their current studies of the contributions of Africans to horticultural advances in early Virginia. They wanted to award Hew an honorary PhD but he refused and asked instead that they award an honorary degree to Ms. Mamie as an ongoing representative of her ancestor's work. She was finally somewhat placated. She agreed to try planting the heirloom tomatoes again in memory of her ancestors.

The kitchen brickwork was almost complete, and Hew was pleased to see that his beehive oven was still intact. They had even convinced the preservationists to allow them to tint the white lime mortar beige to reduce the newness of the look. Sorting out that detail alone took several weeks, but Hew had stayed out of the discussions.

They would start setting roof slates the next week. Hew had insisted on using Welsh royal purple slates in memory of Alexis's ancestors, while the local officials had insisted that the kitchen had to be brought up to meet the current commercial kitchen building code and the original wood shakes were not fireproof. Some of the old rafters were rotten on the ends so they had been sistered with rafters supplied by the West Virginia folks who supplied the replacement log for the cabin.

All of the building services were skillfully hidden and would be covered with new lime plaster on the interior walls and ceilings. They had saved the old hand-split laths and were soaking them in barrels of water. That would prevent the plaster from drying too quickly. Hew had been amused to discover that the old overly pronounced back bands on the interior trim woodwork were actually screeds to form edges to the plaster. He never ceased to be amazed at the old craftsmanship—modern drywall is simply left ragged and the wood trim covers the mess.

The new walls were internally reinforced with stainless steel rods so the new building was up to code. Of course, a building was only up to code until the code changed, but Hew was very comfortable that there would be no more bulging brick walls.

The biggest obstacle had been with the design of the kitchen ventilation system. They had to add a flue into the rebuilt fireplace for the code required exhaust and they had to modify the chimney cap to accommodate the ugly wart that housed the extractor fan. Johann and Hans had convinced the building inspector to allow an in-line fan so the visual aspect was minimized. They added a door into the stainless steel exhaust extraction duct in the attic to facilitate the removal of grease buildup. The makeup air unit was hidden behind closed louvered blinds in a space formally occupied by a window. The louver slat spacing was wider that the old ones, and the preservationists weren't happy, but it was the only solution. They had finally agreed to allow all the slats on all of the windows to match.

The upstairs cook's apartment was updated for a future new "assistant" cook. Ms. Mamie had decided to stay in her nearby modern one-story apartment. Hew added a small high brick walled potagerie beside her apartment for her own use. She could look out of her kitchen window and watch over her flowers and vegetables.

Alexis and two of her friends had just sat down for lunch at the club in Atlanta when a handsome young Black waiter approached their table.

"Jared? Jared Smith?" said Alexis.

"Mrs. Ramsay? What a surprise."

"Yes. When did you start here and did you complete your education as I hoped?"

"Tuesday, and not quite. I have a degree, but not in music. Things were very bad after you left the school. I hated it but I graduated and then I moved to Charleston and started culinary school. I waited tables, bartended private weekend parties, and played cocktail piano to help pay my way. Unfortunately, I still have a big student loan debt and I haven't found a chef's position in town. I may need to move again soon."

"Let me talk to Hew. I may have something for you."

On Friday, Alexis flew Jared and his partner Bruce to Swan Bay. Hew was busy reviewing the window sash and trim repairs on the main house while some of the replacements were still being milled from Swan Bay's supply of old heart pine. The log cabin was finished and Hew couldn't see where the repairs had been made. Overall, he was pleased.

Ms. Mamie loved Jared. He and Bruce would move into the kitchen apartment with him as assistant chef and she would "re-train" him in her ways. Bruce would become the manager for the ever expanding construction force in the old DEA facility. He had an accounting degree and his mannerisms were perfect for dealing with those folks.

ON SUNDAY, ALEXIS, JARED, AND BRUCE returned to Atlanta. On Monday morning, Bubba Hu called the meeting to order. Charlie Hardy, as president of Eberhart's computer division, was up first with his report on cybersecurity. "Our servers are being hit several times a day from the Chinese and Russians."

"Have they gotten through the firewalls?"

"Oh, yes. Absolutely. We set up a series of fake servers and left one portal open. It took them several months, but they made it. We have a team of programmers making fake news and updating those servers. They look real because we keep up with the construction progress so anyone on the ground can report and the visual evidence seems to match the hacked information. We even send and receive fake emails." He smiled. "Hew helped me concoct this ruse. He's a master at hacking himself."

"It's just a little skill I learned from a drug cartel computer programmer while I was in school in Colombia. I never thought I would ever use it."

"So no one has hacked the real servers?"

"No. They're very well protected, air gapped, and located in different buildings. I don't think the hackers know they're even there. The fake ones are extremely good.

"On another front, our personnel security continues to hold. There haven't been any reported attempts on anyone's life." Everyone breathed a sigh of relief. No one else knew about the attempt on Minoru's life.

Jason was next. "The right of way work is progressing smoothly but very slowly. We have to clear more than we initially thought to keep the trees from shading our solar panels and the kudzu is giving us a fit."

"Kudzu?" Minoru was amazed. "You have kudzu in America? My wife would love to get some of that."

Sam was surprised. "What the hell for? We can cover your house in a few weeks if she wants. We call it *mile a minute* because it can grow a foot a day around here. My great-great-grandfather imported it to cover the embankment cuts along our rights of way to control erosion. He thought it was a great environmental improvement, but it's turned into a nightmare in the South. And by the way, speaking of wives, I hate the name Brunhild. Who's idea was that? My Swiss wife's name is Hilde and she's not happy."

"You won't plant that damned stuff on my farm."

"You're out of order. Hans named his new machine Brunhild and we adopted it. She was an ancient German female figure of Amazon-like strength. She's in his favorite opera *Der Ring des Nibelungen* by Richard Wagner. She was a brute. Lets move on, please."

"She'll be happy when I explain how much money it's making her. I'll buy her a new car or something. But why does your wife want kudzu?"

"You're out of order, Sam."

"You opened that door, Bubba. I want to know and it's my company so I can say anything I damned well please."

"Actually, Bubba, we're all curious."

'Okay. Briefly, kudzu is native to Japan and we eat it."

"Now, you're joking."

"No. Every part is delicious. We don't eat the semi-woody vines, but the leaves, the flowers, and the roots can be eaten. The root should be cooked, but the rest can be eaten raw in salads, fried, sauteed, baked, and in jellies. Bring me some and I'll have her cook it for you."

Hew offhandedly remarked, "Kudzu. Why not kudzu instead of corn stalks or grape skins?"

Jason frowned. "What did you say?"

"Well, Kudzu has long fibrous vines. They're longer and tougher than corn stalks and they're readily available. Could they be used for the new composite material for the container covers?"

Suddenly, Sam saw a way to make money. "We've got acres of it. I'm going to call Chuck at Clemson University about this while you folks eat lunch. I've suddenly lost my appetite."

AFTER LUNCH, SAM WAS GLOWING. "WHO would have thought. Bubba's right. Kudzu is also often used as silage for cattle feed. The problem is it's too expensive to harvest because it grows in rough areas and the railroads won't give the harvesting companies permission to use the rights of way. Chuck also gave me a contact at the University of Georgia and she sent me several recipes. She cooks the roots like potatoes, and she also dries them and makes a flour-like powder to use as breading. She even makes kudzu tea!

"Jason has emailed Hans with an idea for an add-on to the front of Brunhild to cut the vines. If nothing else, I don't want those vines crawling up my new piers onto the roadbed. If they cover the roadbed, we would be in trouble. I can sell that crap to the dairy farmers, but if Clemson can use it, we'll save money since we already whack it back anyway and we can ship it to Charleston at no cost."

Jason exclaimed, "If this works, the Japanese will love it too and the airline contractors will start a bidding war. Hew, you and Sam might make billions with this idea."

Hew shuddered at the thought of kudzu tea, but his eyes lit up at the thought of making more money from bio-waste. The Germans would love it too. He then gave a report on the construction progress. That took the remainder of the afternoon, but all was going smoothly and the addition of the club car to the elevated roadbed was a big hit with his guys. Morale was very high.

They used the grill that night, and the food, while not gourmet, was delicious and perfect for that crowd. They had Japanese Wagyu filets that had been flown in for the meeting by the Japanese ambassador. The filets were accompanied by baked potatoes, salad, bread, and cherry pie made from cherries from Hew's orchard. Hew ate the beef as a courtesy, but the high concentration of fats and low number of Omega 6 acids worried him. It also contained about 100 calories more than American beef but he rationalized that one filet wouldn't kill him, and it was very delicious.

❧

AFTER DINNER, HEW AND SAM SAT in the old rocking chairs sipping scotch on the newly-restored porch of the cabin. "It's just like the old one, Hew," said Sam.

"Yeah, I guess so. I'm not one of those people who always say the old 'whatever' was better."

"I'm just amazed that your family held on to this land for so long, What was it? 1638?"

"Captain John arrived here in 1638. This was his third property and it dates to 1651."

"Still, that's impressive. How is it that you have such a fine airstrip here?"

"My great-grandfather loved flying and started a crop dusting business. He worked all over the South spreading poison on every cotton plant, bug, animal, and human in the region. My grandfather stopped that once he understood the health issues. He also stopped growing tobacco."

Sam sighed. "We live and learn—hopefully. One of my paternal ancestors was on the first ship to arrive at Charleston in 1670. I've been to the landing site. It's now a state park called Charles Towne Landing and it's upriver and across from downtown.

"Experts say they were hiding from the Spanish fort at St. Augustine, Florida. The Spaniards constantly roamed the inlets and bays in the area. The natives hated the Spanish and were happy to help the English—or so the story goes. The ship arrived in April of 1670. I made the mistake of visiting in April. The bugs nearly drove me crazy. I would have been on the first ship back! Was life that bad in England?"

"In 1670, as I remember from the stories Tippy Hardy told me—her ancestor was one of the early French Huguenot families in Charleston— the last plague was just ending in England. I suspect those who settled Charles Town had lost many relatives. Also, a great fire had recently

212

reduced the City of London to ashes. It must have been a miserably cold, sooty time in that town. Imagine the acidic smell of wet burned timber all over the city! The Lords Proprietors, as they were called, posted signs in the newly opened coffee houses in London promising wild profits and adventure to anyone who would make the journey. I'm told that the lure of wealth was just too compelling. Life was harder back then, but I've been told that they didn't know much better."

Sam shrugged. "Actually, it was the French who first tried to build a settlement in South Carolina more than one hundred years before the English. They were raiding the Spanish ships and stealing the gold. It was on a point that's now part of the Marine training facility at Parris Island, across the bay from Hilton Head. The remains of the settlement are being dug by archaeologists at the moment.

"The Spanish had discovered gold in South America and the trade winds pushed the gold laden ships up past the South Carolina coast before they turned east toward Spain. The French Catholics and Protestants were embroiled in a civil war so France wasn't able to re-supply the settlement and it mysteriously disappeared. The Spanish then decided to build a settlement there to protect their trade route.

"It lasted a while, but they consolidated their settlers to a new site— now St. Augustine in present day Florida. The English established the first *permanent* settlement in Carolina. All of this has recently been well documented in a new book entitled *American Conquistador* by a man named Ferguson. It's fascinating stuff and adds over a hundred years to the history of the state. I read the book last week."

"I guess the Virginia tobacco profits were worth it."

"Yes. Captain John certainly made a fortune, but the discovery of tobacco was something of an accident at the right time as it turned out. Tobacco suddenly had become all the rage in Europe. The relative ease of growing tobacco and the ease of turning a profit led the settlers to basically abandon all of the other attempts to produce raw materials except for timber, of course. England's big problem was their lack of wood."

"Wood?"

"England had depleted their ancient forests. They had to buy wood products from abroad at high prices. America was to have provided wood at a better rate. There's a small town in South Carolina called

Kingstree. The longleaf pine trees there grew straight, strong, and tall. They were felled for masts for the King's navy. Spain and Portugal were ahead of the race for expansion because of Christopher Columbus. They held South America where they found gold, but they were also heading north."

"I heard a young girl on TV say that if she could go back in time, she would have sent Columbus in a different direction. That ignorant kid didn't realize that she wouldn't exist if Columbus had taken a different route. The natives were still hunter-gatherers. The men hunted and fought with other tribes while the women did all the work. The men simply couldn't be made to do women's work."

"Oh for God's sake! Don't ever say that out loud in mixed company. Alexis would have your head. Here have another wee dram. I think there were many causes including political and religious freedom. Remember, it was freedom *of* religion and not freedom *from* religion. In Charleston, the French Protestants—also called Huguenots, which means ghost because they traveled at night to their secret meetings—are treated almost as royalty, probably because they weren't Catholic. Unfortunately, their past was just as bloody as the Catholics, but this is conveniently overlooked today. Neither sect was above murder in the cause of their religion. Charleston was settled as a gift from King Charles II to those men who helped him regain the throne. He gave his friends all of America south of Virginia and north of Florida from the Atlantic to the Pacific. If you look at a map of the US, you can still see the line of demarkation separating most of the modern states. It's just north of the 35th parallel, but I forget which exact number it is. If my ancestor hadn't saved the life of King James, Charles I and II would never have been born and none of this would have ever existed."

"That's a sobering thought. It's about the 37th parallel as I remember. I don't think they even knew where the Pacific was."

"You're probably right and, anyway, as it turned out, they simply couldn't manage all that land, and eventually the French and Spanish got most of it west of the Appalachians. Virginia and the other colonies were settled as a way to get a foothold here before the Spaniards could claim it. Yes, wood was one of the issues. They had to import other goods that relied on burning wood for manufacturing such as wrought iron too. Owning an endless supply of wood made North America too good to pass up, but you're right about religious and political freedom. New England was all about that. The English who settled South Carolina didn't let religion get in the way except for the Catholics. They didn't want Catholics."

"But what about coal? I know about coal. We burned it to make steam for our locomotives and we still haul it to the ports by the tens of thousands of tons. It's helped make millions for me. They have coal mines in the UK."

"I know. It's been mined there since the Bronze Age, but apparently only in small amounts in the ancient days. They found it by the North Sea and thought it had washed ashore. They followed the veins into the ground, but apparently cutting trees was easier and safer."

"It sounds like the old saying, 'We've always done it that way.'"

"Maybe. Coal didn't gain much in popularity until the industrial revolution, though. It was a cheap alternative for wood. Labor was the big issue in the colonies. Captain John tried bringing indentured servants and most bought slaves. They simply couldn't make the natives do the work."

"Slavery and natives are deep subjects for another day, but you've just mentioned something that rattled my boozy brain. My maternal grandmother used to tell a story about her ancestor who came to Jamestown aboard a ship named *Swan*. He was indentured to the bishop."

Hew laughed. "She may have been partially correct. What a small world. Was his name either Tompkins, Bonner, or Wright?"

"Yes! John Tompkins, but how did you know?"

"He's listed in my ancestor's first 1638 land patent. My ancestor was Captain John Bishop and he paid for your ancestor's passage to America in exchange for a few years work."

"Man! I need to look at those old tobacco fields again in the morning. We really are joined at the hip. I want to walk the fields while I'm here, but now, I'm ready for bed."

BREAKFAST THE NEXT MORNING INCLUDED Ms. Mamie's famous biscuits soaked with farm fresh hand-churned butter, and slathered with her home made cherry preserves made from the orchard growing outside the old kitchen.

Business resumed in the updated SCIF. Jason gave an update on route planning. "We've made a decision regarding the route north out of Charlotte, North Carolina. Since we service all the major ports along the eastern seaboard, we've decided to use our existing main line rights of way. We'll use Charlotte to Washington, D.C. We'll build a transfer facility at Greensboro, North Carolina to move freight onto the north-south line from the Norfolk docks. Basically we'll copy the inland port concept already in construction in South Carolina.

"Then we'll run north from Danville, Virginia to the east of D.C. We don't operate north of D.C., so since we don't own a right of way, we'll follow I-495 east around D.C. to I-95 north and build a short spur to the docks at Baltimore. From Baltimore, we'll run to the docks in New Jersey on the west side of the Hudson River.

"Now, let's look at the revised numbers. The spurs will be costly, but the returns will more than pay off the construction cost." Hew and Sam could see their profits rising. "As far as progress goes, we're on track." Everyone laughed at his pun and he continued. "We'll finish the South Carolina route early. We are ahead with the production of the rolling stock too. We've added solar panels to the tops of all units. Think about unveiling the South Carolina line first as a test, but that's a discussion for a future meeting."

Alexis was next. She first announced the conceptual plans for a big reveal once the South Carolina unit was operational. "We're thinking we should unveil the operation on Christmas Day just like they did with The Best Friend of Charleston. December 25, 2030 would be a good date. Two hundred years to the day would be significant."

"We're going to open long before that, Alexis," said Hew. "Think positively."

She next reported that she had hired a spokesperson to handle the media. That kept Alexis out of the spotlight and hot seat. Sharon, the new spokesperson, was an extremely talented Black woman and had a knack for marketing. She was three quarters of the way through earning a Ph.D. in human resources management and was constantly answering questions from local, national, and international inquirers.

The hungry twenty-four-hour news cycle media was making noises and speculating about how the elevated track would go through Washington. "They're thinking passenger service and want to know how we propose to get through the tunnels into Union Station. We're responding to Freedom of Information Act requests every week."

Jason offered an opinion. "I think it's time for a cryptic news release. I think something like The Southern Railway Company announced today that the existing intermodal line from New Orleans to DC is being upgraded for high speed service on a new elevated platform—don't use the word 'track.' Play up the new passenger service. The government will advertise the continuing Crescent service so that should play well. The passenger group has been told about SCMAGLEV, but Homeland Security had to put the fear of God into the them to keep their media team muzzled about the details."

"Why is Homeland Security involved with passenger service?"

"Troop movement in a time of national crisis, that's why. There will be a connecting track in Alexandria south of D.C.'s Union Station to receive and discharge the newly designed passenger cars to the elevated high-speed line. Passengers won't need to leave their seats."

Alexis nodded. "We'll get it out. That should give the media something to chew on for a while. If necessary, Sharon can point out that our new elevated double stacked high speed intermodal traffic can't fit through the D.C. tunnels."

Jason added, "That should be obvious because those tunnels are being upgraded now and won't be tall enough for the elevated line. Besides, they should have already figured out that the southern tunnel from Union Station under First Street is near too many important buildings on Capitol Hill, so any change to that would disrupt the entire city. Our competitor's freight tunnel under Fifteenth Street is too low for this too, and we don't want to involve them at this point. We'll need to build a new station in Alexandria, though, to handle the passengers who want to leave there."

"Speaking of Capitol Hill, I've heard rumors that you might be called before a congressional hearing, Sam," said Hew.

"Don't worry. Bring 'em on. I'm already a member of the TPB Freight subcommittee working on the National Capitol Region Freight Plan. I won't act contrite like those Wall Street bankers did after the recession, though. I know most of these guys. This project is completely legal anyway. I'll show those blowhard congressional staffers. They're doing all the work anyway, but they don't have a clue. I'll damn them with faint praise at every meeting."

"No, you won't. You'd get cited for contempt. Remember, it's still their money. If anyone goes before a hearing it'll need to be Edward Hardy."

"Maybe you're right. But I still don't like those people."

"I'm getting requests from the trucking lobby and the railroad engineer's union."

"Stall 'em. The truckers will still run short hauls with the trailers after we unload at the transfer facilities. They've got to face facts. The highway system simply can't handle more trucks but Americans are demanding faster deliveries and we're building the answer. The long distance train engineers will go the way of the brakemen and cabooses on these long haul routes. Our competitors will fight that battle with the unions.

"We'll be up and running before the engineers know what hit them. That means, Jason and Alexis, I hate to burst your bubble, but we'll unveil the entire line at one time. South Carolina won't be the first this time. This isn't 1830 and this isn't the Best Friend of Charleston."

"By the way, Sam, whatever happened to those cabooses? I loved to watch them as a kid."

"Progress happened. The word caboose comes from the Dutch language for cabin, or more specifically, cooking cabin. It was an apartment and office on wheels for the train crew. They warmed themselves, worked, ate, and slept there.

"Then, Westinghouse invented the air brakes so the brakeman that used to walk along the tops of the freight cars to set the hand brakes became redundant. All the routing paperwork for each freight car was kept and managed in the caboose, and computers replaced and centralized all that paperwork.

"Those cabooses were dangerous too. Most of the personnel accidents in railroading happened in the caboose by men getting jostled around or falling out of the cupolas. It took an executive order by the president of the U.S., but we finally got rid of the caboose and most of the jobs that they housed. We saved millions."

When it was time to talk about new business, Sam reported that he had managed a deal with the South Carolina State Ports Authority. In exchange for all the property on the east side of the Cooper River in downtown Charleston, he would fund the state's portion of the required new construction on state property at the new port terminal and at the inland port.

"I already own about fifteen acres of that parcel anyway. The feds are paying for the construction, but not the additional land. The state legislature would not agree to just giving the land away. I thought the governor was going to kiss me. It was the easiest negotiation I ever had. The city has been wanting to get their hands on that property for years, but I beat them to it, and Hew, I want you to develop it."

"Thanks. I'll have my team research it. I wish I had known that when I was last in Charleston, but now I have an excuse to go back on your dime. We normally only develop land we own. I thought the feds were paying."

"I can always sell it to you. They are for most of it, but there are several parcels of land the state will need to either buy or take by eminent domain. Then I will get the land and also the swap for everything else."

"I'll consider buying your land too. Eminent domain makes enemies in a state like South Carolina—particularly in the Upstate where they hate government anyway."

"If there's nothing else, I move we adjourn."

"*Sine die* as they say in the South Carolina State House."

"No, Sam. That's a joke. It means without a future date. Our next date is set for the fifteenth of next month—as always,—but you're witty. You can always skip the next meeting.

"Actually, I have forgotten to tell you that Edward has gotten wind of a hearing on Capitol Hill about all of this. He is demanding that you go away immediately. Take Hilde and don't tell anyone where you are going."

"Now why in hell would we do that?"

"Because when the subpoenas go out, we all need to honestly say that we don't know where you are."

"Hmmm. My doctor has already told me to take some time away. By the way, I've heard from Chuck at Clemson. The early studies using the kudzu I sent has been wildly successful. Hew, you and Johann need to quickly get the new research and production facility up and running. This thing is a go and the Japanese are happy with the weight reduction. They want you to build a production plant over there. We'll make billions, Hew. Billions."

"Then leave now, Sam. You can follow it on the news."

On the way out, Bubba Hu invited Hew and Alexis for dinner. They looked at each other, smiled, and accepted as graciously as they could. As they walked away, Hew whispered, "There's no kudzu anywhere on this farm so don't worry."

⁂

THE CONGRESSIONAL HEARINGS BEGAN A MONTH later. Edward was the only person called. He had made himself known as an expert to draw interest away from the others. No one knew who actually owned the construction company but they were really after Sam. They didn't care about engineering and construction beyond the financial aspects.

For three days, Edward answered and avoided their questions. He bombarded them with charts, graphs, and spreadsheets showing nothing out of the ordinary. He spent hours on the history of the previous congressional approvals going line by line through tedious legal jargon, feeding them their own work. At times, things got really heated, but his years of courtroom experience had trained him to keep his composure.

Alexis and Sharon sat in the back row and took notes. Alexis's body guard sat behind her and noticed a person of interest across the aisle. She took out her Israeli-supplied compact and as she looked at her nose, she snapped a few high resolution pictures. During the break, she transferred them to her phone and emailed them to her handlers. During the next break, she got her answer and she immediately texted Pink.

They met in the hotel bar. She had already been replaced by another woman as Alexis's guard. This wasn't unusual, but it irritated Alexis.

Pink asked, "Your guys really think he's a Russian spy?"

"I have positive identification. He's Yuri Agapov—former KGB. He not only is a spy, but he supplies weapons and information to anyone who'll pay him. We know he supplies weapons and bombs to Hamas. He's responsible for the murder of our people. Unfortunately, he has diplomatic immunity."

"Who's the guy he's with? He looks familiar."

"He should. We've just discovered that he's a union organizer. He's just began last week as a bartender on the construction platform. His background didn't show his union ties but one of our guys recognized him from another job."

"Damn, I've had a few drinks with him. Nice but chatty guy. I think he just slipped something black to the Russian."

"It looked like a flash drive."

"You need to leave this with me. We can't have an international incident on our hands. We're at a critical stage."

She nodded.

Pink left her at the bar but didn't guess that Ruth already had her orders to kill Yuri. While he got busy on his computer with the personnel folks getting the union guy removed from the construction crew, she went to her room and put on her disguise. One of her team had been tracking Yuri while she met with Pink and texted her that he was at the bar in a nearby hotel doing shots of vodka.

She walked into the bar and sat near him. It didn't take him long to proposition her. She agreed but told him that she would be in charge. He was delighted.

Once in his hotel room, she quickly went to work. She led him to the bed and ordered him to remove everything except his shorts and he drunkenly complied. She put on a pair of black rubber gloves and he laughed. Whispering into his ear, she loosely tied his hands behind his back with a soft cotton scarf and roughly pushed him onto the bed on his back. He was loving it. She then used another soft cotton scarf to tie his legs to the bed, careful to not leave restraint marks.

She noticed he was starting to become aroused. She took a syringe with an infant needle out of her bag and laid it on the night stand telling him not to worry because it would change the experience beyond his wildest imagination. She took a small vial out of her bag and filled the syringe. His eyes went wide as she approached his face but he was too drunk to react quickly. Sitting on his chest, she carefully inserted the needle just inside his right nostril in his dark nose hair and depressed the plunger. His heart stopped almost immediately.

She started looking for the computer flash drive. It was in the pocket of his jacket. She found his cell phone and using his facial recognition, she looked through it and determined that he hadn't transmitted any information. He didn't have a tablet or computer.

Satisfied that she had all the files, she went back to the body, removed the restraints and using her phone as a flashlight, examined his nose. She spotted a small blood mark. She took a tissue from the box on the night stand, dampened it in the bathroom, and carefully inserted it into his nostril. She inserted the damp tissue on the end of a ball point pen to remove the small blood point and was satisfied that no one would ever notice the puncture among the hair. Only a brilliant forensic pathologist would discover anything except fibers from a common tissue and she hoped his already red blotchy bulbous nostrils would help to cover any other minor irregularities. Her team had decided to use any body orifice that was handy. They tried to never use the skin surface because needle marks were easily found there. They urged her to use an orifice that wasn't commonly examined, but the hairy nostril seems to be the easiest in this case.

She broke up the syringe and wrapped it all in the tissue which she flushed down the toilet. The beauty of the poison was that, at first, it had probably been a failure. It was not stable. They had discovered, however, that if it could be administered extremely quickly, it killed instantly.

The writing on the vial was Chinese. The Chinese had apparently sold it off to the unsuspecting Arabs after discarding it, but the Israeli agents had discovered crates of it following a raid on a suspected Hamas hideout. The Israeli lab tested it but found that it dissipated very quickly before it could be fully analyzed. Not knowing exactly what it was, they tested it on mice and found that the rodents died within minutes. The dissections showed nothing except a heart stoppage. Ruth left Yuri looking exactly like a drunken obese heart attack victim. She went back to her hotel, packed up and was on the next flight from Dulles to Vancouver and from there, home to Tel Aviv.

In Tel Aviv, they found photographs of the construction equipment on the flash drive but nothing that any journalist with a telephoto lens couldn't have gotten. In Washington, the death of a Russian diplomat didn't even make the news. In Moscow, the Kremlin was outraged but their own doctors could find no evidence beyond a common heart attack.

26
DISASTER

Alexis invited Rosalyn and Sarah, her old boss, to have lunch with her at the club. As hostess, she arrived early and sat in the lobby until her guests arrived. She picked through her social media feed until they arrived. As they walked past the bar, something caught Sarah's eye on the TV monitor. "Wait. Could you turn that up, please?"

The bartender obliged. There was a live report from the site of the Academy's construction site. "Oh my God, Alexis!" said Sarah. "That's our school. It looks like something collapsed!"

"I'd better call Hew immediately." Alexis stepped out onto the terrace since phone calls were not allowed inside the club. She came back inside. "He's not answering. I left him practicing his music on the organ which means he probably has his ringer off. I've told him repeatedly to put his cell phone on the music desk, but he refuses. He hates interruptions of any kind. I called our nanny, Marta. She'll go get him to call me."

"Let's get a bottle of Pino Grigio and sit here so we can watch the TV. We can just have lunch at the table here. Apparently it just happened. The first responders are on scene, but the TV bobble heads are just now setting up."

"Why do you call them that? Some of them are cute."

"I know, but have you ever noticed that as soon as the red light comes on and they're live, their heads shake up and down?"

"Ah, yes. I get it."

The news helicopters were circling overhead and they were reporting that it looked like a sudden collapse of the geodesic dome in the "great room." The space joined the technical school and the arts school and was used as the food court. It was setup as a way of combining the students to support collegiality.

Board chairman Kleindic had insisted on a large dome. Alexis had argued for a large clearstory because it would be more energy efficient. Kliendic won, of course. The space was hot as hell and the current construction for the new computer facilities was also adding a massive amount of air conditioning for both the new lab equipment and the great room. Alexis's phone rang. She walked back outside. "Go turn on the TV. The Academy dome has collapsed!"

Hew ran into the library and turned on the 100-inch Sony OLED TV. One of his foundations had funded the new labs. He didn't want to get caught up in law suits and worried that the new cooling units on the roof might somehow be seen as the cause of the collapse.

The three women ate their lunch in absolute silence until Sarah finally spoke. "God help them, but I'm certainly glad I'm not still in charge there. There's going to be hell to pay for somebody."

THE NEWS CONTINUED WITHOUT INTERRUPTION ALL afternoon—except for the commercial breaks, of course. Alexis arrived home after her portion of three bottles of wine to find Hew slumped in his recliner watching the news. "I hope you didn't drive yourself home."

"No. Charlie picked us up. Rosilyn walked home. Pink and Victor will get my car later."

"They should have driven you."

"I didn't want to bother them for such a short trip."

"The TV news anchors have decided absent of any confirmation that the extra weight had caused the problem. They're already looking for someone to blame. There are eight known fatalities including Kleindic, who was there inspecting the nearly finished work. Five of the dead were part of the cleaning crew frantically trying to get the room ready for the news conference. Two were the TV newswoman and her camera man. Harry Kleindic had scheduled an onsite news conference at noon to show off his accomplishment."

"Listen carefully. There's something you need to know about the funding of the new labs." He explained in detail.

"Okay, well, we'd better get out front on this before they put two and two together and come up with five."

"I've been on the phone with Edward all afternoon. He wants us to wait until he can know more. Sit tight for the moment."

⚜

THE SEARCH AND RESCUE CONTINUED AROUND the clock for two days until the chief of police finally announced that they had ceased the rescue portion and were now focusing on a recovery search for more bodies. They believed all personnel were now accounted for. The coroner had confirmed that eight people were dead. Most of the victims were Hispanic, which had sparked cries of racism. The federal government had stepped in to review those complaints and would also review the minority hiring process. There were questions about untrained and undocumented workers.

"Edward says this is going to explode like a highly infectious virus. There will be hell to pay and he thinks it will ultimately land at the feet of the state. As soon as the engineers issue their new reports and the forensic engineers determine the cause of the collapse, they'll release the original contract, but we didn't have any part in the design or construction. We only wrote a check. He wants to wait. He has a team at Bishop Hardy working on finding the paper trail for the design through the process of discovery."

"How long will that take?"

"Could be months or even years. A judge—or judges—since this is now also federal—may need to issue directives if the parties aren't cooperating. Edward wants us to try to forget about it for a while and let our lawyers collect the facts. He said we should go on to England and avoid the press coverage. They've already homed in on the Swan Bay Trust."

"Do they know who or where Swan Bay is?"

"No way. They're scouring the coast of Georgia and all the lakes and

226

ponds in the state. There haven't been many swans on the James River since the 18th century. Almost the entire population of swans ended up on people's dinner table."

27
ENGLAND

Every few years, the choir of the Cathedral of St. Philip traveled to England to be the choir in residence at one of the cathedrals while the resident cathedral choirs of men and boys were on summer holiday. Since Hew was the interim organist at St. Luke's, he worked out an invitation for the St. Luke's choir to join the trip.

As the plan developed, he added the bell ringers for both churches and Grace Church Cathedral, Charleston. The St. Luke's group would go to Truro Cathedral for the first week, and the St. Philip's group would go to Ely Cathedral. The ringers had their own schedules.

Hew was salivating at the thoughts of playing the fine historic Willis organ at Truro. They would meet on the campus of Oxford University for the second week. Hew had purchased a small flat in Oxford the summer of the year he and Alexis had met. They used it for a month every summer, but after the twins were born, they purchased the flat next door and incorporated both flats into one four-bedroom two-bath unit. The Eberhart folks had done a fine job with the renovations. The exterior was repaired but unchanged. The interior was changed to English contemporary country casual. Alexis had seen it on a tour of the private apartments of Blenheim Palace and she wanted colorful stuffed furniture and fabrics in this place. She said it would help brighten all those grey cold days. Hew didn't really like it. He reminded her they were usually only there in June, but he agreed to compromise. If it made her happy, he could endure almost anything for a few weeks each year.

Hew and Alexis included her parents on the trip. They needed three security details. John needed his own detail. Charlie managed to find two young highly trained women who appreciated classical music to cover John. The grandparents would have quality alone time with their grandchildren. Hew and Alexis would need babysitters while they were down in Truro, and her parents jumped at the chance to have the grandchildren to themselves.

The family flew over a week early to make sure everything was in order for the group. Alexis worked her connections with the management at Delta Air Lines and secured a non-stop chartered plane at a great rate for everyone else.

Hew had arranged for his old friend, Colin St. John-Smith, now organist-choir master at Christ Church, to spend the month teaching young John the mysteries of English cathedral music. The Oxford Society of Change Ringers took John to their bell practices in the evenings, so he was in heaven.

Hew's phone rang. Sam Spencer was calling. "Hew, I'm worried. Actually, I'm terrified. My detail thinks I'm being followed. We need to meet and not at Swan Bay or at my place."

"Sam, I'm in Oxford—as in England, not Georgia. Let's call the next progress meeting early and fly everyone over to Cologne. The board wants an update anyway and this will fit nicely. Will this coming Friday work? The board will be meeting then and can add us to the agenda. I'm already scheduled to fly over on Thursday night."

"Works for me. Anyone who can't make it can join us by video conference. I'll go on to Switzerland for a few months too."

Sam's concerns turned out to be an over-zealous reporter rather than anything sinister, but the meeting with Eberhart was very productive. The board wanted a financial interest in the project and Sam and Hew agreed to let the money guys look into it.

The next week, Hew and Alexis's security detail drove them in one of the armored black Mercedes vans to join the St. Luke's folks in Truro. John was already hard at work with his music. "I'm sorry Louise didn't make the trip, but I'm glad she can fill in for me at St. Luke's. Lewis arrives next month so I'll be free when we return."

"I know, but Louise has a sick mother to tend to. She couldn't have left her."

Truro is an ancient city in Cornwall that dates from at least the twelfth century. It's located upstream along two rivers that converge and empty into the English Channel. Hew and Alexis had been invited to stay with a member of the cathedral chapter in her elegant Georgian town house on Lemon St. It was a short walk through the shopping district to the cathedral.

Hew snuggled up beside Alexis in bed. "You know, this is the first real alone time we've had in years," he whispered.

"Forget it, buster. We're not alone in this house either."

The thirteenth-century parish church of St. Mary had been re-built several times. The Diocese of Truro was formed in 1876 and the foundations for the new cathedral were laid in 1880. The main tower and spire were completed in 1904 and the western towers were completed in 1910, which was the effective completion of the building.

The Willis organ of four manuals and forty-five speaking stops was completed in 1887 with the completion of the quire and transepts, but before the nave was built. A smaller organ from 1750 in St. Mary's aisle and an even smaller chamber organ accompany it.

Hew's interest lay completely with the Willis. Known as the Father Willis Organ, it is widely recognized internationally as one of Willis's finest achievements. In addition to the other stops, it has two tierce mixtures, interesting gedackts, and a small but colorful pedal division. The instrument is tonally intact just as Willis voiced it. It's remarkable that Willis voiced it for a not-yet-completed building, but when the nave was completed, no changes were necessary to the organ. The only major change occurred in 1963 when the console was moved to the south side into a new purpose-built gallery. Now, the organist can clearly hear the instrument while being in closer contact to the choir.

Hew had practiced on his Hauptwerk organ in his music room using the Hereford Cathedral sampleset. Hereford's organ is also a Willis, and it is larger, but nothing prepared him for the glorious sound of the real thing in its own acoustic space. Alexis had to drag him away after Evensong every day. He just couldn't get enough.

"This Edwardian English music was written for this type of acoustical space. Too many American organs in dry acoustical rooms just can't make this music sing," he told Alexis.

"I think the St. Luke's and St. Philip's organs do just fine. And we have good heating and air conditioning systems."

"I agree, but this *is* something special. I must say, though, the choir sounded magnificent in this room. It took a day to get used to the reverberation, but it turned out quite well."

"We think those first service mistakes were just due to jet lag."

"That'll work. Let's go with that. We didn't record that one anyway."

Hew and the ringers managed to get to the Tuesday night ringing practice in the cathedral and were warmly welcomed. Truro ringers call the bells in the opposite direction than Atlanta so it took the visitors a few pulls to get it right. Truro has twelve bells with two semitones just like St. Philip's, but the weights are a little different. The Truro bells are heavier, but that didn't keep the Atlanta band from having a go with the ropes. The two extra semitones meant they could ring all twelve, or the lighter front ten bells, or the heavier back ten, or the light eight, or the heaver back eight, or four various rings of six. Hew rang several touches including a touch of his favorite, Stedman. He needed a "minder" to stand behind him for the touch of Stedman Cinques to keep him straight, but when he finished the touch, he was confident that he could have rung a quarter peal of it if he could have stayed another week.

Hew bought the rounds in the pub while they laughed at the backwards call changes. "You Yanks had a Yorkshireman for a teacher. It's no wonder you ring the wrong way." That got more laughs. Hew had a Macallan instead of beer. He just couldn't stand beer.

"JOHN, WHO TAUGHT YOU TO DO that?" asked Colin.

When John answered that his father had, Colin laughed. "I should have known. I taught it to *him*. Your ability to word paint that hymn was beautiful. Now we'll start on the Psalms. Let's go to the Buttery and you can read Psalm One while I have a pint. Then you can explain it to me and tell me how you would register it on this organ."

"The first three verses are kinda joyful, but verse four turns kinda mean. Then verse six is a little of both."

"Excellent. Let's go back and pull a few stops and find the best sound to express these words."

"May I have a dish of chocolate ice cream first?"

"Absolutely. I'll have another pint. We've earned it." Colin paused. "I've got to start working on your diction and elocution immediately. It's not really too bad, but your vowels are too American for our choirs. I've heard some of your Southern choirs sing. Some of them say Go-wad for God and Law-ward for Lord. A double w? Two syllables? God. I'll have none of that. I'll have you singing and speaking proper English before the summer is over. I'll also teach you to roll your R's properly. When your dad first arrived, he had a slight Spanish inflection in his voice, but he soon overcame it." Colin didn't know that Hew's girlfriend had been a languages major and had taught Hew to overcome the Spanish sounds—among a few other things.

❧

THE ST. PHILIP'S FOLKS TOOK TWO chartered busses from the airport up the M11 towards Ely. They stopped for a brief visit in the town of Grantchester just south of Cambridge to visit the scene of the highly acclaimed—at least among American Anglophiles—Public Broadcasting Service's replay of the English TV series of the same name. The author of the books upon which the show was based is the son of a former Archbishop of Canterbury. Having grown up in a succession of vicarages, he knew the ethos very well. The main character is the local vicar who also joins forces with the local police detective to solve crimes.

After touring the church and small village looking for clues from scenes in the series, someone spied the footpath that led to the river where the vicar in the show took long walks with his beloved black Labrador, Dickens. Several pleaded with the driver to go through Cambridge, but he resisted. The traffic in town at that time of day was a nightmare.

Ely Cathedral took them by surprise even though they had all seen pictures during their briefing presentation. They craned their necks to get a view of the octagon as the buses rolled through the flat farmland known as the Fens. Once they settled into their rooms, they walked through the town for the first rehearsal. The cathedral sub-organist met them and gave them a brief history as they walked.

"The cathedral site dates to about 673 when St. Etheldreda founded an abbey here. The present building dates from 1083, but one stone which dates to the 8th century remains at the base of an old stone cross. The building was restored in 2000."

They weren't really prepared for the beauty. The sub-organist continued, "The octagonal lantern at the crossing is the main feature. It dates from after the collapse of the central tower in 1322. It's seventy-four feet wide and one hundred-forty-two feet high inside with large stained glass windows all around. The painted ceilings in the nave are stunning."

Several of the choir boys and men tried to lie on the floor of the center aisle to see it. They tried to scoot down the floor on their backs to follow the scenes of the life of Jesus, but the vergers stopped them. There were too many tourists and they couldn't have everybody trying that.

The crafty guys stopped and apologized, but went back in before practice the next morning before the tours started. When the full moon rose that evening over the flat fens, they were treated to the sight of the orange moon seeming to sit on top of the crossing lantern and shortly after, it seemed to rest on top of the western tower. It was a sight none of them would ever forget.

Everyone had the same positive opinion of the glorious Lady Chapel and sang Morning Prayer in it. It has a fine vaulted ceiling, but the reredos has a modern statue of Mary in a modern blue dress with long flowing gilded hair. They laughed at the idea of a blonde Mary. None of them had ever seen a natural blonde Israeli Jewish woman. Her arms are upraised causing the Americans to dub her "Touchdown Mary" because she looked like an American football referee after someone had scored.

Rob loved the 1850 Hill and Son Edwardian style organ. After having been restored by Harrison and Harrison in 2001, it now has about seventy stops across four manuals and pedal. He not only loved the tonal color and power, he appreciated Harrison's stop layout on the console. It made finding the stop knobs easier for visiting organists.

The groups finally came together at Oxford.

"How was Ely, Roger?"

"Hew, I've never really admitted this to anyone, but I think I had a life-changing experience. I've never really been sure about some of this theological stuff but, as we were walking over to the cathedral that first afternoon, the clouds parted and the entire west front suddenly lit up with the most glorious color I've ever seen. I almost went down on my knees right there on the sidewalk."

"I know the feeling, Roger. It happened to me in the chapel of my school in Bogota. It happened again while we were visiting York. We were walking through the streets of the Shambles on a sunny summer Sunday afternoon. I was still fuming because the tower captain at York Minster wouldn't allow me even to enter the ringing room. I hadn't even asked to ring—I just wanted to see it.

"Suddenly, I looked up and the whole west front exploded with the most glorious golden light I've ever seen on an exterior. The bells began ringing for Evensong and I literally ran up the street to the open door. I've seen the same thing at Notre Dame in Paris. A friend of mine had the same experience there and he did go down onto his knees weeping. It's really an epiphany, in my opinion. Those old medieval folks really knew what they were doing."

The St. Luke's choir began the week by singing at New College and the St. Philip's choir sang in the cathedral. The Oxford cathedral is un-usual. Built in the Romanesque style in the twelfth century, the nave was pulled down centuries ago, leaving the choir, side chapels, and sanctuary intact. It is both the college chapel and the cathedral, and it's the small-est cathedral in England. Worshippers now enter directly into the choir. The organ loft is directly over the entrance and houses a fine four-man-ual Rieger instrument in the 1680 Father Smith case. Hew thought the dimmable uplighting on the curves of the nave arches and vaulting was splendid and much more subtle than hanging fixtures would have been.

New College is a pleasant, magical place. Both choirs and all the ringers stayed in modern accommodations at New College in en-suite rooms. They ate gourmet meals in the New College medieval hall. It's the oldest hall in Oxford. Being a Southerner to the core, as a joke, one of the men asked the waiter for a mint julep, assuming he had no idea what it was. Two of the other guys chimed in and asked for one, too. The waiter returned with a large sterling silver tankard and three silver cups.

When he poured the drinks, they were astonished. He told them that a man from Georgetown, South Carolina, during his mid-nineteenth century stay, was longing for his favorite libation. He gifted the college with the tankard, the recipe, and an endowment to insure that the mint juleps would always be available in the hall. Every June first since then, the scholars are treated to Mr. Trapper's fine Southern drink. They agreed that next to Hew's juleps, they were the best they had ever had.

They were in awe of the 1386 chapel. The St. Luke's folks had never sung in a chapel like this. They mused about St. Luke's needing a chapel. The summer afternoon light coming through the windows was magical.

The reredos has row upon row of statues covering the entire wall. The 1969 Grant, Degens and Bradbeer three-manual organ built in the Organ Reform Movement style is located high up on the choir screen that separates the ante-chapel from the choir and sanctuary. A "V" shaped Positiv division case hangs from the gallery rail behind the organ bench, and the glass swell shades on the main case seem to explode with colorful reflections of the stained glass windows when they open or close.

Several choir members speculated whether this was intentional, because it's very unusual. They were informed that one of the older choir members had said at the time the organ was installed that the swell shades were sending railroad style color signals to the choir below to warn them of the upcoming *piano* verses in the Psalms. The current sub-organist laughed and explained that the organ case designers thought that highly visible wooden shades would be unsightly. The copper horizontal trumpet en chamade pipes project out immediately over the organist's head.

As most often happens, the organ was somewhat changed in the 1980s and again in a 2014 restoration, but Hew enjoyed the clear sounds. Everyone enjoyed the beautiful immaculate peaceful college gardens.

THE RINGERS HAD A WEEK OF intense practice with the Oxford Society ringers. Many of the ringers gained quite a bit of knowledge and confidence. They were treated to tours of the local towers by the Oxford Society members. The most unusual tower was at Merton College Chapel.

This chapel is said to be the oldest college chapel in the world. The bells are famous for being the world's oldest complete ring of eight bells, cast in 1680. The tenor bell of the eight bell ring weighed 25-1-10 in English hundred weight or a little over 2,800 pounds in modern weight, and is tuned to Eb. The largest bell at St. Philip's tower weighs 2,500 pounds so Charlie was comfortable with the slightly larger bell. Eddie even gave it a pull.

In 1680, Christopher Hodson, the London bellfounder, also cast the six-and-one-quarter-ton bell called Great Tom, which hangs in the 1682 Tom Tower, designed by Sir Christopher Wren, at Christ Church College. The ringers visited the huge bell in the afternoon. Going into these towers was like stepping back in time. Very little had changed since they were built.

The Merton Chapel ringing room is in the medieval crossing tower. Access to the ringing room was scary for some of the group. The ringers climbed a dark stone spiral stair built into the wall of the transept, walked through the lead line gutter behind the roof parapet, entered the central tower, climbed through ancient timbers and arrived onto a very dark ledge that ran around the inside of the tower.

There was one small window and a minimum of electric lights. If they dared to look down, they were aghast to see the nave floor far below. They could barely see the people standing on the other side of the space. The whitewashed render on the stone walls helped them to see the other side once their eyes had adjusted to the darkness.

The low ornate railing in front of the narrow ledge had quatrefoils on top of vertical pickets. Someone had added two rows of horizontal white painted iron rails held up by a few slim vertical posts attached above the old rail, but it was still daunting to the Atlanta folks.

"Don't look down," said one of the Society members. "If you miss your rope, don't reach out to try and grab it. Just let it come back to you."

Hew loved the ornate medieval wood trusses and ceiling. There were carved stone-winged angel brackets at the bottom of the wooden fan vaulting ribs that he could touch. The wall at the window opening was so thick that four people could stand in line beside it. He asked, "Am I looking at the organ case down there? I had forgotten about that."

"Yes. That's the new one. The builders put a top on the case. The old organ didn't have a top so we tried to avoid looking at all the pipes sticking up. It was a good way of keeping us behind the rail. No one wanted to fall and spoil a tune during a service, but those spiked pinnacles on the new case still cause some folks to have second thoughts about ringing here."

A nervous chuckle drifted through the visitors. Hew decided to lighten the mood. "I've played both the old and new organs and the little choir organ in the chancel. This new one was built by the American builder, Dobson. The top on the case helps focus the sound down the nave rather than bouncing around up here. It works well. The transepts here function effectively as an ante-chapel/narthex, but the organ sits a few feet above the nave floor allowing the organist's mirror to reflect the liturgical action and the choir director over the heads of the congregation, and it keeps the mechanical parts above the ancient stone paving. There are also three video monitors mounted nicely above the music desk. The distance between the choir and the organ does take some getting used to, but there's a smaller instrument in the quire that's used to accompany the choir. Notice that there's no nave here."

His explanation did little to steady their nerves, but it helped redirect their minds and they started ringing. They soon settled down and enjoyed the sound of the old bells.

After the ringing, several members of the band climbed up the stairs to look at the bells. Hew was surprised to see that the bells were hung around the walls. The center of the bell frame was empty. In most bell towers, the tenor hangs in the center of the tower to balance the dynamic forces of the moving load on the walls. Apparently, the thickness of these walls absorbed the load just fine.

As they were leaving, one of the Atlanta women remarked, "I love these perfectly manicured lush green lawns. I don't even miss foundation plantings."

"Having the stone walkways against the buildings keeps the water run off away from the old foundations and helps to reduce rain water from wicking up into the walls. Foundation plants hold water against the stonework."

ON SATURDAY, THE SOCIETY ARRANGED AN outing day to ring in several of the towers in the Cotswold village churches.

The Oxford Society of Change Ringers is the oldest extant territorial ringing society in the World. They split into teams and were driven in vans by local ringers. Each band started at a different tower to avoid having a crowd in one tower. Ringers call this type event by the term, tower grabbing.

It took at least thirty minutes to navigate the small hedge-rowed narrow country lanes. They were to stay at each tower for about an hour before moving on. The day's plan included two towers in the morning, a group lunch at a centrally located village pub in Chipping Campden known to English foodies as the place to eat, and then two towers in the afternoon.

Hew, John, Charlie, and Eddie were in the same van, and as they approached their first tower, John exclaimed, "Ew. Gross. Something stinks." Eddie and John began to gag.

The van driver was surprised too. It had been misting rain all night, and being local, he realized exactly what the smell was. "Apparently there's been a big communication breakdown. Someone must have forgotten to tell the church wardens about the ringing today. They've let the sheep graze in the churchyard all week and we're all smelling the wet dung and urine. I'm terrible sorry. The tower captain will catch hell for this from my group."

Trying to be polite, one of the Atlanta ladies commented, "It is a bit overwhelming."

"Really, Joyce. I'd say it's godawful, but maybe it'll be better once we get inside."

They ran for the door of the tower trying desperately to escape the smell and the drizzling rain. Hew stopped to look at the stone-lined gutter around the church. The ground was higher than the floor level. The van driver told him that over the centuries, the extra dirt from the grave digging had caused the ground level to rise. He was reminded of the conversation about the Swan Bay potagerie. The caskets had replaced the earth so the grave diggers had just spread the remaining soil out in the graveyard. Sometimes, an observant person could spot small bone fragments in the grass from earlier decomposed bodies.

The gutter was necessary to keep the damp out of the walls. Inside the small closed space of the tower, the smell was concentrated and was actually worse. One of the old ringers casually commented, "She's a bit sharp this morning, but you'll get used to it."

Sharp wasn't the word. They tried breathing through their mouths. They lasted thirty-five minutes before they bolted for the van. As they hastily said their goodbyes, one of the local ladies whispered to Hew, "We're real sorry about this. The rain took us by surprise. Normally, it's nothing like this, but see that large manor house over the field? The lord of the manor owns this church and he hates the bellringers. I'll bet he did this on purpose."

"Take us back to Oxford, Ewan. Even with the windows down its awful."

"I think that's the best idea. I'll call the other drivers and warn them. No need for the others to go there. I'll try to find a substitute tower, and I'll call your second stop to let them know you're not coming."

As they walked into the front room, Alexis's mother yelled,"P-U! Hew! Stop. Go back out and hose yourselves off in the garden. I'll get towels while you two strip off those nasty clothes. Did you fall into a wet dung heap? You smell worse than skunks."

While they showered and dressed, she put two peppermint candies into a pot of water and melted them on the stove. When they came down she told them to use the small swabs and swab some of the warm liquid into their nostrils to clear out the smell. It worked, and they joined the whole group for lunch at the pub with a ringing story they'd be telling for years.

After lunch, Hew's group rang at two more towers. The plan was to end the day at a tower in a village near Oxford to ring for a wedding. Charlotte, one of the Oxford ringers, was driving the van. Hew was in the front beside her.

Her phone rang. It was her husband, the vicar of the church where they were heading. "Better answer that for me, Hew. That's Paul's ring-tone and he only calls if there is a problem."

"Charlotte's phone. Hew Ramsay speaking."

"Oh, Hew. Good. I was hoping you were with her. I need you desperately if you don't mind."

"What's up, Paul?"

"The substitute organist for this wedding hasn't shown up yet. If he doesn't get here, would you fill in? Charlotte says you're a fine musician."

Flattery will win every time, thought Hew. "Paul, I don't have any music with me. What has the bride picked?"

"The only thing she asked for is the hymn following the procession. It will be *All things bright and beautiful*. She wants the first tune."

"The only tune I know is "Royal Oak" but if it's in your hymnal I can play it. I'll just improvise everything else."

"Oh, thank you, Hew. You're a lifesaver and I know the bride will love it."

Hew was the first one up the narrow spiral stair. He stopped off at the choir loft while the others climbed on up to the ringing room. The stairwell was steep and dark and the treads were severely worn. It was so narrow that the only handrail was an old dirty rope attached at various points along the climb.

He looked out across the balcony rail into a beautiful almost unchanged fifteenth century church. Unfortunately he didn't have time to study the beauty before him. As he approached the organ console, he noticed that seven of the draw knobs were missing their ivory name disks.

He sat on the bench—the Brits call it an organ stool—and he looked for the switch. He pulled out his phone, turned on the flashlight—the Brits call it a torch—and began to look under the keyboards. He got a whiff of an unpleasant smell. A small startled field mouse ran out from under the pedal board. He found the button and the organ wheezed to life.

He noticed that the name plate said "Willis" and the remaining stops seemed to be in a similar layout to the other Willises he had played. The reeds were at the top and the quieter stops were at the bottom. This was a two-manual instrument so he assumed that the missing knob names were those most frequently used.

Charlotte had told him that the lady who played was 85 years old and had been the organist there for seventy years. Hew wondered how she still climbed those stairs.

The church was full and he was a bit late so he closed the swell shades just in case and pulled the bottom nameless stop hoping it would be a quiet string—probably an 8′ salicional. He was correct and was rewarded with quiet beautiful string like sounds singing out as he began his improvisation on the hymn tune.

He guessed that the next missing knob was an 8′ Vox Angelica. He was right again. He continued increasing stops as he built up for the mother's entrance. He was impressed with the wealth of stops and the sound was pure unchanged Willis.

Charlotte had agreed to help him with the beginning processions and she signaled that the mothers were ready. He added the three-rank mixture. He realized immediately that it was out of tune and several pipes didn't play, but he was committed. He took the mixture off for the wedding attendants.

Charlotte signaled that the bride was at the door. He grabbed the unknown stop knobs on the great manual and added the 8′ trumpet. Surprisingly, it was in tune. He pulled the 16′ bourdon on the pedal division to add a little bass and got nothing except a few squeaks as several more field mice scurried out into the choir loft.

Charlotte left for the ringing room and Hew, with the bride and her father now safely standing in front of the vicar, introduced the correct hymn. For the recessional, he pulled out all the stops and improvised on the tune "Old Hundredth."

He then climbed up to the ringing room to join the band of ringers. He was surprised to see a small open trap door in the center of the ringing room floor. He peered down and saw the floor of the narthex below with the people streaming out. The clock room below had a matching open trap door. The ringing room was crowded with locals and visitors so he decided that he had done his part. After the ringing ended, one of the locals told him that the men drew straws to be the lucky one able to look through the floor and peer down the bride's cleavage to signal the ringers to start.

At the bottom of the stairs, the vicar was waiting to thank him. He handed Hew an envelope marked "Organist" containing fifty pounds. "Thank you, Paul, but that's not necessary. I'm just glad I was available. Add that money to an organ restoration fund, and by the way, you need to get an exterminator in to clear out those mice."

"That's very generous of you. I'll try to get rid of those pesky mice, but out here in the country, they are rather common, you know. We don't actually have an organ restoration fund, though."

"You do now. Here's my card. Those mice will chew on the leather to build their nest and cause wind leaks. They've also been known to chew on the lead pipes because the lead is sweet and they can also ruin the wiring.

"Send me a quote from your organ builder and I'll pay for a restoration. This is a beautiful instrument and must be restored. Charlotte told me that your organist is 85. Forgive me for being blunt, but we both know that you'll be looking for a replacement soon and you'll never get anyone competent with the organ in its current state."

"I had no idea that it was so bad. Miss Johnson always seems to make it work. I haven't been up there in years. We have our quinquennial report coming up next year. I'll write the diocesan organ consultant and ask him to open a faculty."

"What?"

"You Americans don't have all that bureaucracy do you? The report happens every five years for the parishes of the Church of England. Inspectors go over everything from the roof to the tombstones. A faculty is a study led by the chancellor as to whether a change is actually necessary or helpful."

"So, five years ago, they didn't recommend repairs to the organ?"

"Oh, yes. It's been on the list for the past three reports but we've never had the necessary funds and Miss Johnson always said she could manage. We had to repair the spire fifteen years ago, re-slate the north nave roof ten years ago, and five years ago we had to replace the wiring. Health and Safety demanded that. Unfortunately, we still think those exit signs are unnecessary and obtrusive in this familiar space."

"That's amazing. Why don't I just contact an organ builder and pay them directly. That will save everyone time and cut the paperwork to zero."

"I wish we could but that will violate church law."

"Well, the offer stands. Let me know when to send the check."

On Wednesday after Evensong, the choirs swapped churches as planned. The St. Luke's choir went to New College and the St. Philip's choir went to the cathedral. The Atlanta folks were in awe of the magnificent cathedrals, old parish churches, and chapels.

For the Saturday night farewell party, the Oxford Society offered to host a party for the ringers. Alexis proposed that she and Hew host a party for everyone including their Oxford choir hosts and ringers. After some high level discussions, Hew hired the Christ Church hall. It's considered to be one of the most beautiful rooms in the world, and it's normally closed to visitors.

The Atlanta folks were in awe. The choirs sang the *Gaelic Blessing* by John Rutter. Hew had ordered salad, prime roast of beef with Yorkshire pudding, beef gravy, fresh broccoli, and mashed potatoes with beef gravy. The puddings were small crunchy bread like side dishes cooked in the fat from the roast. For dessert, he had ordered summer pudding made with fresh local berries.

They washed it all down with champagne and pints of Bellringer Ale brewed by Abbey Ales in Bath. The beer was also poured into a large historic brown drinking jug embellished with bell ringing emblems and passed around the table as a common cup. The Atlanta Episcopalians were used to drinking from a common communion cup and didn't hesitate to participate in this ancient ritual. Hew just pretended to drink the beer. John and Eddie weren't allowed even a sip.

Hew gave all the Oxford folks gifts of a St. Philip's red polo shirt featuring the top of the tower on the back and the embroidered name on the front, a St. Luke's blue ringing polo shirt, a green Marietta polo shirt, and an invitation to ring in Atlanta next year. The Grace Church cathedral folks gave the Oxford ringers red polo shirts with their logo of ten gold bells in a circle with two crossed black and white rope sallies. The Oxford folks presented the Atlanta ringers with a signed print of all the Oxford towers and a polo shirt with the society logo embroidered on the front. Hew's print was signed by all the Oxford ringers and was mounted in a gold frame.

On Sunday morning, for the cathedral celebration of the Eucharist, the combined choirs sang Herbert Howell's *Missa Aedis Christi*. They included the Kyrie, Credo, Sanctus, Benedictus, and Agnus Dei. The parts run about 20 minutes, too long for Atlanta services.

For the prelude, John played Howell's 1916 Psalm Preludes Set One number two based on Psalm 37:11. *But the meek shall inherit the earth; and shall delight in the abundance of peace.* He was allowed to improvise while the procession entered. The psalm of the day, Psalm 145:1-10, *Exaltabo te, Deus* was sung to an Anglican Chant as composed by the late American organist, Benjamin Hutto. Ben died at a young age from cancer in 2015 in Washington, D.C. Several of the Charleston ringers had known Ben when he was choirmaster of their former cathedral before the recent schism. They sang Howell's *Like as a Hart* as the offertory, and his *Behold, O God Our Defender* during communion. The concluding hymn was Howell's hymn tune *Michael*. Hew played it and used Howell's own harmonization for the final verse. He improvised the retiring processional in the rhapsodic almost jazz-like arch form style of Howell's using the keys of D minor and E minor alternately, creating a harmonic blur with augmented triads.

The Ramsays had planned to fly to Edinburgh to extend their vacation away from the hectic work of building the railroad. The weather was still bad so they took the train to London with the group and then boarded the fast train to Scotland that uses the historic route of the Flying Scotsman.

They left John and the twins with Alexis's parents so he could continue his studies with Colin. As they were enjoying a leisurely lunch in the dining car, the weather broke and Hew was able to see the towers of Durham, York, and Peterborough cathedrals and spires of other parish churches near the route. He even caught a glimpse of the medieval twisted spire of Chesterfield off in the distance. At times, they were within mere yards of the North Sea.

28
SCOTLAND

They took a cab to their favorite inn, Dalhousie Castle. Until recently, because of outrageous death taxes, the thirteenth-century castle had belonged to Hew's ancestors, the Ramsays of Dalhousie. The new owner turned it into a small luxury hotel.

After settling into their suites, they all met in the library for drinks to meet Hew's double cousin, Sir John Cochrane. Several of the shelves were filled with boxes containing bottles of scotch of every kind from many distilleries. "Alexis, Hew," said Cochrane, "it's been nearly two years."

"I know, but with school last year, we've been busy. That's no excuse, but here we are."

"Sir John, are those really the names of Hew's Ramsay ancestors on that chart on the wall?"

"Yes, but you must call me John. "

They all enjoyed a delicious dinner in the hotel's crypt-turned-dining room and caught up with family events. "I want to take you and Alexis up to the highlands tomorrow," said John. "We'll stay the night at my hunting lodge if that's okay. My son James will drive us in my Bentley."

"That will work," said Hew, "but our security detail will need to follow us. I also want to revisit the Macallan Distillery. I read that they've build a new modern center since I was there."

HEW WAS ENTHRALLED WITH THE NEW distillery. It was the epitome of sustainable design. The modern undulating roof was covered with local grasses and one side wall was mostly floor to ceiling glass. The huge polished copper distilling pots commanded the attention of everyone who entered the room. It was his kind of style. The whole building was nestled into the Scottish landscape. Sir John, however, was not convinced.

"This new visitor's center is too modern for my old Scot's blood. That's too much glass for this climate. I'm glad the whisky wasn't modernized. I do want to buy you a case to thank you for all the Cuban Esplendito cigars you bring every year. Let's get a case of this Harmony Collection Rich Cacao. I've had a wee dram myself. I know you're going to love it."

"No, I couldn't. It's really too expensive. That's about $450 per bottle in US dollars."

"Not another word. Some of their selections sell for $30,000 US. This is not expensive by those standards. Load a case in the boot, James, and buy Hew a dozen of the new nosing glasses with the Macallan seal on them."

Alexis asked, "John, what does the word whisky mean? Is it distilled from corn like bourbon?"

"Nae, Lassie. We distill it from barley and age it in oak sherry casks from Spain. Our word doesn't have an 'E' in it like the American corn liquor whiskey. The word whisky is Gaelic and means water of life."

James left them to make the purchases. "Now, while James is busy, I need to tell you something. We're going to see a nearby castle. It's partially in ruins, though. It's been in our Cochrane family for over eight hundred years, and I'm going to leave it to you in my will. The first wooden fort is said to have been built in the ninth century to try to stop the Vikings from advancing up the river. It didn't work. I suspect your blond hair and blue eyes are proof of that!"

Hew was not amused and changed the subject. "When was this castle built and when did it fall into ruin?"

"Historians think the stone parts of it date from the thirteenth century. The family abandoned it shortly after King Charles II ascended the English throne. They moved to Glasgow to manage our growing shipping business, but they still had farmers working and living on the lowlands. I still own the farms and they are profitable."

"John, I can't tell you how much I appreciate this generous offer, but James should inherit everything. I've got enough property."

"Don't worry about James. He'll be fine but you're going to need to help him."

"How?"

"I'm giving you the old castle. I'll warn you, it needs work, but he'll need you to help him by buying the land. There's 20,000 acres right on the River Spey and you need to buy it to cover the death taxes when I die. The accountants have it all worked out. You deserve it, and I want to keep it in our family. Besides, you're the only one I know who can afford it. You need to know, though, we allow the public to walk and ride on the trails. You can't stop that."

"Hmmm. Let's at least go have a look."

The castle ruins were spectacularly sited high on the west side of the 1,545-foot-high hill called Ben Aigan above a series of bends in the River Spey. It was very convenient to the railroad which crossed the river beside the highway. It immediately reminded Hew of the trip down the Rhine River on the Viking riverboat with the Hardy family.

Even as a teenager, he had appreciated those romantic castle ruins. He thought they looked like giant sculptures in a garden and this one was no exception. He was immediately smitten.

Alexis, however, was shocked. To say it needed work was an understatement. Parts were actual ruins, but she had to admit that the views over the river were spectacular. The heather and brambles had reclaimed most of the interior.

John continued. "I've had an architect draw up some preliminary plans. If you want to turn it into a hotel, you can get about thirty en-suite rooms with a grand banquet hall in the old hall. There's superb fishing in the river, deer and grouse in the heather, and there's room for a golf course, but I'd rather you didn't do that to the land."

"Don't worry, John. I don't play golf. We might put in a swimming pool and a few tennis courts, but that's about it. I want a copy of the plans."

James agreed with Hew. "I'd be happy to help run the hotel. I know how to market it."

"James, open the boot and let's break out a bottle of that fine whisky. Cousin John, we have a deal. By the way, where's the closest airport for my jet?"

"For any airplane? Aberdeen."

"That's about an hour and a half from here?"

"If you're lucky."

Alexis commented. "Maybe we could get Sam to find us a club car, or maybe we can find another old Orient Express club car somewhere in Europe, and we could put our guests on a train like the Flying Scotsman."

"The train goes right by the airport, but you'll need a British carriage for that. Your American trains won't work here, and just so you know for future reference, Flying Scotsman is the name of the locomotive, not the entire train. There are some old Victorian era carriages, and I mean railway carriages—not horse drawn carriages—near here that need to be restored. I know there might still be one from one of the old royal trains. I know the person to contact."

"Yes, John, find us a club or dining car. And find us a horse-drawn Victorian carriage too. That would be fun for our guests. We're going to need a fleet of Range Rovers too. We can have drivers take our guests on driving excursions or they can drive themselves. This is going to be a fun project."

When they returned to Oxford, they presented young John and the twins with Ramsay kilts. They gave Alexis's mother her tartan sash.

"Dad, Mom, I want to learn to play the bagpipes. Gramps bought me my own practice chanter."

Alexis was stunned at the thought of all that noise added to those three organs. "You're going to need to soundproof my studio. I might even need a new one built far away from the house."

Six weeks later, after they had arrived back in Atlanta, James—now *Sir* James Cochrane—called Hew with bad news. Sir John had died suddenly from a stroke and Hew needed to fly to Scotland immediately.

29
MANHATTAN

Hew and Alexis were dressing in their bedroom. "I need to go to New York," he said. "I need to meet with the construction crew in New Jersey about the roadbed, but also, now that Edward has stepped down, the new manager of Bishop Hardy wants to redecorate grandfather X.I.'s old office with Louis XIV decor. I can't imagine that fussy stuff in that building. The movers can relocate the Miesian furniture and the old silk rugs to our Carlisle apartment. The labor unions won't let me touch my own stuff, but I don't trust them with my paintings. I want to personally hand carry the Canaletto and the three Picassos out before we contract with the unions. I'll need to get them out before the damned union guys even arrive to give me their outrageous estimate."

"It's time to redecorate that apartment. It hasn't been changed since Jack Kennedy was in the White House. As I recall from reading the journals, your grandmother used the same decorator."

"I remember hearing my grandfather laugh about that. Apparently he was redecorating our apartment, the White House, and a plantation house near Georgetown, S.C., named Greenfield at the same time."

"That seems odd. Was there a connection?"

"Apparently it was loads of tobacco money. Greenfield is owned by heirs of the Duke tobacco fortune and X.I. was—well—tobacco rich too. Their plantation house has about 10,000 square feet set in three hundred manicured acres. He laughed. "Spending that much money at the same time must have made the decorator orgasmic."

"Of course, the Kennedys had money too." She smiled. "I could use a little shopping therapy myself. Let's take the kids and invite Charlie and Rosilyn."

⚜

ONCE THEY ARRIVED IN NEW YORK, they split up. The guys spent the morning at the American Museum of Natural History while the women shopped on Fifth Avenue and then all met for lunch at Le Bernardin. They all chose the chef's tasting menu. Hew loved the Dover Sole. It reminded him of the dish he used to eat at the Four Seasons Restaurant. It had been in the base of Mies van der Rohe's iconic Seagram building and had attracted the city's power elite.

Lunch, with wines and tip ran slightly more than $3000 for six. Eddie barely touched his but John ate his and his friend's. After lunch, the women returned to the shops and the guys went to the Hayden Planetarium for a few hours.

"Eddie wants to go to the Lego store," Alexis told Hew. "He has his heart set on that Ultimate Millennium Falcon 75192. It's a mere $960. Ridiculous."

"Just be glad he doesn't want the Royal Selangor Pewter Star Wars chess set. It's $2,000. John mentioned that a few months ago. I told him I'd consider buying it when he became a grandmaster of chess, so I'm safe."

"Legos have provided those two with hours of critical thinking and manual dexterity, but John only wanted to build buildings, not starships."

"At least they compromised—John built Jedi cities for Eddie's warriors."

"Do you think John will be an architect?"

"I don't know. Do you think Eddie will be a Jedi? John has stopped playing with the Legos. He thinks the buildings are childish, but then he saw a couple of cathedral Lego models last year in England. He wanted one of those, but I killed that idea. Those things cost a large fortune. At least they don't like the Minecraft video games."

Hew nodded. "Go ahead. We're going to Juilliard to see Mom's old studio and then to St. Thomas for Evensong. I want John to see the place I loved so much. They've installed a new organ since I was a choirboy."

Evensong was glorious as usual. John was enthralled with the choir, the organ, and the building. After the service, Hew took John into the choir stalls to see the new console. The sub-organist was just finishing his postlude. "Hello. Welcome. Want to come closer? It's a beauty. We think Dobson did a fine job."

"Thanks. Yes. I was a choirboy here many years ago and I played the old one."

"I'm Barton Bell, but my friends call me Ding. Come, sit down and play something."

"Let me guess. Boarding school?"

"Of course. Groton. I had to fight them to stop from being called Barbell. Ding was a compromise."

"I'm Hew Ramsay and this is my son, John. I'm the first in my family in eleven generations that didn't go to Philips Exeter. I'm also the first without a nickname. I visited Groton once. I had hoped to ring the bells and play that G. Donald Harrison Aeolian-Skinner instrument, but it was midsummer and there was no one around to help me."

"I didn't learn to ring the bells, but I played the organ during my years there. It's been altered, you know. The console was moved, and the great and choir division have been re-voiced. There were other alterations, but in that space, it's still a fine instrument. Do you play too, John?"

"Yes, sir, and I sing too," John boasted proudly, "but what about that organ in the gallery?"

"Oh, yes. That's our Taylor and Boody three-manual Baroque mechanical action beauty."

"I love baroque music. We have a three-manual Flentrop at home. I play it more than Dad does."

"Oh, wow. While your dad explores this one, let's go up and let you try out ours."

"Only because you won't leave the bench, John. I practice after you've gone to bed, but sure, go on back while I play this one."

Hew tried a few stops and combinations. The hymnal was open to page 401. The music was a tune called *Leoni*, an old Hebrew melody with words by Olivers, who lived between 1725 and 1799. A haunting tune in

A-flat major with four flats, the words begin, *The God of Abraham praise who reigns enthroned above.* Hew loved the hymn and began to improvise on the tune for a few minutes, and then began to play Howells's *Tranquillo, a con Moto.* It was a piece he had recently memorized. It was a short, rather quiet piece, but Hew opened the instrument up in the arch section in true Howells style, added the eight-foot oboe for the solo measures, and then reduced the ending to a whisper.

John and Ding listened from the rear gallery.

"He's quite good," said Ding. "He improvises with great style. What would you like to play, John?"

"There's a song we learned in choir that I want to hear on this instrument in this church. I play it at home, but our acoustics aren't like these. The music is the aria "Largo" from *Xerxes* by Handel, and it has been arranged for the church in a version called *Holy art Thou Lord God Almighty,* but Dad had us sing a version with lyrics for the Thanksgiving Day Service at our cathedral that started with the words, *Thanks be to Thee, Lord God of Hosts.* He said that we might not be able to hold the first word *thanks* for all the measures, and if we couldn't, he would select something simpler."

"Yes, I know the German hymn version, *Dank sei Dir, Herr.* It's originally "Largo" from *Xerxes.* The origins of the hymn lyrics are actually unknown but it's been attributed to Handel. Your dad played the old 'Challenge the Boys' game. Did you sing it in German?"

"No, sir. I'll sing it in English as I play. Tell me what you think."

Astounded at John's bravado, Ding said, "Go for it."

John pulled out and pushed in a few stops on the three-manual instrument and selected the eight-foot quintadena, a stopped flute in which the third harmonic (twelfth) is predominant. As soon as he began singing and playing, the choirmaster and several of the choirboys walked back out into the nave from the south ambulatory to try to see who owned that voice. His voice filled the church with its unwavering clear treble sound. The choirmaster walked up to Hew at the console and asked, "Who *is* that boy? His voice is very nice. His diction is rather Oxonian."

Hew smiled. "He's my son."

The choirmaster cocked his head. "Were you one of Uncle Gerre's boys?"

"I was. I learned the basics of improvisation from him too, but I will never be as good."

"He was a master. Why don't you and your son come back to the school with us? I'd like to offer you a drink. It's always great to talk with our alumni."

Hew was treated to a tour. The lower floors housed the school. The middle floors were all residential facilities for the boys, and the upper floors contained faculty and staff apartments. At the same time, Ding took John on a tour of the school and dorm areas.

The elevator door opened onto the fourteenth floor and Hew was surprised to learn that the choirmaster occupied the entire penthouse. "I suppose Ding is just one level down," he said.

"Not quite. He's a bit further down in a 200-square-foot studio apartment with twin beds, but he gets a free lunch every day."

Hew laughed. Two little girls walked up to their father for a hug and were introduced. "We have twin daughters. They're almost five years old."

Their mother walked in with an infant in her arms.

"They must keep you busy."

The small boy reached out to Hew and just as he was about to take the baby from his mother, the baby let out a loud fart.

"Oops," she said, grinning. "Better let me keep him. That's a prelude to something more."

Hew laughed. "He'll make a fine chorister in a few years with that gas."

"Bloody hell," said the choirmaster. "I'm told it's been that way since the beginning. Each class teaches it to the next and they fart to irritate the gentlemen on the back row. We get the same complaint at every meeting."

"Yeah, that's how we learned to do it. Father Andrew finally gave up trying. He just said that there is a Latin phrase that says we can't change the wind and God made gas for a reason."

"How about a martini?"

"Yes, please. I love a good gin martini—shaken with a twist."

"We've got several gins. Do you have a preference?"

"Botanist, if you have it."

"Of course. Forgive my impertinence, and don't answer if it's none of my business, but Ding tells me that your grandfather was X.I. Bishop and your mother was a legendary keyboard professor at Juilliard."

Hew explained that he had been removed from the choir school before he graduated because his parents moved to Cali and he was forced into a Colombian boarding school. "The only good thing was that I spent three years there playing a Cavaillé-Coll organ—well, that and I became an expert computer programmer. I can improvise on Gregorian chants and play a Catholic Mass in my sleep. Because I was an Episcopalian in a Catholic school, I couldn't receive communion so I stayed in the loft and played while the organist and console assistants went down to receive. How do you know about my grandfather? He wasn't a musician."

"Oh, he's something of a legend here. The stories abound about his entertaining the clergy and music staff here at the University Club at the so called St. Thomas table when you were a student. Something about a famous mint julep made with expensive scotch. He attended Sunday services here while you were in the choir."

"He never told me about that."

"Your time on a Cavaillé-Coll must have been rewarding. Few young organists ever get the chance to even hear one."

"Looking back now, it was. I learned to pull stops on the fly. My Flentrop doesn't have pistons either, but my playing here was not as smooth as I would have liked. I forgot to ask Ding for a memory level and I didn't want to re-set your pistons."

"Some console assistants call the practice of running around the console bench as 'flip, smash, and grab.' Thanks for leaving our pistons alone. As you know, we spend hours setting the right combinations while we are still exploring this glorious new instrument."

"I do remember that it was a bit difficult to hear the sounds because the console's in that alcove, but it seems to be worse now."

"I agree. We are studying a new layout for the console. Eighty percent of the new pipework is now directly overhead of the organist. We may have a newer low profile console built to occupy the space at the west end of the choir pews. It's the location that the architects originally recommended."

"What will you do with the existing console? It's a magnificent piece of work."

"Yes, the woodwork was designed by the building architect. I want to move it to the nave. It will be better positioned for concerts and recitals."

"Great idea. I have spent many summers studying Anglican music and English-style improvisation and Psalm accompaniment with Colin St. John-Smith at Christ Church, Oxford. John spent this past summer studying with him."

"I know Colin very well. I want him to come here for a concert next year. How about your son? Have you been teaching him? It is unusual that being from Atlanta he doesn't sing with a typical Southern nasal sinus twang in his voice."

Hew ignored the criticism. "Yes. As you said, my mother taught keyboard at Juilliard, and she was my early voice and keyboard teacher before I started here. Since we lived across the Park, I was given early acceptance here. My wife and I have been teaching John to sing, and I've been giving him organ lessons. I teach in our cathedral using the Royal School of Church Music curriculum. He's certainly better than I was at his age. He's fearless with both."

"As we heard. How about music theory?"

"I've taught him some of the basics. My degrees are in business so I've never really had formal university theory courses myself except for what I learned here, of course."

"We seem to have taught you well." The choirmaster paused. "I want to audition your son. I think he'd be a natural for our choir."

"His mother will need to be convinced but it will be John's decision, though. We agreed we would never force our children into boarding school."

EVERYONE WAS TIRED FROM THE ADVENTURES of the day so Hew and Alexis left the kids with their nanny and stayed in the hotel. Hew's apartment had a direct elevator to the hotel bar and dining room.

First, they had drinks at the iconic Bemelmans Bar in the hotel. Then they dined in the hotel's newly re-opened restaurant, Dowlings. The updated modern interior still retained some of the original Art Deco touches inspired by the hotel's original interior designer, Dorothy Draper.

They all accepted the waiter's suggestion and ordered the new executive chef's spectacular flambé Steak Diane.

❦

HEW TUCKED JOHN INTO BED. "You're awfully quiet, son. Are you okay?"

"Dad, did you like choir school?"

"I loved it. It was the highlight of my life—until I met your mother, of course. Why? Was something wrong with your visit?"

"No. Some of the boys asked me if I would be joining the choir and I didn't know what to say."

"Is that something you'd like to think about?"

"Yeah. That would be great. Can I?"

"*May* I. Only if it's your choice. You'll need to audition, and one of those will be an overnight stay, but I need to talk with your mother first. Leave that to me."

Once they were in bed, Hew asked Alexis how her day had been.

"Fun, but exhausting. Rosilyn is a great shopping pal. We managed to find a few things."

"Oh, no doubt. We had a great time too. John took to New York like a pro."

"Hmmm. What does that mean?"

"He wants to audition for the choir at St. Thomas."

Alexis rolled over and pretended to sleep. The next morning, she rolled over and whispered, "If John's leaving me, you need to give me a new baby."

"I'll give it my best. We can start that process right now."

30
PENTHOUSE

Hew and Charlie sat on the terrace of Hew's penthouse drinking one of Charlie's famous Scottish Botanist gin martinis after an afternoon of soccer practice. Hew's engineers had included a large gently sloped grassed storm water retention pond on the condo property that was perfect for soccer. Hew and Charlie coached the young kids, but Charlie also coached a group of teens. "I've got a problem and I need your help." A few minutes later, Edward joined them.

"What now, Charlie?" said Hew. "Is this work related?"

"No, but now that you mention it, the Chinese and Russians seem to have stopped hacking our servers. We haven't had an attempt in several weeks. It's strange, but Bubba Hu said that the Japanese ambassador seems to think that the Chinese have lost interest. Their sense of national pride seems to have convinced them that their current system is better than the Japanese system, and the Russians are sticking with the German design they've already stolen."

"Ha. The Chinese system is actually the German version."

"Yeah, but they've convinced themselves their changes are improvements."

"Actually, I plan to bring this up at our next construction meeting. As you know, Eberhart International has always avoided doing business with the Chinese and the Russians. In my last meeting in Cologne, Axel presented a series of interesting facts that the Chinese don't want the world to know. Namely, the Chinese economic bubble may be about to

257

burst. The price of housing in their cities is out of reach for families. Their birth control mandate isn't what they had wanted and developers started building new cities away from the older cities to reduce housing costs. Many of those new cities are ghost towns. The government invested heavily in high speed rail lines to the small, new, but now empty cities.

"China has so far avoided a recession, but it is full of corruption. A very public crash on the new high speed rail line eroded the public's confidence in the trains. Now the debt is huge so I suspect they have given up on improving their high speed rail.

"I'm glad to have them off our backs. We can breathe easier now. Alexis will be thrilled, but we can't break our silence yet. We've still got the labor unions and the mafia sniffing around, and you know how I hate labor unions and goons. They're right up there with drug cartels as far as I'm concerned. We're constantly battling with them on our construction projects.

"Thankfully, they're not a big problem in Georgia. Most Southerners don't like having Chicago mafia chiefs and Yankees telling them what they can do. You know, when the Aeolian Skinner Organ Company started installing their organ in the new Avery Fisher Philharmonic Hall in Lincoln Center in New York City, the unions demanded that only they could install it. The electricians union did the wiring, the plumbers union installed the metal wind lines and pipe work, the carpenters union installed the wood pipes and the wind chests, but the thing never worked correctly. They did allow a professional organ builder to oversee the installation, but the orchestra finally sold the whole instrument to the Crystal Cathedral in California. But that's not your problem."

Edward sat quietly and sipped his martini.

Hew finally broke the silence. "What's going on, Charlie?"

"Nothing that earth shattering. I've got four more kids coming for my soccer clinic this weekend than I have beds. I need to let them stay here."

"In this penthouse? No way! I'm not having four drunken teen boys running wild alone up here."

"Actually, it's two boys and two girls."

"That's worse. Sex, drugs, booze. No. They'll have to go to a hotel."

"It's no worse than what you and I did, Hew. How quickly you forget. Besides, their parents won't allow them to stay unsupervised in a hotel."

Edward mused. "I've been wondering when the stories about this place would finally come out."

"Hotel? Remember that time when…"

"Stop, Hew. Dad doesn't need to know about that."

"What about a hotel?"

"Now you've done it, Hew. We're all adults now. You might as well spill it."

"Okay. It's funny now but back then it was serious. One afternoon, Charlie became seriously horny."

"Oh, like you didn't too."

"Well, yes, we both were. Charlie got the bright idea to go have a drink in the new hotel by Phipps Plaza that had a bar that attracted business women. He thought we might have a good chance with older women."

"Wait a minute. You guys were only seventeen years old. How did you think that was going to work?"

"We had fake IDs and we looked older. We dressed up to look as if we were young business types. I went to the front desk and got a suite. Charlie went to the bar and got a table. It was still a bit early, but we didn't know that. He immediately attracted two women with drinks already in their hands."

Edward sighed. "Of course, he did."

"Charlie had ordered two martinis for us and he invited the girls to join him. I walked in and the fun began. Charlie had his hand on his girl's thigh within minutes. He suggested that we all order another round and take it up to our suite. The girls agreed. Charlie asked them what they were drinking and they said Jackson's gin and tonic."

"Oh, no. I know where this is going. That gin doesn't exist. The bartender would give them straight tonic. Tippy orders that when we're out with friends and she's on call. It looks just like a normal G&T. Go on."

"The drinks came but the girls said they would be more comfortable in their room. We didn't really care so we went to their room."

"Careful, Dad. It's about to get scary."

"Keep going. I know what's coming."

"Charlie started taking his pants off as soon as the door was closed, but just then, one of the girls said they had to be paid up front and

Charlie, as usual, didn't have any money. He asked how much and she said $500 each. I said no way, but he persisted."

Charlie shrugged. "I was really horny and they were hot. Besides, you had plenty of money."

"I turned to leave and happened to look over and saw one of their purses was open. I saw a shiny badge. I panicked and started pulling Charlie out of the room. He was struggling with his pants and protesting, but I got him out. Just as we approached the elevator, two cops passed us in the hall. When Charlie stopped to fasten his belt, he turned and saw them go into the girl's room."

"I realized we had nearly been busted."

"Actually, I told you they were vice cops."

"I told Hew to take one elevator up and I went down. We finally met at the car and came back here. Let me tell you, though, that cooled me off for a while. A few weeks later I met Rosilyn and Hew met Alexis."

"I think I'll leave you guys now. I've heard enough from you clowns. Don't ever tell your mother about this."

After Edward left, Hew sighed. "I haven't forgotten—and we never used drugs—but it was *my* condo so we were very careful." He laughed. "But we really did have some great times up here."

"Yeah, but I don't really miss Suzie. She was pushy. She's now an OB/GYN with her mother's practice here."

"Don't remind me about her. Alexis doesn't use that practice based on Tippy's advise."

"Mom advised Rosilyn to use a different practice also. I wouldn't trust Susie not to blurt something out."

"I'm glad I never had sex with her, but Katie was delightful, and boy did she love sex. Forget this. Why did you bring it up?"

"I can't help it. I think about it every time we come up here—especially out here by the pool. I'll stay here with the kids if it'll ease your old prudish mind."

"Damn you. You know I'm not a prude. Yeah, the pool sex was the best. Okay, but you will be here the entire time they're up here. They don't get keys and you must move all the alcohol into the vault—even yours. Absolutely no drugs. Why not let your out-of-town experts stay here instead of these kids?"

"I would, but they insisted on full service hotels. I don't want to upset that. You look weird. If you're really dead set against it, I'll just tell the kids they can't come."

"No, it's fine, as long as you stay with them. You reminded me about the time I met Alexis. She wouldn't have sex until after we were married. I had a very long dry spell."

"We both did. Rosilyn was the same."

"We conceived John within a few months after the wedding. The girls came three years later. We didn't really think much about the time lag. Don't tell Rosilyn I told you, but we're having trouble getting pregnant. We've been going to a fertility specialist. The tests don't show a problem. The doc thinks we're trying too hard."

"That's hilarious. How can anyone try too hard?"

"He thinks we should slow down and relax, but that's difficult too."

"I know. When we were trying for Eddie, I felt pressure to perform. It's not the same as casual sex, but I doubt women understand that."

"You're right. I was having to leave work in the middle of the day because Alexis's temperature was right. Who would have thought? We didn't have a problem before. It took a little longer with the girls, but we really didn't think much about that at the time. I now think my ancestors might have had similar problems. They had very few children and most were males."

"They don't cover that in sex ed."

Hew laughed. "When we were teens, we got on the job training, and we worked to avoid pregnancy. I even had to take a sperm sample to the lab one morning last month. I asked Alexis to help me but she just laughed and said she thought I could…handle it."

Charlie snorted his martini and got choked.

"I put the little jar in a brown paper bag to conceal it. The waiting room was full of people when I walked in." I handed the bag to the receptionist and quietly told her my name. She pulled the jar out of the bag, held it up to inspect it, and yelled to someone in the back, 'Got another jar of fresh hot semen for the lab.' The whole room laughed."

Charlie spilled the remainder of his martini. "What did you do?"

Hew smiled. "I yelled back, 'Don't drop it. It's worth billions of dollars.' The guys in the waiting room couldn't stop laughing. The receptionist's face turned deep red. I'll bet she won't do *that* again."

"Wow. I've never thought about it but that's actually true. Speaking of future billionaires, how's John getting on in New York?"

"Thanks for changing the subject. I needed that. He's fine. He got a good report last semester, but I understand his temper can be a problem. He texts several times a week with all the news, but he conveniently forgot to mention that he's been removed from practicing in the church for the rest of this term. Ding told me that the rector walked in just as John continuously misplayed a line during his private practice. John let fly a loud curse so he's relegated to practice the piano in one of the school's practice rooms for the remainder of the term."

"What did he say?"

"He yelled, 'You fucking son of a bitch.'"

"He got that from you. I remember, though, that you had the good sense to cuss in Spanish when you were in the church. I'll tell John to practice his Spanish."

"Don't you dare."

Charlie laughed. "As you know, Mom and Dad usually go to Highlands about now for the summer, but they're on a Viking ship cruising between Italy and Greece, so if you and Alexis want to get away for a few days, the house is yours."

"That's a great idea. I loved that ship. It reminded me of what it might be like to spend a week in one of Richard Meier's fine contemporary houses. I'd love a week in Meier's Douglas house high on that hill looking out over the water. Alexis and I don't really get enough alone time. John's going on tour with the choir during the month of June, and we're going to Oxford for all of June so this might be our only chance.

"I'll talk with her. We'll need to go immediately though. We've got another meeting at Swan Bay on the fifteenth. Fortunately, we're way ahead of schedule. We're going to finish construction early. Alexis says it won't be soon enough for her. The media has been relentless."

"What about her lawsuit?"

"It drags on. They finally gave her a date for her deposition. She showed up thirty minutes early just as one of the attorneys called to say she had a sick child and needed to reschedule. Alexis saw her later that same morning at the liquor store, so it was just another stall tactic."

"Did Alexis confront her?"

"No, Alexis was just pulling into the parking lot as the woman was going in to the store so she just backed up and drove to another store. Janet said that was a good move. Apparently, confrontation won't work. We saw the Mink at a function for University of Georgia donors. Someone actually introduced us. What a joke. She couldn't get away from me fast enough. She nearly tripped over a woman standing behind her."

CHARLIE WAS SO TIRED AFTER THE Friday afternoon clinic, he fell asleep at eight o'clock. He woke up about 11 p.m. to a silent condo. He was still dressed, so he decided to check on the teens. One of the bedroom doors was slightly opened. He immediately spotted one of the couples going at it on the bed. The girl was on top with her back to the door and the guy was thrusting. He was so intensely involved, his eyes were closed.

Charlie quietly backed away from the door and went downstairs. He quickly found the other couple naked in the pool. Empty beer bottles rolled around the terrace.

Laughing silently, he went back to bed. Saturday night was a repeat so he decided that he would never let Hew know. He just laughed. Nothing ever changes with teens.

31
ST. HELEN'S

"Oh, Hew, sorry. I thought Mark was playing for the ordination to-night. I was in the hall setting up for the reception when I heard familiar music."

"Hello, Bitsy. No, he called me yesterday. He's not feeling well. He asked me to fill in. I was going to return your call yesterday but things have been hectic here."

"St. Luke's is glad to have you on such short notice. We're still look-ing for a sub-organist. What were you playing? It sounds like the hymn we're singing tonight."

"You've got a good ear. Since the new curate is Irish, I decided to play C.V. Stanford's organ *Sonata, Celtica no. 4, opus 153* for the prelude. It will lead seamlessly into the processional hymn. Stanford was Irish, you know."

"No, I didn't know that. I love his *Mag and Nunc in C* that we some-times sing at Evensong. Why did that last part sound so familiar?"

"That third movement contains two hymn tunes. The first is *St. Pat-rick's Breastplate* and the second is called *Gartan*. It's inserted into the middle of the hymn we sing at ordinations. I do wish there was a trum-pet en chamade up there in the balcony, though."

"Forget it. I'm not giving one. Now I remember. She started singing, *I bind unto myself today the strong Name of the Trinity*. The second tune be-gins, '*Christ be with me, Christ within me.*' That hymn is seven verses long. I always thought that verse six was there just to break it up."

"Nope. It's just good theology."

"I don't think I told you that my family helped establish St. Helen's Church. There was some old Charleston money involved too. Right after the Civil War, my family needed to escape the Reconstruction Era horrors here in burned-out Atlanta so they moved to one of their old plantations in the hills near Sautee, Georgia. One of the old Charleston families had ancestral property there too. The next generation of my family decided the old house was too small for the whole family so they built a big Victorian house in nearby up-and-coming, or so they thought, Helen, Georgia. I was raised in Helen until I married Timmons and moved here to Atlanta. As you know, he and Daddy built Great-granddaddy's family cotton gin business into a huge international distribution company, and I just want to give something back. The parish was founded in 1880 by a group of wealthy people who needed a summer escape from the noise and dust of the rebuilding of Atlanta after the Yankees finally left. They anticipated a growth explosion in Helen that never happened until now, but they built a fine gothic revival church that will seat five hundred. The new organist is highly trained, by the way. She studied in Paris, and she's very good."

"Yes, she is but, as I told you, organists are like chefs. No new chef ever went into an existing kitchen and announced, 'This is perfect. I wouldn't change a thing.'"

She laughed. "They formed an organ committee and a separate acoustics committee which is an Episcopal way of saying they waffled. A war nearly erupted."

"Yeah, it's like the popular stall tactic many Protestants use when they say, 'I'll pray about it.' It often happens that when a vestry forms one committee, an ad hoc anti-committee forms to undercut the official committee. One of my former priests gave me some good advice. You know how we used to read the Palm Sunday Gospel dramatically in parts with several people reading the various voices?"

"Yeah, we used to do that. I didn't like the part where the congregation had to stand up and say, 'Crucify him.' That was uncomfortable."

"I know. Neither did I, but my priest said that was done on purpose because if we could crucify Christ, nothing that ever happens in the church should surprise us."

"That's rather cynical, but now it makes it all seem sensible. I finally put a stop to the bickering. I simply wanted to buy a new organ. I hired a New York preservation architect, told him I wanted him to design a renovation for a new organ and when he gave me his outrageous proposed budget for the design work, I wrote him a check for twenty percent of his fee to get started. We retained the acoustician you recommended. He came in with a battery of computers and testing equipment. He even fired a pistol in the church! He made a believer of the senior warden. Numbers and guns seem to do that with those guys. The numbers don't lie. The problem is, I don't like the new design. The architect came highly recommended, but I should have checked more thoroughly. He's never designed an Episcopal church before. He and the acoustician want to place the choir and the new organ at the east end behind the altar. I want to see stained glass. I don't want to look at shiny organ pipes above the altar. He's also suggested that the new chancel be the same width as the nave and something seems off with that. You didn't answer my question about bells, though."

"I understand, but you know yourself that without some of these changes, you'll be wasting your money. The new organ will function better, but it won't sound much different from the old one. As for bells, on my first visit, I saw an old rope looped over a hook on the wall in the corner of the narthex, but I couldn't find a way to access the tower."

"I should have mentioned that. It's through that circular molding in the center of the vaulting."

"There's a burned out downlight there, but I was wearing a good suit, and anyway, I will not climb a forty-foot ladder. My structural assessment team removed a louver to get access. Fortunately it wasn't full of wasps' nests or pigeon dung. There's no space in the tower for a ringing room, there's no stair, and the walls aren't thick enough to support the weight and motion of swinging bells beyond the old one that's already there. It gets worse. The tower is unstable and so is the chancel. The lime has leached out of the mortar between the stonework. It was probably a cheap mix to begin with, but now the stones are loose. It is precarious and to make matters worse, the chancel foundations are giving way."

"Part of the choir floor collapsed during communion when one of our more portly gentlemen approached the communion rail. Fortunately two other men caught him and he wasn't hurt, but to everyone's amazement, the choir simply walked around the hole, assuming the rest of the floor was sound. There was a big wedding scheduled for the following Saturday at noon and the sexton quickly fitted a piece of plywood over the hole, but the bride wasn't happy. Her mother bought a large oriental rug to cover the plywood, but really, it was too small for the space and didn't look right. It stayed there for months while the finance committee argued with the buildings and grounds committee over the scope and cost of the work."

"I wondered why that rug was off center. That's one of the funniest things I've ever heard. Of course it had to be Oriental. Plain carpet just wouldn't do for Episcopalians. The chancel needs to be pulled down, or as the conservators say, deconstructed and rebuilt."

"They're going to have to pay for that themselves. But what about a carillon or some clock bells, and why can't the kids ring the bell anymore? We used to love to swing on the rope. The harder we pulled, the higher we were lifted off the floor."

"Even a small carillon won't really work. The spire is carried on huge timber columns in the center of the tower that would effectively block the blending of the sound. The rope has come off the wheel because at some point in time, someone pulled so hard the bell turned over and the rope slipped off the wheel. You have two or three options. We can put a stay on the headstock to keep the bell from rolling over, we can stop the bell from swinging and add an electric striker, or we can design a new free-standing tower like this one here at St. Luke's."

"Let me think about that. Just put the electric thing on it for now."

"With regard to the design, if this were a new contemporary church, Johann and I would have a very different recommendation, but since this is an addition to a Victorian building, I think your architect should scrap whatever he's done and start over, but I must tell you ,we no longer feel constrained to divide a church into three Old Testament spaces. Christian theologians now refer to the concept of the priesthood of all believers. We don't set the clergy apart in separate spaces in new churches any more. The Greeks still do that, though.

"Johann says it's certainly physically possible to place an organ behind the altar, but an architect must be very talented to design a reredos that can allow the sound to sing out while simultaneously visually covering the pipework. Some churches are even built in the round with the faithful gathering around the common table, but Episcopalians don't build many of these. I think it's a low-evangelical church idea actually."

"But St. Philip's organ and choir are behind the altar and that works fine."

"Sure, but remember, St. Philip's is actually a modern building with Gothic detailing. The reredos, the muted color of the pipes, the stained glass, and the lighting focuses the congregation's eyes away from the organ pipes toward the table. The stained glass windows put the pipes in somewhat of a shadow since the glass is brighter and more eye catching than the pipework. The colorful vestments on the altar combined with the spotlighting immediately draws your attention to the altar and the reredos partially screens the choir visually." Hew shuttered when he remembered his near miss with death behind that reredos. "I must say, though, it's one of only a handful of successful ones in my opinion. St. Anne's here in Atlanta almost made it, but the pipes peek out rather annoyingly from around and above the reredos. There's a better one at St. Mark's in New Caanan, Connecticut, but it's too modern for St. Helen's. Johann suggests your architect needs to read the Book of Exodus starting at chapter 25."

"I'm not a Biblical scholar. Remind me."

"God gave Moses the first set of complete architectural specifications for the Tabernacle."

"Oh. That's the part about the cubits. I never knew what a cubit was."

"It's a very simple unit of measure like a foot. Basically, scholars believe it was the length of Moses's forearm and hand from the tip of his elbow to the tip of his middle finger. It's considered to be eighteen inches in modern Imperial measurements."

"I measure fabric that way—only I use the distance from my nose to the tip of my finger."

"Well now, see, you're just like Moses."

"Ha. Wait 'till I tell my altar guild broderers about this."

"God made three distinct spaces. The largest one corresponds to our understanding of the nave. It was outdoors and a place for the people to gather for worship. It held the altar for the burnt sacrifice. Christians don't burn offerings. Jesus is the ultimate sacrifice. There was a large copper or bronze basin for the priests to wash their hands and feet before entering the veiled Holy Space. Medieval rood screens performed the function of the veil."

"We light the Paschal candle from a large copper basin on Easter morning. The St. Helen's choir wants to remove our rood screen. They say they can't see the preacher."

"I suspect they think they can't be seen by the congregation. As for the washing bowl, we have holy water stoups for that now. It now reminds us of our Baptism."

"We don't do holy water at St. Helen's."

"The celebrant washes hands at the altar."

"Ah."

"The second and smaller space was called the Holy Space and only the priests entered. It contained a menorah on the north side, a table for the bread and wine on the south side, and a tabernacle for the incense at the east end."

"Oh, no. No incense at St. Helen's either. And those candles and that table would be in the way of the choir seeing the organist."

"Well, today, because the monks occupied this space in medieval times, it's most often used now as the space for the choir. It's also the proper place for the Pascal candle since we don't use a menorah. The choir space, as it's now called, is usually less wide and less tall than the nave as a reminder of the smaller space in the description of the Tabernacle. The third space, the Holy of Holies, is smaller still. It contained the Ark of the Covenant and God's throne called the mercy seat—we now call it the Mensa—was on top of the Ark. It was God's earthly dwelling place. Today, that corresponds to the space east of the communion rail where our high altars sit. Its proper name is the sanctuary."

"Wow! You sound Jewish. How do you know all this?"

He laughed. "I have been asked that before. Several years ago, Johann was asked to meet the administrator of the Atlanta Jewish Temple to evaluate their thoughts for a new youth space. I tagged along because I had never been in the Temple."

"That's the one with the dome on the hill on Peachtree Street at Brookwood Station?"

"Yes. It was designed by Philip Trammell Shutze, and it's fantastic. When we walked into the meeting, the administrator immediately recognized that we weren't Jewish. He apologized profusely but said they really needed a Jewish architect. I recommended several in Atlanta and then asked if we could see the Temple. While we were there going on about the interior detail and the organ, the administrator casually said that the young Jews didn't like all the formality. He was trying to decide how to make a large meeting room work for the younger crowd, but they were not happy with the plans. We asked to see the space. It was a big boring box of a room with a low, standard office-type suspended acoustical ceiling, fluorescent lights, streaked beige sheetrock walls, and dirty beige asbestos floor tile. Johann suggested they build simple wood fence-post-like columns, hang curtains between the columns and transform the space into the outer court of the Tabernacle of Moses and Aaron. He suggested removing all of the lights and painting the ceiling sky blue with uprights mounted behind the new curtains along the walls. The administrator was astounded to say the least, and asked him why he would do such a thing.

"Johann suggested that the young people were still wandering in their own desert and weren't ready for the Temple. The administrator asked if we were sure we weren't Jews. To answer your question, though, I was trapped in a Catholic boarding school in Colombia for three years. The monks drilled us in Biblical studies. This architectural stuff and the Psalms were the most interesting. I know the Psalms backwards and forwards."

"I think I'll throw a little dinner party and invite you and Johann to meet with my architect. I'll tell him to bring his plans and some extra tracing paper."

⁂

AT THE DINNER PARTY, JOHANN SHOWED everyone a small book. It was an 1899 leather-bound first edition entitled *Church Building* written by the great American architect, Ralph Adams Cram. The old spine was faded and broken but the well-studied book was otherwise intact. The chapter on the chancel and its fittings included pictures of the fittings and architectural plans of a typical chancel of a proper neo-Gothic church. Cram was very highly opinionated with a huge ego, but he was considered the absolute American authority on this subject. Johann pointed out the credence table on the south wall of the sanctuary where the bread and wine were kept before they were consecrated. "This is the Christian location of the table of the Showbread in the Tabernacle. You'll also want to design a small cupboard near it made of cedar and fitted with a key. It's where the remaining consecrated bread and wine are stored in the event of an emergency communion. In some faiths, the consecrated elements are placed under the cross or even in a separate chapel. There must be an eternal candle over it to signify that the consecrated elements are present. A fire always burned in Moses's time in the Holy of Holies to signify the presence of God. The saints and angels on the east wall behind the altar are there to symbolize that the entire church, living and dead, join around the table at the Eucharist. We don't really care for organ pipes visible behind an altar. They're fine for Methodists, Baptists, Presbyterians and others, where a sermon is the focus of their worship, but in a liturgical church, the altar and its entire immediate setting must focus one's attention entirely on the table. You need to build an addition and re-order the east end by pushing it eastward by three bays. I suggest that the organ pipework be moved to the south side and the choir and organ console be located across from the pipes on the north side. Look at the location of the organ console in this idealized chancel plan! That's exactly where St. Thomas in New York is planning to relocate their console. It was the original console location. Old Ralph Adams Cram knew a thing or two about neo-Gothic church design. There can be a very large opening from the pipework into the nave but, with this arrangement, the organist can clearly hear the instrument and the choir members can hear themselves better."

The architect resigned the next morning. Bitsy asked if the report were finished and Hew said yes. He asked if she wanted a copy.

"Oh, God, no, Hew. It would only bore me to tears. I trust you and Johann implicitly. I'll ask the rector to put you on the next vestry agenda. You can address them directly. They don't know that you made the studies for the complete building. I only told them about the organ and the acoustics."

271

"That's fine. Actually, we studied the building on our own after Johann began to see things that concerned him. We couldn't just walk away and pretend we hadn't seen the issues. I'm afraid you and they aren't going to like the report."

"Well, I'm only concerned with the music. They're on their own for anything else, but if they don't hire you two, I'll pull my funding."

Hew sighed. This wasn't a meeting he looked forward to.

⁂

THE VESTRY MET THREE WEEKS LATER. The meeting was held in the parish house library which looked like a small old English medieval hall. The walls were lined with bookshelves made of heart pine. The flooring was the same pine but mostly covered with large oriental rugs. The vaulted hammer beam ceiling was up-lit to show off the craftsmanship. There was a fire in the stone fireplace at the far end of the room. A large Elizabethan oriel leaded glass window commanded most of one of the long walls. There were several wine colored leather sofas and chairs in front of the fireplace. The large round Oak table sat in the window and was lined with leather chairs and everyone was dressed in coats and ties for the occasion. Everyone seemed to be curious about the report. The current gossip around the parish was that Bitsy was up to something.

Hew scanned the books on the shelves while waiting for the preliminaries to conclude. Most of them were theological works. Some were in his library. He recognized Diarmaid MacCulloch's *Christianity*, and his *Thomas Cramner*. He had read those. He also recognized *The Shape of the Liturgy* by Dix and *Loves Redeeming Work* by Williams. He had read those too. His eye spotted the worn faded gold colored dust jacket of *The Power of Their Glory* by Konolige and he almost laughed out loud. The gold color was not an accident in his opinion. His grandfather had insisted that he read it. He sighed when he remembered that it was about the time period in the Episcopal Church when many congressmen were churchmen. It was the time of his great-grandfather and his grandfather. Those days were long gone now. His attention was drawn to the proceedings. After the opening prayer and a short Bible study on the sin of usury which Hew thought was odd for this occasion, the meeting opened with

272

the minutes of the past meeting and the treasurer's report. Tom Barker, the treasurer, reported a positive balance and was pleased to announce that the trust investments had made a fine profit. Everyone applauded. Hew laughed. Apparently it was not a sin to make interest on their money but paying interest was a sin—at least in this rector's opinion. He wondered how they would finance what he was going to tell them without borrowing heavily.

Introductions were made and Johann passed out the two-inch thick annotated and illustrated conditions report. As Hew began to speak, Johann taped large scale drawings and images to the faces of the bookcases.

"Gentlemen,"—there were no women on this vestry—"I'm just going right to the heart of the matter without sugarcoating it. We've done a thorough assessment of your church and the building is in serious condition. Bitsy initially asked me to evaluate the situation for a new organ. In the course of checking the acoustics, we began to see things that bothered us. The steeple is sinking and is leaning four inches toward the north side aisle. There are no foundations under the steeple. The walls, also without a foundation of any sort, are made of brick and faced on the exterior with stone veneer. The plaster on all the interior walls is simply attached to termite eaten wood laths and is no longer firmly attached to the brick. That's one reason the acoustics are bad. The walls are no longer solid. The plaster vaulting in the ceiling is extremely thin and does not help the acoustics either. The ceilings aren't insulated which runs up the utility bills. The mortar between the bricks is dead and they are just sitting there by gravity. I had the same problem with the 1650 brick kitchen on my Virginia farm so I know how shocking this news is.

"The air-conditioning system is noisy and worn out and the electrical system is in very poor shape. It hasn't been in code for decades. Nothing is grounded and the wires are cloth-covered. Some of it is still active knob and tube in the attic. The high roof trusses over the center of the nave are about to collapse. The ends rotted long ago from backed up gutters and were repaired by simply scabbing on new ends nailed with iron nails. Those nails are failing and the trusses have started to sag. Johann has drawings and images to show but frankly, this building needs to be deconstructed and rebuilt. We can probably save the tower, but you need to act quickly. We've studied the possible costs and we suggest that it will be less costly and quicker to rebuild."

All hell broke loose around the table. The rector banged for order. Finally Tom, the treasurer yelled. "Who are you to come in here and tell us this? Has Bitsy set us up with her grandiose scheme for a new organ? Frankly, the current organ sounds just fine to me. We could put her money to work feeding the poor."

Hew thought, *Hello, Judas. I wondered when you would join the meeting.*

"Furthermore, Mr. Ramsay, who paid for this study? I didn't authorize it and I'm certainly not going to pay for it. It's utter nonsense. This church has stood since 1880 and it will stand for another hundred years. This is the most outrageous thing I've ever heard!"

Johann saw Hew's ears and face turning deep red. He knew about Hew's temper. "Thank you, gentlemen." he said. "This is obviously a bit too much to take in at once. Hew and I will just take our leave and await your decision. Thank you for your time."

"Decision? What decision? Hell, man, there's no decision to be made. And I can tell you right now that we won't do anything without at least three bids."

Hew began to collect the reports as Johann took the drawings down. When he reached Jake Tillingham, chairman of the building committee, Jake was tucking the report into his briefcase.

"I'll take that if you don't mind," said Hew.

"But I do mind. You gave it to me and I'll need it to get other bids and we'll need it to do our value engineering."

Hew reached for the report. "Tom just stated that he had no intention of paying for this report, so I'll not let it be used to bid against me. There are serious liability issues here."

"Liability for you maybe, but not for us."

Hew grabbed the report. Jake resisted and ripped the cover off but Hew got the report.

"I need this report!" yelled the chairman.

Hew leaned down, whispered something to him in Spanish and stood up, placed the torn report in the box with the others, turned and strode out the door.

Hew's security detail was sitting in the van with the heater running. Hew and Johann slammed the documents into the back and climbed in.

"Hew, my Spanish is rusty but I thought I caught the word *culo*. Did you call Jake an ass?"

"No."

"Well what exactly did you say?"

"I told him where I would ram the report if he didn't give it to me."

"Oh, God, Hew. You and your temper. At least he didn't understand."

"No, but the rector did. Did you see him laugh?"

"Well, you burned that bridge forever."

As they drove down Highway 75 toward Atlanta, Hew spotted an old brown building that he remembered seeing earlier on the drive up. The old partially burned out neon sign announced it as a steakhouse. "Turn in down there, Jacob, I'm starved. I'll buy us all a steak."

The building had never seen a coat of paint, but there were four cars out front and the lights were on. As they walked up onto the porch, Hew saw a large confederate flag nailed to the wall beside the door. Having spent quite a bit of time on Southern construction sites, he went into character. Four men, shotguns propped beside their chairs, were sitting around the old black pot bellied stove sipping brown liquor from mason jars. There were four more rebel flags on the walls.

"Howdy boys. Is the kitchen still open? We heard that the best sirloins in North Georgia are here and we're starved."

One man looked up. "Where y'all from?"

"Alanta. We're contractors and have been looking at property up in Helen. Any of y'all work construction?"

"We all do. Come in and sit yourselves down. Drink? What are you building."

"I can't say at the moment, but if we do, I'll be back. Got any single malt scotch?"

They all laughed. "We got PBR, Bud Lite for the ladies, Jim Beam, some gin and vodka, and sweet tea."

"We've still got a long drive to get back home so the Jim might be a bit too much for the road but if you have a little tonic, I'll have a double gin and tonic."

"Me too," added Johann.

The Israelis asked for tap water. When they finished their steaks, Hew remarked, "This place lives up to its reputation for sure." He left a fifty dollar tip on the table.

❦

SEVERAL MONTHS LATER, A RARE MAGNITUDE 5.8 earthquake near Mineral, Virginia shook much of the east coast. Hew's phone rang the next morning. He was afraid it was bad news from Swan Bay. The quake had barely been felt in Atlanta.

"Hello, Bitsy," he said, relieved to hear her voice.

She was sobbing. "Oh, Hew, it's just awful. Parts of St. Helen's collapsed last night. The tower is now leaning six more inches and there are large cracks in the clearstory walls. Three roof trusses fell right over my family pew. My mother's beautiful stained glass window is completely destroyed and the big organ pipes fell onto the great wind chest. It's destroyed. We need you immediately."

"I'm very sorry to hear this. I also heard that there's damage to the National Cathedral, but I can't help you. I blew up any bridge we had there and there's no going back. I refuse to work with those guys."

"I've talked with the rector and senior warden. They want to meet with you and Johann at your earliest convenience. The rector heard whatever it was that you said to Jake and he agrees with you."

"No…"

"Just listen, Hew. I won't fund the new organ unless Johann designs a new building. The county building inspector has condemned the church so there's no going back. Jake and Tom had hired a bunch of local guys from down Highway 75 and they just wasted about a quarter of a million dollars. They drilled the walls and put in bolts with large nuts sticking out on the outside. They were planning to just paint the plates on the inside. One of the guys said that his wife was an artist and could 'fox paint' the walls to match the exterior stone. Imagine that. He didn't even understand the term *faux*. The outside bolts and plates are already rusting. They dug a small trench beside the north tower wall and poured concrete. None of it worked. They've been fired. Jake's company is transferring him to Atlanta anyway. Tom has been replaced. When can we come see you and Johann? We need you to intervene with the insurance company. We had earthquake insurance through the diocesan umbrella policy, but they're saying that the damage was due to long-term maintenance neglect."

Hew knew exactly who the contractors were. "Okay, Bitsy. For you, I'll agree to listen to them. I'll be in my office all next week. I'll get Edward to meet with the insurance company. As Chancellor of the Diocese, he knows that policy inside and out. There's no way anyone could have known about the foundations, the old mortar, or the ends of the trusses. Hell, Johann dislocated his shoulder just trying to get to the latter. Edward can probably get money for the destroyed organ too."

THE MEETING BEGAN WITH APOLOGIES ALL around. Finally, the discussion turned to timing and funding. Edward explained that he would take the lead with negotiations with the insurance adjustor but the guy had already learned about the structural issues and the inadequate attempts at repairs. He assured them that they would get a significant payout but it probably wouldn't be enough for the entire work. "Deferred maintenance is a hard issue to negotiate, but we do have the preliminary report which should help immeasurably. Unfortunately, Jake re-negotiated the termite contract and excluded the most important clause. It covered the responsibility of the termite company to repair any subsequent termite damage. He saved a few hundred dollars annually but the cost now is in the tens of thousands. I can't recover that."

Parker, the senior warden, groaned. "Jake called the insurance company and reported the loss. Why did the termite coverage fail?"

Hew cleared his throat. "Well, basically I think he crowed about his expert knowledge and told them too much, but that's not unusual for an amateur. They set their payout limit on the basis of that poorly planned phone call. I've seen this before. The treasurer takes the lowest bid from insurance companies without understanding the terms thinking he has saved money. You have a regular run of the mill commercial fire and loss policy and a bad termite policy. The Episcopal Church Insurance Fund was established by J.P. Morgan in the nineteenth century. He correctly understood that Episcopal churches, unlike commercial buildings, don't depreciate. The church insurance guys will come in, evaluate the property, set the terms and value, and then set the premiums. They insure it for full replacement value at the current cost of construction. If you ever have a loss, it's a great value. They also pay design fees and the cost of any code mandated upgrades. If you had let Edward review your policy he would have recommended you take it. If you had used a contractor to evaluate the cost of rebuilding a total loss, he would have advised you that the insurance company had evaluated the cost to rebuild very low. In the big scheme of things, it would have been a great value. Now, though, you will need to raise a substantial amount of money."

Johann spoke up. "As regards the termite treatment, the HVAC ductwork is located in the earth under the floor slab around the perimeter of the outside walls and along the foundations of the nave columns. Water and condensation from the uninsulated stained glass windows and the old HVAC blower units under the windows have been draining through the floor and into the ground for years. When the company drilled for the treatment injections, they drilled into the ductwork and pumped the treatment into them rather than the earth. Over time, every time the system has come on, it has been blowing the poison into the air. Even the organ pipes have the poison in them so every note that's played blows a little more poison into the room."

Betsy screamed. "Oh, shit!"

The rector coughed again. Hew got up and poured Bitsy a glass of water. He resisted looking at the rector.

"It's okay, Bitsy," said Hew. "The industrial hygienist we used assured us that the airborne concentrations are not dangerous."

Parker abruptly changed the subject and asked Hew about his preliminary budget.

"Parker, it wasn't a budget. It was an early estimate and it was prepared before this latest catastrophe. We might not be able to save the tower now."

"Fine, but we need to budget something. We can't go in open ended."

Hew took a long breath. Judas had arrived again. It was time for a frontal attack to put this issue to rest.

"Parker, a church budget is a planning target. Unfortunately, most church treasurers and finance committee folks see the budget as an absolute. If the youth group gets the opportunity mid-year to take a once in a lifetime trip, and it costs a thousand dollars more than was budgeted for youth activities, what happens to the budget?"

"Well, usually a few parents chip in and cover the cost."

"Yes, but that doesn't answer my question. The parents write a check to the church and the cash flow isn't negatively affected, but the treasurer shows the line item as a loss—expense over budget. It gets reported to the parish as a busted budget and everyone is made to feel that something bad happened."

Parker moved up in his chair. "Well, yes, but for the past several years, we have been able to report that we were under budget and started the current year with a very positive cash flow."

Hew looked at the senior warden. "In my mind, that's poor stewardship. You were entrusted with the people's gifts and you didn't use them. There's a parable about that."

The rector cleared his throat but didn't speak.

"So I guess you're not an annual pledge person."

"That's correct. We make an annual gift in January to keep cash flowing."

No one said anything. Hew was about to announce that he would decline to take the project when Bitsy broke the awkward silence. "Hew, I've never thought about it like that, but I see your point. Churches shouldn't operate according to commercial financial rules. Those are mostly set up for tax laws. The budget has never been changed mid-year to accommodate unforeseen expenses—or savings for that matter. We need to review that policy. For now though, we need to retain you, Johann, and all the consultants to re-visit the problem and get us going. We'll let the matter of cost wait until after Edward has done his best and you're ready to give us a contract with a healthy contingency. I'll pay for this study."

Everyone gave a silent sigh of relief and the meeting ended on a positive note. Hew hoped that there would soon be a new senior warden.

⚜

A WEEK PASSED AND BITSY CAME to Hew's office. "The vestry voted that the work will be going ahead as you and Johann suggested," she said. "During the annual parish meeting, the rector nominated me as senior warden since Parker's term is expiring. I'll make history as the first female on that board. I thought you would like to know."

"That's great. Now someone with some sense will keep them straight. As I told you when we visited the church, the liturgy was fine and the choir was excellent, but the acoustics were terrible. The acoustics are the most important stop on any organ so you folks were in trouble there. The organ pipe chamber was truly in a hole—two holes actually. The antiphonal division was probably the best part of the instrument acoustically. It's small, but it sits up high in a small west gallery and speaks directly down the central axis of the nave. That's always the perfect place for an organ. The heating and cooling system is from the middle of the twentieth century and it's extremely noisy, and I don't think I've ever heard a cheaper sound system. It looks recent but the finance committee must have bought the parts online."

"I have no idea what that means."

"Basically, those speakers just scatter sound everywhere. Small pew-back speakers would focus the output towards the congregation and not toward the walls and ceiling. The speakers would be set to digitally delay the sound so that the amplified sound would reach the people at the same time as the natural room acoustic.

"I talked with the organist and played the instrument. It's really loaded with ranks of pipes of every tonal color, but the electrical components need to be replaced. I believe I said that unless they improve the acoustic environment, they should just replace the switching system and get a good voicer in to clean it up. Maybe some ranks of pipes need to be replaced.

"Basically, the thing has had so many additions, it really doesn't have a good ensemble. The acoustician suggested they add high density foam insulation above the vaulting and Johann agreed, but now we can just get it right from the start. A new digital delay sound systems do a much better job of distributing the sound of the spoken voice. It's monaural rather than stereo so it can't be used to amplify music even though many places try to use it that way. "

"Well, now we have a chance to pull it all down—except the iconic tower—and get it right."

"Deconstruct, Bitsy. Let's stay with the word deconstruct."

"Whatever. Johann understood perfectly. He's quite a blessing. The new pew-back speaker design idea is visually subtle and will work well too, and the old unsightly black box ceiling-hung speakers will be history. I always thought they looked like hemorrhoids."

"God, Bitsy. That's a horrible but astutely correct visual description. I'll never get it out of my brain."

"Well, in my early life before I married Timmons, I was a nurse. Nothing much bothers me. I've seen it all. Based on Johann's advise, all the old banged up woodwork that we can salvage will be stripped and sanded, and as he suspected, we have beautiful honey colored straight grained heart pine. We're not going to stain it back dark."

"Yeah, the Victorians got that detail wrong. They thought the old medieval woodwork was always black, but in fact, the Gothic craftsmen used wet green oak straight out of the forest and left it natural unless they painted it in reds and greens and other vivid colors. What the Victorians saw was dirt and soot. I saw repairs being made to the choir woodwork in St. Paul's, London. They're leaving the repairs to Grinling Gibbons's masterpiece as natural colored European lime. The rest will be left black."

Laughing, she added, "The decibel level of the new mechanical system will be at about 30 Db just as the acoustician suggested. That's concert hall quality. I can't wait."

"Johann also convinced them that the church wasn't big enough for the growing congregation. It's packed on most Sundays even with three services, and that didn't help acoustically, so he's suggesting moving the chancel back to add more pews by building a new chancel addition with much heavier materials to reinforce the acoustics. The organ builder won't start the installation until every last speck of construction dust has been removed."

"We've decided to split the organ into two separate instruments with a baroque mechanical action organ in the new west gallery. It will be built by Fisk and will be a two manual and pedal stand alone instrument. The old antiphonal division will be reused and will continue to be connected to the chancel console, and an English/American classic style organ will be located on the south side of the chancel with large openings into the nave. After interviewing several builders, we voted to accept Cornel Zimmer's proposal. He will keep most of the good pipework and replace the rest. He will actually reduce the number of ranks to allow all the pipework—except the pedal pipes—to stand on one level. That will improve the ability to maintain everything. Reusing the best undamaged pipework of the existing organ placated the insurance adjustor. Those old wooden pipes are made of very fine, wide Honduran mahogany boards. It would have been a shame to throw them out. You're going to love it. You and John can play joint recitals."

"Ha. Fat chance getting me to ever play a recital. We hope to be able to underpin the tower and try to straighten it. The new west gallery will actually strengthen the piers of the old tower by tying them together. Johann found the remains of an old stair to the gallery while he was measuring the building so that proves that the old gallery was larger than the current one."

"When the local guys started work on the tower, they discovered that the pinnacles were rotten. They were built of pine covered in lead sheets but the lead had cracked from movement and expansion and contraction. The crockets and finials were made of cast iron and had been simply nailed onto the wood with iron nails. Those nails were rusted and they discovered several crockets in the shrubbery around the steeple. Many of the pinnacles fell in the earthquake anyway. No one knows how long they had been in the bushes, but they each weigh about fifteen pounds. If someone had been hit in the head by one of those falling hunks of metal…"

"I saw the report."

"That reminds me. My conservators also found a layer of school bus yellow paint on the crockets and spire, Bitsy. What was that about?"

She laughed. "That was a mistake and was quickly covered up. Back in the late 50s and early 60s the rector always took his family to England for the summer. The last thing he did on the day before they left on one of the trips was to send the painting contractor the number for the new paint color. In his haste, he sent the wrong number. The spire and crockets had always been painted a grey-beige stone color to match the base. The painters started at the top painting the yellow."

"What did they do?"

"The wardens sent a telegram to the rector and he was embarrassed. The paint contractor had already purchased all of the yellow paint, but he graciously suggested that he had enough grey paint left from another job at the North Georgia Military Academy to paint our spire so we changed it from a limestone color to battleship grey and it's been repainted that way several times."

"Well, unfortunately, the last paint that was applied was an Elastomeric paint. It was state-of-the-art paint chemistry at the time but it has now been shown that it doesn't breathe and therefore holds moisture. The moisture has damaged the materials and must be removed."

"Maybe we can return the color to the original."

"Johann found a boat builder in Charleston who will replace the crockets, finials, and pinnacles with fiberglass using the old decorative pieces as molds. We're told that as long as the church keeps it painted to block the UV rays of the sun they should last another hundred years."

"That's fine. I like that solution. What are those crockets for anyway?"

"They are foot and hand-holds so workmen could climb the pinnacles and spires to make repairs. They're said to be modeled from ladyslippers."

"What? They don't look like a woman's shoe to me. No one today would try to climb up those things."

"They're not shoes. They're flowers, and no, today's safety regulations wouldn't allow that. I'm glad it's working out."

〰️

32
PLANNING

The Brunhild construction team met at Swan Bay for the monthly meeting. They no longer thought there were foreign threats but still met in the SCIF.

They were ahead of schedule. The Charleston line was ready.

"No. I'm not going to say it again," said Sam. "We will not open it before the whole project is ready."

"But Sam," Alexis pleaded, "The governor himself calls me personally. He wants answers and I don't know what else to tell him."

"All right. Leave him to me. Truthfully, though, the rolling stock isn't ready. Those huge carriages are still being tested in Japan on their existing system. At least the kudzu covers are working perfectly. Hans even found a way to further reduce the weight of the under carriages. Using the smaller wheels helped too. They looked into using the composite kudzu material for use in the container frames and bodies but we concluded that it would involve bringing on the shipping companies and they have tight contracts with the steel worker labor unions. I won't go there and we really don't need to. Hew, you and Johann really rose to the occasion on the new building. It was way ahead of schedule and is already producing. Clemson thinks the design will win major awards and the airlines have started a bidding war over the use of the material. Let's move on."

The remainder of the meeting was uneventful. The line was finished from Birmingham, Alabama to Danville, Virginia. The push to New

Orleans was scheduled to finish in a year. The push from Alexandria, VA to the New Jersey docks would take an estimated fourteen months. They allowed for possible delays around Washington and Philadelphia. "Well, let's work that out ASAP. No delays. I'll get the president on it if the problem is with the Feds."

"Our concern is with rush hour traffic. Our guys can't get to the sites."

"Hell, we run a railroad. Put a regular commuter train up on Hans's tracks."

"Good idea, Sam, but the feds will want us to jump through all the safety regs."

"Fine. I'll get the president to issue a temporary order giving us permission. This is still under the national security order."

Bubba Hu announced a game-changing item under new business. "The Japanese ambassador told me that the son of the emperor wants to open the line."

Alexis blanched. "I've never planned an event with royalty."

"Don't worry. The embassy will handle all the details. We've got to decide on the location. All you need to do is buy a high quality red carpet runner and a flag pole for the Japanese flag."

Alexis groaned. Hew spoke up."How about the SC Inland Port? He can fly into their airport which is less than a mile from our facility. We can launch three trains at once to the north, south, and east."

"That'll help appease the governor. We need to get our government on board, so to speak."

Everyone laughed at that. The train jokes seemed to roll at these meetings. "I can get Dad to arrange drinks and dinner the Poinsett Club in Greenville. It's one of the best venues in town. It was greatly enlarged in the early 1970's with a large grand ballroom and paneled bar, but there are several smaller elegant dining rooms. I just need a number of guests to decide which room to reserve."

"Fine. I'll let the ambassadors know."

⁜

AFTER DINNER, HEW AND SAM MET in the old cabin for after dinner drinks. Winter was coming and the staff had built a nice fire in the old brick fireplace. "That was a great meeting. I think that after we unveil the new trains, we can dispense with our protection details. On another subject, I've got some bad news for you. We won't be pursuing the downtown Charleston ports property."

"What? Why not? I'm counting on you to make me millions."

"I don't think you and I will live long enough to see it finished. The opposition will be massive. We did a historic buildings survey, a historic land survey, an environmental analysis—it's a contaminated brownfield site—and we've met with the city planning staff, the Preservation Society, Historic Charleston Foundation, and the adjacent neighborhood groups. I actually agree with the Preservation Society and the Foundation. Their positions make sense, but unfortunately, they keep saying they don't want to see reproduction buildings. They want to see buildings that fit the context. The problem is, they either can't or won't show examples to us. The neighborhood groups only want to see a park, and they demand that if any more buildings are constructed, they must look exactly like the old buildings right down to the window panes, shutters, massing, and historic colors.

"There is one lingering issue and that concerns the proposed new cruise terminal. They've been fighting the state port folks in court for several years over the driving of a single additional pile and there's no end in sight at the moment. If that weren't enough, the city staff is an even bigger problem. They're passive aggressive bureaucrats. They sit expressionless in the meetings and at every meeting and hand out sheets of new requirements. Many contradict the ones that they gave us the last time. No one controls them. The city council can't be bothered. They are a law unto themselves.

"Tippy's brother thinks that we may be looking at a minimum of fifteen to twenty years to get a building permit for anything. Oh, and I forgot to mention the Board of Architectural Review. They're a piece of work. For example, a property owner had a fine 1814 wooden single house that recently burned. The front façade and three old brick chimneys were left partially standing. The city insisted that he rebuild exactly as it had been, and they demanded that he shore everything until construction permits were issued. He hired three structural engineers before the city agreed to the findings of the third one. The cost for the shoring was proposed to be over $400,000 and the city tried to issue a $1000-a-day fine for not starting. He sold the property and the city staff immediately let the new owner tear down absolutely everything. These folks are hired by the mayor and have let a little bit of power give them absolute dictatorial power. They serve themselves and no one can stop them.

"I've got an interesting project in Scotland that's moving into planning. I'm going there next. I'm going to start that work in the spring. I'm sorry, but Eberhart is not going to continue with this Charleston work."

"I can't have my money tied up that long. What do you suggest?"

"Tippy's brother suggests that you sell it. Offer it for bid to the highest bidder. Someone will bite."

"I don't know. My few acres there alone are worth some money. Maybe I can use that as a bargaining chip. I'll talk with my attorneys."

33
REPORTS

Hew convened the first meeting of the Scottish team he had assembled for the feasibility study for restoring and improving the castle. He had provided trailers—caravans as they were known locally—for the team members, and this meeting was held in the project office meeting trailer. It was a bit small, but the hotel in Craigellachie had provided a draped table, a projector, a small table for the laptop computers, and a podium. Hew made a mental note to buy himself a UK-powered computer and projector. The top of the table was covered with reports and drawings.

"We have a big agenda today so I want to ask you to dispense with the platitudes and usual opening preludes and dive straight into your briefings. We all know each other, so just begin. I know you're all happy to be a part of the team so no need to tell us that. First up is archaeology. What have you discovered thus far?"

"I'm Brian from Dig Scotia." He had been educated at Cambridge, but his old accent came through on many of his words once he started talking. "We've only begun—scratched th' surface so ta speak." He chuckled at his own joke. "But we have already made interesting finds. Our team includes archaeologists, osteoarcheologists, funerary archaeologists, and palynologists. We started at the river since that's the way our civilization began. We have found traces of an early iron age settlement, and parts of a Pict and Celtic village down by the river."

Hew could suddenly see his project spiraling out of control. He was only interested in the castle. His Scot's budget was under attack. "Excuse, me, but I'm not familiar with these 'ologists.'"

A quiet snicker rippled through the crowd.

Brian's tone was borderline condescending. "For those of you not really familiar with these terms. Osteoarchaeologists study bones, or as they like to say, 'the truth in our bones.' Funerary archaeologists study ancient burial practices, and palynologists study ancient dust particles that are strewn around such sites.

"As we all know, clans are the networks of the descendants of these early people, and by the way, the word *clan* comes from the Gaelic word for children. We quickly found small earthen works—now circular berms mostly. They're characterized by the fact that they have a small, now barely discernible depression which was the door to the dwelling. Over time, this opening has allowed rain water to drain from within the circular work. We've excavated two of them and they've proven to be the remnants of stonework. They're full of artifacts from the earliest times up until the castle were built. Sorry, Hew. *Was* built for you Americans." More giggling. Hew ignored it.

"The river floods have probably washed away most of the settlement, but these were higher up on the banks. The Spey River floods regularly and the water level has risen and fallen over the centuries. One of our greatest finds came last week when we found the prow of a Viking longboat buried in the mud of the riverbank. The Romans are not known to have occupied this area, but we assume they explored it. Most people know about Hadrian's wall, but they don't know about Antoine's Wall. It were—sorry, *was*—further north of Hadrian's."

"Don't worry about the grammatical differences, Brian. I understand. Just get on with it."

"Okay. It were an earthen mound with ditches and possibly topped with a wooden palisade. It stretched basically from what is now Edinburgh to Glasgow and is thought to be the northern termination of the Roman outpost. They never were able to control us highlanders." That brought a chuckle from the home team. Hew was going to want a word, as the English say, with this guy.

"The current village dates from the reign of Charles II. The bothies are constructed from the ruins of the castle. The stones show marks of having been previously used."

"Excuse me. Bothies?"

"Sorry, sir. A bothy is an old Scottish word for a small cottage."

"Then what's a croft?"

"A croft is the house of a *shepherd*. You own both bothies and crofts. We've only researched a few of the bothies. We are still exploring that area but it's likely that the villagers lived inside the castle fortifications rather than down by the river before Charles II's reign. The Viking raids would probably have caused them to abandon the old Celtic and Pict settlement. By allowing the native trees and brambles to grow along the banks, they may have fooled the raiders into continuing to move on. We believe the first construction built high on the mountain was a place of refuge and was built of wood."

"Brian, do you think it were a broch?"

Hew was exasperated. "What's a broch?"

"We'd need a brochologist to make sure, but I dinna think it. Brochs were on the western coast mostly. If I find dry stacked stones then there might have been a few later iron age wheel houses here but we need more time to investigate."

Hew asked, "What's a wheel house? Are there wheelhouseologists too?"

"No. First, brochs are only found in Scotland—no where else in the world. They were round stone towers and were double-walled struc-tures with a passage containing the stairs between the two walls. They were dry stacked—no mortar—and were extremely thick. They're from the Iron Age and were absolutely ingenious. I'd expect to find one at the coast by the mouth of the river or on top of Ben."

"Remind me about the Iron Age."

"It were the time from 1200 B.C. to about 600 B.C.—well afore the Vikings."

"Can you date it more specifically to this site?"

"Depends. The people of every age always used the same local clay for the pots. The Vikings used stone pots so we can tell their stuff, but it's hard before them. The outer wall stopped the wind and rain and the inner wall provided dry warmer living spaces on several levels. There's one still standing in Scotland and it's 13 meters—sorry, Hew—about 44 feet high and 20 feet in diameter. They were huge. A wheel house is also from the Iron Age. They were round also, but low. The chambers were divided with spoke-like stone walls. It seems probable, though, from the construction type found here that your ancestors were probably defenders and protectors rather than warriors. As a small wooden palisade, it would have served as a refuge to hide from the Vikings. It was in the dense forest and probably couldn't have been seen from the river. We're still exploring that. With a little advanced warning—they probably posted a lookout on top of the hill because he could have seen all the way to the sea on a clear day. Fires with telltale smoke in the fort could have been quickly extinguished until the raiders passed. Stone castles didn't appear this far north until the middle to latter part of the twelfth century. This location appears to have been a defendable place rather than a place from which to launch an attack. We doubt that, even as large as it is today, it ever housed a garrison. The building conservator will explain more about that. We've got years of work ahead of us."

Hew cringed. Next up was the historian, but after forty five minutes, Hew diplomatically cut her off. Her details were almost Biblical with all the begetting of the generations. She enjoyed her details.

"Thank you, Mirren. In the interest of time, we'll forgo the further details of your very interesting finds. I really look forward to reading your full report on my maternal ancestors. It's a subject I've never had time to explore. I'm glad you told us that no battles were fought here, and I can assure you that we will have a complete ancestral history exhibit room for our guests to explore."

Next up was the building conservator, Baird Campbell. Hew really liked him. He was on the team at Swan Bay and worked for a Philadelphia conservationist's firm. He had a bachelors degree in Architecture from Clemson University, a masters in Preservation Technology from Boston Architectural College, and a PhD in Preservation from the University of Edinburgh. His dissertation was on medieval Scottish masonry.

"My team is collaborating with all the others and I must tell you that we're all getting along nicely. I think the bottles of Macallan you've been providing every evening has helped build camaraderie." That got a round of applause and a few 'hear hears.' Overall, Hew was happy with this group. Following his cousin James's suggestion, he had deliberately found Scottish experts for part of the work as a way to build trust in an area of suspicious highland country folks.

Baird continued. "We agree that even though this ultimately was a rather large castle, it was built as a safe place. It's tucked into the hillside rather than commanding a position at the top of the mountain. This position allows surveillance of river traffic. The castle is constructed mostly of local sandstone from the hillside. This sandstone is a good building material because it is resistant to weathering and as we all have discovered, the mountain mists foretell immediate rain. There's an old poem, 'If Ben Aigan hae a cap, be sure yer be gettin' a drap.'"

"Remind me what Ben Aigan means, please."

"It means the hill of the cleft or notches. The early stonework is full of hematites which are iron oxides. That makes those stones very hard and gives us the predominately reddish sandstone color. The construction indicates the tall rectangular tower house portion was built in the second half of the thirteenth century. Historians know it as a peel tower. These towers were basically keeps or places of refuge. Your ancestors don't seem to have been waring people."

Mirren nodded in approval. "Fast moving raiders worked during daylight and moved on. This mountain location probably wasn't worth the effort to climb."

"Is it possible to be more precise with a date?"

"Yes, I was just coming to that. We retained the services of dendrochronologists from Oxford University. They use small borings from timbers to date the trees. They have dated the timelines in the roof beams and floors joist to the winter of 1255. The trees were cut then and as you know, the builders used green wood so we're very confident in that date."

"Wow. That's about as precise as it gets. That means the stone walls were probably under construction before that. Fascinating stuff."

Baird kept on. "Subsequent generations made significant additions. In the interest of time, I'll just say that we believe, based on size, that about 75 people lived here before the family moved to Glasgow to a more upscale modern seventeenth century city house. The old Catholic church records now in the local archives show a Cochrane baptism on May 15th of 1565, but nothing afterward. We suspect that baptisms after that were private. The records of Glasgow show the Cochranes living there in 1670. Many people restored and enlarged these castles in the 19th century after Sir Walter Scott and others romanticized castle life. Those owners added more rooms and fanciful turrets and battlements, but not your family. We suspect the fire sped up the decision to leave."

"Fire?"

"Yes, absolutely. I'll get to that in a moment. This later period of restoration created a whole new architectural style called Scottish Baronial, but the Cochranes were long gone by then. We have the paperwork from when they built their fine city house on what's known as Tobacco Row in Glasgow. The people who stayed here hauled the fallen stones down to the ancient village and built themselves new stone cottages closer to their fields and pastures. That's why there's so little rubble. The bothies, um, cottages, are in fine condition. Those people were, of course, field hands. In the earlier days, this was a safer place than down by the river.

"We now know that the beautiful extant space called the hall was not, in fact, originally a hall, but a large chapel capable of holding at least 75 people. We found that the beautiful delicate undercut hand-carved oak linenfold panelling on the east wall is full of deathwatch beetles. The beetles also infest many of the wooden floors and roofs. The paneling has been dated to the late 16th or early 17th century so it was added sometime after the Catholic Church was abolished here."

"Excuse me again. You're saying the paneling dates to after the last recorded baptism and before the move to Glasgow?"

"That's correct. The beetles' infestation must be addressed immediately, but when we began removing one of the infested panels, we realized that we had accidentally found an access panel to a space behind the paneling. It was a priest's access panel. These are commonly referred to as priestholes, which were used for hiding a Catholic priest. This was a capital offense and would have resulted in the death of the Laird and the priest if one had been discovered. Local searches were common I might add.

"We discovered religious artwork carved into the stone behind the paneling. It was a stroke of luck that we found the right panel. There is Gothic coloring and gilding on the stonework too. The space was originally the sanctuary in the chapel. It was large enough for a priest to move about comfortably during the Mass. We'll know more as we remove more of the panels. If possible, they will be conserved, but the amazing discovery of a priest's hole behind the panels is quite significant. The space was not crudely cut into the wall telling us that it was not hastily constructed after the old religion was outlawed, but it was very finely finished. There is a window with both clear and stained glass still in the wall. It's covered with stone on the outside—probably from the time the old religion was banned. The panelling was probably added to conceal the hiding place."

"How was the priest hole accessed?"

"That was the most ingenious thing of all. The paneling was set away from the stone so when anyone tapped on it looking for a hollow sound, they soon realized that every panel sounded the same. The hole was off center of the wall too. Each panel is large enough that a slim man could just squeeze through."

"So not good old Friar Tuck, then?"

That got a chuckle and a question. "Who was Friar Tuck?"

Mirren answered. "He is a mythical kind-hearted member of Robin Hood's band of merry men. He distributed the stolen wealth to the poor. The Disney cartoon film portrayed him as being extremely rotund."

Baird continued. "Each panel was set into quarter sawn oak stiles and rails with a small reveal around the panels that disguised the operable panel from all the others."

"Okay, I hate to keep interrupting, but this is fascinating. What do you mean quarter sawn?"

"Before machines were invented to saw timber, oak and other woods were cut—split I should say, across the growth rings. It made the work easier. Think about the end of a cut log. You see the circular growth rings. Now think about that as a pie and cut the slices of the pie into wedge shapes. It creates beautiful straight grained boards on the long flat sides. The problem for modern timber cutting was that there was too much waste in making the boards flat rather than wedge shaped and it was easier for the machines to cut round logs. Unfortunately, it made modern lumber more susceptible to rot because too much of the soft wood is exposed.

"There were small loose pegs at the intersection of every rail and stile. If someone completely removed the four pegs, latches fell into place and the panel couldn't be removed. If the pegs were pulled out slightly—just until a small resistance was felt, the panel could be moved forward and removed. We managed to work the pegs carefully without disturbing the work. Once we found four pegs that seemed more loose than the others, we took the gamble and started to carefully pull them out. We were lucky."

"Sounds like pulling out organ stops. On some old instruments, the organist could pull the draw knob out half way to play only one rank of a two rank mixture. Ingenious. How did the priest get out if someone pulled the wrong peg out?"

"He had release levers inside that lifted the latches. He could also open the adjacent panels so the family could see the service through the screen."

"We have something like that at the cathedral in Atlanta—without the panels, of course."

Alexis laughed. "In Atlanta, we try to hide the choir. The priests would never stand for being hidden."

Everyone laughed then. "It really was ingenious."

He then bent over and pulled a large heavy box from under the table and placed it on the draped table. He deliberately did not open the lid. "Inside the priest's hole, or old sanctuary, we discovered a gold communion set, crucifix, two gold flagons—one large and one small—and two gold candlesticks with gold bobeches. There's a large gold ciborium and even a small pocket-sized gold ciborium about the size of a tobacco tin that still contains a few communion wafers. The wine and water had dried up long ago. The vessels were set up as if awaiting another Mass. These were probably left because the priest never returned."

"At least we won't need a priest-ologist to tell us what this is."

No one laughed. "It was hidden in a niche that was concealed behind a tightly fitted stone that had not been set in mortar. The unconcealed part of the niche is surrounded by finely carved columns holding up a series of arches. This is divided into two spaces. The lower one contains the Sedalia or priest's seat, and the higher one—at about table height—contains a rare two-bowl piscina. We believe one sink was used for the priest's ablutions and the other one was used to wash the sacred vessels.

Both drains communicate directly down lead pipes into the ground. The Body of Christ must be buried in the earth. The details of the niches are picked out with gold."

Hew shuddered at the thought of the fate of that priest. "The communion wafers were probably consecrated at the last Mass and reserved for quick use in the event of a sudden emergency. Treat them carefully. I'll talk to a Catholic priest about them. Was the altar-ware and Sedalia niche on the south side?"

"Yes, it was. How did you know?"

"Read "Exodus." That's a common location for the communion vessels and elements. Today we call it a credence table. What's a bobeche?"

Alexis answered. "I know that from my altar guild duties, but ours at home are made of glass and are easy to clean. They're small round shallow dish-type collars with holes in the center that fit over the base of a candle to catch the drips of wax from drying on the ornate candlestick base. Wax is difficult to clean off of candlestick crevices without scratching the metal. If wax gets on the metal, it has to be gently heated until the wax melts. Then it can be blotted with a soft cloth. The polished brass Pascal candle stand at St. Luke's has a very large deep bobeche. The verger fills it with colorful jelly beans for the acolytes on Easter Day. You should see the congregation looking for a jelly bean when they pass by going to the communion rail. By then, of course, the beans are long gone." Most of the team members had no idea of what she had just described.

Baird continued. "These are quite sophisticated for the time and are engraved with fine delicate Celtic crosses. Let me open this box. There's one more thing. I brought the entire set for you to see."

He removed the lid, pulled on a pair of white gloves and dramatically and delicately removed an old yellowed cloth that covered one of the vessels. He was relishing this moment. "This is an old vestment for the chalice. The center of the square cloth is worked with gold thread into a Celtic cross within a circle. It precisely fits over the paten. The embroidery in the circle around the gold cross was originally red. This type embroidery is known as Opus Anglicanum. This is extremely rare and probably dates to the late 12th century."

Everyone gasped. Hew and Alexis were speechless. Hew tenderly held the large chalice and paten up to the light and turned them in his hands. They were in pristine condition. Hew turned the chalice upside down and remarked, "Did you notice this, Baird? It's engraved with hallmarks and the Latin word *fecit* which means 'I made this.' It's dated 1265. This is priceless. We'll need an expert in early hallmarks to tell us who the goldsmith was. Tell me about the cloth. How did they make gold thread?"

"At our request, The Worshipful Company of Broderers in London sent a woman here to examine this piece. It's a piece of fine linen and it's in an extremely delicate condition now. They believe the work started by placing gold coins between two thin pieces of the skin from a young lamb and pounding the coins until they were thin. If you've ever seen sheets of gold leaf, these were about three times that thickness—give or take."

"Oh, yes, I work with gold leaf all the time in my art restoration, but I've never pounded my own."

Murmurs of approval drifted through the room.

"They cut the gold into small strips about 3.2 mm wide. That's about 1/8 inch Imperial. They likely rolled the gold between their fingers around a silk thread and then pulled the thread tightly through the linen. As you can see, it's still bright, but please don't pick it up. The linen is very fragile."

Alexis smiled. "We still use similar vestments, but none of them have real gold threads. I'm going to try to make some. I love to do needlepoint while we're flying. Hew can do the pounding though."

Not knowing what else to say, Hew stumbled with his words. "Then where is the hall?"

"It's part of the ruins. The fire probably started in the kitchen. We know this because one of the ruins beside the original hall was the kitchen and neither are adjacent to the chapel. The current hall/chapel is precisely oriented east to west. The old hall is not. Sanctuaries were always oriented precisely toward the east. That's the direction of Jerusalem, the rising sun. Many believe it's the direction from which Christ will come again.

"The large six foot long and eight foot high arch that remains in the kitchen was the opening to the now destroyed fireplace and chimney. It's the largest stone arch in the building, but there's still a small baking oven hidden in the pile of rubble. There are holes where the old wrought iron fireplace cranes would have been mounted and we've found shards of 13th century pottery in the kitchen. There are shards of later cookery as well. The archeologists will bring in another team to explore this area, but we're convinced that we're correct."

"Don't tell me. There are kitchenologists too."

"Actually, we don't call them that, but yes, there are specialists. Oh, and there's a shaft in the tower that would have been the latrine. There are seats in the walls at each floor and a pit at the bottom with an access hole for periodically cleaning it out. Usually they would open to the moat or river, but there was neither here."

Alexis turned up her nose. "Don't tell me what those 'ologists' are called. That shaft would have been for the men. The ladies used chamber pots. They would never sit on those nasty drafty holes."

"You're probably correct. There's no sign of the niches ever having had doors."

"Let's adjourn for lunch. My mind is reeling. The hotel at Craigellachie has provided box lunches and bottles of water. Baird, let's take our boxes outside. I want to examine the stone walls." Hew directed Baird away from the crowd and they selected a clean dry flat spot on the old ruin and sat down. "This has been extremely exciting. I'm going to make you the project manager with a proportionate raise in salary, but I want you to diplomatically direct all the research to the castle. While I'm interested in the Bronze Age, family history, and all of that, I'm not focused on it at the moment. We'll pick that back up later."

"Thank you. I understand and it will be done."

"Great. Now tell me what I'm looking at here. This just looks like a pile of rubble."

"It's actually quite sophisticated. The outer stones are much darker. They contain the most iron ore and are therefore the hardest. Hardness is determined by color. Notice that while they are rough cut, the grain is all laid horizontally."

"I see that now. I've never noticed that."

"The infill is actually rubble, but the infill stones are laid with their grain vertical. That makes these 2.5 meter thick walls much stronger. The mortar is interesting. Historic mortar is made from burning limestone in a process known as slaking. It's a dangerous process and your ancestors would have purchased it elsewhere because your sandstone doesn't work. The lime that's produced is mixed with sand and water to make the mortar. It's very caustic and modern masons hate it. It's mostly been replaced with Portland cement today. That's why most modern stucco and concrete cracks. Portland cement shrinks about seven percent by volume as it cures. Lime, on the other hand, cures very slowly in the presence of oxygen. In thick walls, it may remain soft and pliable for centuries. It absorbs minor movements in the walls even after it has dried. The medieval masons likely rubbed pig's fat on their burned hands every night. Also, notice that about every three meters in height, the stones are of a better finish."

"I did notice those bands. I assumed they had either weathered differently or were replacements."

"Good guess, but no. Those are regulating courses. They are exactly level and provide true horizontal and vertical bases for the next work. Also, every meter along one of those courses, a much longer stone is set lengthwise or ninety degrees to the faces of the wall. Those are bonding stones and help tie the faces to the infill."

"I saw something like that during the restoration of the brickwork at my farm in Virginia. I believe they called it English bond. This castle was very well built."

⁂

THE MORNING SESSION HAD GONE BETTER than Hew had expected. The afternoon session included questions and comments from Historic Scotland and the local preservation community. Hew prepared himself for battle. This had all the earmarks of requiring the patience of Job. First up was Historic Scotland. "Dr. Ramsay, sir, I'm Dr. Malcolm Knox, Board Chair of Historic Scotland. Thank you for inviting us to your most excellent presentation this morning. As a descendant of the Cochranes I'm hopeful that you'll be treating this property with the respect it deserves. The reports are promising, but we dinna know what your intentions are about, Sir. I look forward to your appearing before us for the planning consent. Please enlighten us. Who are you and what are you wanting to do with the castle?"

Hew remembered the entries in Capt'n John's journals about his dealings with the Knox followers before he left Scotland. He decided to treat this man with respect. "Those are fair questions. I have Scottish DNA on both my paternal and maternal side. My paternal ancestors are Bishops and Ramsays from Midlothan. You've already heard about my maternal ancestors. That's why we're here.

"My name was changed from Bishop to Ramsay when I was a teen-ager in America in an effort to protect me from my family's enemies. My baptism record shows John Bishop XII. I'm a direct male descendant of Sir James Bishop, born about 1470 and Sir A.L.D. Ramsay, born about 1464. My DNA runs deep. I took the name of my ancestor, Charteris Hew Lady Elizabeth Ramsay of Clatto, Midlothan, Scotland. One of her relatives saved the life of King James VI during the Gowrie Conspiracy."

Malcolm nodded approvingly. "And what about your family, Mrs. Ramsay? Do you have such a distinguished Scottish ancestry?"

Alexis answered matter of factly., "Oh, yes, a wee drop. I'm a Williams of the Welsh coal miner Williamses on my dad's side—not the mine owners, but the workers—but they really knew how to sing. My mother's maternal line is directly descended from the prominent Scottish historical figure, John Knox."

That got Malcolm's attention. He began to warm up to Hew and Alexis. "And your intentions for the property, sir?"

"I inherited the castle and purchased the acreage to bail out my cousin from the draconian death taxes. By way of reference, I inherited an 8,000-acre farm in Virginia. It's been in my family since the mid-17th century. We recently restored it, exceeding the best preservation guidelines America has. I believe that building codes and guidelines are starting points, not finishing points. A build that only meets code is the worst building allowed by law."

Dr. Knox smiled.

"I know a little about brick and timber. We've replanted a portion of our old tobacco farmland with native pine trees since we no longer grow tobacco. During the recent research process there, archivists discovered that my ancestor, Captain John Bishop, learned to grow tobacco after arriving in Virginia by indenturing himself to Thomas Gray, whom we also believe was a relative. Capt'n John quickly rose to prominence once he had paid his debt. My cousin, from whose estate I purchased the property, suggested that I turn this castle into a hotel, but the research and feasibility is just starting. I want to hear from you folks first. My educational background is in business and sustainable real estate development with a terminal degree from The London School of Economics, and yes, it's a PhD although I prefer not to be addressed as Doctor. I prefer to live in the background without accolades. I'm president and CEO of an American component of Eberhart Construction of Germany. We only build environmentally sensitive works. I have absolutely no intention of wasting years of my life and vast sums of money in court battles over this property. I will say at this point, I would like to restore the extant buildings with new roofing, timbers, doors and windows. I plan to employ local craftspeople wherever possible. I would like to properly manage the remaining native forest and plant more trees, but I absolutely have no desire to rebuild the ruins. They will be managed, but I have no intention of turning this treasure into an Ole Scotia theme park."

The room erupted in applause when Hew sat down and Mr. Knox cleared his throat. "Well, Doctor, er, sir, as I said earlier, we look forward ta hearing about your plans as they are developed."

Hamish Douglas, the local preservationist spoke next. "We dinna approve of more hotels. Nothing can disturb the look or trails of castle. I ken 'at to be a problem."

The group moved to the hotel bar.

LATER, AFTER THE GROUP HAD DISBURSED, Hew confided to his cousin. "That was entirely too easy."

James sat at the grand piano in the now empty hotel bar playing a tune Hew recognized.

"What are you playing? I've heard that tune."

"It's an old 19th-century Scottish folk tune recalling the Jacobite era about Bonnie Prince Charles named *The Skye Boat Song*, or *Over the Sea to Skye*. You probably heard it as the music from the TV series, *Outlander*."

"Oh, yes. I loved that series and that song. Alexis thought it was too bloody."

301

James began to play and sing, "*Speed bonnie boat, like a bird on the wing, onward! the sailors cry; Carry the lad that's born to be king over the sea to Skye.* Don't worry. They were just being nice. The battle's just starting. You'll need your own boat to Skye if you're not careful."

"Hmmm. I might compose a fantasia on that tune when I get home. James, why do you think the family just left that gold communion ware in the chapel?"

"I know that at some point, the family converted to The Church of Scotland to appease Knox's crowd, but we always assumed that happened after the move to Glasgow. Now, I'm thinking that after the paneling was built, the family converted and the later generations just forgot about the old ways. How do you plan on making a hotel invisible?"

"Easy. We're going underground. I deliberately left the land conservationist out of the meeting. He's already told me that the land below the castle is highly disturbed and will be easy to build on. Much of it looks like open pasture, but it is actually rubble used as fill from the old quarry. By going underground, we will avoid driving piles or digging deep foundations to reach good rock. We'll plant the new roof to restore the pasture and the only thing that's visible will be the glass walls along the river view and we will cant those windows to avoid reflections from the sun. It's a northern exposure, anyway."

"Hauling that much dirt up the mountain woulda' been a back breaking job."

"Yeah, but the soil isn't very deep and the dirt was plentiful along the river, and buying stone and hauling it up the mountain would have been worse. Don't tell the ologists about this yet. That dirt is probably full of old artifacts."

"Aye. We Scots are good at saving money. Why do you think the kitchen and great hall fell into ruin?"

"I asked Baird about that over cocktails. He surmises that the kitchen fire—probably in the middle of the night—was extensive and too expensive to rebuild. It must have come at a time when they were thinking about moving. We always used to worry about the kitchen at Swan Bay because the cooks went to bed and left the grits to cook all night long. The roof here was timber framed and was covered with tile shingles. A few shingle shards are in the rubble. The better ones are still on the roofs of the bothies. The wind probably blew the embers onto the roof of the hall. He suspects the larger hall was covered with wooden shingles to reduce the weight on the timber framing and to save money."

James grunted.

"There are partially decayed pieces of oak shingles and fine thick oak framing members buried in the rubble. The walls of the tower are much higher so it probably escaped the fire."

"What'll you do with the gold pieces?"

"In the long term, I don't know, but tomorrow they will go into a bank vault in Aberdeen and then to my vault in Virginia. The cloth is going to Oxford to conservators Alexis knows and trusts. Your Mr. Knox couldn't take his eyes off of the gold, though. He actually caressed 'em."

⁂

AFTER DINNER, HEW AND JAMES DECIDED to walk to the nearby pub for a few more. Hew wanted to experience more of the local flavor. As they made their way in the crowded room toward an empty table, several of the local women started looking at Hew and giggling. When James walked up to the bar to place their orders, one of them came up to him. "Is that the new laird?"

"Aye. Would you like to meet him?"

"Aye."

All four of them walked over, drinks in hand. Hew stood for the introductions pulled up more chairs, and once they sat down, the giggling got louder. "We see the resemblance, sir."

"Resemblance to whom?"

"Ach. Ye mustn't a heard th' legend then."

"What legend?"

"Yer ancestor's legend. Yer a Cochrane for sure, sir. When the Vikings first sailed into th' river, they stole, raped, and murdered. One tall curly blond, blue eyed Viking raped seven women in one day. He were a bull o' a man for sure. One thirteen year old girl gave birth to a tall blond headed blue eyed boy. She were th' first he raped. Th' other women had girls. They started calling the boy Cockram. Thas where yer surname comes from."

Hew realized that the girls were completely drunk. "How's about raising yer kilt and let's see if ye measure up t' yer name?"

Another one was running her hand up the inside of his thigh. Hew slapped her hand away as forcefully as he could. He jumped up nearly knocking over the table. "Bloody Hell, James, let's get out of here."

As they walked back to the hotel, James asked, "What was that about?"

"She ran her hand up my thigh."

James chuckled. "Twenty years ago your reaction would'a been different."

"Twenty years ago she would have been still in diapers."

They both laughed. "Put no stock in the legend. The name's changed spelling many times. The Cochrane's, the Bishop's, and the Ramsay's are all lowland Scots. The land here come from the marriage dowery of a Highland Laird's lassie to yer ancestor."

"Hmmm, well, some of the DNA is still there."

"Aye, cousin. Aye." They both laughed.

⚜

THE NEXT MORNING, HEW, ALEXIS, AND James met with the financial and marketing team. Sir John had found two railroad carriages and Hew had them under option. He discovered that the route was a regular passenger route so he would probably need to build a small station too. The building of a hotel was not as straightforward. The pro forma numbers showed that they needed at least fifty rooms and the occupancy would need to be maintained at a high level to turn a profit. They doubted that the location without a golf course would make it. "Guys, fifty rooms won't be a problem. We can probably go as high as seventy-five without overloading the property. The castle rooms can be used as meeting rooms and the chapel can be used for weddings."

"But do you realize how many wedding venues there already are in the UK? What will make yours stand out?"

Alexis spoke up. "We'll market it differently. It's a retreat from the busy modern world. Almost monastic." Hew winced at those words remembering his boarding school in Bogota. She saw it, but it was too late

304

to retract them. "Out here, you're away from everything. Our chef will be second to none, and James will ensure a first rate Scottish experience. We'll offer package deals with non-stop flights from anywhere to Aberdeen aboard our private jet and our rates will be ridiculously low. We don't need much profit. We only need to break even."

"NO PROFIT? What if you run at a loss?"

"That's the gamble we're ready to take. Alexis is right."

"Sounds like you're determined. Just try to keep the construction costs down."

"Don't worry. Eberhart will build it but we will use select local craftspeople to do some of the work. We're meeting with the design team this afternoon."

"We know what that means. You don't do cheap."

Something was troubling Hew's mind about all of this, but he couldn't figure out what it was.

JOHAN, HEIDI, AND HANS ARRIVED ON site by helicopter from the Aberdeen airport and Hew, Alexis, and James met them. Johan and Heidi, now a married couple, were ecstatic about the property. Hans, as usual, didn't show much emotion. "The idea of going underground is fantastic. We can develop the ruins as passive gardens and use them as a site for a large marquee for outdoor events. We can use the existing historic entrance as the new entrance. We'll access the ensuite rooms through tunnels from the castle.

"I think we should locate the ballroom and kitchen on the slope above the castle at the other quarry site. It's still raw, and maybe we can use the rock face as part of the rooms. The only glass we will need can be in the pre-function area, and that can be with operable skylights. Service will be easier up there. We'll also need a large indoor pool with a big retractable skylight like the ones on the Viking cruise ships, and we'll need a full service luxury spa. We'll put the hotel's back of house services there too. I don't want the guests to see the garbage."

"I'm glad you bought all the acreage. We'll need it!" Johann then translated for Hans, and Hans replied through Johan, "I like that concept, but I worry about water seepage from those rock faces. Either we develop the water as a feature, or we build new rock walls away from the existing."

"Or perhaps both?"

Heidi's creative juices had been flooding her brain."Hew, let's continue the International Style but perhaps we'll use some of Rennie Mackintosh's furniture to give a more Scottish look. I want to see the same pale grey Scottish wool on most of the walls. I agree that this won't be a theme park. Maybe we'll have your tartans made into throws and pillows. The art needs to be local but I don't want to see literal landscapes, old castles, deer, ducks, dogs, or dead salmon staring at me."

Alexis laughed. "Thank you Heidi. This isn't a place for Mies, but Mackintosh is perfect. I don't like all of his work, though. His Deco Berger armchair isn't for me, and I don't care for most Art Nouveau fabrics either. Perhaps we'll commission some contemporary local art work for the public areas."

"I agree. I don't really care for his Argyle chair, but his other work, including those boxy Cassina Club chairs are great. I want each guest room to have two custom designed recliners with high backs. Alexis is correct. I want those rooms to be as serene and monastic in feeling as possible, but every space will have the best in internet access and TV. The ballroom and meeting rooms must have first rate AV and lighting. Let's build a SCIF too. We need to attract security-minded clients.

"Tell Hans we'll use ground water heat source and heat recovery as much as possible. Solar might not work in this rainy climate in the winter. Oh, and every guest room needs a fireplace so check out the local gas sources. Johann, we need to hide the vent stacks within rock work. Maybe a dry stacked stone wall? On another subject, I want to restore the chapel. We'll get an organ built for the musician's gallery. I want the Bishop of Aberdeen to give it a proper Scottish Episcopal Church consecration, but we'll keep that to ourselves until after everything is finished and we have opened."

34
FRAUD

The monthly meeting of the construction team they had nicknamed the Brunhild Construction team met in New York City in the conference room of the senior partner of Bishop Hardy. It had been Hew's late grandfather's office. Hew cringed when he saw the furniture and artsy giclée scenes of Paris. The meeting opened with the usual preliminaries. Jason gave the status report.

"We're on target to complete the last thirty miles to the docks along the Hudson River in two months—weather permitting. Last winter was brutal but we've made up about half of the time we lost. There have been no injuries to date. We did have one incident that you need to know about. Hew will brief you on that."

Hew nodded. "Many years ago, while I was in high school actually, members of the Eberhart design team and I created a computer program to monitor worker productivity."

"Isn't that the one where you made your first billion, Hew?"

A quiet chuckle ran around the table. "Actually, I've made two billion five hundred million, plus or minus, if you really want to know, but I didn't keep all of it."

Now they laughed out loud. "We've been using it successfully on this project and in the early days, we caught a few, but everyone has really fallen into line since then. Jason is actually referring to my second program. We've been using a beta testing of it for the last six months both here and on Eberhart projects in Atlanta. Only Charlie, Jason, and

307

I know about it. It watches the purchases and uses of materials. Every computer in the purchasing departments and every computer in the production areas are linked to this program running in the background. It's not perfect yet because we need to set up a system to tag each piece of material and that's taking time to implement. There are too many questions from suppliers but we're making progress tying their existing systems into a new one of my design. We're negotiating fees, and we're being generous, but those who don't agree will quickly find themselves off of our preferred supplier list."

Sam grunted.

"To date, this project has been clean except for one guy and he has been terminated. It turns out that he was mobbed up anyway. Pink was able to dig that out. He'll never know that we know, though. I'm very proud of our folks and at the end of the project, we'll find a way to quietly reward them. Unfortunately, we had to let a longtime employee go in my Atlanta office."

Bubba Hu began his report. "The rolling stock testing is complete and the first shipment of powered units is on the ocean bound for the port of Charleston. They're wrapped and we'll keep them that way until we're ready to place them on the roadbed. They'll be shipped from Charleston to the inland port at the appropriate time. So far, no one is watching the production facility on the old Charleston Navy base. It's time, though, to begin installing the electronics in the container carriage frames and in the roadbed. Everything has been tested in Germany and the shipment to Japan was successful for testing the units there. We're still under budget."

That got a warm round of applause, but Sam sighed. "I wish we could have been there for the test run."

"I know," said Hu, "but it was just too risky. As it is, there will be questions when we start inserting the electromagnetic modules into the slots on the roadway. There are damned drones overhead everywhere along the route now. One bit of news is for your team, Alexis. The son of the emperor has decided not to attend, citing pressing business in Switzerland. Since the opening will take place at the South Carolina inland port, the Japanese ambassador will represent the country. He will fly into the Greenville-Spartanburg Airport and fly back to DC. He'll only be on the ground for a max of four hours, weather permitting. I understand the American and German ambassadors will accompany him. It won't be much more than a photo op."

"That's a big relief. We'll still have a small dinner party that evening for this team, though. I've sourced a red wool runner if you still want it. My dad has reserved the room for the dinner afterwards. We're working on a series of barbecues along the route for the workers."

After they concluded the meeting, Hew treated everyone to a catered meal in his penthouse apartment in the Carlyle Hotel.

After dinner, when everyone else had left for their beds, Charlie asked Hew to join him on the terrace for a cigar. "We've got a bit of a problem. Dad called me after the meeting today. You will be served when you return to Atlanta. That woman we fired from accounting is suing for false termination."

"Hell! This sounds like Alexis's never-ending suit. She doesn't know what we have on her, does she? She doesn't know about our beta testing of the purchasing software does she?"

"No. Only you and I know that."

"Good. Remind me of our records."

"She worked for us and her family hardware business simultaneously from her desk in our office—on our computer using our cell phone. She was double-billing time in addition to milking our suppliers to help her parents. She, for instance, attended several weeklong national trade shows for building materials and hardware. In several of those weeks, she billed 58 hours in 40-hour periods. She typically billed fourteen to sixteen hour days split between us and her parents.

"Since we didn't have her billing for her parents, and they didn't have ours, no one noticed, but she used our time to purchase goods for them. That's documented with our new software. It wasn't until I dumped her computer just before you fired her that we found the problem."

"But she was initially terminated for letting a client skate."

"True, but she mailed her time sheets to her parents using our mailing materials and postage machine. We have records of that too. She's going to get hit with mail fraud when we countersue. She'll never know what hit her until it's too late. Oh, and get this. She took our laptop home with her, saying she could work off-hours at home and be away from the phones. She didn't know that her teenage son was texting and emailing his girlfriend from our laptop. It's the most XXX-rated stuff I've read in a long while. They were looking at porn and having sex while the parents were at Bible study, and then the next day, reminiscing about it in juicy detailed emails. They had signed some sort of purity pledge at their church so they were *only* having oral and anal sex."

"Okay, well, that has nothing to do with her suit or our defense, so just erase it. She's got enough problems without that."

"Get our lawyers to hit her hard and quick. I want this settled ASAP. If necessary, we'll pay her legal fees just to make it go away, but not a dime more."

35

DEPOSITION

"Hello, Edward," said Alexis on the phone. "The trip to Scotland took my mind off the suit but I guess you want to hear about my deposition today. Let me put you on speaker. I was just about to tell Hew about it and I don't want to repeat myself."

"Sure. Go ahead. I've already talked with Janet, but I want your version. I heard you gave 'em hell."

"I wouldn't say that. It lasted six hours. I was as polite as Melody in *Gone With the Wind* until Amos came across the table at me.

"First, he was thirty-five minutes late. The subpoena was for ten a.m. I forced them to start at five after ten without him by telling them I was nearly nine months pregnant with twin boys and I might need to leave at anytime. That got their attention. We went through the usual 'who are you' stuff and the second team started asking questions. Six sets of lawyers all asking basically the same damned questions.

"I had already told Janet that two of the Academy people had lied in their depositions so it became a matter of my refuting their statements. I was calm, clear, and polite. My statements were simply matter of fact without any emotion. Amos waltzed in as if nothing were wrong and immediately got irritated that we had started without him. Janet shut him up. He was fuming and sat down and pouted. It took the others another hour to finish, and then he wanted to start at the beginning. Janet forcefully told him he could read my answers in the transcript.

"'So,' he said, "is it true your husband is one of the wealthiest men in

North America, Ms. Ramsay?'

"I was sitting back in my chair and I replied, 'My husband isn't part of this matter and neither is his net worth.'

"He jumped up from his seat, pounced across the table, and got in my face. 'I'll ask you anything I please and you'll answer.'"

"Janet objected, but I calmly replied, 'Amos, sit down and get your curdled cream coffee breath out of my face. You almost made me vomit. You're a condescending misogynistic bully and your tactics don't work on me. I'll have Janet file a complaint to get you removed from this case if you try that stunt again.'

"He responded, 'Now, my dear, let's not go all pregnant female here. I know your emotional state.'

"I responded, 'At exactly which point in these proceedings did I become your dear? How dare you try to assume you know anything about my emotional state!'"

"With that, he stood and announced the deposition was over and walked out. After that, Janet congratulated me. She said that she had never seen anyone handle themselves like that before. She said my responses were brilliant."

Hew and Edward laughed. "A lawyer does that when he has nothing," said Edward. "He was trying to trip you up and it didn't work. Brava, my dear." Hew spilled his scotch and the guys rolled with laughter again.

Alexis didn't think it was so funny.

36
SUCCESS

Sam had actually been secretly hoping to unveil the new trains on Christmas Day as a nod to the first passenger train, the Best Friend of Charleston, but the embassies wouldn't agree. The date was set for Saturday, March 12.

The day dawned cool and clear in upstate South Carolina. The elevated platform at the transfer facility at the inland port was two miles long and a quarter of a mile wide. There were twenty staging tracks and a Y-roadbed arrangement that allowed trains coming or going east to Charleston to move smoothly onto or off of the main North-South line. Five large cranes stood like their avian namesakes ready to lift the first ceremonial containers from trucks onto the magnetically powered flatcars. Three completely shrouded locomotives stood on the roadbed. The sleek shark nosed units contained the computers and electronics that responded to the main servers in Atlanta which allowed the driver-less units to work. They were ready to head to the ports of New Jersey, New Orleans, and Charleston.

Sam was almost giddy with anticipation. He had successfully eluded the truckers' unions, the longshoremen's union, the Chinese, the Russians, and the railroad engineers' union. In a few hours, they would know that the railroad had taken back the long-haul freight business.

Sam's family had held a grudge for generations. The railroads owned and maintained their own property, but the federal government had paid for the interstate highways. The truckers, while paying taxes, still got a better deal than the railroads even though the railroads paid taxes too. One train engineer could do the work of hundreds of truckers. Now, neither would be needed.

At eleven a.m., the Southern Railway Company Board of Directors and their spouses began to leave the tent where waiters in white shirts, black coats, and Ramsay-tartan-patterned bow ties had been serving Bloody Marys, mimosas and pastries. A marching band and bagpipers from the Military College of South Carolina entertained the gathering crowd of about a thousand curious spectators. A pool of reporters and TV cameras would send the ceremony live to media outlets around the world.

Alexis and her team had managed to build the secrecy to an international news frenzy. Everyone wanted to know what the secrecy was all about. At 11:55, her one-hundred-foot-long bright red Scottish wool carpet was rolled out and Sam and Hew led the ambassadors of the US, Germany, and Japan, and the governors of the states, along the route onto the stage. Their spouses accompanied them, although a very pregnant Alexis was visibly uncomfortable. At noon, the signal lights along the entire system roadbed turned from red to amber. Sam walked to the podium and asked, "Would everyone please rise for the presentation of the colors and our national anthems, please?"

The flags of the three countries were raised and the three national anthems played by the band. Hew had been adamant that no soloist would warble their own self-serving versions of the anthems. There had been some concern that veterans of World War II would be upset at seeing the flags of Japan and Germany fly alongside the Stars and Stripes, but the governor assured Sam that those flags had been flying in many places in SC for years without incident.

Speeches followed. At 12:45—the South Carolina governor's welcoming speech was entirely too long—the spouses of the three ambassadors moved forward to the three locomotives. The shrouds were removed and Sam saw his machines for the first time. He gasped. Someone had decided to paint them in the forest green and white livery of the old Southern Railway locomotives that had been retired when the passenger service ended. The 24-carat gold stripes and lettering gleamed under the cloudless blue South Carolina sky. The Charleston unit carried the name Best Friend in honor of the Best Friend of Charleston. The other two units were named Somei Yoshino in honor of the Japanese cherry blossoms, and Edelweiss. Sam was glad his dark polarized sunglasses hid his tears of joy.

Hew was amused. He sensed that this was Alexis's work. The three locomotives were christened with champagne, and along the route, the signal lights turned from amber to green. The large cranes then moved to ceremoniously load containers onto flatbed carriages and cover them with gleaming polished silver colored lightweight composite covers made from kudzu that had been developed by the Clemson University research team. The covers would reduce wind resistance and keep the coal, gravel, and pulpwood containers from losing their cargo from the high speed suction.

Sam knew immediately that they would look like the old passenger trains of the 1940s and 50s. Unfortunately, one of the cameramen used a telephoto lens to show the crane and noticed there were no windows. He then trained his lens on one of the locomotives and noticed that there were no windows there either.

The whole world now knew that this was a fully automated system and text messages began to fly. The locomotives began to move slowly on the embedded tracks using small retractible flanged wheels until their speed allowed the SCMAGLEV system to take over. Then, in a silent flash, they were gone, leaving the crowd speechless. The world would now know that those tracks embedded in the platforms were there to get the trains started. Alexis had not lied to the press—she simply hadn't told the whole story. Sam stepped to the podium and explained exactly what they had just witnessed. The crowd, amazed at what they had seen and heard, dispersed slowly. Many waited to see if the Charleston train would actually reappear as Sam had boasted.

The dignitaries moved back to the tent for a champagne brunch. Food trucks rolled in to treat those members of the public who wanted to stay and wait for Charleston's unit to return. The crowd moved back onto the stage an hour later to witness the flash as the Charleston train returned.

Crowds had also gathered in North Charleston on the dock and in boats in the harbor to witness the event. It was only when the trains reappeared at the inland port that everyone knew that they had really witnessed a historic event.

It was momentous for Alexis as well. Just as the other returning trains passed, her water broke, so she and Hew missed the dinner at the Poinsett Club that evening. Instead, her father rose to announce to the 150 guests the happy birth of two grandsons, William Douglas Ramsay and Robert Daniel Ramsay. Their DNA results showed them to be 99.9999% identical. The boys weighed nine pounds, ten ounces and had blue eyes and curly blond hair. He assured them that mother and boys were well and that Alexis was in good spirits. Toasts ran on for thirty minutes.

The chef had included tender shoots of new kudzu in the salads. Even Sam agreed that they were tasty. Kudzu was becoming the newest fad in high end restaurants across the country. One chef in Charleston had started offering a cold kudzu soup on his menu at an extremely high price. The Spoleto Arts Festival crowd couldn't get enough. The conservative Wildlife Festival folks wouldn't touch it. Clemson University plant and animal science folks began harvesting it and selling it at a profit. Sam laughed all the way to the bank.

Sam left early to fly to New Jersey to start a series of barbecues along the route for the workmen. He ran into trouble immediately. The railroad union leaders had seen the livestream and had discovered that the new trains were unmanned. They threatened an immediate strike when they realized that the cranes were completely computerized too.

Sam's board had anticipated this. He still had to deal with the longshoremen's union, but he immediately negotiated a significant raise for all remaining train crew members. He gave a generous early retirement bonus to anyone who wanted to leave and assigned those who stayed to the surface routes as openings became available.

Times were changing. They had already been experiencing labor shortages so this move filled the vacancies. As for the unions, he acknowledged that working conditions had been rough in the 1890s but there would be no working conditions with the new system. Computers don't need benefits or hourly operating rules. His problems with the truckers were just beginning, but he was ready to fight to the bitter end with them. They had been unmerciful to the railroads once the interstate highway system opened. The public interstate highway drivers would help him with that fight. The president had agreed not to raise gas taxes on private automobiles. The taxes would be passed along to the companies shipping the freight. After all, they benefitted from the decreased shipping times. The increase would be small and spread out over years since the government wouldn't be paying for the maintenance of the new system.

All of the residents of the small towns along the route praised the new silent trains. Many had trouble sleeping at first because of the silence, but they quickly got used to it. They enjoyed not having to sit at the street crossings while long slow freight drags rumbled by. No one missed the diesel horns. The residents of the city of North Charleston were ready to elect Sam mayor. The new venture was a success.

Jason had discovered a way to have the Japanese high speed system work with the new American system. By modifying the design of the undercarriages, containers no longer needed to be offloaded from their carriages onto the ships and then loaded onto American carriages. One carriage type fit both standards. This saved time and labor. The automobiles and other imports and exports arrived even faster. Since he had installed standard railroad tracks onto the elevated roadbeds, he and Hans also invented a system that allowed the new carriages to be rolled using gravity down ramps and into freight yards at grade. It was a variation of the old system but this one was now completely computerized. This allowed surface transport by standard traditional rail or truck and saved even more time. Sam and his board were impressed. Jason was given a bonus and a seat on their board as a reward. Hans was given a bonus and elected to the board of Eberhart International.

MABLE SMITH AND LES WILSON SAT on the plastic covered sofa in their rusted singlewide trailer in an industrial area near Atlanta's Dekalb-Peachtree Airport, watching the late evening news. She was smoking a joint and petting her rat terrier, Sissy. He was finishing their bottle of bourbon. He'd had a busy day as a ramp rat at the airport.

"Les, look at this shit," said Mable. "That's that bitch, Alexis Ramsay. She's looking like she's gonna pop any minute. What the hell's Miss 'got rocks' doing there sitting with all them mucky de mucks?"

"Hell, I ain't got no idea. What's a 'got rocks'?"

"Oh, you know, dumb ass. Rocks equal money. Bitch got me fired. Said I was drinking on the job. Called the captain. Got you fired too over a little half a chicken salad sandwich. Damn her hide.

"I got Tommy to leave the back door unlocked so's you could get you a little free supper from the stuff the office bitches left in the break-room refrigerator. They're always leaving some good stuff cause they're always on a diet and can't be seen eating a whole sandwich. It wasn't no big deal. They wasn't no cameras in there last time I looked."

"Yeah. yeah. I done tried to shoot her and missed."

"You was drinking on the job. You said you was drunk."

"Bitch walked in the bathroom just as I was taking a little nip. My bunions was hurting something fierce. All that walking on them concrete floors. I just needed a little pain killer. She trapped me and wouldn't let me leave. The captain came in right after she called. He fired me on the spot. I hate that bitch."

"I heard she embarrassed Amos in that legal stuff. Word is he'll let her die of old age before he finishes that case."

"I wish we could help him out and send her on her way to Hell."

37
CASTLE

The presentation was finished. Hew's team had done a fantastic job. There was a large model and beautiful plans and renderings. They had thought of everything. The model was in two pieces to allow it to be easily moved. It was even lighted to show the night effect. The total cost to date for the presentation was about $150,000.

Hew and Johann flew to Aberdeen. James met them and drove them to the hotel in Craigellachie where the planning consent meeting would be held. They were sitting in the bar having a dram. "Johann," said Hew, "something is still nagging at me and I can't understand what it is."

"No need to worry. They'll throw something at us for sure that we can't anticipate. I think the worst case is we'll have ta pull the application and regroup."

At two a.m., Hew heard the old clock in the village church chiming. He sat straight up in bed. It finally came to him. It was the conversation he and Sam had had about the early settlements in the American colonies. Labor. Would there be enough nearby to staff the hotel? The site was rather remote from Aberdeen and the railroad passenger service could get them to Keith, but that's was a nearly two-hour train ride both ways assuming the train was on time, plus they would need to run a pickup service to the station. They might convince Scottish Rail to build a station by the river bridge, but he was sure he would be asked to pay for it, and if the weather were bad…

At breakfast, he broke the news to Johann. Johann sat silently as he watched a masterpiece of environmental hotel design and all of the accompanying awards vanish. He put his fork down and muttered, "Why didn't anyone know that before now? We need ta get a study done. We need ta pull tha application."

"Not entirely. Would you get on your computer and change the Powerpoint to only include the restoration and conservation of the old castle? We won't introduce the model. I think we can still get these people on our side with a reduced scheme. If we ever work out the labor issues, we can reapply. I'll figure out a new speech."

That evening, the hotel meeting room was packed even though it was a bitterly cold snowy night. The smell of alcohol and hot bodies wearing wet wool kilts permeated the air. Hew wondered if they had come to re-enact a highland battle with him as the enemy. The mood seemed hostile.

He calmly walked to the podium and spoke clearly into the microphone. "Ladies and gentlemen, thank you for coming. Dr. Knox, I wish to announce that we are hereby removing the application for planning consent for the hotel. We will only address the repair and conservation of the castle and it's environs."

The room erupted with yelling and applause. Hew had found the temperature of the crowd and he was convinced that a hotel would never have gained approval. Ninety percent of the crowd left the meeting. Hew continued and told those left that his plan was to repair and weatherproof the existing spaces still under roof. All openings would be closed with panels of satin finished black stainless steel. All rotten and beetle infested woodwork and timber would be replaced to match the original using as many local craftspeople as possible. The stone rubble would continue to be excavated by the archeologists as would the bothies and the old village berms, but there were no plans to add wiring, plumbing, or heating to the castle. It would be left as it was the day after the Cochrane's moved out.

He almost won total approval. The commission would not allow the occupied bothies to be disturbed. He could only research the bothies as they became empty. That rarely ever happened, though. One generation simply took over after the older ones had died. "Hew, you came out mostly unscathed. You ain't never gonna get tha hotel, though."

"I got that loud and clear, John. I don't know what I'll ultimately do. I hate to see it just sit there."

"Ye could build yourself a small vacation bothie in the ruins."

"The last thing I want is another house. Alexis's idea of roughing it is a hotel with no room service."

38
DISCOVERY

Hew called his wife from Scotland. "Alexis, I just got off the phone with Edward about the Academy's geodesic dome disaster. The judges put the fear of God in all these attorneys. They're so many of them, the court rented a hotel ballroom in Atlanta to hold the first hearing. The attorneys then broke out into small tables and started the paperwork. They're attorneys for the Academy, the victims, the contractor, the subcontractors, the civil rights groups, the material suppliers, the insurance companies, the lien holders, the bonding company, and then there are the minor suits."

"Minor suits?"

"Yep. One such suit is with one of the TV reporters who while live on camera, stepped back into a ditch without looking and broke his leg. Edward's group was able to quickly establish the paper trail on the construction. That was relatively easy compared to the rest, but simply put, it goes like this. As we know, I only provided the funds so my involvement did not have anything to do with the construction. We're clean.

"Amos, the Academy attorney, didn't bother himself with the details. He subbed it out to an old friend and I do mean old. He presented the construction contract to Harry Kleindic, now late chairman of the Academy board, who quickly signed it and initialed and dated each page per Edward's requirements. The problem, as it turns out, is related to the original construction. The engineers designed the dome with stainless steel connectors but Kleindic followed the construction manager's suggestion and approved less expensive aluminum connectors. You know what penny pinchers these folks are. He looked like a hero to the board. Over time, the connectors slowly but surely cracked and failed and the windstorm that morning was the final act. The dome failed suddenly and completely. He was hoisted with his own petard."

"And suddenly you're quoting Shakespeare's Hamlet. It means he was blown up by his own bomb."

"I thought it sounded appropriate. The judge has excused Swan Bay Trust without prejudice so we're clear. The trials will drag on for years. According to Edward, the state will ultimately get hit with the payments. Oh, and get this. The state Attorney General and the US Attorney General have both hired Bishop Hardy as consultants. We went from being a defendant to being a prosecutor in one heart beat. Edward will be the lead. Fortunately, he has kept his law licenses current. He'll have a great time with this."

39

TRIDUUM

The services of Holy Week at the cathedral took on a very somber tone with the Thursday evening service known as Maundy Thursday. Even though there was a bright rose-colored full moon—the first full moon after the equinox always signaled the coming of Easter. The sky was completely overcast and about as dark as it ever gets in Midtown Atlanta. It was the first of the three—Tri—days—of services before Easter.

The word Maundy is derived from the Latin word for "mandate," recalling Jesus's new commandments to love one another. It begins as a normal Eucharist but quickly moves toward darkness. The lights in the cathedral gradually grow dimmer. There is a foot-washing ceremony commemorating Jesus's washing of the disciples' feet before the last Passover supper.

This was a new addition to the service and many of the old members didn't want any part of it. The cathedral altar guild rushed to find enough sterling silver bowls to keep the lines short. They didn't want the service to drag on. Alexis loaned them two of their matching antique bowls and they resorted to buying two new ones from Beverly Bremmer's silver shop. They also purchased new white Egyptian cotton towels for the priests to wipe the wet feet.

Alexis was amazed to see so many of Atlanta's finest remove their very expensive shoes to walk down the aisle. The musicians were completely silent during this part. The cathedral was absolutely silent. It was extremely moving. The service ends with the stripping of the altar and sanctuary of all the finery leaving a bare table and a cross covered with a black veil. The altar is then washed. The choir, now robed in only black, silently processes to the narthex and the remaining lights, except for one, go out. The only light is dimly lighting the blackened cross.

The unaccompanied choir sings *Were You There*. At the verse, *Were you there when they laid him in the tomb?* the remaining light was suddenly turned off and the cathedral was plunged into total darkness. The new dean of the Cathedral of St. Philip, The Very Reverend Dr. Thaddeus Carson, wanted five minutes of black silence. They compromised on one minute. The narthex lights came on and people almost ran to get out of the "tomb."

The Good Friday service was three hours of somber music, readings and homilies. The dean insisted that the lights would not be turned on. Several in the choir tried to protest and said they would use their cell phone flashlights. The dean heard this rumor and promptly walked into the choir room and demanded they leave the phones and any other devices in the choir room. He also introduced a Saturday night service to try to spread out the Easter crowds. It wasn't a new service at all, but it was new to the cathedral.

The Great Vigil of Easter would begin at sundown on Saturday of Holy Week following an old Jewish tradition. It was a service with long readings of Old Testament lessons and there would be baptisms with a celebratory champagne reception in the hall after the Eucharist.

Thad started lining up the babies well in advance. He wanted a big crowd for this first one. He had Hew prepare the children's choirs to sing. Hew thought it was too late in the day for the little kids, but their singing always brought out aunts, uncles, and grandparents. It was a clerical marketing ploy. They even let one of the older kids play the small continuo organ to accompany the youngest choristers.

There were to be twelve babies, and the new Ramsay twins were on the list. The Ramsays were flying to New York for Easter at St. Thomas Fifth Ave. It would probably be John's last Easter with the choir. He was growing rapidly and Hew remembered that his own puberty had started early.

Alexis had decided to let the twins be baptized. Hew had wanted to wait and have it at Westover Church in VA as the other children had been, but Alexis convinced him that most of their friends were in Atlanta. Hew agreed, but he insisted that all the luggage be loaded on the plane early so they could leave directly from the service. Her parents drove to Atlanta. Edward and Tippy drove over from Charleston and would go on to Highlands for a few weeks. Mary and Jeffrey flew down from Swan Bay. They would accompany Hew and Alexis to New York. Alexis's brother, Doug Jr. and his family, and Maybell completed the entourage.

The service was in four parts and began in a dark cathedral at sundown with the lighting of a new fire in the atrium under the vaulted skylight. All the candles and lights had been extinguished at the end of the Maundy Thursday service of stripping and washing the bare altar. The choir still grumbled about not being able to see the music.

The cathedral was packed with parishioners and families of the twelve babies and the choristers. A large copper brazier had been set on a new wrought iron stand in the atrium, allowing just enough room for people to safely pass by. The brazier was filled with the dry leftover palm crosses from Palm Sunday. A single wooden match lit the dry crosses. The remaining ashes would be used for the next year's Ash Wednesday service. The large white pure beeswax candle, known as the Paschal candle—from the Greek word, *Pesah,* meaning *the passing over*—recalls the Jewish Passover. Christians are reminded of the passion, death, and resurrection. It symbolizes the coming of the New Light into the world.

The Paschal candle was carefully dipped into the fire to light the wick and then held high. During the lighting of the candle, the deacon sang the rather lengthy *Exsultet*, and then, as the choir and clergy processed down the aisle—stopping three times as the deacon chanted the ancient words, *"The light of Christ"*—they passed the new fire down the rows to the congregation's small individual candles. The congregation responded each time chanting, *Thanks be to God.* The light in the room was ancient and mystical.

Nine Old Testament lessons and nine Psalms were to follow. Most priests only read a few, but the Dean insisted on having them all read or sung. Ten of the babies were getting restless, but the twins slept peacefully. Maybell had rubbed an old remedy on their gums that she said would help them sleep. The reader, Beatrice Ramsbotham-Jones, known as Bea, was an middle aged English actress of note. She married late in life and moved to Atlanta to her husband's large house on West Paces Ferry Road. Hew loved to hear her read.

As a concession to not having the baptism in Virginia, he had persuaded the dean to use the King James readings. She had the perfect voice for that, but one of the lessons contained the ancestry of Abraham. When she started reading Genesis, the seed of one generation multiplied as the stars in heaven. As she carefully read through the verses, ten of the babies began to wail loudly and Ramsbotham-Jones got tickled. The congregation began to laugh. Finally, the dean said, "Thank you, Bea. We get the idea. We can see the results of the begetting right in front of us. Let's move on to the dry bones reading and then the baptisms."

When time for the twins' baptism came, The Hardys and the Beverleys, their godparents, walked with the family to the font and gathered around it. The dean swapped the current *Book of Common Prayer* for Hew's well-worn old family 1559 book and recited the ancient words. The family was once again regenerated.

The service ran an hour and a half. Hew wanted to get to the plane, but just as they started down the corridor, both boys let go and filled their diapers. It ran onto their white christening gowns and into their white booties.

"Oh, wow," said Alexis. "Hew, you take Dougie to the men's room and I'll take Robbie with me. Clean him up as best you can but we'll need to stop by the house to give them baths. We can't get on the plane like this." Hew held Dougie at arm's length while everyone around him quickly backed away laughing. Dougie let another round go. This one covered the cuffs of Hew's suit pants.

Once home, while Alexis and Marta, their nanny, bathed the boys, Hew and the others had a drink. "I wonder what Maybell gave them. I'll ask her when we get back. It's well past her bedtime. She's asleep by now." Hew looked around. "This is one advantage of having my own plane. We'll be an hour late but the plane will wait." Everyone laughed.

"Why don't you fly out of Hartsville-Jackson?"

"Much too crowded. This one's closer to home."

꧁꧂

LES WILSON WAS WORRIED. HE HAD gotten word that the departure was going to be late. He opened the cargo bay and crawled in to make an adjustment to the timer. The two car loads of the group gathered in the terminal lobby. Hew was planning to build his own hangar with a lobby but he had never gotten around to it.

Everyone had said their goodbyes at the church. Only Jeffrey and Mary would be flying with them. The babies began to cry. "They're empty. I need to feed them," said Alexis.

"Do it on the plane. We're late. Tim's extremely eager to get off the ground before the full fury of this storm hits."

"We're not that late. I'll have more room here. I'll just lay them on the sofa and give them their bottles."

"Mrs. Ramsay, I'll take the girls on board and get them settled for the night," said Marta.

"Fine, Marta. Go ahead."

"Mommy," said one of the girls. I need to use the potty."

"Me too, Mommy," said the other.

"You two can use the potty on the plane."

"Noooo. It bounces too much. I need to go NOW."

"Okay. Marta, go on and get their beds ready. Mary, would you please take them to the bathroom and don't let them play around. Hew's pacing the floor."

Hew was turned with his back toward the jet and was talking to Jeffrey when the explosion blasted through the terminal. Something hit him in the back of the head and the concussive force knocked him into Jeffrey. They were both hit with hot glass pellets and fell together to the floor.

Alexis was facing the sofa arranging the twins. She was blown into the sofa and also pelted with pellet-sized hot balls of the exploding tempered glass. Her tall black leather boots protected her legs and her full length black mink coat caught most of the pellets.

Unfortunately, the glass was not also safety glass. The noise could be heard for ten miles. The fire ball was blown upward by the fifteen knot wind from the southwest, but another plane was rolling past Hew's jet headed for takeoff and took the brunt of the blast. The low walls and pitched roof of the building also helped to deflect much of the blast.

People living in the high rise apartments in Buckhead and downtown heard the explosion that rattled their doors and windows. Some of them ran to look. Those on the northwest side saw the fireball. Almost immediately, a message began to roll on the bottom of their TV screens. **"EXPLOSION AT DEKALB-PEACHTREE AIRPORT. CREWS IN ROUTE. DETAILS AT 11."**

Hot metal shards ripped through both planes and ignited the jet fuel. Because Hew had called to say he was going to be an hour late, they had rolled his jet back away from the terminal so other planes could be boarded. Mary came staggering out of the ladies room with the girls in tow, Elizabeth clutching a wad of toilet paper. Her panties were still around her knees. "I'm not finished, Aunt Mary. I need to wipe."

The copilot, Lance, came staggering out of the men's room. The crotch of his grey slacks was wet and his fly was open. It took him a minute to understand what had happened. His training kicked in and he immediately took charge and called 911. The tower had already called it in and the crash vehicles were rolling. He got Mary and the girls outside into their car, found her keys in her purse and turned on the heater. He went back inside but he decided not to move the men. He tried to help a dazed Alexis to her feet but she immediately collapsed, screaming in pain, and he decided to let her alone. He grabbed the screaming twin infants and their bottles and took them to Mary. He heard more sirens coming out Clairmont Road.

What remained of the building worried the first responders and they had quickly called for backup. They needed more ambulances but they took a gamble and started moving the injured. They triaged the three and decided Hew was in the worst condition. They strapped him to a board, put him in a cervical collar, and moved him first. Next, they strapped Jeffrey onto a board and put a cervical collar around his neck. Finally, they put Alexis on a stretcher. Mary, still in the car, was shaking and in shock, but she managed to call Edward and Tippy.

"Oh, God, NO, Mary!" screamed Tippy into the phone. "We heard a boom. Oh, Jesus. We thought it was thunder. Tell me they're alive. Tell me they're alive."

"I…I don't know, Tippy. I don't know." She started to cry.

"Mary! Mary! Listen to me. Stop crying and just listen. There's a big storm coming. Tell the EMS to transport them all to Grady Memorial Trauma Center, STAT. If they argue, hand your phone to them and I'll tell 'em. I'll start calling specialists. Concussions from a blast can wreck a human body in ways you can't imagine. They'll be in expert hands, Mary. You go in the first ambulance with the kids."

"I need to see about Jeffrey."

"NO. You get in an ambulance with the kids. I'm extremely worried about the kids. You and I are their godmothers. Take charge! Jeffrey will be in good hands."

Even though Tippy was retired, she still had good friends at the hospital. She called her former partner and lined up neurosurgeons, internists, and pediatricians. Edward was using files on his cellphone to find his copies of their powers of attorney and health care powers of attorney.

She drove like a bat out of hell while he read the documents. She knew every turn and light. She had driven the route for thirty years. He called Charlie. Charlie called the cathedral dean, Thad Carson, on his private line. The dean called the archdeacon because the care of the diocesan and cathedral staff and families were under her jurisdiction.

The crash team quickly extinguished the fires but the wreckage was too hot to immediately investigate. A carefully guarded secret, Hew's jet was constructed with explosion panels in an attempt to keep the jet fuel bladders from rupturing. Apparently hot fragments of Hew's jet ripped into the full fuel bladders of both planes. They began to check on the airport employees.

"Everyone accounted for?" said the team leader.

"No, we can't find the new guy, Les Wilson."

"When did you last see him?"

"He was loading the luggage into that jet's cargo hold."

The rescuers look at each other. "How long has he worked here?"

"He started about three weeks ago. He moved here from a construction job. Said his back wouldn't take that much work anymore."

They pulled up the contact info on their database and sent a patrol car to his house to check on him just in case.

A drunk and wailing Mable staggered to the door, mumbling.

"It's Les. I know it's him. I heard the explosion. I know it's him what's dead. I bought them bomb parts myself. That C-4 stuff looks just like the modeling clay I played with as a kid. I didn't think that it would really work. He said it would go off over that damned farm in Virginia. He's so stupid I had to work out the timer." She stopped and cried out. "I just hope he took that Ramsay bitch with him. I tried to get him to just shoot her. I told him to pay someone else to build that bomb, but oh, no he wouldn't listen to me. He said could do it."

She was immediately handcuffed and led to the police car. The officer's body cam recorded the entire confession. She wailed, "Are you taking me to the morgue to ID his body? We're supposed to be celebrating. I can't move my arms. Why are my hands behind my back? What's happening?" She vomited all over the patrol woman's shoes and passed out.

Media reporters with cameras were lining up outside the hospital. Others were at the airport reporting live on the 11 o'clock news. One of their guys had followed the first ambulance. He had picked up the chatter on his radio. The eleven p.m. news reported at least four dead in two airplanes. The reporters rushed inside.

Tippy's's quick thinking had already organized everything. Fortunately, it was an unusually slow for a Saturday evening full moon but it was still early as emergencies go. The trauma center was a level one trauma unit and could handle almost any emergency.

Alexis, Hew, and Jeffrey were already in three of the eight critical care rooms. Mary was in a separate sub-critical room. The girls had been taken to the pediatric unit and Tippy had insisted that the babies be sent to the NICU.

Edward was the only person in the waiting room. Charlie, Rosilyn, Archdeacon Cindy, and Dean Carson arrived at almost the same time. Cindy immediately notified the rector of St. Luke's. One of the nurses who knew Tippy ushered everyone into a small office to avoid the media.

AT 1:30 a.m., Tippy walked in with the first report. Edward and Charlie knew from experience not to interrupt her when she was in her physician reporting mode. "They're all alive. Hew and Jeffrey are in the ICU. The babies, the girls, Lance, Alexis, and Mary have been admitted. Mary's been sedated to calm her down. Alexis has a cracked vertebrae at L4, three broken ribs, a broken tibia, and glass pellets in her scalp. She was leaning over the sofa about to give the boys their bottles. We think she was hit from behind by that large round wooden coffee table. Her arm must have hit the wooden edge of the back of the sofa. She fell on the babies so she protected them. The table and the soft cushions probably protected her from the full concussive force. She's on her way to surgery. We don't wait around with broken bones anymore.

"The other plane took the worst of the blast. It was a small single engine prop plane. That pilot and his two passengers were incinerated. Mary and the girls were in the bathroom. The tail of the second plane was slammed into the bathroom walls, but they're not seriously injured. Lance was in the men's room next to the ladies' but he should be fine. He was knocked into the concrete block wall. The size of the small room kept him from hitting the floor. Fortunately, he didn't hit his head on the sink. No bones were broken, but his shoulder will need to be watched.

"We suspect Jeffrey hit his back on the block wall before his head hit when Hew was slammed into him. Jeffrey was conscious but groggy and in shock. He is verbally responsive and his pupils are reactive. He's awake now, but we're watching him. He'll be stepped down from the ICU shortly. They both have too many glass pellets in their head, face, and neck to count. Their winter clothes protected everything else. We're waiting on Jeffrey's medical records to be faxed from his doctor in Williamsburg.

"Hew took a hit to his occipital lobe. We think it was from something relatively soft. Otherwise, he probably would be dead. The rescue team leader told me that the position of the other plane and the roof of the building probably helped reduce the injuries. He's unconscious but without a subdural hematoma. We're watching it very closely just in case, but they're going to medically induce him into a coma until they're sure he's not in danger. Fortunately, we took X-rays first looking for broken bones and found a small GPS device behind his right ear lobe. Since we didn't have a medical record for it, we decided to remove it. It's good we found it before we started the MRI. It might have caused catastrophic damage. It was old and was not compatible with our modern devices."

"Oh, God," said Edward. "X.I. had it put there as a precaution before they went to Colombia. That's how Jeffrey found him and his parents. I had completely forgotten about it. He did mention it when everyone got one for the railroad project. I just assumed he had gotten a new one."

"He's getting scanned as we speak," continued Tippy. "The glass walls on the front and rear of the building exploded. We'll do a scan of his abdomen to rule out internal organ damage. We've cut their hair to get to the pellets and they'll shave the area of Hew's occipital lobe in case it starts to swell and they have to quickly operate. We're scanning his cerebellum and brain stem again for pellets. Probably because of his height, he somehow got the worst of it. Now, there are six and possibly seven fatalities. Three were in the other plane. The wing of the second plane was shoved through the waiting room windows.

"The NTSB and FAA folks will arrive tomorrow but their findings could take months. If that plane hadn't blocked some of the explosion, we'd be looking at a much worse scenario. Hew's pilot Tim, their nanny Marta, and Becca, the receptionist…are all dead." Charlie gasped and Tippy continued. "Hew's powers of attorney and a DNR are not on file. We can't find any records for him. I don't think he's ever been admitted before. We can't find a personal physician either."

Edward spoke up. "I've got the legal forms with me on my phone, but he doesn't seem to have much in the way of medical records."

"That must be a mistake," said Tippy.

"No, Mom," said Charlie. "Hew hasn't seen a doctor since we were seventeen. He doesn't trust them."

"Why the hell not? I'm insulted."

"You forced us to go to that guy when we were teenagers. I wanted to go to my pediatrician but you said no. The new guy was way too into our junk. He spent too much time fondling us. Hew stopped going and never saw a doctor again."

"Oh, for God's sake, Charlie. How stupid could you boys be? You're an adult now. It's okay to say the word genitals. Dr. Wisemon is a very well respected urologist. I asked him to check you two for venereal diseases. That's why I made you go every year. I knew about Susie and Katie, but I didn't know about any others. I was trying to keep you safe. What he was doing was just good practice."

"How did you know about all that?"

"Susie's mother caught you two having sex in their playroom one afternoon. You were only thirteen, but we discussed it and decided we couldn't stop it so we didn't say anything to anyone. You're not light bulbs that can simply be unscrewed."

"But you never explained about that particular doctor to us."

"No, I assumed he discussed it with you as a part of patient confidentially and I didn't want to embarrass you. You men can be such idiots when it comes to your genitalia."

"Did you know this at the time, Dad?"

"Well…I…"

"Listen, you two can have that long overdue father-son talk later. I've got a very fragile patient here and I have no time to listen to this nonsense. Maybe you can teach your old dad some new tricks." She turned to Edward. "What are we going to do about this DNR? We're not really doing anything heroic to keep him alive. He's breathing on his own, but what if he arrests, or we suddenly discover a large hematoma? Do we relieve the pressure on his brain? Do we revive him?"

Edward shook his head. "Hell, Tippy, I don't know. That's your department. I've got his will and copies of his arrangements here on my phone. What do you recommend?"

"Let me get them printed. I don't think Hew would want to be kept alive by machines. If he's declared brain dead, we'll take appropriate measures at that time. I think if there's a chance of restoring him to health he would want us to try—and I think Alexis would agree."

"Fine. Do that."

"Now to continue, Tim was in the cockpit. He was not strapped in and was slammed against the windshield and broke his neck. Marta was standing directly over the luggage area getting the children's beds ready. They never knew what hit them. Becca was standing behind the receptionist desk. Her neck was shredded by a metal fragment. She bled out instantly. The rescue team didn't immediately find her. Questions?"

"You said perhaps seven."

"Remind me about the occipital lobe."

"There's a baggage handler that's unaccounted for. The detectives will be looking for information. We won't let them question our patients, so Edward, you can update them with the basics." She turned to the dean. "Thad, the occipital Lobe is the section on the back of your brain that controls your vision. You know where the brain stem is." She turned and put her hand on the back of her head.

Edward had been standing, but he fell back into his chair. "Oh, God, not again. How many murder attempts can poor Hew withstand?"

The dean took his hand. "Let's have a prayer for the injured and the dead. It's Easter morning."

Tippy continued. "Charlie, after your dad talks to the police, take him home. You're playing for the Easter services. There's nothing more you can do here tonight. Thad, why don't you and Cindy come with me. You can offer prayers over the injured and then you need to leave for morning services."

"We'll add all the names to the Prayers of the People list."

The police detective spent about thirty minutes with Edward gathering information on the victims and where they were going. Edward suddenly remembered John. He needed to call New York. Tippy retrieved Hew's cell phone and Charlie found the number. The phone was unlocked. After his near death experience in the cathedral, Hew had never set a password on his phone again. A security guard at the school answered. Edward instructed the guard to keep John secured in the school until more was known. Edward feared it was another attack on the family like the one in Colombia.

He remembered that Alexis's parents were driving back to Greenville. He didn't have their cell phone numbers so he decided they would be safer in their own house. He didn't even think about Alexis's brother. The detective wouldn't discuss the bomber, saying it was too early in the investigation and no remains had been found.

As they drove, Charlie and Edward finally had the father son sex talk. "So when did Mom tell you about Susie and Katie?" said Charlie.

"Do you remember the trip to Asheville for a wedding when we left you boys at the house in Highlands? Your mother sensed something then. You were entirely too eager to go to the mountains and be stuck there with nothing to do. She told me while we were driving to pick you up. I couldn't believe it. She found one of Susie's long blond hairs on the floor of the powder room just before we left for home."

Charlie started laughing and that started Edward laughing. "We had some great times with those girls," said Charlie.

"Stop. I don't need the details. That hotel story was enough."

⁂

EASTER SUNRISE WAS UNUSUALLY WARM AND very stormy. The sun was obscured by thick clouds and torrential rain. There had been several devastating tornados in northern Alabama overnight and the Atlanta area was under a tornado warning. As the 8 a.m. service was about to begin, Thad stood under the skylight in the cathedral's atrium waiting with the choir for the prelude to end.

The rain suddenly stopped and the clouds began to part, but the bleak sunrise sky turned an eerie shade of green, which usually preceded a tornado. Thad pressed on. The Atlanta Symphony trumpets, trombones, and Charlie's timpani heralded the opening processional hymn.

The congregation rose to sing, *Jesus Christ is risen today. Alleluia.* During the staff planning meeting, Hew had argued for *Christ the Lord is risen today,* claiming musicologists declared it was more about resurrection than about suffering. The six verses would allow more time for the full procession to get down the aisle. Thad immediately dismissed the idea. "Hew, those words are not in the hymnal. The Methodists sing those words. We always sing it our way."

"But, it's a little too…Catholic."

"Not another word. I just love the way Rod slows down the line, *Now above the sky, he's King.* The congregation and choir really belt that line out. They love it. They practically scream the next Alleluia. Let's move on."

The EF3 tornado hit Atlanta at 8:06 a.m. just as the cathedral congregation had finished the last triumphal verse. The last of the brass concluding fanfare that Hew and Charlie had composed was ending.

The tornado tore through an area west of the Dekalb-Peachtree airport, which recorded wind speeds of 155 mph. The area, which was mostly industrial buildings, was demolished, and Mable and Les's trailer park were destroyed too. Nothing of their trailer was left so any evidence of bomb-making was gone. Mable's little dog and his doghouse were missing, but the bedraggled dog showed up three days later looking for Mable.

The trauma center became very busy. When all was accounted for, there were 25 fatalities and many more injured.

Thad handed a slip of paper with the names from the explosion to Bea as she stepped in line for the procession. There were collective gasps at all three services when she read the names. Everyone had seen the morning news. Alexis's parents were drinking coffee in their home in Greenville watching when details of the explosion came on. Anne immediately called Doug Jr. in Atlanta.

"No, Mom," Doug Jr. said, "we're still in bed. We came home and went straight to bed." He turned on the bedroom TV. "Oh, my God. I need to call Edward. I'll call you back. Stay put until you hear from me."

"Doug, grab our bags," said Anne. "I've got a bad feeling. Let's go."

"But we don't know…"

"Get up. We're leaving. Junior can call us on our cell."

They were just crossing the state line on I-85 when Doug Jr. called them back. "I finally got Edward. It was Hew's plane but they're all alive."

"Oh, thank you, Lord. THANK YOU!" She began to cry.

"Put me on speaker, Mom. I need to give Dad directions."

Doug yelled, "Oh, no. Dammit. That's way downtown. I'll never find it in this weather. Dammit, as soon as I get back home I'm buying a new car with GPS."

"Just come here. We'll wait for you. We need to shower and dress."

At 11 a.m., a police detective returned to the hospital. He was able to speak with Edward, Lance, Mary, and Jeffrey. None of them knew anything useful. He told them that Mable had confessed. This was a case of a local vendetta by disgruntled former employees. Alexis had been the target.

"We need to call John," said Mary. "He'll wonder why we're not in church."

"I called the school last night. He knows, but I'll call now and let them know that he's no longer in danger."

"It's 11:30. The service is underway, but he's scheduled to be the cantor and sing the versicles at Evensong. Maybe he can still make that. He's really been looking forward to it. Hew and Alexis were…" She started crying. "He's getting his tone by hitting himself on the side of his head with a tuning fork. It's a process he learned while working with the choirs in England. How ironic, given that Hew has a brain injury."

Jeffrey hugged her to console her. Tippy ordered another sedative.

40

JOHN

Ding sat down beside John at breakfast and whispered, "Let's go into the school chapel and talk."

The choir chaplain was waiting there. John just sat there for a moment as they carefully explained the situation. "No. I'm here to sing. That's my job. Dad would expect me to do my duty."

"Unfortunately, until someone from Atlanta calls to advise us differently, we can't let you out of this building. Go on back to your room and wait."

John jumped up and stormed out of the room. Instead of going back to his room, he went into the piano practice studio and began banging the keys.

Edward called at 2 p.m. Ding found John in the piano studio. "John, STOP! What in the name of all that's holy is that racket?"

"I'm composing a work to help guide the bomber into Hell."

"That should do it." Ding paused. "Mr. Hardy called. You're free to sing. Let's go. You've worked up quite a sweat. Hit the shower and we'll head over to the church."

At 4 p.m., the choir processed into the choir stalls as Ding improvised music appropriately joyful for Easter Day. John started to pick up the tuning fork and lightly tap it against his head just behind his ear, but someone had replaced it with a silver salad fork. John realized the practical joke immediately and smiled. He simply started right on pitch from memory without the tuning fork, and sang in his clear treble voice.

"Oh Lord, open thou our lips." By accident or design, Ding's improvised processional music ended on the exact note John needed for his pitch. He looked around to try to catch someone smiling or hiding a giggle, but he didn't see anyone.

After the service, Ding asked, "You were a little slow starting. What happened?"

"My tuning fork wasn't in the choir stall. "

Ding gave him a curious look. "No matter. You recovered nicely. Pack up. I'm going to accompany you to Atlanta. We've got to head to LaGuardia as soon as possible."

"Commercial?"

"Yes, well, your plane isn't available, is it? I'll plan to spend our spring break with you in Atlanta. I want to see the music room you keep talking about."

ON MONDAY MORNING, JOHN AND DING walked into Alexis's room. She was awake and sitting up. Her head was bandaged, as was her arm, and she was wearing a back brace. As John started to say, "Hi Mom," his voice cracked. Ding recognized immediately that this wasn't emotional. *John's days of singing with the choir have just come to an end*, he thought.

As they were leaving, Tippy and a new doctor walked in. "Alexis, this is Doctor Raj. He's going to be Hew's otologist."

"Sorry, his what? Hew has cancer?"

"No. 'Oto,' not 'onco.' He doesn't have cancer. He's going to assess Hew's ear and hearing."

"Oh, no. Don't tell me he's deaf. Please don't."

"Now Mrs. Ramsay, don't jump to conclusions. It might just be in one ear, but either way, we think we can repair the injury. When he's able, we'll do a full audiology workup. We've got a new anechoic chamber so we can record even the faintest of responses. We have a team of ENT's, otologists, neurologists, and audiologists on standby. We have the latest in diagnostic tools." She paused to let Dr. Raj speak.

"A glass pellet entered his middle ear through his ear drum and is lodged just behind his ear drum in the space known as the tympanic cavity. The three smallest bones in the human body are located there. The one closest to his brain is called the stapes and it resembles the stirrup on a saddle. It connects to the cochlea in the inner ear which works with the nerves to his brain. We can see on the scans that the pellet has broken part of the stapes and is not allowing the sound to be conducted to his brain.

"Fortunately, it did not penetrate to the cochlea. He's very lucky. We'll go in through his eardrum, with a procedure known as a stapedectomy, and basically replace it with a titanium prosthesis. He should be as good as new. It's a procedure sometimes called an oval window fenestration."

"But fenestration is a French word for windows. A single window is called a fenetré."

"Yes, well, I didn't invent the term but I've done hundreds of them on people with otosclerosis," said the doctor. "Those folks often have a hereditary disease that causes the stapes to harden and stop vibrating. It may be also be caused by measles, stress fractures, or immune responses. Beethoven is thought to have suffered from it. The new prosthetic works like a charm."

"Does Hew have that?"

"We'll know more after we do surgery, but his scans show the break. He'll have an audiogram and a middle ear conduction test known as a tympanogram too. We can't start until he is fully awake and able to respond to the hearing tests."

John and Ding left Alexis and went to the ICU. They wouldn't let Ding see Hew, but they did allow John in for a few minutes.

ALEXIS AND THE BABIES WERE RELEASED on Tuesday. She faced rounds of physical therapy, but Tippy had arranged for the therapist to come to the house. She was glad to get home to the girls. The girls met her at the door with flowers they had picked from Maybell's flower garden, wanting to know when Marta would come home. Alexis had a difficult time answering that. Fortunately, Maybell took over the work that Marta had done.

Tippy finally drove to Charlie and Rosilyn's on Tuesday morning to change clothes. She had been in scrubs since Saturday night. She gratefully took the cup of freshly brewed coffee Rosilyn offered. "My God what a nightmare. With the tornado too, we were greatly understaffed. They called in every available doctor and nurse in the Atlanta region. I've done three surgeries myself. We were busier than a newly hatched swarm of noseeums at a Charleston oyster roast in April."

"You always have great one liners, Tippy. What are noseeums?"

"I forget that you're from north Georgia, dear. They're tiny flies. Some places call them midges, but not in Charleston. They're also called flying teeth—the piranhas of the air. They're dark grey, about one to three cm long, and are hatched in stagnant water or marshy areas just like mosquitos. They come out when the temperature reaches about 70 degrees. They bite like crazy. Fortunately, they aren't know to carry diseases like mosquitos do but they make outdoor life miserable for coastal folks. Once their life cycle is complete, the mosquitos arrive." She paused.

"We can't do anything about Hew's ear until he wakes up and we can assess his hearing, but the very good news is that he was slowly being brought out of the coma just before I left."

She continued. "When the babies were admitted, they had a slight temperature, but it increased. They had an intestinal virus and were put on IVs to keep their fluids up. Three other babies at the church service had the same virus. Hew is still in the ICU, but the neurosurgeon is satisfied with his progress. His concussion was difficult to pin down exactly but they've settled on a stage called mild. Concussions, or mild traumatic brain injuries known as a mTBI, are now classified as Mild TBI, Moderate TBI, or Severe TBI. We'll know more when he comes out of the coma. His team doesn't want Hew to get upset and spike his blood pressure.

"We're still not sure that his blood vessels weren't damaged. The hospital had a case a few weeks earlier where a woman presented after falling and hitting her head on a city sidewalk. Her scans were normal and she was released, but she suffered a fatal aneurysm three days later. We don't want to have a repeat with Hew."

She went up to the guest suite, kicked off her shoes and was asleep in less than a minute. She slept for the rest of the day.

❦

ALEXIS WAS SITTING ON THE TERRACE drinking tea when Ding walked out and asked to sit with her. "Thanks for bringing John home," she said. "I'm sure you had a better plan for your break. You're more than welcome to stay longer, and I'll welcome the extra hands, but if you need to leave, I'll get Edward to arrange a flight."

"I'm glad to help. I had planned to stay in New York. It's expensive to leave for such a short time."

"I know John enjoys having you here and frankly, your practicing with him takes his mind off Hew."

"He still can't practice the organs in the church because of his outburst, but I've given him a very difficult score to start learning here. I'm forcing him to play the French piece on a French sampleset on the virtual organ instead of his beloved Flentrop. It's Dupré's *Variations on a Noel*. It took me forever to learn it. It even uses the top C on the manuals so we always need to ensure that particular note is in tune before we start. If it's not, the piece will be ruined. He'll be busy for a while and I told him that if I hear any cussing, I'll make him stop altogether."

She laughed and winced. "Don't make me laugh. My ribs are sore. Hew cusses in Spanish and Gaelic. Sometimes when he's practicing, the words spew out in long strings. Fortunately, we don't understand, but Marta..." She changed the subject. "Isn't that piece called *Sing we now of Christmas* in English? I think Hew tried to learn it one year just before Christmas and gave up. His excuse was that he didn't have enough time to learn it."

"Yep. That's the piece. Sorry. I didn't mean to bring up bad memories."

"It's okay. I do hope you told him to keep the volume down with the headphones. Hew's always reminding him about that. After everything I've learned about audiology in the last few weeks, I could write a master's thesis. Tell me about you. Where's home?"

"I don't allow him to use headphones for that very reason. At St. T's, we're not in the rock band business. I'm from a little coal mining town in the mountains of West Virginia known as Barton, after my maternal ancestors."

"That sounds interesting. My ancestors were slate miners in Wales. How did you get to St. Thomas?"

"This could take a minute. May I fix myself a gin and tonic?"

"Certainly, and if you don't mind, put a drop of gin in another tea cup for me while your in the bar. Add a little tonic and a twist while you're at it. Don't tell Tippy."

He brought her a proper gin and tonic with a twist in a cut crystal Baccarat Harmony triple old fashion tumbler with a white linen cocktail napkin on a highly polished sterling silver tray.

"You do cocktails in a fine style, sir. Thank you."

He laughed. "I couldn't find plastic cups or old jelly jars in that china shop you call a butler's pantry." He sat down in the cushioned contemporary outdoor lounge chair beside her and took a sip of his equally appointed drink.

"Wow, this is delicious, Ding. What's your secret?"

"An old friend from North Carolina told me to add the lime to the tonic before adding the gin. Apparently gin doesn't infuse with the lime juice so it doesn't get properly mixed."

He continued. "I'm from a coal mining family. I'm descended from two of the first pioneering families of West Virginia. Our land grants from the king date to 1734. The settlers wanted to be as far away from the eastern political and religious conflicts as possible. In 1861, they broke away from secessionist Virginia and were admitted to the Union as a free state. The negroes had discovered coal chunks on the ground and burned it to dry salt from the mud and sand from the river beds, but after becoming a free state, they left the saltworks and begin as paid laborers in the coal mines. By 1880, America discovered the high quality West Virginia coal and the coal industry began requiring a massive number of miners—many of them boys under 12.

"My family owns a mine but we play down our money because Granny doesn't want us to strut around town. She says it's bad for morale, but I know it's a very poorly kept secret. We and all of my relatives live in small wood frame houses just like everyone else. We have to drive two hours to Morgantown, West Virginia to the airport to go anywhere. We keep a small jet there away from prying eyes, so your situation is a little too close to home for me. We have a winter house in Jamaica but no one's there at the moment, and it's still cold at home. I like the warmth here."

"Have you discussed this with Hew?"

"No. We only talk about John and music, but from what I've learned, he wouldn't be too happy about my other source of income. Of course, America is cleaning up the industry, but we still ship massive numbers of tons of coal overseas and those countries aren't ready to change.

"Organists are becoming a rare breed. I'm living on my church income and investing all of my family profits. My granny is technically the mine owner. My dad is second in line and my older brother is third so there's very little chance that I'll ever inherit the company. I've never told them this, but if I were to inherit it, I would sell it faster than my fastest arpeggio. I probably won't be able to support a family on an organist's salary unless I manage to land a plum position in a large church or marry a rich woman. Do you know any rich girls? A southern Episcopalian girl would be nice."

"Ha!" said Alexis. "No, but I'll start looking. I could use another G&T, please. Are you dating anyone at the moment? We can bring her here if you like."

He left to go to the bar to mix another round. "To answer your question, no, not at the moment. There was a girl at Oberlin, but after graduation, she found a teaching job and moved to San Francisco. I couldn't find a job there so…you know. I live like a monk now. I don't want to spend the money for a New York apartment even though I can afford it."

"Do the others at school know about your background?"

"When asked, I usually just say that my dad's an accountant and my mother's a school teacher. That's actually true. My dad has a running battle with the railroads over the haulage rates."

"Hmmm. Hew's just recently built the new roadbed for the high speed trains along the east coast. He knows a little about coal. If you talk to him, you might be surprised. He's had to come to terms with the money he's inherited from his family's role with tobacco farming. If you're conflicted, he might be able to help. I'm sure he would listen even if he can't help."

"I won't lie to him, but I hope it never comes up. There's nothing I can do to help the situation." Ding paused. "Would it shock you to learn that I love country music? I grew up on it. I play a sweet little mandolin handcrafted by a man in western Tennessee. I'm also hell on a banjo too. There isn't a pipe organ within fifty miles of our town, but Granny has a little reed pump organ—a harmonium—in her front parlor where the organist pumped the bellows with their feet. It didn't work, so when I was ten, I took it apart and discovered that rats had eaten the leather bellows. I rebuilt the bellows using old bed sheets coated with flexible rubber cement, and I replaced the straps on the foot pedals with fiberglass straps from an old lawn chair.

"Mountain kids learn to fix things at an early age. That organ still works. I knew that I was somewhat different from the other boys in town, though. I loved the mountain music but I'm just not into hunting and fishing—or baseball and basketball."

She laughed and winced again. "You're among friends here. I am somewhat surprised by your love of country music, though. Don't you find it to be racist?"

He cocked his head. "Is rhythm and blues racist? Is reggae music racist or is it just cultural? Black gospel? That music is really about the truth of racism in my opinion. Jesus loves everyone. I learned the meaning of the word joy at an early age. Jesus, Others, Yourself. I suppose that because country music is mostly written and performed by white people about white problems it might be considered by some to be racist but I can't think of it that way. It's in my DNA."

"Oh, sure. Everything can be blamed on DNA now, but it's a learned choice. I think the lyrics to that music are at least covertly racist. If you had been raised in Cuba, you wouldn't think that, would you?"

"I'm sorry, but I disagree. I love Latin music too. Covertly racist? Well, you may be on to something I've never considered. Speaking musicologically, when the Europeans came to North America seeking a new way of life, they brought their religion, music, prejudices, and cultural preferences with them. In the hollers and on the ridges of Appalachia, the settlers were separated from the easterners by choice. They continued to play the folk music of their homeland and they continued the speech patterns of their homeland. Some English historians consider the speech of the mountain folks to be the closest thing to Anglo Saxon speech left on the planet. Our verb tenses don't work in modern American schools. The isolation preserved that."

"But Ding, come on. That was at the height of the Baroque era in Europe. Our ancestors came from an enlightened time."

"There's good and bad music in every genre, Alexis. I've learned to appreciate every genre. You should consider doing the same. The new cities of America—Boston, New York, Philadelphia, Williamsburg, Charleston—were enlightened and had fine performances of that type of music, but the people who settled in the mountains were simple European country folks.

"Mountain country music is mostly ballads and dance tunes, but it became popular in America during the 1920s with the spread of radio and modern recording devices. The term 'hillbilly music' is the derogatory term for our music but now it's mixed with western music and is therefore identified as poor White. There are many styles and substyles but I still prefer the historic form."

"But the singers use a very nasal sound. I find it irritating."

"I teach voice too. Country music is best performed by people who have mastered the southern twang. It's part of our speech history. The lyrics of country songs and even the blues are usually about a lost love or about someone or something who 'done me wrong.' Poor people were always ruled by someone else whether it was a king or a boss. Their freedom was tentative at best. In their experience, someone is always pulling their chain and they're never responsible for their own lives.

"Men sing it using their speaking voices so it's hardly ever a low bass or a high tenor sound. It doesn't strain the vocal cords if you were born to the twang. Women sing it in a mostly alto range. The sound is developed above the vocal cords and is therefore a nasal sound as you described."

She laughed and grabbed her ribs. "Wait. When I was a kid, Greenville TV stations were full of male quartets singing gospel music. Dad only liked the Welsh male choirs. Their sound is very smooth compared with the harsh nasal sounds of the southern quartets. When I was a child, I don't think many people in Greenville had ever heard an English cathedral choir of men and boys."

"Those *are* different genres." He laughed. "I can still sing shaped notes too."

"We always changed the channel when a Billy Graham crusade came on."

"My whole family came to our house to watch Billy Graham. We had one of the only TVs in town."

"So how did you get to Groton for prep school?'

"My granny made my parents send me there. She believed I needed to be the one in the family to keep the books like my dad. Funny how that turned out."

"Hew and I were astounded when John sang that type of song at Douglas's funeral."

"That was his YouTube premiere, wasn't it? He's had over a hundred thousand views now. The boys at school love it."

"Don't bring that up with Hew. Maybell sings a different song but I don't think it's in our hymnal."

"Can you hum a few notes?"

She began and after three notes he started to sing—without the twang—in his fine bass-baritone voice, *"Precious Lord, take my hand, Lead me on, let me stand, I am tired, I am weak, I am worn; Through the storm, through the night, Lead me on to the light: Take my hand, precious Lord, Lead me home."*

"You sound just like George Beverly Shea. Your crescendo with the words *through the storm* and then your whisper *lead me on through the night were perfect*. I must admit that perfectly describes my feelings at the moment."

"I understand. Shea was born in Canada where his father was a preacher, but my family loved his American gospel songs. He could play the organ too. He's mostly remembered from the Graham crusades and it's thought that he sang gospel music to more people than anyone else on earth. I remember that song from my childhood. You don't know this, but it was written in 1932 by a man named Dorsey. The lyrics are calling for guidance through a difficult time of personal tragedy. Herbert Howell's *Michael* is similar, although it is so much better musically, but you're right. It's not in our hymnal because it's a song of personal devotion. Our hymns were written for corporate worship. These two songs are internationally loved though. Germans love these American songs."

"Ding, do you consider religious music as racist?"

"No, but it's prejudiced."

"What the hell does THAT mean?"

"Only that Christian music is all about Christ but some believe that other religions aren't necessarily about Christ at all."

"Well, I did hear a bishop once say that the church would be the last bastion of prejudice, and that eleven a.m. on Sunday morning was the most racially divided hour on Earth."

"I think he was right."

"Hmmm. Maybell's husband died recently. Now I understand. So, this music has always been that way even before the era of slavery. Fascinating. My friends won't believe me, though. By the way, when we were in New York a few weeks ago, the choir sang the *Vierne Messe Solennelle*. The music was superb but the *Kyrie* had me weeping."

"Thank you. That was the last Sunday in Lent. We don't sing the Kyrie on Palm Sunday so we decided to go for it that Sunday. Vierne was born nearly blind, but soon after he was appointed titular organist at Notre Dame, he wrote this Mass to be played on the outstanding Cavaillé-Coll organ. The entire Mass is a bit long for St. Thomas. We substituted another piece for the Gloria because it runs a bit over eight minutes."

Alexis laughed and winced again. "Hew said the priests don't like that much down time. I'll remind him of that if his vision's not…" She stopped the thread of her thoughts. "He played a Cavaillé-Coll in his school in South America. He said Vierne dedicated that work to Dubois. While the choir sang, he took out his muted cellphone, found the score and followed. I have to make him keep his arms down when he does that. The people around us don't need another conductor. We sing some of Dubois' works here at St. Luke's. The congregation just loves it. Hew's in discussion with several organ builders about restoring the Cavaillé-Coll he bought from his old school in Bogota for the other music room."

"He's never told me that. We'll need to talk when he comes out of the coma. I wish it were playable now. I'm playing Jehan Alain's *Deuxième Fantasie* for the prelude in two weeks. I'd love to practice it on a real French organ. The other music room? You mean the storage room with the other virtual console?"

"No. I'll show you when we go downtown. It's in his bachelor pad." She laughed again. "God, that hurts." She shifted slightly. "He had an apartment built for himself while he was still in high school on the top two floors of a forty-story condo tower one of his trust's owns. That room was built for the Flentrop. It's an exact copy of the organ they built for Harvard. When we built this house and moved everything, he filled the empty bookshelves in the old penthouse with matching panels. The acoustical engineers in his firm are studying the possibility of canting those panels to add diffusion to the walls. Personally, I think a French romantic instrument would be too large for that space."

"I can't wait to play that! Anyway, the Kyrie itself runs about six and a half minutes, but it comes at the beginning of the service and it sets the tone for everything afterward. I always pity the homilist who comes after it. It's hard to top. Playing those chords made my fingers feel like a golden eagle's talons. I can just imagine Vierne smashing those old tracker type keys trying to pound every ounce of expression out of the organ." He spread his fingers into a curved rigid look.

"Hew says too many organists simply bash the piano keys. He learned piano from his mother and he insisted that John learn to play it too."

"That probably comes from playing the tracker organs. Some of them are extremely difficult to play with full organ and coupled manuals. Having two organs is a luxury, but it was written that way for the Notre Dame de Paris's two organs. One of the sub-organists played our gallery organ. The music just climbs and soars with French romantic chromaticism. At the end, the tenors have a screaming high F—well, E#—in the score, but you know, it's wild, and they love to shine. They were effortlessly spot on pitch."

"Y'all rose to the occasion. I don't think I'll ever forget it."

"Granny rewarded me by teaching me to sing and play. I grew up learning to play hymns and sing shape notes. After my parents sent me to Groton to boarding school, I found my passion with the organ in the chapel. I also discovered English cathedral music. Next was Oberlin and the whole world of organ music. Then I won a few competitions and now I'm at St. T's. My older brother will take over the mining business. He loves it. I don't."

"You'll always be welcome here. But Edward is arranging a jet service until we get a new plane so just let me know. As Jeffrey always says, 'Just get back up on the horse.' How's John behaving at school? Hew was so mad when he heard about the cussing he wanted to pull him out of school for the rest of the semester. I talked him out of that silly notion."

"We're certainly glad you did. His education comes first. He's really been on his best behavior. We've taken a little pity on him and are allowing him a little practice time two hours a day two days a week on the school's three-manual Hauptwerk instrument much like the two here. He's restricted to learning to accompany the music that the choir will sing that week. He's also learning to play the cello. We bought the custom built Hauptwerk instrument from the Ortloff Organ Co. to use in the church during the two-year interval while the old organ was being removed and the new one was being installed. We use the Hereford Cathedral sampleset. The instrument is located in the basement in a room near the gym, so he can't really be heard if he does get rambunctious. Both the students and the faculty use it because we can practice during times when it wouldn't be convenient to walk over to the church. It's also located in an electronically dead spot in the basement. That means no cellphone, email, text, or social media will work in the room.

"Now that his voice is changing, if he continues to behave, we might let him accompany the choir versicles at Evensong on the little four rank Taylor and Boody continuo that sits in the choir aisle. It's a lovely instrument, but the keys are extremely sensitive to the touch."

Just then, John walked out onto the terrace to ask Ding a question about the Dupré. As they talked, he told them that he didn't want to go back to New York. "My voice is changing and I can't sing, so what's the use. I don't want to walk around during the services with a stick in my hands. Dad will need me when he comes home."

Alexis immediately protested. "Oh, no, you don't. You're going back and that's final. Your dad will need peace and quiet when he comes home. Besides, you don't want to let down the soccer team, do you?"

"Mom, get real. We haven't won a game in all the years I've been in school. It's just exercise. I can do that here with Uncle Charlie."

"Actually, John, we've been thinking of a new position for you, but don't you ever again refer to your acolyte classmates as stick walkers. You know the school will keep you on. Your education is important to us too. We think we'll create a new position and we'll call you a Junior Assistant Organ Scholar."

"Wow, I could start playing the organ again."

"Not yet. You're still under suspension for the rest of this term, but you would assist us by turning pages, organizing the music, pulling stops—especially on the Taylor and Boody gallery organ—occasionally pumping the bellows for early music performances, and keeping the organ music library in order. The English refer to a position like this as a 'dog's body.' You do as commanded. Next year, you can begin playing preludes and postludes on occasion."

'Okay. That'll work. I love dogs's bodies. They never let me down. I already know how to pump the bellows. I did it in Switzerland and our organ at Swan Bay can be hand pumped. Let's go see if Dad's awake. This news will cheer him up."

41

THE MINX

Rachael Fox, head of the Atlanta Academy for Technology and the Arts, known behind her back as 'the Minx,' was feeling horny. It had been a while since she divorced her husband and she was having to pay him alimony every month. Their marriage began to fall apart after she had earned the moniker.

One of her friends told her that a new hotel in town had a bar that collected young attractive wealthy men. She was told there was a convention in the hotel of young guys in seminars for the Georgia bar exam so she decided to go check them out. She knew she was considered a cougar, but that just added to her fun.

She spotted her target the minute she walked in. He was seated at the bar with an empty stool beside him. She ordered an extra dirty martini.

"Extra dirty?" said the man. "I like a woman who knows what she wants." He was tall, well-built, and dark. Just her type. She had no idea that he was a vice cop.

They'd talked for a few minutes when she suggested, "Let's get another one and take it to your room and get better acquainted away from all this noise."

He nodded and carried their drinks to a room. He asked her to hold one while he got his room key card out of his pocket.

"Oh, let me get the card out," she said.

She reached into his pocket and groped him in the process. When they were in the room, he asked for a $500 payment.

"I hadn't planned on paying," she said, "but after what I just felt, I suspect you're going to be worth every penny." She opened her purse and quickly took out a credit card. He handed her his phone. She swiped it through a little attachment on his phone and entered the amount.

As soon as she hit Send, the door burst open and two uniformed police walked in. They cuffed her and led her out through the busy hotel lobby. A reporter who was just walking in to check out the bar scene recognized her. He called a buddy at the precinct.

"Get ready. The next big story is about to walk through the door. Be sure to get good pictures of her in cuffs. It's our old political friend, the Minx."

42
RECUPERATION

Hew sat up in bed, talking with Alexis, when a new doctor walked in. He had a wicked headache, was nearly deaf in one ear, and his vision was blurry, but the neurosurgeon was mostly satisfied with his progress. They were still concerned about his vision, but they couldn't fully evaluate it until he was conscious.

"I'm Dr. Evan Ewing, Mr. And Mrs. Ramsay. I'm head of neuro-opthalmology here at Emory and my team of specialists will evaluate your vision now that you're awake."

"I've never heard of a neuro-whatever."

"It's a relatively new field. We have five additional years of clinical studies beyond med school. We study diseases of the brain that affect vision. We're one of the top ten centers in the world. Your condition isn't a disease, but we're very interested in the effects of concussive damages from blasts like the one you suffered. We will also consult with retina and cornea specialists at the appropriate time. We use state of the art ocular coherence tomography, structural and angiographic imaging, and neuroimaging among other tools."

"I just want this to go away as soon as possible."

"I understand. Your first session starts in an hour, but you might as well relax. The ENTs haven't even started with your ear yet, but have no fear. You're in great hands."

Two hours later, Hew was sound asleep when the police detective and Tippy walked in. Tippy suggested they all walk outside the room.

The detective told Alexis that the explosion case had been solved. She was astounded to learn that she had been the target.

"This bombing was a federal crime so the FBI and the NTSB will be taking over. Your pilot was also a pilot for the Drug Enforcement Agency and his murder kicks this whole crime up to the feds. Mrs. Wilson will be tried, of course, but they've got enough evidence to put her away for life."

"I had forgotten that Les Wilson worked for Hew's grandfather when they were busting drug runners. I want them to send her to a prison up near the Alaskan Arctic Circle."

"She wants to see you. She wants to ask your forgiveness."

Alexis sat there for a few minutes. "She doesn't need mine. I'm not God. He forgives. I won't see her. We won't be in court, either."

Tippy was standing beside her. "But we must love our enemies. Let it go. If you don't forgive her, it will eat away at you. I know you, Alexis. Rise to the occasion and be the better person."

"I suppose I don't hate her, but I hate what she did. I'll think about it, but not right now, and yes, Tippy, you're correct."

After a week of testing Hew, the doctors had not found anything serious. He had been cautiously walking the corridors with a strong male physical therapy nurse until his leg muscles were almost back to normal. He was ready to go home, but still needed to have ear surgery. He had a month's growth of beard and his normally blond hair was coming back gray. Alexis was with him when the doctor came in.

"We find no issues with your vision beyond the fact that you now need bifocals."

"You mean I need glasses. Okay, fine. Just get me out of here."

"Has anyone talked with you about your blue eyes?"

"Certainly. Well, no. What do you mean? Is there a problem?"

"No. Not in your case—at least not yet."

Alexis frowned. "Not yet?"

"Let me explain. This is a new field and we're very interested in following it. You presented with issues that prompted us to study it. Genealogists believe blue eyes all descend from one common ancestor thousands of years ago. There are genetic markers that have been recently discovered. Obviously, you have them. Blue is actually a lack of pigment

355

in the iris and due to the lack of pigment, we now believe that blue eyes make you susceptible to melanoma of the eye, macular degeneration, and/or hearing loss, and our European colleagues are beginning to see a link to Type 1 diabetes. Fortunately, you're not diabetic, but the risk for the other conditions seems to increase as you age.

"You have been a great case study, but you are fine. We also took a blood sample and tested for 47 genes for variants now associated with cancers since you have no living relatives with known genetic disorders. We don't want melanoma to surprise us. You only have one variant on the MUTHY gene and that's of uncertain significance since there are too few known cases to be a subject for study at the moment. We will insist that you always wear sunglasses when you're outside. We'll prepare a prescription."

Alexis thought for a moment. "What about my kids with blue eyes?"

"Yes. Absolutely. They need to begin seeing an ophthalmologist as soon as possible. We'll be happy to take them as patients here." He turned back to Hew.

"Your ear surgery is scheduled for tomorrow morning first thing. Three more days, baring complications, and you'll be ready to walk. No head showers, no swimming, no getting your ear wet in the rain and no flying until you're cleared. Just go home and sit, but studies are beginning to show that the lack or low levels of melanin may lead to acquired sensori-neural hearing loss. We'll be watching carefully for that. We want to see you every six months from now on."

⚜

A week had passed and Hew was severely depressed. The ear surgery had been successful and the hearing test showed that his full range had been restored. The doctor came in with the results and proudly exclaimed, 'God damn, I'm good.'

Hew laughed for the first time since Easter Eve, but he really did want to go home. He just wanted to sleep in his own bed but his doctors told Alexis to keep him quiet once he was at home. She decided he needed a new look first. "We're going to your barber. I can't look at that beard another minute."

356

"Fine. I'll get a buzz cut too. I don't want to look at gray hair."

Hew kept trying to understand the blast. The last thing he remembered was talking to Jeffrey about something but he couldn't remember what. His mind from that moment until a few days after he came out of the coma was almost a total blank. He had fuzzy memories of people coming and going but that was about all.

He kept trying to understand why the Chinese or Russians had targeted him and his family. Was it a mafia hit? He thought Sam would have been a more likely target. He knew that the Russian rail system was mostly ancient. Eberhart had refused to do business in Russia because, among many reasons, whenever the Russian military moved, the whole public transportation network came to a grinding halt and Eberhart was not sure that construction products would ever arrive on time.

Hew decided that it must have been the Chinese. He blamed himself for agreeing to build the project. He put profit before family. That had nearly gotten them all killed. He just couldn't forgive himself. He was miserable and he was making everyone around him miserable, but he was so deep in despair he couldn't see that.

Hew had trouble learning to use his glasses. He could see distances with no problem, but the middle distance and the music desk was a big problem. His doctor changed his prescription to trifocals.

Alexis heard noises coming from the library. He was sitting at the table with his laptop cussing in Spanish and she ran down the stairs to investigate. In a fit of rage, he had thrown his glasses across the room with such force they had smashed against the stone fireplace. "Damn stupid glasses. The middle part isn't big enough to see the damned computer, goddamnit!"

"What are you writing?" she asked.

"Nothing. It's just some thoughts." He tried to close the computer but she grabbed it and looked at the screen. "Oh, my, God. You're writing your own obituary and your funeral plans."

She started reading. The obit was short—just a few simple lines—typical for an introvert. The funeral plans, on the other hand, were very detailed.

If I'm terminal, let me die in my bed in the old cabin at Swan Bay. Place my body in the front room overnight draped with my tartans and carry me to the old cemetery and bury me in a pine box beside my mother. Edward has my end of life details. No extraordinary measures are to be used. Use the old family prayer book and let the piper play 'Going Home' while the procession leaves the front parlor, then he's to play 'MacCrimmon's Lament' going up the hill, and then 'Flowers of the Forest' on the walk back. Do not embalm me but dress me in my kilt so my ancestors will recognize me. Have a grand party in the ballroom.

If I die elsewhere, cremate me and take me to Swan Bay at a convenient time. At some convenient time, the family might want to have a service at St. Philip's here in Atlanta. It should be an Evensong on a late afternoon that doesn't inconvenience the choir. Begin as follows:

Change ringing bells — half muffled. Leave the tenor unmuffled.

Prelude:
Toccata and Fugue in D minor BWV 565 by Bach.
Nimrod by Elgar.
Peaceful Meditation II by Paul Fey — with the chimes as written.
Cortege and Litany by Dupré. note: The bell notes shall be played on the chimes on the organ or orchestral tube chimes if the organ chimes aren't in good repair."

"Wait," said Alexis. "Why the organ chimes? I've never heard anyone but you play it that way."

"My mother played it that way. Actually, Dupré wrote three versions. He originally composed it for piano and then organ. He wrote one version for organ and orchestra that used the percussionist's tubular chimes for the bell sounds. That's what Mother preferred and that's the version I prefer."

She continued reading. "Who is Paul Fey?" She read aloud. *"The bourdon bell in the crossing tower shall then toll the nine Taylors."*

"Paul is a young organist who currently lives in Leipzig. The score is in my iPad on Forescore. John will know about it. *The processional shall be the Croft — NOT the Merbecke. It is to be sung by the choir, not a cantor.*

"Now wait a minute. This prelude starts in a dark place."

"Yes. From darkness to light with the Dupré. And the Croft suits the old Rite One in the 1928 *Prayer Book* better. I insist be that rite be used. Print the whole service in a booklet."

Alexis continued to read.

> *The opening hymn is 'All People that on earth do dwell' by Vaughn Williams with orchestra, organ and choir verses to be followed immediately by 'Oh what their joy and their glory must be.'*
> *NO REMEMBRANCES.*
> *The Psalms shall be 23 by Goss in Anglican chant and Psalm 150 by George Talbot. Tell the organist to let it soar out like they do at St. Thomas.*

"Wait. Two psalms? I don't want to sit through that. I'll be grieving too much."

"They're both short. You'll be okay."

> *She read on."The lessons shall be the appointed ones for the day or whatever the dean selects. The Office hymn before the Magnificat shall be 'Michael' by Howells with his harmonization on the final verse. The organist may also modulate magnificently between verses. The Mag and Nunc shall be from Howells's Collegium Regale. The collects and prayers shall be the usual. The anthem shall be 'And I Saw Another Angel' op 37 No 1 by Stanford.*

"Stanford?"

"I was trying to decide between that and Balfour Gardiner's *Evening Hymn.*"

"Nope. Extremely beautiful, but too much Latin. No one will understand it."

"Then I guess *Tallis's Spem* in Alium is out too."

"Don't even mention that one. Eight choirs of five voices each? Forget it. Too much practice required." She read on.

> *The next hymn as the priests move to my cremated remains shall be Hyfrydol's* Alleluia Sing to Jesus *with an improvised play over introduction and an improvised interlude before the final verse. The*

organist shall let her rip. Then the priests shall say the committal followed by the choir singing Parry's I was Glad with brass and Charlie's timpani and finally the congregation will sing the hymn Blaenwern, 'Love Divine' by Wesley with the brass quintet and Charlie's timpani and cymbals.

"Should we sing it in Welsh? There's no Scottish music here."

"Don't make fun of me. The Scottish music is reserved for the burial. I'm saving you the grief of having to decide at the last minute. The retiring procession shall be Paul Fey's Fanfare for a Farewell *followed by his* Westminster Toccata.*"*

"I've never heard that Toccata."

"He used the correct notes of the Westminster clock chime unlike Vierne. Oh, I almost forgot. NO HOMILY."

"Okay, Buster. That's it! We're getting out of here. You're too morbid right now. No more practicing until you get new glasses. Pack up. Charlie and Rosilyn will drive us to Highlands to stay with Edward and Tippy until you have calmed down. Tippy'll watch your ass like a hawk. I'm tired of this too, you know. You aren't the only one who suffered. We've all been walking on eggs around here."

"There won't be room with Eddie too."

"He's gone to Sullivan's Island with his Mazyck cousins. He says there's nothing to do in Highlands. You're going."

Hew started laughing and couldn't stop. He was remembering that Charlie used to say the same thing before the girls showed up for their epic sex-filled weekend when Tippy and Edward left them alone in the mountain house. They'd gone to a weekend wedding in Asheville. Alexis didn't understand, but she was happy that he was finally laughing.

⚜

The doctor prescribed a new set of bifocals and a full-sized pair of middle distance glasses exactly suited to the music desk and a computer screen and they were delivered to Highlands. Since the Hardys didn't have a piano or organ, Hew took his portable Casio keyboard, headphones, and laptop so he could sit on the screened porch and practice.

The music began to restore his attitude. His hearing was fine. He had panicked for a moment on the drive up when his ears popped from the change in altitude, but once they arrived, he didn't have a further problem. The procedure had been a complete success.

Alexis ordered several sets of glasses including polarized, UV protected dark tinted mirrored sunglasses. She wanted to be prepared. He didn't like having to carry three pairs of glasses around. She got him a chain to go around his neck. "It's like a damned dog collar," he said.

"Just shut up and wear it. It's your new reality."

43
THE SETTLEMENT

Hew sat on the Hardy's terrace in Highlands, watching the sun set over the Blue Ridge Mountains. It had rained that morning so the normal blue haze that gave the mountains their name was gone and the air was cool and crystal clear.

He should have been happy that his family was alive and healthy, but he just couldn't fully shake the depression and Tippy was ready to prescribe meds.

Edward walked out and joined him. "Beautiful isn't it, Hew? This is my favorite time of day. The western sun lights up the southern valley in a magical way. It's almost a religious experience."

"I suppose. The Scots call this time of day the 'gloaming.' Actually, now that you mention it, the sunlight on those rock faces does remind me of the setting sun on the west facade of those English cathedrals. The old stonework actually turns gold and glows." Hew sighed. "Edward, why did the Chinese want to kill my entire family? Do you think they'll try again?"

"Chinese? It wasn't the Chinese, or the Russians."

"Don't bullshit me, Edward. We've always been straight with each other. I need to know what to do next and I just can't figure it out. Was it one of the labor union mobs trying for revenge because of the SCMAG-LEV contracts? It was a mob hit, wasn't it?"

"Did no one tell you? It was local. They were after Alexis, not you. The rest of you folks would have just been collateral damage."

"What the hell are you talking about? No one hates Alexis!"

Edward explained the whole situation. "I'll show you the police report."

Hew stood up, walked over to the terrace rail, looked over and sighed. Alarmed, Edward yelled, "Come back here and sit down. He texted Tippy and asked her to bring his laptop and Hew's reading glasses out as quickly as she could."

"Oh, for God's sake," said Hew. "I'm not going to jump. Calm down. It's fifty feet to the ground. That would make a mess on those rocks."

"Fine. Just come back here and read this."

He read it twice. "It's really final."

"Yes. They also found two skull fragments. The DNA on one matches Marta. The other matches Les Wilson, the bomber. They matched the slug from the hit on your van with a rifle belonging to Les. The slug had bounced off onto the grass. Pink found it. The tornado carried the rifle into a suburb. A man living there found the rifle when he removed the tree that had fallen on the roof of his garage. Being a gun dealer himself, he gave it to the sheriff who alerted everyone along the path of the storm." He nodded. "It's really over."

Tippy's brother, DeVeaux Mazyck, and his wife Missy, had driven up from Charleston and arrived just as drinks were being prepared. They were all old friends and Tippy had already given them all the sordid details of the explosion and the aftermath. They were pleasantly surprised to see Hew looking happy.

Hew and Alexis were sitting with them quietly sipping cocktails, enjoying the cool summer breeze, and watching the shadows on the trees deepen in the valley as the sun set over the mountains. "DeVeaux," Hew said, "the last time we were in Charleston, the Episcopal church battles were still in the courts. How's that going? Are you going back to your old parish?"

"Yes, to the first question, and no to the second. We're permanently settled at Grace Church Cathedral. Has Tippy told you about the family?"

"Not much. Has something changed?"

"Our son Isaac has finally found a partner and they will be married at Christmas at Grace."

Alexis jumped up and hugged Missy. "Congratulations. I know you'll be glad to get him settled."

Hew walked over to shake DeVeaux's hand. He toasted the happy couple. "Slainte' Mhaith and Cheers!—Good health and fun."

"Yes. It's taken a long time and too many boyfriends, but they are both mature men and we're delighted. You all will be invited of course, but I've got to warn you, our house is already full."

Everyone laughed. "Don't worry Alexis, you and Hew can stay with us at Bishop Gadsden. You might even want to retire there too."

"Oh, not yet, Tippy. Not for a long time."

They all laughed as the alcohol began to do its work. "Now as to the second question, let me give you a little history since Atlanta has mostly been spared this disaster."

"We had a bit of it early on over the issue of the ordination of women, but those folks left and built their own church. They took a huge chunk of parishioners out of our cathedral, but we've managed to recover."

"South Carolina was founded in 1670 and the Church of England was the official religion. As such, the land and the buildings were financed with tax funds. The furnishings and fixtures were paid for by the parishioners and several gave glebe lands to support the priests."

"Remind me about a glebe."

"Basically it's land from which the priest was supposed to derive his income. Most of those lands in Charleston have now been squandered away unlike Trinity Wall Street in New York, which still owns most of their land in lower Manhattan. In South Carolina, they simply sold the land rather than cough up money from their own pockets to pay their bills. It's basically a form of cannibalism."

Everyone laughed. "Well you must remember that they were broke after the Civil War."

"Yes, but the selloff began before the Civil War, and remember, we're talking about the great-great-grandchildren of the sons of anarchy at the moment. They were the first to secede from the Union."

Alexis chimed in. "Not all of us still carry that torch. One of my ancestral grandmothers was born in South Carolina on the day of secession. They named her Carry Secession Andrews."

"That's a joke, right?"

"No. She did have the good sense to call herself Carrie, though."

"Those old ideas of prejudice and privilege haven't gone away. Anyway, after the war, the Anglican parishes were adrift until Samuel Seabury of Philadelphia was ordained bishop by the Episcopal Church of Scotland. He was able to provide Episcopal oversight to the churches in the new states. The 1778 post-war constitution of the state of South Carolina simply gave all of the then currently occupied lands and buildings of the Anglican parishes to the parishes—Article 38 if I remember correctly."

"Gave?"

"Yes. They further stipulated that the gifts were forever. Other states had confiscated the Anglican property and forced those parishes to buy them from the states. The Anglican members of the South Carolina legislature pulled a fast one. Of course, in the twentieth century many of the old South Carolina colonial parishes relinquished that right when they ratified the Dennis Canon and assigned their assets to the national church. In the 1780s, the former Anglican parishes in the Northeast began to form a new national organization to be called The Episcopal Church. Southern clergy had mostly been patriots, so the Charleston churches were invited to join and they banded together to form a diocese, but not until they had long protracted discussions over the form and theological wording of the liturgy. They basically argued over every word, comma, and period of the *Prayer Book*, but finally, they agreed. They didn't pay much attention to governance beyond their own personal needs.

"Now, you need to understand that the Charleston churches were founded while the Church of England was basically what we today might call low church evangelicals. That started to change in the Church of England in the 1840s after several dons at Oxford University began to challenge the extremely lax eighteenth- and early nineteenth- century liturgical practices. They pushed for a return to a more formal form of liturgy with Holy Communion rather than lengthy sermons as the central core. There are even eighteenth-century references to the people sitting in the balconies of St. Martin in the Fields in London watching as liveried servants scurried to and fro delivering mixed drinks on silver trays to the folks in the high rent box pews on the nave floor. The drinks were said to help with the 'tedious parts of the service'—the sermon."

They all hooted with laughter. DeVeaux commented, "I actually saw a similar reference to the services in the brick church called Pon Pon Chapel south of Charleston down near Walterboro. It was a country plantation church so the concept must have been common in the Church of England parishes around the globe."

"I wouldn't mind reviving that practice. I thought the balconies were for slaves."

"No, that's a common and rather romantic but now rather racist idea. The 1711 St. Philip's Charleston building was first built without the side balconies. They were added as the parish grew. This fact is recorded in the old vestry minutes. It apparently never occurred to anyone to hold two services. An old oil painting of the interior made after the 1835 fire shows white faces in the side galleries and the west gallery shows a fine organ—the 1833 Erben—behind the small faces of robed choir boys."

"Apparently that was a fine instrument," added Hew. "It only lasted three years. According to the newspaper of the day, it was 26 feet high, 14 feet wide and 10 feet deep. It had three manuals and pedal. It had 24 stops. I love old Erben organs. There are three left in South Carolina and two are in Charleston. St. Philip's has a very rare Appleton Organ in the chapel. It's one of only two left."

"Not to gloss over the pain and suffering, but the Oxford reform didn't come easily to say the least, and most of the Charleston parishes simply ignored it entirely.

"In Charleston, worship simply stopped during the Civil War. Grace was the last to close after a missile fired from James Island struck the east clearstory wall, but the parish was the first to reopen."

"Oh, yes. Grace sent their Erben organ to First Presbyterian in Columbia for safekeeping. They bought a new organ after the war ended. Can you imagine how important music was back then? The South was destitute but they found the money for a fine instrument. The Erben case survives today in an old AME church on Sumter Street near the Baptist Hospital, if I remember correctly."

DeVeaux added, "Yes, the organ case is still there. The pipes—except for the facade pipes—are long gone. Several times, squads of Union soldiers would stand in the center aisle at Grace until the rector prayed for the President of the US. One Sunday the federal commander himself ordered the prayer. Dr. Pinckney, the rector, replied, 'I will gladly obey your order. I know of no one who needs praying for more than the President of the United States.' The soldier was not aware that the Episcopal service included that prayer as a common prayer."

"That rector was Pink's ancestor," said Hew. "I've heard him recall this same story from his family. All their children learn it."

"It was a most difficult time for the people—Black and White. South Carolina tried hard to erase all the work of Reconstruction. They wanted to restore the culture to pre-war conditions as much as possible."

"They're still trying," quipped Edward.

Tippy added, "No doubt. And there were frequent episodes of typhoid and yellow fever during that time too."

DeVeaux continued. "Storm clouds began to gather again in the late 1970s when the national church began discussing the issue of a new *Book of Common Prayer* accompanied by a new hymnal. Many of the old parishes refused to use the new books."

"I remember that. The theology schools pushed the idea that our generation didn't respond to the old 'stained glass' language."

"What the hell is stained glass language?"

"Oh, words like atonement, propitiation of sin, regenerate, and other Elizabethan terms."

"I am of that generation and that never entered my mind."

"About the same time—1979—the national church passed a new canon known as the Dennis Canon because during the 1960s and 70s some parishes left the Episcopal Church over the issue of the ordination of women. The real battle started with this. The so-called Dennis Canon gave the property deeds over to be held in trust by the Episcopal Church. Each parish had to agree. What's happened recently relates to the ordination of homosexuals. That was the last straw for many. Our diocese split and the split was extremely painful."

"Let me tell this, DeVeaux. I've just in the last few years finally come to terms with this. I finally realized that if my ancestors could get in a little boat to flee France for their religious freedom, I could drive a few more blocks north in my air-conditioned Mercedes, but my family is all buried in the old graveyard. We've been baptized, married and buried there for more generations than I can remember. We still sat in the family pew. This is like a death in the family except we still have to drive past the old church. After the split—and you all will remember this—you came to Charleston for the presentation of the return of the old silver to Grace Church."

Hew and Edward squirmed. Hew's grandfather had returned the silver anonymously. It had been recovered from a drug lord's private home vault in Colombia shortly after his parent's murders. "Oh yes. I remember that weekend. We had a great time."

"Well, *we* didn't. We put up a good front, but we had just moved to Grace. At first, we thought we could just ride out the storm. We thought we could just fire the rector if it got too bad but then we began to realize it wouldn't be that simple. The old sanctimonious bishop was a driving force behind the issues and we realized that it would take three or more vestry elections to get the right people in place to make the change. Like most of our friends, we didn't really care about the priests' lofty theological issues, but Isaac started refusing to go to church. Most of our friends and family were and are determined not to let the clergy drive them out. It wasn't really personal to them and we never really listened to the sermons anyway. Daniel and Issac had always loved taking turns as the crucifer, but Daniel's girlfriend had casually remarked one day that girls weren't allowed to be the crucifer because girls weren't allowed behind the communion rail. I had never noticed, but she was right."

Edward sighed and mumbled, "First Corinthians Fourteen."

"I'm sorry," said Missy. "I didn't quite get that."

"Oh, Missy, sorry. It's just more conservative proof-texting. It's a line in the chapter that many modern theologians no longer attribute to Saint Paul. It says women must remain silent in church. These men select passages of scripture to support their pre-existing biases. Evangelicals have raised it to an art form. A sad art form, I might add, because too many people believe them."

"I've always thought of Saint Paul as something of a paradox. He certainly seemed to dislike women."

Hew chimed in."In the King James version, Paul admitted to being a liar to advance the cause of Christianity. Later versions have pasteurized that passage. He even claimed to have conversations with God. Many clergy make the same claim, but apparently, Paul never met Jesus. Paul was a flawed human just like everyone else."

"Oh I know. These guys think the ends justify the means. We heard our former clergy boast about discussions with God from the lofty pulpit and even in casual conversation. Frankly, that's above my level of under-standing or care."

DeVeaux shrugged. "We even had a chairman of the building com-mittee try to hide eight-hundred-thousand dollars of hurricane insur-ance money so he could seed the construction of his dream to build a large facility for contemporary worship. He simply skimped on some of the repair projects. Fortunately the vestry saw through his scheme and refused to fund the new building."

Missy continued. "We tried everything with Isaac. He finally blurt-ed out that he was gay and he refused to attend a church that wouldn't accept him. He told us that he thought he could agree to go to Grace Church. He and Daniel rang their bells for weddings and funerals and he went to their bell practices. It was our second Sunday there and the service was very different.

"I love my boys no matter what and we told them so, but it's taken me a while to get used to the liturgy. It's more formal than we were used to. As far as Isaac goes, I'm just glad he's happy. I must say, though, the people have been so loving and understanding. I can't imagine not being there. They simply took us in and never questioned us. I've joined the flower guild. I'm also embroidering a new kneeler cover with a bell mo-tif, so I'm at peace. DeVeaux is on the finance committee. Isaac's partner sings in the choir. I've finally seen all the joy in the liturgy and sermons."

Edward joined in. "The State Supreme Court has finally ruled—again I might add. Several of the parishes and other property will be returned to the Episcopal Church. The federal courts have returned the name and other rights to us. Several other churches are still fighting in court but basically, it is over. It basically came down to the exact wording of each parish's resolution to the Dennis Canon. Priests are beginning to move away and vestries are being dissolved. One of the first groups to leave took the trash cans, the wall art, the kitchen utensils—basically every-thing that wasn't attached—and the keys. They've yet to turn over the bank accounts. They turned off the electricity and internet without no-tice. Another parish took all of the audiovisual equipment, but the new priest was glad to see that stuff removed from the church. It actually saved him from having to pay someone to get rid of it.

"One parish actually absconded with the grand piano! New priests will be assigned until the parishes can form new vestries and call new priests. Some of the parishes will probably be dissolved and those buildings will probably be sold. There are deferred maintenance issues that will be expensive and the diocese will need to support these parishes until they can get back on their feet. We in the diocese are trying to heal the wounds but it won't be easy. We try to speak to each other in peaceful, prayerful terms."

Missy sighed. "I refuse to let my religion come between me and my neighbor. I'm supposed to love my neighbor more than my church. It won't be any easier for those who have now lost than it was for those of us who had to leave, but some of them are our family and some are old friends, so we just don't discuss it. We try to love everyone. I realize that many of my friends and relatives are members of churches of other religions. Many of our friends aren't religious at all. We all have to be comfortable with our own beliefs, but I'm just really surprised at the clergy. In hindsight, I suppose it really was there all along and we just didn't really see it."

The Atlanta folks sat there in silence sipping their drinks and thanking God all that hadn't happened to their diocese. Edward finally broke the silence. "The bishops either fueled or quenched these fires, but I think it's always been this way. Since the earliest times of Christianity, people have always tried to frame God according to their own beliefs. The church is composed of flawed people who are trying to find their way. How many millions of people have died fighting over a way to protect God? God doesn't need our feeble attempts of protection. It's not even possible.

"The word *catholic* means many things to many people. The same is true of the word Anglican, but the Anglican Communion does not recognize these American break-away parishes as being Anglican. Their use of the word is, frankly, meaningless. I've heard them referred to as AINOs—Anglicans in name only.

"I think you're correct, Missy. We should all ask ourselves if what we—and they—are doing really is looking out for the interest of our neighbors. Do any of our actions fit the commandment to love our neighbor?"

"So what has actually changed?"

"Apart from many many hurt feelings and an ocean of tears? Not much. The breakaway parishes still use the Episcopal *Book of Common Prayer* and the *1982 Hymnal*. The smug priests and bishops think they won a battle for God. They're no longer priests in the church and really can't consecrate communion or give blessings but everyone seems to just ignore that."

Hew said, "That's true, Edward, but even James VI, while king of Scotland, disapproved of the word Anglican as it applied to the Scots. Of course, he had to change his tune when he ascended to the throne as James I."

Edward laughed. "This is just the latest in an ongoing cultural sea of change and conservatives are fighting back. These people actually believe they're defending God."

"You're right, Edward," said Missy. "God doesn't need anyone's protection. That's just hubris. It's the other way around. A few of the parishes finally won the right to keep their property and break away so we must graciously give them that right. The law has spoken and frankly, our diocese probably couldn't have sustained all of those properties anyway. Too many more people would have simply left. I'm just sad about the amount of time and money that was expended. There was so much pain, heartbreak, and division for those of us who couldn't stay in our beloved churches, and now some of those who tried to take parish property and assets away have lost their battle anyway. We endured ten years of fighting."

"Missy, we feel your pain," said Hew. "It was particularly painful in your diocese yet the Upper Diocese of South Carolina managed to weather the storm as did we in Atlanta. I'm reminded of lines from old hymns. *Through many dangers, toils, and snares I have already come.* And another that goes, *"By schisms rent asunder, by heresies distressed, yet saints their watch are keeping, their cry goes up, 'How long'."*

"How long, indeed, Hew, but in my opinion, it's no wonder so many people are giving up on the church."

"Well, that's true, but..."

Edward's phone rang. "It's Judith. I'm going to put her on speaker." Edward already knew what was coming but he hadn't expected it quite this soon.

"Alexis," said Judith. "We have a settlement offer. Edward can fill you in but you're going to love it."

"Edward? Why does he already know the details?"

"I asked him to join me in trying to wrap this up. He's been a tiger. We should have involved him earlier. I've got to go meet a client for drinks and dinner, but I'll need you here by the first of next week to sign everything before the next Academy board meeting. Congratulations."

"Thanks. Why before the next board meeting?"

"He'll tell you. That may be even better than your settlement."

After she hung up, Alexis looked at Edward. "Spill it."

"It's complicated, but it's the largest settlement in the history of the state. It will take an act of the state assembly but that will absolutely happen tomorrow. I remembered that I had notes from the time that the Academy was created. I had information about all the wasteful spending, but I had forgotten about it so I had my old assistant pull it out and organize it. She called one of your friends still at the Academy—there are only a few left—and he was only too happy to provide the backup documents from storage. Two weeks ago, he was going through the latest credit card statements and discovered a bombshell. Rachael used her Academy credit card to pay the vice cop!"

"No! Even she's not that stupid."

"We'll never know. I contacted my two friends on the Academy board and gave them a briefing on this whole sad tale. They called Amos and told him to shut down this vendetta with you before the next board meeting or they would make it all public. They can't afford to have Rachael take the stand in a trial."

"How much?"

"I'll get to that, but that's not all. Tomorrow, the legislature will lift the cap on liability payouts. Even the legislators who are attorneys can't be seen as opposing justice for such a heinous premeditated crime. The feds may even go for the death penalty. If they don't, the state of Georgia will try her for all the deaths and they will certainly get it. Now, here's the interesting part. Even our friends on the board don't know all of this.

At the next board meeting, our friends will make a motion to go into executive session and conclude this privately. Alexis, since you brought the suit, you and the board will sign a confidentiality agreement. Once that's done and they return to the regular session, the state attorney general will walk in, fire Rachael, and dissolve the entire board."

"That'll certainly become public. The reporters at the meeting will love that. Who will run the show after everyone's fired?"

"That's the only bad part. They've delegated me to re-institute the board. Since Kleindic is dead, I will select the names of the members and I will submit them to the legislature for approval, but I will tell you without the slightest pain of embarrassment of cronyism that your two board member friends will be put forward as members of the new board and they and I will select the other board members from a list of names put forward by the Georgia State Assembly. The next chairperson will be elected from the new board members. No one wanted another group of autonomously elected board members pushing their own political agendas. We'll argue that we need some continuity. I'm also under strict orders to spend as little as possible."

"People will lose their jobs."

"A few will. Those who were instrumental in your downfall will find that their positions have become redundant. Those who remained loyal to you will keep their positions if they so desire. As the old proverbial saying goes, 'Revenge is a dish best served cold.'

"There's one other thing. They want you and Sarah back in your old jobs. Oh, I almost forgot. The marketing organization, Rockin' in Alana, is under the microscope. Seems that they've been footloose with their spending on private trips and promotions. There's been no real accounting for years and the funds have been used for personal travel and entertainment trips cloaked as promotional necessities. They've been making frequent trips to Nashville and Europe on private jets. They even have a private fund stashed in a bank in the Cayman Islands."

Hew was aghast. "Why?"

"Their excuse was that they needed it as a way to offset the dollar to English exchange rates, but it looks dubious to me. We'll probably never know because they bring in so much tourism money the governments look the other way. This will die the usual way once the press gets bored."

"I'm not surprised. I can't answer for Sarah, but my answer is no. I'm happy to be a stay-at-home mom. We haven't found a new nanny yet, and I might just quit looking. My children deserve a full time mother."

"If I had been a stay at home mom, Charlie wouldn't have started having sex at thirteen," said Tippy.

Hew squirmed and tried not to laugh. He turned back to Edward.

"HOW MUCH?"

Edward scribbled a number onto a piece of paper and passed it to Alexis. She dropped her G&T onto the terrace and glass shards flew across the slate floor. Hew and Tippy grabbed the paper from Alexis and started laughing.

"Keep in mind," said Edward, "this is only your portion. The other victim's estates and the airport will get a huge chunk too. Some of this will pay the enormous hospital and doctors' invoices, and some of it will fund your new Gulfstream G650ER jet. The cost per day on your ICU bed was nearly $2,500 and that doesn't include the specialists.

"Judith will be paid a third of the gross. We decided to expand your original suit and the judge, after reviewing our brief, was only too happy to oblige. During the discovery for the documents against the Academy, we found several more interesting items. Because Mable had been an employee at the Academy, her comments allowed us to tie the bomb with her termination.

"They planned your murder as retribution. When he changed jobs and moved to the airport, Les failed to erase his histories on his work computer. Dekalb-Peachtree Airport is not going to be held liable. To save money, the owner of the other plane had refueled using automotive fuel—gasoline—rather than aviation fuel. That contributed to the fire so his estate won't be suing you personally, Hew.

"Rachael and Amos had also used their cellphones and computers to plot their revenge against you for filing your suit. They discussed strategies to keep you tied up for as long as possible, citing the fact that you didn't need money. That, of course, only allowed Amos more fee. Their correspondence shows an intent to delay justice and shows they were plotting to increase their own salaries in the process. They deliberately withheld critical information from the board too. You are due every penny. Amos will be disbarred."

"Tippy," said Alexis, "I'm so sorry about the broken martini glass. I'll buy you a new set."

"Oh, hell, no. I buy those at the local thrift store. We don't use the good stuff up here anymore. Forget about it. Now, who's hungry? We're having those North Carolina mountain trout Hew and Edward caught in our stream this afternoon. Edward cleaned and gutted them and I filleted them. Go start the grill, Hew. It's time you start being useful again."

Hew laughed and then they all did too and Edward broke another glass. The old order of friendship had been restored.

They ate supper on the screened porch. The late May temperature had dropped from 72 degrees at four o'clock to a cool 66. The house blocked most of the breeze that earlier had been delightful on the open terrace. Edward built a fire in the porch fireplace.

"These fish are absolutely delicious. How did you prepare them? I want the recipe."

They complemented the meal with several bottles of Sauvigon Blanc from the Cade Estate Winery on Howell Mountain in Napa Valley that Hew had furnished from his cellar.

Tippy laughed. "Edward and Charlie go to the local hatchery every year and get the fish to stock the stream. They were cooked in a shallow foiled lined baking sheet over low heat and topped with lemon infused butter, capers, a little extra virgin olive oil and a squeeze of fresh lemon juice as a finish. We stopped at Costco in Greenville and bought the olive oil. There's is sourced from a single grove unlike most oils that are blends from several groves. Missy found the cauliflower and yellow squash at the farmer's market yesterday and she turned the cauliflower into a mashed concoction that tastes like mashed potatoes. She also made the lemon meringue pies." She looked around. "I'm getting chilled. Let's have dessert inside by the other fire."

"I use the Eureka lemons from our garden," said Missy. "I prefer them to the usual Meyer lemons. These are the first of the season and they're actually early. They are very tangy and cut through the fish extremely well for a nice finish." She smiled. "You know, we've been coming here for years, but I'm just now beginning to appreciate this mountain contemporary architecture. I'm so used to our English antiques I never appreciated how absolutely comfortable Johann and Heidi's contemporary furniture just adds to the comfort. This soaring ceiling and the sloped glass wall allow us to see the stars without reflections. It's pure magic."

"Thanks. We've always loved it here."

⁂

ALEXIS AND HEW CRAWLED INTO BED and she snuggled up to him. "Are you really back?"

He sighed. "Yes. I'm sorry I've been such a pain in the ass, but it's really over. I've used up eight of my nine lives. We've got to decide how to spend number nine."

She reached down and fondled him. "Let's start now."

"Oh, yeah...let's."

44
CELEBRATIONS

"Folks, thank for the hospitality," said Hew. "This place was just what I needed. Well, that and Edward's explanation of the bombing."

"The settlement didn't hurt either, Hew." They all laughed.

"I really need to run up to Swan Bay. Jeffrey and I have an unfinished conversation. I just this moment remembered our discussion just before the blast. Why don't you all fly up with us? DeVeaux and Missy have never been to Swan Bay. We'll make it a quick weekend trip."

All agreed and they drove down to the Oconee County Airport at Clemson since Highlands only had a heliport at the hospital. They stopped on Main Street in Highlands for bags of fresh pastries for their breakfast.

Dinner at Swan Bay was the usual sumptuous feast in the grand dining room. Due to the unseasonably cool late May weather, there were fires in both fireplaces and the light from the bee's wax candles in the eighteenth-century polished brass chandeliers and wall sconces cast flickering shadows around the room. Most of the leaves were removed from the table for this supper. A fine antique handmade white Belgian lace tablecloth covered the fine Chippendale table.

The restoration team had tried to convince Hew that the candles were a fire hazard. He firmly refused their suggestion for gas logs too, but the chimneys now included stainless steel liners with modern dampers. Jared, the new young chef had suggested adding downlights over the original Chippendale sideboards. Hew simply ignored him.

Jeffrey and Mary joined their eight old friends. With very little notice, the new staff had prepared a fine repast under the watchful eye of Ms. Mamie.

During dessert, Tippy turned to Hew. "Remember that Viking trip we made down the Rhine River when you and Charlie were teens?"

Of course, Hew remembered—he had lost his virginity on that trip. "Sure, Tippy. Why?"

"I've been getting mailings from Viking ever since and I recently saw a trip on the Rhône from Avignon to Lyon that looks like fun. We should all go. How long has it been since you and Alexis took a vacation without the kids?"

Edward chimed in. "Yes. It's like a floating house party." Everyone agreed to let Tippy book it. Hew agreed to fly everyone to Europe.

During the night, just before dawn, Hew sat straight up in bed, soaked in sweat. His nightmare had returned. This was the third time since the bombing. He got out of bed wearing his usual baggy soccer shorts and tee shirt and padded barefoot down the grand staircase.

After the restoration, Alexis had convinced him that the family needed to use the house as it was originally intended. The old cabin was simply too small now and the guest quarters, while very nice, were more like a fine hotel than a home. Hew and Alexis slept in the old main bedroom on the second floor behind the ballroom. The babies were across the hall in the old nursery, and the girls were on the third floor. When John was there, he still slept in the old cabin.

The sun had not yet started to glow in the eastern sky. Hew stood in the damp grass of the great lawn and let the cold morning dew tickle his feet. When he looked up, the billions of bright stars reminded him of how small he was. He couldn't see stars like this in Atlanta because of the light pollution. It was one of the things he loved about Swan Bay.

He suddenly felt the warm presence of generations of his Scottish ancestors standing silently in a circle around him. They seemed to be resolute and firmly set in their ways, but he was not afraid. He had several decisions to make and their presence was comforting. He suddenly knew what John had felt at Douglas's funeral.

Alexis quietly walked up behind him and wrapped him in a large Ramsay tartan cashmere throw. "Is it the same nightmare?"

"Almost. This time I saw the end. I saw my ancestors waiting to help. This time, I woke up alive in a tight black box. I was gasping for air but the air only smelled like pine. I was buried alive in the cemetery here."

"Let's hope it really is the end of the nightmares. In the other ones, you woke up but you didn't know where you were. Tippy thinks it is a reaction to your coma."

"I hope so, but now I know the order of the solutions to my questions. My ancestors gave me two of the solutions."

"What questions?"

"The first is the immediate future of Swan Bay Breeding Center. The second is the future of that albatross of a castle in Scotland. The third is the disposition of my Cavillé-Coll organ."

"Start with number one. Let's go to the kitchen and warm up. It's cold out here."

Ms. Mamie and Jared, the new young new chef, were already hard at work. The big pot of grits had been simmering all night. Hew whispered to Alexis, "We'll talk later."

"Ms. Mamie, you shouldn't be up at this hour. Let the young guy cook breakfast."

"Humph. He finally understands the grits and this last batch of biscuits is his best yet."

Jared spoke up. "She thinks she's tough as nails, but we get along just fine. She's just like my grandmother. I'm learning stuff they never taught us in school. Mr. and Mrs. Ramsay, let me make breakfast for you. How do you like your eggs?"

"I'll fix 'em," said Mamie. "You can watch. Grandmother, my ass. Ha. I'm a great-great-grandmother now. Hew eats two soft scrambled eggs with no salt. He won't eat my grits or my country ham and red eye gravy neither. I cured that ham myself, but no-o-o. Not this city boy." She cackled and smiled. "I thawed a pack of last year's blueberries for the pancakes."

"Mmmm. That sound just right. You know me too well, Ms Mamie. The biscuits smell great. Pass the butter. Do you still have a jar of your cherry preserves?"

"I had to fight those people to keep 'em from chopping down my cherry trees. Construction folks are always looking for the easy way out."

"Ms. Mamie, I love your grits and country ham. I'll eat Hew's too. I'll take some extra red eyed gravy if you don't mind. I'm a Southern girl."

After breakfast and a shower, Hew met with Jeffrey in the old cabin to discuss the future of the breeding center. "I'm sorry, Jeffrey. Yesterday at breakfast, I suddenly remembered that you were talking about retirement just before the, um, you know."

"I thought you might have forgotten. Yes, Mary and I want to retire. She inherited forty acres of farmland across the river and we've had Johann design a smaller version of Edward's Highlands house. It's going to face south down the river so we can have a full array of solar panels on the pitched slate roof. It will be raised above the flood plane and constructed of handmade Virginia bricks but with large glass windows. He calls it Contemporary Tidewater Virginia style. It will have a great room, a small study, and our bedroom suite on the main floor with two ensuite guest rooms above. The guest rooms will be located along a balcony that over looks the vaulted great room. There will be a long row of operable clearstory windows over the balcony on the north slope of the roof. There will be an elevator, of course. Tippy wants you to design a virtual organ setup."

"That sounds great. I understand. I know exactly what she wants. I don't know who I'll get to manage this place, though. As you know, I know absolutely nothing about horses and I absolutely despise having to sit through those long boring dinners here when we wine and dine the owners. All that talk of siring and mounting and foaling bores me to tears."

"I have a solution I think you'll like. Mary's nephew, Jackson—he's actually her grandnephew—has just graduated from the University of Virginia with a masters in equine studies. His wife has her masters in business administration. They would love to take our places and move in here. He will go to vet school in the fall."

"That really sounds hopeful. I'll need to think about it and meet them."

"Of course. Here's a prospectus she's prepared. They already know and love the staff here. The vets will enjoy working with them. You might still need to be trotted out—pun intended—from time to time to schmooze with a few of the wealthier owners, though. They like to know the real property owners."

"I guess that can be arranged—on rare occasions. Okay. I'll give you my answer in the morning."

Hᴇᴡ ᴀɢʀᴇᴇᴅ ᴛᴏ ʟᴇᴛ ᴛʜᴇ ɴᴇᴡ generation run the breeding center. On the following Thursday morning, the Mazycks flew back to Clemson and drove to Highlands to retrieve their car. The rented jet returned to Swan Bay in the afternoon after having collected Alexis's parents in Greenville and they all flew to New York to attend John's graduation from St. Thomas Choir School.

The diplomas and prizes were awarded on Saturday. John had received two letters at their home address that Hew didn't understand. One was from Le Concours International in Chartres, France, and the other was from the Haarlem Summer Academy. He knew nothing about either festival, so he called Ding and asked him to look into it. On Friday evening, Hew called Ding again and was told to wait until the prizes were announced and he would understand. At the end of the prize awards, the head of the school asked John and Ding to step forward.

"John Ramsay, you have been invited to attend the Haarlem Summer Academy to further your organ studies and, as a part of the Concours International d' Orgue de Haarlem, you are invited to perform your Psalm composition on the Muller organ in St. Bavo's Church." Hew gasped and Ding just smiled. "And you have also been invited to compete with an improvisational composition given in recital by the Grandes Orgues de Chartres Association as a part of Grandes Orgues de Chartres Le Concours International in Chartres Cathedral during the summer series. This festival is known as the Olympics of the organ. Congratulations."

There was polite applause. Alexis was puzzled. Hew was ecstatic. Ding asked for the microphone.

"If I might just say a word or two about these awards…This is a tremendous award for John of course, but also for our school. The Haarlem school and festival are home of the oldest organ awards in the world. It was founded in 1955 and many of the world's finest organists have performed there. Likewise, the Chartres festival was founded in 1971 and is something of a restoration of the old Grande Prix de Rome—not the auto race I might add." That got a chuckle from all the parents. "I'll add that I had nothing to do with this and I have never heard this composition."

John took a bow and blurted out, "Dad we'll need a choir in Haarlem. Can we take all the boys? Please?"

Hew didn't have an answer except to say, "I'll discuss this with Ding." Hew didn't have a clue how this had come about.

Hew and Alexis invited Ding to join their party for dinner at the restaurant Daniel on East 65th St. Hew still hadn't gotten over the closure of The Four Seasons restaurant in the Seagram building. Over cocktails, Hew asked Ding, "How did this happen? Someone at the school must have known."

"Really, I don't know. My contacts told me that someone sent a recording and a copy of the score to these committees. Apparently the person who sent them was a former Grand Prix winner."

"Oh, of course. My old organ teacher, Father Arturo. He's the only one who had the recording and score. He had to have sent it that same afternoon we were there. He died during that night." Hew paused. "Father A. What a great priest, mentor, friend, and organist. May his soul, and the souls of all the faithfully departed, through the mercy of God, rest in peace and Rise in Glory." He sighed. "When is it?"

"They are both held in July but according to the schedule, John's performances don't conflict with each other. This is quite an honor."

"I know. I was fortunate to have been given an afternoon to play the Haarlem organ myself. I wonder if the same organist is still there. John will love it." He murmured, "Collette."

"What?" said Alexis. "Who's Collette?"

Hew was embarrassed that he had whispered her name out loud. She was one of the girls he and Charlie had picked up in Holland. They were both French organ students. He had gladly given her his virginity too. He and Charlie had experienced two nights filled with sex.

"Oh, nothing, Alexis. She was a visiting organ student who turned pages for me." He quickly changed the subject. "John's right. It's a choral work. We'll need the boys if you can arrange it. I'll pay, of course. We want you there as well, if you can. Let's order. I'm starved."

They had the seven-course tasting menu with several bottles of fine wine. During the courses, Ding commented, "It won't be a school trip, but we can contact the parents individually. I can be a chaperone and perhaps I can get one of the housemothers to join us. Most of the boys have summer plans, but I think they'll jump at the chance for a free trip to Holland."

"We can provide the plane, hotel rooms, and food, and we can take a parent or two if that will help. We leave from here tomorrow for a month in Oxford. We were planning to split July between the Royal School of Church Music course at Duke University in North Carolina then fly to Scotland, but I'll change Scotland until August. This will be a great fun filled summer."

"You'll love the Duke Chapel. It was designed by one of America's early Black architects, Julian Francis Abele. It's a neo-gothic masterpiece and is as big as an English cathedral. He studied architecture at the University of Pennsylvania and was the chief designer of the Philadelphia firm of Trumbauer, but because of the segregation policies in the South at the time, he is reported to have only visited his great masterpiece once. Are you the course organist?"

"I'm glad he got to see it and I hope those days are finally coming to an end. We despise racism in all its forms. No, Alexis and I will be singing with the adults. I do hope I get a chance to play the magnificent Flentrop organ."

"That won't be a problem. They always let the musicians have an open console afternoon to play the instruments. Don't miss the chance to play the chancel 1932 Aeolian Skinner. It's a masterpiece itself. They almost lost it, you know."

"Lost it? How? Why?"

"The story goes that after the Flentrop was installed in 1976, some of the organists only wanted to play it and not the chancel instrument. The acoustics in the chapel had been improved by sealing the old stone vaulting and their tastes had changed to exclude music for which the Aeolian Skinner excelled. One of the alumni wanted to give a closed circuit TV system so the organists could see the chancel. They reportedly quipped they didn't want a camera because they weren't concerned with the service down there."

"Typical musicians' egos. They weren't serious. They couldn't easily accompany the choir from back there."

"Right. One of the old guys wanted to by a new instrument to re-place the aging instrument just to support the services, but reason pre-vailed. The authorities refused to remove the old organ. I had a good friend—he died recently—who was president of the faculty senate and he had to approve anything that was built or renovated on campus. They called him the 'space czar.' George flatly refused to remove the organ and gladly approved its restoration. He was an Episcopal musician born in Charleston and baptized at St. Michael's as well as an English litera-ture scholar."

"We're looking forward to it. I particularly want to sing the Sowerby again."

THE SUNDAY SERVICE AT ST. THOMAS the following day is known as the Valedictory service. The head of school gives the address.

The morning broke with clear blue skies, a warm temperature, and a slight breeze out of the west. Hew decided to walk to church down Fifth Ave. along the side of Central Park. He hadn't done that since childhood with his nanny. Alexis vetoed that idea, so they compromised. Hew and Edward walked and everyone else rode in their secured vans.

It was an unusually quiet morning for Midtown. As they crossed 54th St., Hew thought he heard bells. As they walked closer to the church, he remembered that St. Thomas had a small twenty-six-bell carillon. As a chorister, he was always busy at the other end of the church and hardly ever saw the front. As they approached the front steps, he thought he recognized a Bach chorale but he couldn't place it. They entered the nar-thex and he forgot about the bells.

During the announcements following the Peace, the rector told ev-eryone that a parent had given another chorister scholarship during the awards on Saturday. It was for the full $500,000 and would be placed in the endowment. He hoped that during his incumbency, the entire choir could be completely endowed. Everyone applauded.

The rector had no idea that Hew had a cashier's check for three-million-five-hundred dollars in a plain white envelope in his pocket. He simply placed it in the alms basin during the offertory as an anonymous gift for seven chorister scholarships—a memorial known only to himself for those killed in the airport bombing. At first, he decided not to include Les, the bomber, but after thinking about it, he decided that perhaps something good could come from it.

After communion at the conclusion of the valedictory service, the eight graduates knelt at the communion rail and the head of school placed a small pectoral Celtic cross around the necks of each boy. The rector then announced that at the conclusion of the last hymn, one of the award-winning graduates, John Ramsay, would give a final recital on the gallery organ as the postlude. Hew and Alexis exchanged quizzical glances. Neither had known.

The rector invited everyone to stand. He made the sign of the cross and blessed them and the congregation with the words, *Go in peace to love and serve the Lord.* The recessional hymn was "Ora Labora"—Come Labor On. It had been written by the great English-born organist/choir-master, T. Tertius Nobel, who founded the St. Thomas Choir of men and boys. While the trebles were singing the descant on the final verse, John rushed up to the rear gallery. Hew wondered what he would play.

Almost everyone sat and stayed for the recital. John quickly removed his choir robes and, to allow himself complete freedom of movement, flung them over the top of the wood and iron railing beside the steps leading up to the console platform. *I'll have to speak to him about that,* thought Hew.

John played the first three notes on the pedals and Hew smiled. C, G, E♭. Bach's monumental *Passacaglia Fugue in C Minor.* BWV 582. Hew hardly breathed for nearly fourteen minutes as John expertly and confidently played. Afterward, during the standing ovation, he turned to Alexis and whispered, "Take everyone on to the hotel. I'll be there in a few minutes."

As Alexis led everyone toward Fifth Avenue, Hew turned and walked up into the choir. He bowed to the cross and took his old seat—front row, seat three, right side behind the pulpit. He sat down and bowed his head while he replayed John's recital in his mind.

The last time Hew had played this piece was here on the old organ. He was tricked into leaving a week later and he had not really memorized the work. Father Arturo didn't have a copy in Colombia, but he listened over and over to a recording of E. Power Biggs playing it on the Harvard Flentrop. That's what sealed the idea of owning his own copy of the great instrument.

He never got the chance to try it again, and after his leg was damaged, he believed that any attempt to hold the low C for the several measures at the conclusion of the piece would invite a disaster. He simply couldn't be sure he could hold that note.

John's pedal work, though, had been amazing. It was clear and full, but appropriately dark. The phrasing was immaculate. He could hear Ding's teaching. The finger work on the manuals was likewise amazing. Hew was sure that he detected the work John had been doing on the cello with the flowing of the notes.

Many organists have a tendency to let the louder variations overpower the reoccurring pedal theme but John had managed to provide plenty of power when necessary while letting the reoccurring pedal theme be clearly heard.

Hew looked up at the monumental reredos just as he had done for years during the tedious parts of the hundreds of services he sang in. He remembered trying to count all of the more than sixty stone figures standing in their aedicules as the ranks upon ranks of figures rose eighty feet to the peak of the stone vaulting. He had been taught that they represented the legions of saints in the Church Triumphant who joined the congregation around the table at every Eucharist, but he always wondered what they were thinking as they gazed without seeing toward the rear gallery.

It rather selfishly occurred to Hew that this monumental architectonic and structurally robust piece of musical genius moved much like his own life. From the dark pedal opening through the light and dark manual variations, the work marched on, unbroken, toward the light and joy of the ending. At once he felt a peace he hadn't known was still possible after all these years. He stood, walked into the aisle, turned, bowed to the cross, turned again, and walked out.

He arrived at the Carlisle penthouse just as everyone was finishing their first flutes of champagne. He walked over to the bar and selected two nosing glasses and poured two wee drams of The Macallan Rich Cacao single malt whisky from the harmony collection and handed one to John.

"This will be the first, and for many years the *only* time you're going to be allowed to taste this, but after todays superb performance…"

"Wait. Wait." Edward rushed to the bar and began filling more nosing glasses for everyone else. They all raised their glasses for the toast.

Hew could tell from John's pleasing expression after smelling and then tasting the liquid that he had unwittingly unleashed a Scotsman.

Sir James offered an old lowlands Scottish blessing often attributed to Robbie Burns."*Some hae meat an canna eat, And some wad eat that want it: But we hae meat, and we can eat, And sae the Lord be thankeit.*"

James had brought fresh highlands Venison from the castle herd and fresh Dover sole from England.

After eating the sautéed Sole as the fish course, Hew congratulated the chef telling him it was the best he had ever had including that from the old Four Seasons restaurant.

The chef had grilled the venison filet for the main course. Everyone was pleasantly amazed at the taste. Ding had asked the hotel's pastry chef to bake a cake for the celebration. It was a chocolate sponge covered with white fondant. He had sent over a copy of the first page of the Passacaglia and asked the chef to find a way to include it. The chef had piped the border around the top of the cake with alternating swirls in the colors of the choir insignia, and he had written the word *Congratulations* in chocolate script. For the music, he simply piped the lines of the first few measures in chocolate and filled in the notes with more chocolate.

Hew looked at it, thinking it was some inside choir joke. "What's the song?" he asked.

John smiled. "Hum it."

"Da De Da. That's the Passacaglia. You've even included fugal lines in the borders!" Hew grabbed Ding's hand and hugged him. "You're now officially a member of our little family."

"Hew, John has a rare gift. Technique can be learned but he really is musical. He connects emotionally with the instrument and lets the music talk. Not everyone can do that."

"I can't help, but I think his work on the cello helped."

"True. He has a difficult time with the quadruple stops on the strings but he'll get there. When he plays with the string quartettes, he shines with the Bach."

John looked at his watch and exclaimed. "Oh no! We've got to go. Everyone get your coats. I can't be late."

Alexis stopped him."Go where? We're not scheduled to go anywhere else today. The girls need a nap."

"No, Mom. Please. It's a surprise. You'll love it. Hurry."

Ding intervened. "John, you and Hew go ahead. I'll get everyone else there in time. I'll explain. Your mother will be there."

John gave the directions to the security driver of the van. "John isn't that the address for Riverside Church? Are you giving another organ concert on that massive instrument?"

"No. I'm giving a carillon concert and it starts at three p.m."

"When did you learn to play the carillon?"

"One afternoon, I had been turning pages for Mr. Bell in the gallery and as we were leaving, I heard little bells. The carillonneur, or carillonist, as some now call it, was playing on the practice clavier. I had never been in there so I peeked in the door. He invited me in and I started taking lessons. The batons are farther apart than most keyboards and the sharps and naturals are the same color so it took a little practice to get comfortable. There was an open day coming up and Mr. Bell let me participate. The group also played the carillon at Riverside Church. I had never heard of it and I was hooked! It's the world's largest carillon by weight with 74 cast bronze bells. The largest bell weighs 40,000 pounds and oddly is called the *bourdon* just like the organ stop. Mr. Bell told me the word is French and literally means bumblebee."

"Yes, it's a buzzing sound."

"So I was allowed to take lessons in both towers. Mr. Bell went with me and took lessons too. He also goes with me down to Trinity Church, Wall Street for change ringing bell practice and he lets me ring there for weddings and Saturday quarter peals."

"Yes, I know about that. I allowed that during your first year here, but I hadn't been told about this."

"I wanted it to be a surprise."

"Well, you have succeeded. What will you play?"

"I have three pieces. I premiered my original composition this morning before the service."

"Was it the one that sounds like a Bach chorale? I heard that, but I didn't know it was you."

"Yep."

"Well, don't tell your mother. She'll be mad that she missed it."

"No problem. She'll get to hear it on the big bells."

"So what are the other pieces?"

"They're both by Roy Hamlin Johnson. The first one is *Te Deum Laudamus for Carillon* and the second one is *Summer Fanfares*. You'll really love that one. It sounds like a sudden summer rain storm. It's wickedly difficult. Mr. Bell gave up on it saying he just didn't have the time to devote to it. It contains three note chords that must be played with open fists. My fingers are longer than his."

They rode the tower elevator to the twentieth floor and climbed the stairs to the playing cabin arriving at 2:45 for the usual 3 p.m. Sunday concert. John even had special shoes—beach shoes—just for the pedals. Unlike the organ pedals, these are short and only require toe work so the shoes don't have raised heels.

Everyone else arrived in the park adjacent to the tower just as the bourdon bell struck three. Hew was amazed at the clavier and just shook his head as John played with what he could only assume was great skill. The Te Deum had a crescendo in the middle part. Hew was astounded to watch John pound the batons and stomp on the pedals. He assumed that, like a mechanical action organ, the clappers hit the bell with more force when played that way, but John used almost all of his body weight on the pedal passage. He never knew that a musical instrument could require such brute strength but he decided that a 40,000-pound bell needed all that force to sound properly. Alexis was thrilled that she had agreed to come.

⁂

THE MONTH IN ENGLAND FLEW BY. John spent his days with Colin practicing the organ in Christ Church. Being small, the cathedral has a very short reverberation time compared to the larger cathedrals so he had to work hard on his technique.

He needed time away from the cathedral, however, to better understand the French sound and console layout. They played every organ at the university including a few historic instruments in the museum, but finally they took the channel tunnel train to France so John could play a series of real French organs. They attended a Sunday Mass at Chartres just to listen to the organ.

Alexis thought it was hilarious that Hew had taken the first name Charteris. Some of Hew's ancestors were Normans from Chartres who helped William conquer England in 1066.

Hew walked into Christ Church Oxford late one afternoon while John was playing something on the organ. It sounded vaguely familiar. He climbed onto the organ bench just as John ended the piece. "What's that you were playing?"

"It's a tune Mr. Bell told me about after he learned that you had worked on the railroad. It's called…"

"I've been working on the railroad all the live long day."

"Yep. I'm improvising."

"I think we should add a theater organ sampleset. You'll love the train whistle and the chuffing. Come to think of it, we'll go down to the Fox Theater on Peachtree Street. They still play the old organ from the silent movie days."

"Oh, come on, Dad. No one would pay to go to a silent movie."

HEW AND JOHN SPENT MANY EVENINGS ringing bells with the Oxford ringers. John conducted his first peal on ten bells at St. Thomas's Church, Oxford. Alexis spent her days working in the art restoration lab. As a surprise for all his hard work, Colin made arrangements and took John and Hew by train to Cambridge to play the newly-restored organ in King's College Chapel.

Unfortunately, the trains in England mostly run north-south so there was no direct train from Oxford to Cambridge. They had to go via London. As requested, they arrived very early at the chapel before the tourists entered. The young organ scholar led them up to the loft and stayed while all three of them put the instrument through its paces.

John had never seen a console built into the short side of an organ case. He was enthralled and bonded immediately with the organ scholar.

Hew took videos thinking John might need one in the future. They left the chapel with the organ scholar in tow, crossed King's Parade, and sat at a table by the windows at the Copper Kettle—a 1929 Mediterranean café also known as Agora (Greek marketplace) that has a spectacular view of the eastern and southern facades of the college chapel.

They all ordered the salmon and scrambled eggs from the brunch menu as suggested by the scholar. The adults drank English tea while John drank unsweetened iced tea with lemon. John and Hew were impressed to learn from the scholar that football, or soccer, was first played in England at Cambridge, and was based on an ancient Chinese game.

After visiting several more of the colleges including the Department of Architecture, which surprised Hew when John requested the visit, they caught an afternoon train back to Oxford. As they sat enjoying their gin and tonics, John casually asked, "Can we go down to Lansing College tomorrow for a visit?"

"*May* we?"

"Hew," said John. "We've had this conversation before and I'm not going to change. You're being stiffly pedantic and anachronistic. No one uses that anymore except in formal work. This is a casual request."

"In that case, the answer is emphatically a formal NO. Do not ever call either me or your mother by our first names again. It's very disrespectful."

"Okay, Dad. I'm sorry. I just want to see the school. Johann talks about it all the time. I want to enroll there."

"In England? No. Besides, it's too late for this term."

"Your dad's correct. It's too late."

"But I want to follow Johann's studies. I want to study architecture at Cambridge too. The school's just down Trumpington Road from King's College Chapel too. I might get to be an organ scholar too. I could be the first American organ scholar."

"Ah. That's why you made us walk down there. Sorry. There's already been an American organ scholar at King's."

"There's nothing for me in Atlanta anymore. Eddie and my other friends have moved on. They go to places I don't enjoy. It's like we're living in parallel universes. Besides, you and mother have another family now. I'll just be in the way. My sisters hardly remember me and I've barely met my brothers. Charlotte wants my room."

"I can't believe that you think this way. Stop feeling sorry for yourself. I know how hard it is to leave your fraternity of friends at St. Thomas. I experienced the same emotions. Of course, you're still very much a part of our family. I'm hurt that you would even think that. What have we done to make you think that?

"Charlotte's not getting your room. We're adding a new suite for your mother and me while we're in Europe this summer and we'll divide our old spaces. There will be five equal ensuite bedrooms plus our suite. It won't be a problem. We're refacing the front stone work with a honey-colored rough faced ashlar stone so the addition won't appear to be an add on. It will look less rural and more urban.

"Besides, if you really feel crowded, you can have one of the rooms downstairs. You're going back to Holy Innocents School and that's it. End of discussion. Besides, your mother and I are going to North Carolina. There's no time."

"But Johann told me that American schools of architecture have watered down the bachelor's degree to the point it's not much more than an art or music appreciation course of study. I would be bored. He says that the old five-year curriculum was intense and they have just made the new courses so the students can transfer the course credits as electives when someone drops out.

"One of the guys in Johann's office suggested that I study either at Notre Dame or the American School of the Building Arts in Charleston. He said I could get a solid foundation in classical design and then take a masters at Clemson in modern work."

"I know the old curriculum was intense. I know the students who dropped out back then had to basically start over because their architecture credits wouldn't transfer, but we've got four years before we need to make a decision."

John pouted for the remainder of the train ride.

ONCE THEY RETURNED FROM DUKE UNIVERSITY, Hew and Alexis gathered the family's luggage and took the nonstop early train from Oxford to

Paddington Station, London. It was a quick cab ride to St. Pancras Station but they needed two cabs to transport the entourage. Exhausted from hauling luggage and three small kids plus two grandparents through the early morning English commuter rush, they visited the first class lounge. It was nice, but Hew and Alexis were more than ready for cocktails and lunch aboard the Eurostar Channel Tunnel high speed train from St. Pancras station to the Gare du Nord station in Paris. He had booked Business Premier tickets which included drinks and lunch.

Alexis and her mother chose the Piper-Heidsieck Champagne. It was said to be rounded and balanced with an added depth of pinot noir. They loved it. Hew and Doug chose a Surrey Hills Silent Pool Gin martini. They agreed that it was a fine choice and had a second one to make sure. The girls got apple juice and Alexis and Anne gave the babies their formula. After a quick diaper change, the boys promptly went to sleep. The girls read quietly while waiting on lunch. John chose tomato juice. Like Hew, he hated sweet fruit juices.

For lunch, Hew, Doug, and John chose the hot option of beef tagine, couscous with courgettes, peppers, apricots, and sultanas. Hew and Doug chose the 2018 Val Dejean Malbec Comte red wine. Alexis and her mother continued with the champagne and ordered salads. John ordered more unsweet tea with ice and lemon. The girls ate peanut butter and jelly sandwiches their grandmother had made for the trip.

For dessert, they all had the dark chocolate and salted caramel delice with a small bit of honeycomb. John's taste had matured during his years in New York and Alexis was afraid he was becoming a food snob. They all slept for the remainder of the trip.

Hew drove a rental van from Paris to Chartres. They were all warmly welcomed. John's performance was an improvisation. He was given a theme to base his work on. John played very well, but didn't win a prize."I just couldn't get the organ to speak to me, Dad," he said.

"If it's any consolation, Ding says the French organists don't think the instrument is very good. They think it's difficult to get good sounds from it." Hew wasn't unhappy. He thought John was still too young for such accolades, but the experience was priceless. He had secretly recorded it on his phone video.

The train ride from Paris to Haarlem was frightful. Just after they had crossed the border from Belgium into Holland, the train made an unscheduled stop and an alarm sounded. Everyone jumped up and rushed out of the carriage. While Hew and Alexis were fumbling with the young kids, John immediately took charge of his grandparents and all the luggage. He understood the conductor. The train was on fire.

They were standing on the platform in a very small Dutch station with a name they couldn't pronounce trying to shield their ears from the European sirens while trying to understand the schedule. A lady approached Alexis and asked where they were going. When she told her, she simply said in slightly accented English, "Follow me."

Hew was kicking himself for not taking the fast SCNF train from Paris to Amsterdam. He could have rented a car and driven from there to Haarlem with less hassle, but that trip included a change in the Amsterdam airport and he didn't want to go through that. He had bad memories of that airport from his teenage trip.

Ding was waiting in the hotel. Smiling, he asked, "How was the trip? Did you win?"

"The train from Paris caught fire in the middle of nowhere, and, no, I didn't win, but we had an adventure we'll never forget. It was all great fun."

Alexis growled, "I'm glad you think so."

After checking everyone into the hotel and reviewing the arrangements for the choir, Hew, Colin, Ding, and John walked to St. Bavo to meet the organist, Karl.

"Of course I remember you, Hew. Where are your girlfriends?" Karl chuckled and John looked surprised. He had never considered that his father might have ever had girlfriends.

"And this is your son? Why am I not surprised? I still play your outstanding composition. I'm still not sure I have it right. Perhaps you will give me another lesson?"

"You're too kind. I haven't played it in years."

"Let me go get my copy. I want you to play it again. Introduce your friends to the organ until I return."

"What composition, Dad?"

"Oh, it's nothing you've ever heard. It's something I composed when I was trapped in school in Bogota."

394

They started pulling stops and listening to the sounds. The organist returned with the original autographed copy. Ding and Colin looked at it and exclaimed in unison, "You wrote this? We had no idea. It's autographed JBXII. No one knows who that is. It's been driving all our friends crazy. Play it."

"Those were my initials before my name change. John Bishop the thirteenth. JBXIII." Hew reacquainted himself with the instrument and began to play. When he finished, they all were astonished.

Colin finally spoke. "That's the way this copy is annotated, but mine's in French. These markings are in English. I've been playing it correctly all along. Well, mostly."

"I composed it on the Cavillé-Coll at my school, but this score is marked up for Karl and this instrument. I don't speak his language unfortunately."

"Is that the same organ you recently purchased? What are you going to do with it?"

"Yes. I had a call from the property manager for the Archdiocese of Atlanta last week. We have the beginnings of a plan in the works for a new church in Atlanta."

"Hew, after John's recital, I want you to play this as an encore. The audience will love the father-son connection."

"Oh, I don't know. It's been years since I've played it."

"Come on, Hew. We'll be your console registrants."

To everyone's surprise and delight, Hew's new Gulfstream G650ER had been delivered and Edward took the liberty of arranging the first nonstop transatlantic flight for the Hardys and Beverleys. Hew was happy to be able to discontinue the rental jet. The rentals were fine planes, but they just weren't his.

While Hew had still been in a coma, Alexis and Edward had ordered the new jet with the interior configuration number four. It seated 15 and slept six but with crew, could carry up to 19. Edward, Tippy, Charlie, Rosilyn, Mary, and Jeffrey were the first passengers.

All the choir boys, the rector, and the organist/choirmaster had arrived by separate flights. John had diplomatically invited the organist/ choirmaster to conduct the choir.

The concert was a success. After hearing a series of technically perfect virtuoso but sometimes bombastic performances, the audience loved John's quietly beautiful arrangement of Psalm 121. The boys sang beautifully and filled the old church with glorious sound as only pure treble voices can do. The mostly Dutch audience wasn't familiar with Anglican Chant, but they loved it. After a moment of absolute silence, the audience suddenly sprang to their feet with thunderous applause. Karl introduced Hew and told them about the encore. They were equally enthusiastic.

Karl, Colin, and Ding discussed the performances with Hew over several gin and tonics made with Dutch gin. Karl told them that John's composition delighted the Dutch audience because it was the only one on the program that reminded everyone that the organ had been built not only to outperform the instruments in other towns, but also to accompany the congregation's Psalm singing.

"Yes, I'm sure we'll be singing it during Evensong at St. Thomas for years to come."

"I'm going to add it to our Psalm cycle at the cathedral as well."

"Hew," said Karl, "your composition demonstrated sounds on the organ no one has ever heard. They loved it because you challenged the tried and true."

"Now that I have a copy with your registration in English, I'm going to re-visit this."

They all laughed. Hew had rented a ballroom in the hotel for the farewell dinner. None of them would ever forget these events. All the guests flew home on commercial flights in first class, thanks to Hew. John went to the Haarlem Academy for two weeks of intense study and Hew and the rest of the family flew in their new jet to Glasgow.

After Alexis finished getting the kids to sleep, she joined Hew and James in James's library in the old Cochrane mansion, where they were sipping a wee dram of 25-year-old Macallan. The men rose when she entered the room and James poured some in a nosing glass for her. "Sláinte Mhath, Alexis."

"Do dheagh shláinte, James."

"Very good, Alexis. We'll make a proper Scot of you both before long."

"James," said Hew, "we've devised a scheme for the old castle. We need your input. The hotel idea is dead but what about a college? I want to meet with the folks at Edinburgh University about building a college for the study of archaeology within the ruins. Johann had a scheme that will put the living quarters and classrooms underground by digging out the old quarry waste areas. Since the windows were a main problem with the preservationists—"

"Not to mention the tourists."

"Yes, not to ever mention them again, this scheme utilizes a sunken courtyard so nothing is visible from the surrounding area. It won't be a huge college although I have since decided to ask Clemson University in South Carolina to consider adding programs in sustainable architecture and historic architectural design. Clemson has a thriving concept called the "fluid campus." The architectural school has campuses in Italy, Spain, and Charleston. It's well established. I didn't intend to use the old castle for anything but as we worked through it, I thought the old hall/chapel would make a great auditorium/lecture hall, and the dungeon would make a great little pub."

Alexis laughed. "And, of course, he wants to put an organ in the musicians' gallery."

"We'll use a Scottish organ builder, of course."

"Of course. I know just the firm,"said James. "They're based in Glasgow and I suggest you let them relocate a redundant Scottish historical organ instead of building a new one, but you're getting ahead of yourself. I agree it a fine idea. We'll set up an appointment at the university. The vice chancellor is an old friend. He'll be most happy to listen to your scheme."

"Shouldn't we go straight to the chancellor?"

"Oh, no. The chancellor is none other than Her Royal Highness, The Princess Royal. You probably won't see her until the dedication." James paused. "I've something to show you. It's the old family Book of Hours."

"What's a Book of Hours?"

"It's a medieval devotional book of canonical prayers."

"How old is it?"

"We didn't find a date but it's sure to have come from the castle. It's covered with a sheep skin leather false wrap and lettered to read *Canterbury Tales* so it was hidden from prying eyes." He carefully laid it in Hew's hands. "Take the wrap off. Those old Catholic priests could have been killed for just having it."

"My God! This is a beautiful perfectly preserved illuminated leather cover! The pages have worn gilt edges from use, but the illuminations are incredible and the lettering is in Latin. Have you had experts study it?"

"The pages are vellum. No, we didn't want the attention."

"I agree. It's surely from the castle. What a treasure!"

THE VICE CHANCELLOR GREETED THEM ALL. "Thank you for coming Sir James, Mr. And Mrs. Ramsay. I'm stunned at your gracious proposal. Our College of Arts, Humanities & Social Sciences is very similar to the Clemson program. Our archaeology and sustainable design studies will work nicely with theirs.

"I suggest master's and PhD students for your site. That area has a wealth of pristine Pictish, Viking, and highland artifacts just waiting to be discovered. Leave this information with me. I'll need to first meet with the various historical groups and get them on board. If that works, I'll take it to our board and then to the department chairs. Finally, I'll contact Clemson. I must say, though, I think we'll be able to navigate through the minefield very quickly."

Alexis spoke up. "Thank you. I might add that we will give travel scholarships to all the students. There may be opportunities for your students to study at Clemson as well."

"That will certainly be very welcome. I'll be in touch."

When they were safely back on the road, James told them that the Princess Royal would be briefed immediately. "With this much money in play, it will not take long to get approvals, but if I know anything about how this system works, she'll approve and everything will fall quickly into place."

Alexis turned to Hew. "Well, that's two out of three. What about Father A's old French organ?"

"I had an email from the director of facilities for the Archdiocese of Atlanta last night. They've approved Johann's design for the new church. It will be more traditional than he usually likes but he understands. All my plans are underway."

⚜

During the flight from Scotland back to Haarlem the cabin phone rang. "Where are you, Hew. We need to talk as soon as possible."

"We're flying over the English Channel. What's up?"

"I've just signed a new contract with the feds. You're back in the railroad business as soon as you sign your contract."

"That sounds great. Send it to Edward. I'll be back on Monday and if he's approved it, I'll swing by your office and sign it. Where are we going to build next?"

"It's so big it'll be phased. First, we'll build from New Orleans to Chicago via St. Louis and Louisville. We'll build an interchange where I-55 crosses under our line. Next we'll build from New Orleans to Seattle via Houston, San Diego, LA, and San Francisco. Maybe we'll go on into Canada. From Seattle, we could run up to Vancouver and across to Toronto using their existing trans-Canada route. Hell, if we run up to Maine from New Jersey and run from Toronto to Newfoundland, we could jump across underwater to Greenland and then to Ireland and—"

"Stop, Sam. I need to schedule a meeting with Eberhart International in Cologne for this. How quickly can you get here?"

"Well, probably in two weeks. The president wants a feasibility study done from Seattle to Vancouver as soon as possible. He's already talking with Canada, Greenland, and Scotland. He wants tunnels from Newfoundland to Greenland and ultimately to Europe. We'll be very busy." Hew could see his net worth skyrocketing.

45
LE RHÔNE

Hew's mind was spinning. The idea of adding that much railroad construction work to their lives worried him. He also had to oversee the Scottish project but the real love of his projects was the old French organ that needed a complete restoration.

He really did need a vacation so he welcomed the opportunity to leave the railroad planning alone for two weeks to concentrate on Alexis and just enjoy the company of good friends away from all their distractions. Edward and Tippy drove to Atlanta from Highlands and joined Hew, Alexis, Charlie, and Rosilyn for a quick flight up to Swan Bay, where they stopped long enough to pick up Mary and Jeffrey.

Tippy had insisted on going two days early in case there were delays. DeVeaux and Missy couldn't leave that early so they flew commercial. Hew's party flew into Avignon's small executive airport and took a cab to the hotel. They would board the boat the following day.

DeVeaux and Missy weren't as lucky. When they arrived at the airport in Charleston, the Delta gate agent told them that there was an air traffic controllers' strike in Paris. Their flight from Paris to Marseilles had been cancelled, which meant, in turn, that their flight from JFK to Paris had also been cancelled. After an hour and a half on the phone with Viking emergency travel services and the Delta gate agent, they were re-booked on a KLM flight from Atlanta to Amsterdam for the following day. They went home to wait.

Hew's party slept in and spent the day wandering around Avignon. They visited the massive medieval pope's palace. Alexis was amused when their tour guide called the large fireplace in the banquet hall a medieval "microwave." As they left the palace, the guide pointed out three average-looking teen girls and told them the girls were known as local pickpockets. That evening, they walked to the famous ruined bridge and Alexis serenaded them with the old French song, *Sur le Pont d'Avignon*.

Meanwhile, DeVeaux and Missy's problems continued. The KLM flight was an hour late leaving Atlanta which meant that instead of two hours in Amsterdam they had only an hour.

Dinner aboard the flight, though, was delicious. After both of them enjoyed two signature KLM Very High Fashioned cocktails made with Dutch Genever Barrel aged Bols Curacao Dry Orange and Angostura bitters, their nerves began to settle and they dined on an appetizer of poached lobster in tomato vierge sauce with cauliflower purée and shaved fennel salad followed by a main course of ravioli served with Alfredo sauce, pumpkin, and wild mushrooms. Dessert was a simple dish of fresh strawberries dipped in chocolate.

Even though his seat reclined into a completely flat bed, Deveaux couldn't sleep at all. He worried about the connection in Amsterdam. Edward, Hew, Tippy and Charlie had warned them about Amsterdam's Schiphol airport—due to problems on previous flights. The line to clear customs was long and slow and Edward had had his credit card numbers stolen there.

Instead of calling it skee-pol, he called it "shithole" airport. There was no line for first class passengers and they didn't recognize Global Travelers either. The lines were already impossibly long when they arrived with only forty minutes and another long walk before their flight was scheduled to leave. Fortunately, a quick line had just opened for people with short connection times.

The first official looked at Deveaux's boarding pass and said no. Missy tried a more kind-looking young lady who said yes. They made it with minutes to spare, but their luggage didn't. Their flight took them to Marseilles and then they had to find the train station to get to Avignon.

The signs were mostly in French and poorly marked. Missy had taken three years of French in high school but that had been years before. A bus that took them to the train station but all the ticketing information was in French and the station agent had left for the day. Finally, they found a young French girl who took pity on them and bought their tickets for them at an automated machine, paying for the tickets with her rail pass card. They thankfully gave her fifty euros for their forty-euro tickets.

After another two hours on a slow train, the exhausted couple met their friends at the delightful Hotel L'Horlodge in the center of Avignon and walked to dinner. Their luggage arrived at the hotel the next morning and they all took taxies to the quay and boarded the boat to Arles.

Once settled in, they all met in Hew's large suite for champagne. They then had their first group dinner. The food was as fine as Hew had remembered it.

In Arles, the morning tour involved walking through the old city to the Roman coliseum. The outer ring of arches around the structure opened to a covered walk that circled the arena. Hew had never seen so many classical details in one building, many of them still in great shape after two thousand years of constant use. Missy was amazed that the plant everyone in Charleston called Confederate jasmine was in bloom there and the scent was heavenly.

Outside the church in the main square, the frieze over the main portico had carved stone figures of people walking to either Heaven or Hell. Those on the left included happy pregnant women while those on the right of the main door included people in torment. Vestiges of red paint were still visible at their feet.

Van Gogh had once lived in the town and was there when he cut off his ear. They visited several sites including the hospital where he recovered. Their delightful tour guide told them that the Dutch pronounced his name as van *Houck,* as if they were clearing their throats.

Most of the group took the tours to the local wineries but Hew wasn't interested in looking at old barrels of wine. Instead, he and Charlie took the tour to the Roman aqueduct. The stones were stacked without mortar. While the two-thousand-year-old structure was magnificent, they really enjoyed the museum. The Roman water systems were impressive.

After listening to the explanation of the lead pipes and the deaths from lead poisoning—the latin word for lead is plumb, as in plumbing—

Hew decided to pack up all their lead crystal stemware and pewter cups when they returned home.

There was a replica of a hot bath and one of a public toilet. The marble toilet seat was continuous with no partitions. Hew was reminded of his hellhole boarding school in Colombia, South America. What surprised him, though, was an explanation that Romans wiped themselves with a sponge fixed to a short stick—a sponge dipped in water that ran below their feet and was reused by other people. He suddenly understood the significance of the Bible passage of the crucifixion in which the Roman soldiers used a long pole with a sponge dipped in vinegar when Jesus cried, "I thirst."

Life aboard the boat sailing up the river with old friends was delightful. They all drank too much wine, which was always included with the meals, and they had too many cocktails in the beautiful lounge, but they also enjoyed sitting on the top deck watching the boat go under low bridges and through very high locks. They drank beautiful Kir Royales and met new friends. The Rhône water level was high and even though the wheelhouse can retract into the boat, they still only had six inches to spare under several of the bridges.

Every day included a new town with many fascinating sites. They lit candles and said a prayer in the churches along the way for a dear friend who was in the hospital. At Saint-Jean-de-Muzols, they all boarded a beautifully-restored 0-6-6-0 steam train for a morning ride into the wilds of France along the cliffs of a wild and scenic raging river. The old wooden coaches were quite a contrast to the leather seats on the new jet.

At Colombier-le-Vieux-St-Barthelemy-le-plain, the old engine was turned by young engineers pushing on a restored turntable by hand. In Vienne, they marveled at a Roman temple with most of its detail intact. Even the much of the fluting on the Corinthian columns was still sharp.

The last stop on the river was at Lyon. While everyone else went on the afternoon tour to another winery, Hew and Charlie set off walking to find the church, Eglise St. François de Sales. They could see the top of the dome from the boat.

They walked a few blocks and crossed the river. They walked a few more blocks to 11 Rue Auguste Comte, the church. Hew wanted to visit because he'd heard it housed a perfectly intact Caville-Coll organ and he hoped to hear it, as the old organ he had purchased from his old boarding school was very similar. He was not disappointed. Someone was practicing. Suddenly, the organist began the famous Widor *Toccata*. Widor's father had been organist there and had taught his son to play.

Hew remembered Father Arturo, himself a French classically trained organist, telling him about the structure of the toccata. Even though the *Toccata* was composed years later in Paris, the story was that the city of Lyon had a funicular that traveled from the river up to the Basilica at the top of the hill. Like most young boys, Widor was fascinated by large machines.

"The word toccata is an Italian word that means to touch. Look at the first line. What do you see?"

"Repetition."

"Good. Play the notes like well oiled gears of the funicular going round and round without a break. Watch me and listen. Now look at this section marked 'pp.' That's quieter because the funicular goes into a tunnel, but don't stop playing. Now look at the pedal line. It sounds like thump thump, thump thump. That's the sound of the brakes of the funicular being applied from time to time as it is coming back down the hill. Then go for full organ on the finish."

The organist finished beautifully. Hew decided then that he needed to hire a French organ builder to restore his instrument. Now all they needed to do was find the funicular and take a ride to the top, which they did.

The next day, they all flew home. Hew was satisfied and well-rested, and Alexis had had a wonderful time.

46
CONVIVIUM

Hew walked into the butler's pantry from the garage. He'd returned from Swan Bay after putting the final touches on the castle scheme, the contracts, and discussing the Canada and transatlantic tunnel idea.

He dropped off a large cooler filled with fresh Scottish Salmon, fresh venison, a bowl of fresh Swan Bay cherries hand-pitted by Ms. Mamie using her favorite little antique cherry pitter, and a case of a white Burgundy Coté de Rhône dessert wine.

As James had predicted, everyone, including Clemson, had quickly approved the castle scheme. The locals weren't entirely happy at the thought of having drunken students in the area, but the universities assured them that they would keep the students in line. Besides, they'd said, graduate students and doctoral candidates tend to be a bit more settled than undergraduates.

Hew walked into the kitchen where Maybell, their new chef Richard, Ewan—the new English house manager/butler, and Alexis were finalizing the plans for the evening's dinner party.

"Who's that playing the violin with John?" asked Hew.

"Hello to you, too, darling."

He laughed. "Sorry," he said, grabbing her and pulling her into a long and passionate kiss.

Finally, she pulled away. "That's Ama. She's a fourteen-year-old prodigy like John."

"Her technique is lovely. She's playing the piano just like my mother did. I'm amazed."

"Yes, and she's a beautiful girl. She's loaned John her copy of Leopold Mozart's book on violin studies."

"*Gründliche Violinschule?*"

"I don't know the name, but it's an English translation of the book he wrote for his son, Wolfgang. Ding told him that by studying stringed instrument bowing techniques, he would become even better at playing Bach on the organ."

"I detected that during his concert at Saint T's. That's fantastic, but I'm giving you fair warning. I will not buy him a Stradivarius."

Alexis laughed. "Says the man who owns three pipe organs and two Hauptwerk organs with God knows how many different samplesets, but I doubt he'll go that far. Anyway, I've met her parents and they're lovely people. He's an architect and she's an attorney. Ama's older sister is a freshman at Clemson. You'll love getting to know them. He's very environmentally aware and he loves single malt scotch. Ding made John study the piano and cello while he was on suspension from the organ. She's brought out his hidden talent. He's going to start his cello studies again so they can go to strings camps next summer."

"So I'll take that as a conformation that going to England to school is no longer being discussed. Great. What else is happening?"

"John announced that he's changing his name to John Bishop XIV. He's decided that he doesn't want the family name to disappear and if we don't approve now, he'll do it when he turns eighteen. I've already got Edward working on the documents."

"Well, that's settled. What about the other kids?"

"Elizabeth spends her spare time painting. She's taken over half of my studio. Ama is teaching Charlotte to play the violin. Robbie spends every waking moment reading the classics in the library. John pushes him out of the library when he wants to practice. He's had me move the Saarinen womb chair and ottoman into his room. He's happy to be away from all the music."

"He's two years old. Is he reading Homer in the original Greek?"

She playfully punched him. "Of course. He's *my* child too. I have found a series of classics written for preschool kids. The story line is basic and the pages are filled with colorful illustrations by a very fine artist. Mother recommended the books. The boys climb in my lap while I read. Dougie jumps down as soon as the book's finished. Robbie stays and asks questions. After I leave, he sits there looking at the pages. I've heard him making up his own stories to fit the pictures."

"John is teaching Dougie to play soccer. Charlie has already taken him under his wing and, oh, get this—John is teaching Dougie to play the organ. He's discovered a curriculum from the Brigham Young University School of Music called *Organ First!* It teaches kids to play the organ as their first instrument. You need to add a second headphone jack to one of the virtual consoles before I go crazy. He can already play the C major scale—over and over and over."

"I assume everyone is coming tonight?"

"Yes, we'll be twenty four for dinner. John has announced that he, Eddie, Ama, and Eddie's friend Melissa want to be footmen."

"Where did *that* idea come from?"

She laughed. "They've all been binge watching *Downton Abbey.* Apparently it's a thing now at Holy Innocent's School."

"That should be a hoot."

"True, but they've been practicing. It was comical at first, but Ewan has whipped them into shape."

"If I may say so, sir, they're quite good," said Ewan.

"I drew the line at uniforms, though," said Alexis. "I'm not paying for that. No one is dressing formally tonight anyway. I think that shocked Ewan."

"It's your house, Madam. I shall learn to adjust."

"John and Ama selected the contemporary Tuxedo dinner ware by Charles Gwathmey and Robert Siegel. I agreed, but I drew the line at the Arne Jacobsen contemporary stainless steel flatware. We don't have twenty-four place settings. We're using several mixed patterns of sterling just to make things a little less formal. Why don't you go shower and have a nap? We're almost ready here."

"I love those white dishes with the little black squares. I'll shower, but I want to practice. I've got a composition running through my brain based on Clemson's fight song. I want to try it on that theater organ sample set that John installed."

Alexis turned up her nose.

❧

THE GUESTS BEGAN ARRIVING AT SIX. Alexis had planned on serving cocktails on the terrace but the threat of rain changed her mind. Recent torrential downpours had produced a bumper crop of mosquitos. Instead, they gathered in the great room. John had offered to play cocktail music on the piano, but Hew said no—he hated hearing highly-trained musicians reduced to playing cocktail music when no one was listening, or worse yet, talking louder to be heard over the music.

He felt the same way about preludes and postludes in church. He flatly refused to play them except in the Catholic cathedral across from St. Philip's. Catholics always entered to pray, unlike the Episcopalians who turned everything into a cocktail party.

He agreed to let John and Ama provide a small concert after dessert. Alexis introduced Hew to Ben and Ginny Darlington, Ama's parents. Hew introduced them to his Swan Bay mint juleps. Being a single malt scotch drinker, Ben loved it. Ginny sipped hers.

"Amelia just texted," said Alexis. "The bishop has been involved with something unexpected. They're on their way, but they'll be a few minutes late. She said to proceed without them."

"Absolutely not. We'll all just have another drink. Etiquette demands that he sit at the head of the table so we can't start without them."

"That's fine. Chef won't put the salmon on the grill until the cucumber soup course has started anyway."

At 8:10 p.m., Ewan announced that dinner was served. After everyone was seated by the footmen, John stepped forward and announced, *"The Lord be with you."*

Alexis was startled. Hew couldn't wait to hear what would come next. He remembered being surprised when he was asked to bless the food for the first time. He had simply played the piano and sung.

Everyone at the table except Bitsy Hollingsworth and her husband, Timmons responded, *"And also with you."* The Hollingsworths response was *"and with thy spirit."*

"Let us pray. May he who blessed five loaves and two fishes to feed five thousand, now bless us that we may be a blessing to five thousand more. Amen."

Hew almost laughed out loud. He knew that prayer—Father Andrew had taught that blessing to the boys in the choir at St. Thomas in case they ever got caught short when asked to bless the food.

"I see that St. Thomas teaches more than just music," said the bishop. "Bitsy, still using the old language at St. Helen's?"

"Absolutely. You know we'll never change. I use it at St. Luke's too. I'm not changing my pronouns in the doxology either. He is he. Besides, why change the word *he* for the word *God* and then sing the word *Father*. It's pointless, in my opinion, and it reminds me of the fourth-century Arian controversy about the trinitarian concept. Tom Roberts always shot me the evil eye from the console, but it's one of my personal acts of devotion. I don't cross myself or genuflect or any of that other high church stuff so this is it."

The dean nodded to John. "Thank you for that blessing. Usually people ask the clergy, but we're in sales, not service. You'll be a fine priest in your own home one day I'm sure." Then he segued to "We all thank God that Hew, Jeffrey, and Alexis have survived their *late unpleasantness*."

Edward rose to offer a toast. "Please raise your champagne glasses and join me in congratulating John on his graduation and his successful summer in Europe."

John took an exaggerated bow. Hew chuckled.

A cold cucumber soup made with fresh cucumbers from Maybell's high brickwalled *potager*—the French word literally means for the soup pot—was served with a Napa Valley Howell Mountain white wine from Hew's grandfather's cellar.

Hew picked up the old wooden box beside his chair and opened it. He carefully pulled out the castle communion ware and passed it around the table while he explained. Everyone gasped. He opened an envelope with high resolution photographs of the linen chalice and paten vestment and explained that it was too fragile to carry but it was now at the British Museum for conservation. He also had photographs of the old *Book of Hours*. There were gasps all around.

"What will you do with this? It would work quite well in the chapel at Saint Philips."

"Nice try, Thad, but as a concession for my new college, I had to agree to place all of the communion ware on permanent loan to the museum in Aberdeen. They drove a hard bargain. Fortunately, they don't know about the medieval *Book of Hours* James has in his library in Glasgow."

Everyone loved the fish course of fresh wild salmon poached in the French white wine. "I can only assume these fish were recently swimming in your river."

"The River Spey isn't my river, but, yes, several of my tenants caught them early yesterday morning. They can't get any fresher here in Atlanta."

"Let me tell you all why we were late," said the bishop's wife.

"Now, Amelia, don't start that at the table."

"Why not? It's hilarious. Everyone will love this. Cuthbert, our Cavalier King Charles Spaniel, suddenly started barking at the floor. I couldn't get him to stop. He was having a fit, but something was bumping up against the underside of the wood floor. I made Mark go look. He came back in all wide eyed and said there was a large snake in the crawl space."

"She's not exaggerating. That thing was eight feet long and it looked at me!"

Bitsy shuttered and exclaimed, "I hate snakes. What did you do?"

"I called the city and they told me to call a critter exterminator. The guys came and for an outrageous fee of almost four-hundred dollars, they set a steel cage trap with a whole, still-warm roasted chicken they picked up at the local supermarket. The snake went right to it. The whole thing took an hour but it's gone. It was a python!"

"They're not native around here."

"The guys think someone's pet got too big. Imagine having so little concern for your neighbors."

"I'll have nightmares now. The serpent really—"

"Bitsy, don't even think about finishing that statement. I'll excommunicate you."

"Hell, we all know what she was going to say about Adam and Eve, and you couldn't do that no matter what she said."

"Bishop, some of us have been wondering about something. When you celebrate communion at the cathedral, you make the big wafer snap. It echoes across the entire cathedral and certainly gets everyone's attention. We absolutely know the body has been broken. How do you get it to do that? Everybody else just seems to tear it."

"It's a little secret they teach us at bishop's school. I can't reveal it."

"Oh, hell, Mark. I'll tell them. There's no such thing as a bishop's school. He puts the wafer in the toaster oven at home to dry it out so that it snaps cleanly. Sometimes, he forgets it. The fire trucks have been to our house on several Sunday mornings when we can't get the smoke alarms to shut off. It's a joke in the neighborhood now."

"St. Helen's folks call it cracking the cookie," said Bitsy.

"Now, Bitsy, *that* blasphemous comment *will* get you excommunicated!"

Everyone hooted.

Laughing, the bishop continued. "Tell me about the construction progress. I've been meaning to get up there to check it out."

Johann jumped in. "Your Grace, call me at your convenience and I'll give you a detailed tour. Everything is going very well."

"Johann, please call me either Bishop or Mark. I prefer Mark—especially in social settings such as this. We don't really use the honorarium in America."

Hew sighed. "Unfortunately, Mark, we weren't able to save the tower. It was in worse condition than the engineers thought. We were able to deconstruct the wooden spire timbers and reuse them."

Not to be outdone, Bitsy added, "Yes, Mark, but they were able to increase the tower height by forty feet and we added a twelve-bell peal for English change ringing. Hew kindly sponsored a retired ringer to come over from England to teach our band. That also allowed us to increase the height of the nave. We now have a proper triforium that contains the spotlights, and the return air-conditioning duct work. The re-dedication is set for next August on St. Helen's Day. Everyone is very happy. The rector is writing new lyrics for the hymn tune *St. Helen's*. We're on schedule and on budget—well, except for the little change order Johann dreamed up."

"Oh," the bishop exclaimed. "You mean for the new vestiarium? I wholeheartedly approved that change."

"What's a vest...something?" asked Missy. "We don't have those in Charleston."

Johann explained. "It's Latin for clothing or closet. They're the spaces where the priests and others put on their vestments. The choir will still use their existing vesting and rehearsal rooms. There'll be a new handsome space for the clergy so they can have a few moments to, as the rector says, 'get their heads in the game in silence.' The walls are paneled with straight grained oak faced doors for the vestment closets. There are full length mirrors on the insides of the closet doors. A Catholic priest friend saw a picture of this room and said it could only be an Episcopal sacristy because of all the mirrors."

Everyone laughed. "There's a very large semicircular chest for the copes and there's a kneeler for private prayer set in a small niche, and there's a small desk with a chair for making last minute notes and filling in the attendance register. There are other spaces for the lay folks and the acolytes to vest. The old vestry was built in the nineteenth century for a single priest. It's too crowded now."

"Timmons is giving a new set of vestments in memory of my grandparents," said Bitsy. "He's such a dear. The fabric is called Comper strawberry gold. It was designed by Sir Ninan Comper. We've ordered four copes in various sizes with different hoods. There will be chasubles, dalmatics, tunicles, stoles, and other matching pieces. One of the chasubles will be fitted with small hidden hooks so it can be either lengthened or shortened to fit the priest. There will be a gorgeous full Jacobean covering for the altar. Johann also designed a large new octagonal sacristy with a very high medieval type wood roof, and a separate space for the flower guild with large coolers and a very deep custom stainless steel sink. For the first time we'll have a proper piscina in the new sacristy too."

Amelia had seen this fabric in London and mentally calculated that these vestments would easily cost more than a hundred-thousand dollars.

"Grace has a piscina in their new sacristy," said Missy. "At our old church we just poured the leftover wine into the graveyard."

"That's perfectly permissible," said the bishop. After the Eucharist, any remaining consecrated wine not needed for emergencies must be buried. It must never be poured into a sink connected to a sewer. That old sacristy was also built for an age when there was only an occasional Eucharist. I can't wait to use it."

Johann smiled. "I always say that a sacristy is to an altar as a kitchen is to a dining room table."

Wanting desperately to change the subject away from religion, Alexis said, "Josilyn, tell everyone about your commercial."

She smiled. "Well, some of you may have heard this, but last year, I was shopping at Phipps Plaza. I was feeling great that day. I was wearing my green Diane von Furstenberg dress with the little parrots on it. I was wearing my bright green Ferragamo heels with my new Gucci green leather purse when I spied a woman with a clipboard making a beeline toward me.

"For some reason, I decided to talk with her. She asked if I would answer a few questions and I said yes. She asked if I ever fried chicken and I said yes, occasionally, because Charlie loves my fried chicken. She asked about the oil I used and I said Crisco. She asked why and I said because my mother and grandmother always used it.

"To make a long story short, she came to the house, met Charlie, and asked us to make a commercial for Crisco. We agreed and her production team decided to shoot it on our back terrace. We were seated on a little Charleston wrought iron and wooden slatted bench between the little Japanese maples. They were in full glorious fall color too. Our place was overrun with trucks and production people. They paid a location fee and even paid us to wear our own clothes. They cooked the chicken in my kitchen but we quickly learned that it was cooked for the camera and wasn't fit to eat. I gave my lines and Charlie had to take a bite and say, 'Our chicken never tastes greasy.'"

"Try to say that with a mouthful of greasy undercooked chicken," said Charlie, grinning. "It took me forty-five minutes to get it right."

"To make matters worse," said Josilyn, our dog Toby kept running up to Charlie's spit bucket trying to steal the chicken."

"Oh, no!" cried Amelia. "You never want to give chicken bones to a dog."

"I know," said Josilyn. "Charlie finally had to lock him in the pool house but he whined so loudly that the chef picked the chicken off the bones and gave him a bowl full. To make things more complicated, Charlie was wearing a powder blue Oxford cloth button-down shirt and the grease was dripping down his shirt. They had to cover it with a white napkin to obscure the spots. He went through at least two dozen napkins."

"I quickly learned that the operative word was *tastes*," said Charlie. "It never *tastes* greasy."

Everyone erupted in a fit of laughter. The cocktails and wines were loosening up the crowd.

"So when will we see it?"

"Actually, never. We got several royalty checks but last week we got a letter saying they had decided not to air it."

"Did they say why?"

She laughed. "They decided we didn't sound Southern enough."

Bitsy chortled. "Well, bless their little Yankee hearts."

The conversation quickly went down hill.

Chef prepared the Venison Wellington from a recipe in The Ritz London cookbook written by John Williams, MBE. It was prepared using 4½ ounces of goose liver from Swan Bay's recently restocked geese, 11¼ pounds of fresh Scottish venison fillet, puff pastry, duxelles, chicken mousse, and a wine sauce made with a red Cote de Rhône and a dash of port. It was sliced at the table to reveal the filet—cooked rare. Served with Yorkshire pudding and steamed fresh broccoli, it was a hit with everyone.

During the salad course of Maybell's fresh tangled greens with a champagne dressing made by the chef, Amelia asked, "Has anyone heard about that guy that calls himself an Anglican archbishop?"

"If I may suggest, dear, don't go there. We never make fun of other people's religion and we never discuss politics or religion in polite society."

"This isn't making fun. These are facts. They'll love it."

Alexis added, "Mark, we are just an extended family here. We haven't thought of ourselves as polite society—especially around this table—in years."

Everyone agreed.

"Is that the guy who started that mega church down I-20?" asked Tippy.

"Yes," said Thad. "He came to the cathedral for a while but he didn't tell me he had been in Holy Orders. He convinced five hundred of our parishioners to join him in leaving the church."

"You said *had been*. How does that work?"

The bishop touched Thad's arm. "Better let me take this one. He graduated from a seminary in England and worked for several years in the mission field in several African countries. I was informed that one of the bishops there consecrated him as an archbishop and sent him to the USA mission field."

"Mission field? Bishop, we're not a mission field."

"Of course we are. The entire world is a mission field, but according to the ultra conservatives we are not orthodox."

Hew grunted. "Hogwash. I've never considered myself or the Episcopal Church to be orthodox. The Archbishop of Canterbury does not recognize him so he is not in communion with the Anglican Church, but I doubt his followers actually know that. He has about five-thousand members now and they have built that large cathedral-like building. They bought an abandoned big screen theater and the adjacent office building and moved in. Then they built the big church."

Tippy nodded. "We saw that on the drive back from Charleston. They've also got a huge neon billboard on the side of the interstate. They call it the First Anglican Cathedral of the Americas."

"Yeah, but that's not the good part."

"Now Amelia..." said Mark.

She ignored the admonition. "One of the wardens came home early one day a few months ago and walked into the bathroom just as his wife was backing out of the shower. Her butt was covered with red welts."

Hew squirmed uncomfortably as he remembered being beaten by the priest in Colombia.

"She confessed that when she went to the archbishop for advice, he turned her over his knees and spanked her." All the women at the table gasped. "Her husband did some research and discovered several others had been whipped. The archbishop was fired immediately."

"Are they members of one of those breakaway groups?"

"Oh, no. They're breakaways all right, but they aren't affiliated with the others. He says they're too liberal for him."

Hew joined the discussion. "I suppose I can tell the rest. They're twenty million in debt and people are leaving in droves. They filed for bankruptcy and the Roman Archdiocese has assumed the debt and taken over the property. Johann did a building analysis and we'll be stripping the building back to the steel frame. That imitation stucco was delaminating from the substrate and the water intrusion is massive. Johann had designed a new traditional Romanesque style church for a different site but now we'll reconfigure their interior to a traditional plan and I will donate my old Cavaillé-Coll organ. It will go into the proper gallery but the clergy want a smaller instrument in the choir for the daily services. I've introduced him to Schoenstein. They've built several beautiful small French-style organs of ten stops or less that will work perfectly. I saw a similar one at the church in Vienne, France on our trip."

As they were finishing the salad course, Rob, the cathedral's canon for music asked, "Alexis, I want to conduct Buxtehude's *Membra Jesu Nostri* next year on Good Friday and I want you to sing second soprano. And Bitsy, I'd like for you to sing alto. Would you both consider it, please?"

"Rob, next year at Easter, I want to be as far away from Atlanta as I can be."

"Oh, I'm so sorry, Alexis. I didn't think about that. It's just that I want to use the new little continuo organ Hew gave the cathedral. It would be perfect in this work. Buxtehude wrote the work for two sopranos, an alto, a tenor and a bass. The instruments are two violins and a basso continuo consort."

Hilde spoke up. "That's a wonderful composition. We heard it in Sion two years ago in the Protestant Lutheran church on Good Friday. It's very moving."

Sam grunted. "Yeah, I remember that. It was an hour long. I nearly froze in that drafty church. Your father called it the body parts concert as I remember."

Bitsy was shocked. "Body parts concert?"

Rob tried to repair the image in her mind. "It was written for Good Friday and it contains Biblical passages that relate to the crucified body. It translates as the most holy limbs of our suffering Jesus. It was based on the *Salve Mundi Salutare* and is considered to be the first Protestant oratorio. There are seven cantatas and each is about a part of Jesus's body. Specifically, his feet, knees, hands, side, breast, and heart, and face."

The bishop interjected, "Rob, as wonderful as that sounds, and here I bow to your excellent command of repertory, may I just suggest that you consider something more focused on the *good* in Good Friday rather than the suffering? Perhaps you and Thad could write a new piece. I'd be happy to preach the three-hour service and the choir could sing your composition between each part."

"Certainly, bishop. I'm sure we can. Hew can help."

"Oh, no. I'll be on the other side of the world with Alexis. I don't want to be here then, either."

"Pardon me," said Heidi, "but as you know, I was a Swiss Mennonite before I met Johann. My ancestors fled to Switzerland before World War Two. Why do you call the day of the crucifixion good?"

"Better let me answer this one," said Amelia. "Mark and Thad will talk too long. It's called *good* because on that day, by His death, Christ took away all our sins. It's the day all believers were born again and we call *that* good. I suppose we could have called it grateful." Everyone murmured their agreement.

The footmen began expertly clearing the plates as Ewan, Richard, and Maybell moved in procession from the kitchen toward the antique Chippendale sideboard with the dessert course. Ewan carried the large sterling silver butler's tray with the Burgundy wine in the sterling silver wine coolers and Richard proudly brought in the fresh Black Forest cake he had just finished.

The cake was a round mass of fresh whipped cream covering the sides and top of six thin layers of fluffy chocolate cake with layers of a cherry reduction sauce heavily laced with Kirsch between each layer. The top was garnished with curls of dark chocolate and Ms. Mamie's carefully selected unstemmed red cherries that had been dipped in a clear corn syrup to enhance their color.

Maybell carried a stack of antique dessert plates in contrast to the contemporary tableware. Just as they were passing the kitchen and just before they turned into the dining room, Amelia asked, "Has anyone heard from Sandra? I haven't seen her in weeks. Is she still dating that Italian count?"

Bitsy shook her head. "Oh, no. She's in England with Lord somebody. She dumped the count. He's handsome, rich, and has impeccable Italian manners but she said he couldn't f—" She saw Eddie start to giggle and quickly faked a cough. "Um, *find* his way around town worth a damn."

Eddie completely lost it. He had heard the gossip on the tennis court from the women he was teaching at the club. Charlie and Rosilyn glowered at him and he had to leave the room. But Charlie couldn't help himself and started to laugh. He'd heard the gossip in the men's locker room.

The entire table broke out in riotous laughter. Because almost all of them knew Sandra, everyone else except the other three footmen read the f-word between the lines. Those who didn't know her understood perfectly. Charlie reached for his silver water goblet and knocked his Lalique Angel wine glass over, spilling wine on the placemat and onto the table.

The $150-each glasses had the body of an angel in the stem that was faithfully copied from the Smiling Angel statue on the west façade of Reims Cathedral and the wings were etched up the sides of the bowl. The contemporary placemats were cotton, that had been commissioned from a weaver in Seneca, South Carolina. They were shades of green with a cobalt, ultramarine blue, and white line meandering down the center along the length of the mat—inspired by the view from the terrace.

When the laughter began, Ewan had quickly turned the dessert procession around to wait until decorum could be restored. Maybell was giggling. She had heard it at the butcher's from Sandra's cook. Richard, professional that he was, carefully sat the antique Irish Waterford cut leaded crystal cake stand on the granite kitchen island and quickly used the clean white cotton towel on his arm to mop up the wine and remove the soaked placemat. Eddie brought a fresh placemat from the butler's pantry, but he was still stifling a giggle. Bitsy was red with embarrassment and rose from her seat.

Charlie was embarrassed but he was still laughing. Hew, seeing Bitsy's discomfort, rose from his seat and gently said, "Bitsy, sit back down, please. We all understand the situation. It's fine."

"Yes, Bitsy," said the bishop. "This is the most fun I've had at dinner in a long time. You've made the evening. The conversation at most dinner parties I'm invited to is stiff and, frankly, boring. You've made my day."

Alexis told Charlie not to worry. "The kids spill things all the time and the mats are washable."

Bitsy gratefully sat down and Rosilyn quipped, "Now that the subject of sex has been broached, I'm reminded of the time Amelia brought a *Playgirl* magazine and a bottle of Merlot into the cathedral kitchen."

Bitsy groaned. "Oh, my Lord."

Amelia defended her actions. "Well, we were new here and I just wanted to liven up the girls' rainy afternoon. Cooking church suppers doesn't have to be a bore."

"It certainly made our day," said Bitsy. "Some of the old girls hadn't seen anything like those naked guys in years."

More laughter erupted. Even the footmen couldn't hold back. After order was restored and dessert finally finished, everyone returned to the main room with tea or brandy, to marvel as John and Ama played Mozart's *Violin Concerto No. 5* in A major, 1st movement.

⁂

HEW WAS EXHAUSTED FROM THE TRAVEL. He and Alexis were finally snuggled into their California king bed.

"Well, that was fun," said Hew. "Ama's parents may never come back, though."

"Don't worry. They're great sports. Ginny told me at the door that they haven't had that much fun in years."

"Sounds like all is well. You had everything in perfect order—except Amelia and Bitsy of course." He laughed. "Of course, you'll never get those two in order. The evening was absolutely perfect. What a great group of friends." He paused and looked at his wife. "I've made some decisions too. After our meeting in Cologne, I told Sam that I will be retiring. I'll be forty in June and I don't need another death threat. Johann will take over Eberhart North America. Eberhart International will take over the international construction. They will buy half of my stock in the existing SCMAGLEV project and still give me thirty percent of the annual profits.

"The accountants are happy and tell me that money will more than fund the Cavaillé-Coll organ restoration. The Catholic bishop has agreed to dedicate it to Father A. Johann's new design has increased the reverberation time in the new church to five seconds so I've agreed to fund a new state-of-the-art sound system to keep the priests happy.

"I'm putting my profits from the kudzu project into the Scottish castle school. It's a win-win for Clemson and there's nothing for the

419

state legislature to fight and grumble about. I'm going to spend quality time at home and I'll use the quiet time in the house while the kids are in school to compose." He searched her face. "You haven't told me what you've been doing besides running after the kids."

"That's great news," said Alexis. "Who knew that a simple comment about using something an obnoxious as kudzu could solve such a huge issue. The Japanese engineers say that the long fibers in the vines allowed them to reduce the weight another five percent. I've been thinking about your situation ever since Sam's phone call. Your hospital stay was a wakeup call for us both." She kissed him. "Two things—well actually three. I took Tippy's advice and wrote Mable a letter telling her that I have forgiven her."

"That was very kind of you. Who would ever have thought that a half-eaten tuna salad sandwich would have resulted in so many deaths. I'll bet that hunk of C-4 he used wasn't much bigger than your sandwich. What's letter number two?"

"I wrote the judge asking him to sentence her to life without parole rather than executing her. I also asked him to send her to a prison as close to the Arctic Circle as possible. Edward assures me that the judge will do just that. On a positive note, I'm helping IFACS clean and conserve the Blashfield painting over the St. Luke's altar and I've been asked to sing the mezzo-soprano Angel part in Elgar's *Dream of Gerontius* Op 38 with the Atlanta Symphony in October."

"Fantastic. That painting of the Good Shepherd carrying the lost lamb is stunning. On another positive note, all of this has allowed us to work together on a major project. I really enjoyed that. Our stories intertwined in an almost fugal composition. I might even compose one based on it all. I'll call it 'The Kudzu & C-4 Fugue.'"

Alexis laughed so hard she almost rolled off the bed. "Please use your headphones. I don't ever want to listen to that."

He ignored her sarcasm. "Are you performing the original Elgar text or the Anglican revision?"

"I didn't know there was an Anglican revision."

"Yep. The Anglican clergy at the time objected to some Catholic theology in the text and it was revised for use in the three choirs festival in 1900."

"That's ridiculous. No, I'm sure we'll sing the original. It's considered to be his masterpiece. I think religion will be the last bastion of prejudice."

"Hmmm…I think you're right. The bishop told me as much. By the way, James had to give the vice chancellor a dossier on us. Apparently no American has ever walked in to the university with a proposal of that magnitude. He included details of the Swan Bay equestrian breeding program. We'll get an invitation to the royal box at Ascot. You'll need a hat."

He casually rolled over and she punched him in the back. "You'll need one too, buddy boy. By the way, Edward sent the paperwork. John's name change is final."

"I'm sure he's happy. What else is he doing?"

"I didn't want to mention this now, but since you've asked, he wants to spend the summer in Mechelen, Belgium at the Royal Carillon School."

"I think that's okay." He laughed. "From what I saw, they'll probably pay him to teach."

"Well, as it happens, Ama is spending most of the summer at a strings camp in France."

"Oh, bloody hell," said Hew. "I just remembered. I hate top hats. It'll make me look like I'm eight feet tall."

"No problem. James can escort me or he can find me a young handsome Scottish stud in a kilt and a Prince Charlie jacket."

"Sorry. The invitation will be strictly confined to the names on the invitation. The Secret Service is already vetting us."

"Oh, well, a girl can dream."

"Fantasize is more like it. Sex dream?"

"You have abandoned me for two months. You've got to make up for missed opportunities. What's that word you like? Regenerate?"

"No, it's too late for us for that. No more babies. We need another family wedding first. The word you're looking for is Resurgam. It will be John Bishop XIV's turn next."

"No. He didn't add the Roman numerals. Ding convinced him to drop them."

"Why? It's his birthright."

"Think about it. I.V. What's an I.V.? I'll tell you, and I agree with Ding. An I.V. is a drip."

"Oh, God. Well, I missed the American boarding school nickname nonsense." He grabbed her around the waist and turned her over.

"Nevertheless, the Bishops will rise again."

❧

THE END

Acknowledgments

My thanks to my wife Becky who lived through this process and gave me uninterrupted time to write.

Thanks to Richard Parsons who read an early incomplete version and made constructive comments.

Thanks to Dr. Robert Poovey for information about the St. Luke's, Atlanta choral history.

Thanks to Dr. Murray Somerville for information on the organ at New College, Oxford.

Thanks to Grace Church Cathedral Canon Organist and Choirmaster Nicholas Quardokus for insight into the choir school at St. Thomas, Fifth Ave.

Thanks to Thomas Tisdale who introduced me to Vally Sharpe.

Thanks to Vally Sharpe who agreed to be my editor. She had to bring my fifty-year-old rusty rules of grammar into the twenty-first century.

www.ingramcontent.com/pod-product-compliance
Lightning Source LLC
Chambersburg PA
CBHW020429130626
46549CB00001B/47